Praise for *Color of Violence: the INCITE! Anthology*

Color of Violence is a fantastic anthology from an amazing organization—it's a must-read for academics, activists, and everyone in-between!
—Jessica Valenti, author of *Full Frontal Feminism*
and Executive Editor of *feministing.com*

The essays are biting, candid, and honest in their assessment of very real inadequacies on personal, familial, and governmental levels to promote a safe world for women, as well as how the white, middle-class feminist perspective can actually be deleterious to the needs of women of color. Highly recommended.

—*Midwest Book Review*

This beautifully produced and exquisitely edited anthology is a mind-bending experience to read. More than two dozen brilliant, committed women and trans activists write with passion and righteous anger, but also great skill.
—Roxanne Dunbar-Ortiz, longtime activist and author
of *Blood on the Border*, *Outlaw Woman*, and *Red Dirt*

I am beholden to the contributors of this volume for their attempts to shift a poisonous culture that debases us all. It is possible—and indeed this anthology makes one believe it is probable—that women of color will lead us through and beyond our collective ignorance.
—Shannon Cain, Executive Director, Kore Press

I read this book with a very particular project in mind. However, I like to choose my reading…such that it also will end up…giving me the sort of general radical political education I would want to have anyway. Particularly for those of us with relative privilege, it must be an integral part of our politics to challenge ourselves with material produced from other standpoints, that takes us out of what we know and have participated in directly ourselves…. This book can be a crucial piece of political education for any activist in North America.
—Scott Neigh, author of *A Canadian Lefty in Occupied Land*

Color of Violence

Color of Violence
The INCITE! Anthology

INCITE! Women of Color Against Violence

South End Press
Cambridge, Massachusetts

Cover concept and photo of Neena Pathak: Josh Russell
Cover design: Design Action Collective
Page design and production: Alyssa Hassan
                    and the South End Press Collective

Discounted bulk quantities of this book are available for organizing, educational, or fundraising purposes. Please contact South End Press for more information.

Library of Congress Cataloging-in-Publication Data

Color of violence : the INCITE! anthology / INCITE! Women of Color Against Violence.
    p. cm.
  Includes bibliographical references and index.
  ISBN-13: 978-0-89608-762-0 (alk. paper)
  ISBN-10: 0-89608-762-X (alk. paper)
1. Women--Crimes against. 2. Minority women--Crimes against. 3. Feminism.
I. INCITE! Women of Color Against Violence.

HV6250.4.W65.C627 2006
303.6082--dc22

                                        2006024094

Printed in Canada by union labor on acid-free, recycled paper.

11 10 09 08 07   2 3 4 5 6

Contents

III. Building Movement

Acknowledgments

INCITE! would like to thank all the women of color who continue to organize against violence and fight for a more just world. Without this movement, this anthology would not exist. We thank the countless women of color who have attended color of violence conferences, organize in local chapters, support INCITE! financially and politically. We thank all the contributors to this anthology, including those we could not include because of space constraints.

South End Press has been fabulous to work with. We are so impressed with its political integrity and commitment to social justice movement–building. Jill Petty, who served as our editor, worked countless hours to help shape this anthology. We thank her, and wish her all the best in her new life path.

We would particularly like to acknowledge all the women who have served on INCITE!'s national steering committee since its inception: Val Kanuha, Kata Issari, Sherry Wilson, Loretta Rivera, Mimi Kim, Isabel Kang, Beth Richie, Clarissa Rojas, Andrea Smith, Simmi Gandhi, Paula Rojas, Barbara Smith, Elham Bayour, Jamie Lee Evans, Jamie Jimenez, Andrea Ritchie, Nadine Naber, Michelle Erai, Julia Sudbury, Ann Caton, Prosh Sherkarloo, Tammy Ko Robinson, Janelle White, Nan Stoops, Shana Griffin, Inhe Choi, Ije Ude, Nada Elia, Eunice Cho, Kabzuag Vaj, Trishala Deb, and Alisa Bierria. Those who served as coeditors for the anthology include: Andrea Smith, Nadine Naber, Andrea Ritchie, and Clarissa Rojas. Those involved as coeditors at other stages include Beth Richie, Julia Sudbury, Val Kanuha, Michelle Erai, and Isabel Kang.

The following chapters were published previously:

The essays by Sarah Deer, Haunani-Kay Trask, and Stormy Odgen appeared in a special issue of *Social Justice*, "Native Women and State Violence" (eds. Andrea Smith and Luana Ross), vol. 31, no. 4, 2004.

Dorothy Roberts's essay is a version of an earlier piece, "Feminism, Race, and Adoption Policy," from *Adoption Matters: Philosophical and Feminist Essays*, edited by Sally Haslanger and Charlotte Witt (Ithaca, NY: Cornell University Press), 2004.

A previous version of "The Forgotten '–ism': An Arab American Women's Perspective on Zionism, Racism, and Sexism," written under the auspices of the Arab Women's Solidarity Association, San Francisco Chapter, appeared in *Time to Rise*, edited by Maylei Blackwell, Linda, Burnham, and Jung Hee Choi (Berkeley, CA: Women of Color Resource Center), 2001.

Rosalinda Fregoso's essay is a version of an earlier piece, "Toward a Planetary Civil Society," from *Mexicana Encounters: The Making of Social Identities on the Borderlands* (Los Angeles: University of California Press), 2003.

Traci West's essay is a version of an earlier piece in *Wounds of the Spirit* (New York: New York University Press), 1999.

The Color of Violence: Introduction

Andrea Smith, Beth Richie, Julia Sudbury, Janelle White,
and the INCITE! Anthology Co-editors

Many years ago when I was a student in San Diego, I was driving down the freeway with a friend when we encountered a Black woman wandering along the shoulder. Her story was extremely disturbing. Despite her uncontrollable weeping, we were able to surmise that she had been raped and dumped along the side of the road. After a while, she was able to wave down a police car, thinking that they would help her. However, when the white policeman picked her up, he did not comfort her, but rather seized upon the opportunity to rape her once more.

Angela Davis's story illustrates the manner in which women of color experience violence perpetrated both by individuals and by the state. Since the first domestic violence shelter in the United States opened in 1974, and the first rape crisis center opened in 1972, the mainstream antiviolence movement has been critical in breaking the silence around violence against women, and in providing essential services to survivors of sexual/domestic violence. Initially, the antiviolence movement prioritized a response to male violence based on grassroots political mobilization. However, as the antiviolence movement has gained greater prominence, domestic violence and rape crisis centers have also become increasingly professionalized, and as a result are often reluctant to address sexual and domestic violence within the larger context of institutionalized violence.

In addition, rape crisis centers and shelters increasingly rely on state and federal sources for their funding. Consequently, their approaches toward eradicating violence focus on working *with* the state rather than working *against* state violence. For example, mainstream antiviolence advocates often demand longer prison sentences for batterers and sex offenders as a frontline approach to stopping violence against women. However, the criminal justice system has always been brutally oppressive toward communities of color, including women of color, as the above story illustrates. Thus, this strategy employed to stop violence has had the effect of increasing violence against women of color perpetrated by the state.

Unfortunately, the strategy often engaged by communities of color to address state violence is advocating that women keep silent about sexual and domestic violence to maintain a united front against racism. Racial justice organizing has generally focused on racism as it primarily affects men, and has often ignored the gendered forms of racism that women of color face. An example includes the omission of racism in reproductive health policies (such as sterilization abuse) in the 2001 United Nations World Conference Against Racism. Those forms of racisms that disproportionately impact women of color become termed simply "women's issues" rather than simultaneously racial justice issues.

There are many organizations that address violence *directed at* communities (e.g., police brutality, racism, economic exploitation, colonialism, and so on). There are also many organizations that address violence *within* communities (e.g., sexual/domestic violence). But there are very few organizations that address violence on both fronts simultaneously. The challenge women of color face in combatting personal *and* state violence is to develop strategies for ending violence that *do* assure safety for survivors of sexual/domestic violence and *do not* strengthen our oppressive criminal justice apparatus. Our approaches must always challenge the violence perpetrated through multinational capitalism and the state.

It was frustration with the failures on the part of racial justice *and* antiviolence organizations to effectively address violence against women of color that led women of color to organize "The Color of Violence: Violence Against Women of Color" conference held at University of California–Santa Cruz on April 28–29, 2000. The primary goals of this conference were to develop analyses and strategies around ending violence that place women of color at the center; to address violence against women of color in all its forms, including attacks on immigrants' rights and Indian treaty rights, the proliferation of prisons, militarism, attacks on the reproductive rights of women of color, medical experimentation on communities of color, homophobia/heterosexism and hate crimes against lesbians of color, economic neo-colonialism, and institutional racism; and to encourage the antiviolence movement to reinsert political organizing into its response to violence.

Few events have been as profoundly important to the antiviolence movement in the United States as this conference. It was initially conceptualized as a small gathering for impassioned women of color activists who were fed up with having our contributions ignored, taken for granted, and in many instances sabotaged by an increasingly mainstream social service–oriented agenda.

As news about the event spread, the conference grew both in significance and in scope. Women of color from across the country urgently called the organizers asking to be included in the discussion, imploring us to find a larger venue, and insisting that we consider the establishment of a longer-term strategic response to their anger and disappointment. This wellspring of interest made it clear to the cofounders of INCITE! that this conference could not simply provide opportunities for a small groups of women of color to reflect on our experiences; instead, we had touched, and needed to tend to, a collective raw nerve.

In the years leading up to "The Color of Violence," women of color came to understand that the once-radical analysis of violence against women had narrowed so greatly that almost all remnants of a social justice approach had virtually disappeared. The legacy of the lesbians of color, particularly Black lesbians, who built the movement had disappeared from the collective memory of the mainstream movement. Instead, women of color in the antiviolence movement were engaging in "high-risk activism." Women of color tend to occupy roles in the antiviolence movement that place them on the frontlines of the work, and in situations where they must negotiate complex and at times adversarial relationships among and between their organizations of origin, their home communities, other communities, formal institutions of power, and perpetrators and survivors of violence.

Cultural workers and scholars addressing gender violence and the oppression of women of color are also often faced with marginalization in communities of color and women's communities, as well as within their academic and cultural communities; thus, their work can be identified as high-risk, too. In fact, it could be maintained that women of color involved in antiviolence mobilization share particularities—the motivation to negotiate and build solidarity with other women of color, the ideologies of resistance that contribute to taking action to transform systems, and the salience of race and class (and their intersection) in confronting gender violence—that, combined, make it more likely that these women will find themselves engaged in high-risk roles.

As a result, many women of color had left the antiviolence movement by the time the conference was convened in 2000, feeling forced out because of exhaustion and feelings of betrayal. These women of color had been attempting to do radical work in the face of deep contradictions inherent in the prevailing white feminist responses to violence, which refused to accommodate analyses of race and class. At best, the women of color who continued to do the work felt unappreciated and misunderstood, and many felt under personal and political attack as they attempted to provide support for women of color who had survived violence but had no other resources except programs controlled by white women. Even in programs where women of color were in leadership or working with white women acting as allies, the prevailing ideological conditions in the antiviolence movement made it incredibly difficult for women of color with a radical vision of structural oppression to do radical antiviolence work.

Within this context, "The Color of Violence" became an extraordinarily significant event. In unexpected ways, it offered myriad opportunities to advance radical analyses of violence developed by women of color while re-igniting a radical social justice movement to end violence against women. Two thousand women of color attended the conference; more than two thousand had to be turned away. The success of this gathering and commitment of the attendees disrupted the mainstream movement's hold on the energies of women of color. At "The Color of Violence," power was shifted from those who claim authority over antiviolence work, and women of color survivors of violence were empowered to speak the truth of their experiences.

From this conference, INCITE! Women of Color Against Violence formed to continue efforts to develop strategies to end violence that addressed community and state violence simultaneously. The overwhelming response to this conference suggests that women of color (and their allies) are hungry for a new approach toward ending violence. INCITE! held follow-up conferences in Chicago (2002) and New Orleans (2005) in which thousands more attended. Many of the articles from this volume come from presentations at these conferences.

INCITE! stresses the importance of transcending the "politics of inclusion" to actually address the concerns of women of color. As the antiviolence movement has attempted to become more inclusive, attempts at multicultural interventions against domestic violence have unwittingly strengthened white supremacy within the movement. All too often, inclusivity has come to mean that the sexual or domestic violence prevention model, developed largely with the interests of white middle-class women in mind, should simply add a multicultural component. Antiviolence multicultural curricula are often the same as those produced by mainstream groups with some "cultural" designs or references annexed to the pre-existing format, and most antiviolence programs servicing communities of color are constructed exactly like those in the mainstream, with the addition of "community outreach workers" or bilingual staff.

An alternative approach to "inclusion" is to place women of color at the center of the analysis of and the organization against domestic violence. That is, what if we do not make any assumptions about what a domestic violence *program* should look like, but instead ask: What would it take *to end violence against women of color*? What would this movement look like? What if we do not presume that this movement would share any of the features we take for granted in the current domestic violence movement? As mentioned previously, when we shift the center to women of color, the importance of addressing state violence becomes evident. This perspective then benefits not only women of color, but all peoples, because it is becoming increasingly clear that the criminal justice system is not effectively ending violence for anyone. In fact, *The New York Times* recently reported that the effect of strengthened anti-domestic violence legislation is that battered women kill their abusive partners less frequently; however, batterers do *not* kill their partners less frequently. Thus, ironically, laws passed to protect battered women are actually protecting their batterers.

When we shift the center of analysis, there is no permanent center of organizing. Rather, by constantly shifting the center to communities that face intersecting forms of oppression, we gain a more comprehensive view of the strategies needed to end all forms of violence. The articles in this volume reflect an attempt to shift the center, to better understand how various forms of intersecting oppressions contribute to the creation of a violent world, and to devise the strategies necessary to end violence.

The first section of this book focuses on reconceptualizing violence against women beyond interpersonal forms of sexual and domestic violence. As Andrea Smith has argued elsewhere, if we look at the history of women in color in general and Native women in particular, it is clear that sexual violence has served as a tool of patriarchy *and* as a tool of racism and colonialism. Consequently, it is problematic to assume that the state, in the form of the criminal justice system, can effectively address violence against women. Historically, it has been the primary perpetrator, particularly against women of color. In "Federal Indian Law and Violent Crime," Sarah Deer demonstrates how federal policy, supposedly designed to protect Native women from violence, entraps Native women in further violence.

Julia Sudbury's "Lessons from the Black Women's Movement in Britain" considers the deleterious effects of reliance on the criminal justice system as the primary strategy for ending violence against women. While antiviolence activists often conceptualize the state as a protector, standing between women and violent males, Sudbury argues that this has not been the case for women who defend themselves against potentially lethal intimate violence. For women convicted of defending themselves against a violent partner, the criminal justice system becomes a site of secondary victimization. And for all women prisoners, the state acts as a punitive perpetrator of violence, subjecting women to invasive body searches, emotional and physical isolation, and physical and verbal abuse. Sudbury calls for the antiviolence movement to develop a radical solidarity with women found guilty of "offending" the state, and suggests that women of color must resist the criminalization of survival strategies by women of color.

Nirmala Erevelles' "Disability and the New World Order" further develops the links between globalization, violence against women, and ableism by analyzing the material conditions within which the social category of "disability" is constituted, and the ideological effects that these constructions have on the reproduction of race, gender, and class oppressions. In particular, Erevelles elaborates on the relationship between poverty and disability in Third World contexts. She reflects on the underlying assumptions behind structural adjustment programs (SAPs), delineating how SAPs impact women living in poverty and contribute to the social construction of disability in Third World contexts.

In "The Color of Choice," Loretta Ross argues that reconceptualizing state violence also impacts how we look at reproductive justice for women of color. She challenges the prochoice framework and articulates a reproductive justice agenda for women of color that addresses white supremacy as it intersects with attacks on the reproductive rights of women of color. Dorothy Roberts's essay, "Feminism, Race, and Adoption Policy," further investigates how these logics contribute to a racialized gender violence within adoption politics.

Andrea Smith argues that much of the tension in women of color organizing is the result of simplistic understanding of white supremacy. In "Heteropatriarchy and the Three Pillars of White Supremacy," she argues that white supremacy operates through three distinct logics—slavery, genocide, and orientalism—that impact communities of color differently. Women of color organizing, she asserts, will be more effective if it is not based on shared victimization, but rather on strategic alliances based on how we are particularly impacted by what she terms the "three pillars of white supremacy."

Nadine Naber's work addresses the connections between gender violence and state violence in the form of militarism and colonialism. Naber further investigates primitivist analyses of women of color, focusing on Arab women. She asserts that the discourse around "female suicide bombers," particularly prevalent after 9/11, is part of an ideological framework that represents Arab women either as passive victims who need to be saved from Arab men or as barbaric terrorists who, according to the 2003 Interfaith Summit on Zionism (Washington, DC), "hate Jewish children more than they love their own." Instead of entering debates within mainstream feminist discourse about whether or not we should "support" suicide bombing, Naber argues, we should ask: What are the conditions that give rise to suicide bombing? This excerpt from Noura Erekat's poem, "Three Home Demolitions and One Pending Order," poignantly portrays some such conditions, as well as the will to survive and resist the violence of Israeli occupation:

> The second time they came
> I stood in the doorway
> Israeli bulldozers need to crush me
> If they wanted to trample my home
>> Again

But the soldiers didn't care that I was
Fifteen and female
Long hair just made it easier to pull me away

They spit on Mama but she wouldn't move
Not her baby's home she screamed
She looked so strong, I swear
I thought her fingers would shoot lightning
It took three soldiers to take her down
Expose her breasts to the watchful sky
Spill her hair from her God-fearing hijab
And push her into the wailing dirt

Having reconceptualized violence against women of color, it becomes important to address the myriad forms violence takes, particularly as it is perpetrated by the state. The essays in the second section, "Forms of Violence," reveal violences against women overlooked in traditional activism and scholarship.

Andrea Ritchie's essay, "Law Enforcement Violence against Women of Color," contests the notion that the criminal justice system can effectively protect women. In her analysis of police brutality, she notes that the mainstream anti-police brutality movement tends to focus on men as victims, while the mainstream antiviolence movement does not defend women who are victimized by police—particularly when the vicitimization occurs as police respond to situations involving domestic violence.

In "Crime, Punishment, and Economic Violence," Pat Allard demonstrates how seemingly gender-neutral anti-drug laws serve to oppress women, particularly women of color, who are attempting to survive an exploitative economic system. And in "Pomo Woman, Ex-Prisoner, Speaks Out," Stormy Ogden further explores gender violence committed by the state in her essay on Native women in prison. Writing as a former prisoner, she analyzes how the incarceration of Native women in California can be understood as a continuation of the genocidal policies the US government has implemented against American Indians. Her essay reveals the extent to which the mainstream antiviolence movement, through its implicit support of the criminal justice system, helps to promote additional forms of violence against violence survivors who are prisoners.

Dana Erekat, S. R., and Dena Al-Adeeb address the impact of military violence on West Asian and North African women, particularly since 9/11. Their voices highlight the history and experience of surviving and resisting colonial violence. Renee Saucedo and Sylvanna Falcón address the gendered forms of violence that are perpetrated by the INS and Border Patrol. Saucedo looks at the tactics of sexual terrorism within INS raids, while Falcón's essay explores the rampant gender violence faced by women at the hands of the Border Patrol.

Rosa Linda Fregoso's "The Complexities of 'Feminicide' on the Border" explores the intersecting logics of capitalism, national boundaries, and misogyny that have resulted in more than one thousand unsolved murders of women, primarily poor and indigenous. She complicates the explanation provided by critics of

Third World development policies—that the murders are simply the outcome of the introduction of maquiladoras to Mexico. The implication is that as transnational corporations introduce Western values and ideas to the Third World, they break down traditional gender roles. Fregoso argues that these interpretations, while critical of the Western development model, reinscribe primitivist notions of women in Mexico.

"The Forgotten '-ism'," by the Arab Women's Solidarity Association (AWSA), further explores the colonialist representation of Arab women in Zionist ideologies. This essay argues that Zionism—the belief that Israel should be a Jewish-only state and exclude the Palestinian peoples indigenous to the area—is responsible for policies of genocide against Palestinians that have relied heavily on gender violence. They note that mainstream feminist organizations have nonetheless failed to address the colonialist and apartheid policies of Israel when they might condemn similar practices in other countries. A consistent antiracist, anticolonial politic, AWSA argues, must recognize Zionism as an axis of oppression.

Within the context of Hawai'i, Haunani-Kay Trask argues that much of the colonial violence suffered by indigenous women can be understood as a "quiet violence" in which women of color are killed slowly through oppressive social structures. In particular, Trask focuses on the damage caused by nuclear testing in the Pacific, which has wiped out many Pacific Islander communities, with no public outcry. She argues that the strategy for addressing this violence is national self-determination that recognizes the United States as a settler colonial country, rather than reform within the current US system. Neferti Tadiar extends Trask's analysis to argue that the US war on terror is not an indication of "declining" democratic ideals in the United States, but rather a reflection of the United States *as* war. She notes that the United States is fundamentally structured under a colonialist ideology that holds that most peoples are not, in fact, human.

In "The War Against Black Women, and the Making of *NO!*," Aishah Simmons traces the eleven years it took to make her powerful and revolutionary film on Black women and sexual assault, and chronicles the fierce resistance and resourceful activism that Black feminists have always drawn from in matters regarding justice, visibility, and community accountability.

Recently, many antiviolence advocates have reconsidered their reliance on the criminal justice system as their primary strategy for ending violence. However, as Clarissa Rojas argues in "The Medicalization of Domestic Violence," there are innumerable ways the antiviolence movement can find itself coopted by the state. One such way is simply shifting from a criminal justice model to a medical model for addressing violence, even though the medical model both individualizes and pathologizes women who are victims of violence. Rojas further contends that while both approaches are problematic, each has been aggressively promoted to antiviolence activists as *the* model for ending violence.

Having established an expanded analysis of violence against women of color, the anthology moves to address the following question: What strategies are necessary to truly end violence against women of color in all its forms? In section three, "Building Movement," the contibutors offer possible models for organizing from a more comprehensive and holistic analysis of violence. While there are no simple solutions to these issues, these essays explore strategies that both challenge state power and rely on grassroots political organizing. These strategies also assume that part of the work of ending violence is the creation of communities that will hold perpetrators accountable.

Currently, anti-prison advocates often argue for "restorative justice models" as alternatives to prison for addressing crime. "Restorative justice" is an umbrella term describing a wide range of programs that attempt to address crime from a restorative and reconciliatory framework rather than a punitive one. That is, in contrast to the US criminal justice system, which focuses solely on punishing the perpetrator and removing him or her from society through incarceration, restorative justice efforts involve all parties (perpetrators, victims, and community members) in determining the appropriate response to a crime. However, as articulated in the Critical Resistance/INCITE! statement on gender and the prison industrial complex, these models often depend on a romanticized notion of "community" that seldom exists in practice. In the absence of this ideal community, there is no guarantee that restorative justice measures will actually hold perpetrators of gender violence accountable. Consequently, many survivors find themselves further victimized by these strategies, as they are often pressured by community members to "reconcile" with the offender with little regard to their safety or need for justice and accountability.

TransJustice contributes a statement that highlights the importance of a gender binary system in maintaining systems of capitalism, violence, and exploitation. Patriarchy, under which men are entitled to oppress women, depends on the acceptance of the construction of two and only two genders—men and women. Thus, this statement illustrates that challenging transphobia and the gender binary system is central to the work of the antiviolence movement.

Emi Koyama presents the bold critique that the domestic violence shelter system itself replicates the dynamics of abuse it seeks to eradicate. She argues that most shelters police women in a manner similar to the criminal justice system, and that the system particularly victimizes women who are already criminalized, such as sex workers and transgendered peoples. Koyama further suggests that an alternative approach, based in harm reduction, would not require survivors to act like "model citizens" in order to receive assistance, but would recognize, interrogate, and work with the conditions within which women actually live.

Sista II Sista in Brooklyn and Communities Against Rape and Abuse in Seattle describe models of organizing against violence that rely neither on the criminal justice system, nor on restorative justice models. Instead, they focus on grassroots political organizing strategies that attempt not only to circumvent the state, but also to oppose the violence the state inflicts in the forms of police brutality and the prison industrial complex. Traci West maintains that one of the sites critical to target with these grassroots strategies is spiritual/religious communities. She notes that because the Black church in particular has often implicitly or explicitly promoted violence against women, it remains an important location for organizing and transformation.

Puneet Kaur Singh further demonstrates that our work against violence today comes from a legacy of women of color who have created a space before us. The

Combahee River Collective, a group of Black lesbian feminists, began meeting in 1974 to confront violence against women and girls. Thus, from the very inception of the antiviolence movement in the United States, Black women, and Black lesbians in particular, have been both central actors and challengers to the approaches and practices of the predominantly white antiviolence movement. Finally, long-time organizer Elizabeth Martínez reflects on her history of women of color organizing and calls on us to be hopeful, rather than despairing, because we have opportunities to build a better future for everyone. Her hope is reflected in the poetry of maiana minahal.

It is indeed hope, fierce resistance, and a belief in the power of women of color united in the face of the profound devastation wrought in the lives of low-income women of color, their families, and communities in the aftermath of Hurricane Katrina that inspired the INCITE! New Orleans chapter to build the Women's Health and Justice Initiative, which includes a clinic for low-income women and a Women of Color Organizing and Resource Center. This effort reflects the leadership of women of color struggling for the survival of their communities where government and non-profit responses to the state and interpersonal violence that followed in the wake of the storm have been systematically racist and sexist.

The historic Treme community in New Orleans, the first free community established by Black people in the US and home to hundreds of Black women and their families, many of whom are poor, hosted INCITE!'s Color of Violence III conference in March 2005. Our hearts continue to go out to the families and communities that graciously welcomed us, and we continue to provide them with as much support and as many resources as we can so that they can rebuild the rich and vital communities that have been devastated.

Unfortunately, due to strictly technical limitations, a full-length chapter providing an analysis of the feminization of disasters and displacements as experienced by women of color during and following Hurricane Katrina and sharing the struggles and successes of the INCITE! New Orleans chapter in rising and rebuilding does not appear in this anthology. INCITE!'s initial analysis of the raced, classed, and gendered dimension of this catastrophe is posted on our website, and a full-length article featuring the voices, analysis, and organizing efforts of the women of INCITE! New Orleans can be found in South End Press's anthology on Hurricane Katrina, *What Lies Beneath*.

Another critical issue not addressed in this volume is the impact of the non-profit-industrial complex on the antiviolence movement. This subject is vast enough to warrant another anthology, which INCITE! will be publishing with South End Press. Entitled *The Revolution Will Not Be Funded: Beyond the Non-Profit Industrial Complex*, this work challenges antiviolence activists to develop organizing models not dependent on the non-profit/NGO model that currently dominates antiviolence organizing (as well as social justice organizing in general) in the United States. For the antiviolence movement in particular, the non-profit model has contributed to the transformation of a complex, political, grassroots struggle against violence into a sprawling network of social service providers.

All of these essays represent our collective struggle to rethink strategies for eliminating violence. The question we ask as women of color is not how do we set up a model antiviolence intervention program, but what will it take to end the violence against us? This anthology places women of color at the center of analysis and argues that neither white-dominated discourses on gender violence nor male-dominated discourses on racial violence provide the comprehensive analyses required to develop effective strategies to end racism and sexism. It is the hope of INCITE! that this work will provide a space to continue dialogue around strategies and analyses that can end violence and oppression against not only women of color, but against all peoples.

In the end, "The Color of Violence" conference reminded feminists of color that as we take power, we must remember that our goal as women of color is not to secure promises of more diverse workplaces, or inclusion in white feminist organizations. Our goal is nothing less than the liberation of our peoples. And if we are truly committed to ending violence against women, we must start in the hardest places in our own communities. These are the places where the mainstream movement has not made an impact. We can't look for the "easy alliances," or be the "friendly colored girls" that antiviolence programs and male-dominated community-based organizations demand us to be. As women of color activists, we must not deny the parts of ourselves and our work that is the least acceptable to the mainstream movement and to our communities. We must not let those who reject our liberation as a people coopt individuals and our work, and we must remember that our antiviolence movement will never be "legitimate" in a patriarchal, racist society.

Indeed, we have made very important progress. But that progress has cost women of color a lot. Too many deals have been cut that undermine our legitimacy. We have built too many coalitions with people who don't understand our work, we have collaborated too much with our enemies, and we have accepted too much abuse—so much so that twenty years into the antiviolence movement, the situation for women of color in prisons, at home, and on the streets is as dire as ever. Our movement's relevancy and our integrity as women of color are only as solid as our work against the oppressive, dangerous systems that imprison women. So we must build a solid base of feminists of color, and engage in independent mass mobilization around specific campaigns. Our work must be founded in a radical analysis and we must resist cooptation. Our work is not about populating ethnically specific programs, not just about reparations for the past, not just about multicultural interventions, and not about reform. Our work is about justice and freedom.

I

RECONCEPTUALIZING ANTIVIOLENCE STRATEGIES

1

Rethinking Antiviolence Strategies
Lessons from the Black Women's Movement in Britain

Julia Sudbury

In April 1998, women activists from Southall Black Sisters,[1] a Black[2] women's organization at the forefront of breaking the silence around violence against South Asian women, picketed the Royal Courts of Justice in London. Their banners proclaimed their slogans: "Our Tradition, Struggle not Submission" and "Free Zoora Shah!" Five years earlier, Zoora, a Pakistani woman living in the conservative Muslim community of Bradford in the north of England, was convicted of murder and sentenced to life with a tariff (minimum time served) of twenty years.[3] Zoora's story broke the stereotypes about South Asian women that have been a legacy of the colonial era in India. She was not passive, veiled, or submissive. Instead, she defended herself against a physically violent, sexually abusive, and financially exploitative man by poisoning him with arsenic. Zoora's case raised a strategic dilemma for women of color involved in activism against violence. The antiviolence movement has directed many of its demands toward the state, campaigning for specialist women police officers, domestic violence training for police and judges, and harsher sentences for abusive men. These demands share a common vision of the state as protector, standing between women and violent males. But for women convicted of defending themselves against a violent partner, the criminal justice system becomes a site of secondary victimization. And for all women prisoners, the state acts as a punitive perpetrator of violence, subjecting women to invasive body searches, emotional and physical isolation, and physical and verbal abuse. The challenge for women of color activists was to conceptualize the campaign for Zoora's freedom in a way that also created solidarity with other women found guilty of "offending" the state. Meeting that challenge has led to different approaches to resisting the criminalization of survival strategies by women of color.

Colonial Legacies and Patriarchal Violence

Like many violently abused women, Zoora's story starts many years earlier. In the early seventies, she came to Bradford, England, from rural Mirpur following an arranged marriage. She was beaten by her husband, and forced to undergo several abortions in order to avoid the birth of a girl. She was eventually thrown out by her husband's family and found herself homeless, unable to speak English and without any income to support her young children. When pregnant with her third child, she was befriended by Mohammed Azam, a married man who helped her buy a house since she was unable to obtain a mortgage in her own name. Although Zoora by then had her own income from working in a factory, she became financially dependent due to this arrangement and Azam quickly used this to his advantage, forcing her to have sex and becoming violent when she refused to obey him. Azam was also involved in trafficking drugs from Pakistan and when she traveled home on a visit, he demanded that she carry heroin. When he received a prison sentence for trafficking, he pimped her to former prisoners on their release. In her words: "I was used as a mattress by all the men in the community."[4] Zoora turned to community elders for help, but Azam's brother was a prominent leader in the Bradford Council of Mosques and she was told that nothing could be done. On Azam's release from prison, Zoora became anxious because he had persuaded her daughter to enter "a business relationship" with him. Zoora had obtained arsenic in Pakistan believing that in small doses it would make Azam sexually impotent. Instead, she gave him a large dose and he died the same day at the hospital. In her original trial in 1993, Zoora denied killing Azam and did not reveal her experiences of abuse and exploitation:

> She denied it because it was too shameful to admit the kind of abuse she was going through and she was part of the criminal underworld, this man is a convicted drug dealer involved in crime, his brother is a leader of the Bradford Council of Mosques, he's a community leader, he's got all the protection he would want. She didn't feel she could speak up and not risk her life and her children, so she didn't say it.[5]

In 1998, with support from Southall Black Sisters, Zoora appealed her conviction on the grounds that she was suffering anxiety and severe depression at the time of Azam's death. The court found her testimony about the extensive sexual and physical violence that she had survived "not capable of belief," and upheld the original perception of Zoora as a dangerous and malicious woman who had willfully planned Azam's death. In 2000, after considering testimony provided by activists, including her daughters Naseem and Fozia Shah, then Home Secretary Jack Straw cut Zoora's tariff from twenty to twelve years, with a parole date of 2004.[6] At the time of writing, Zoora continues to serve time at an open, low security prison in Yorkshire. Her case for release on license was due to be reviewed in 2006.[7]

The failure of the campaign to free Zoora Shah must be understood against the backdrop of another case that changed the way women who kill their abusive partners are dealt with in English courts. Kiranjit Ahluwalia was born into a privileged Sikh family in rural India. She moved to England in 1979, and settled in suburban London. In 1989, Kiranjit was sentenced to life for the murder of her physically, verbally, and sexually abusive husband. Because Kiranjit had set him on fire and she had appeared detached to authorities immediately after the event, the prosecution attempted to depict her as a calculating and sadistic murderess. In her appeal, however, Southall Black Sisters amassed extensive evidence arguing that the traditional legal construct of "provocation" should be expanded to include the cumulative effects of a history of violence, and maintained that Kiranjit's behavior was influenced by battered women's syndrome. This campaign revealed Kiranjit's shame about being a battered woman, her unwillingness to seek help due to her sense of *izzat* (honor), as well as her desperation and isolation as an Indian woman, and it helped reconstruct Kiranjit's image. Although the case for provocation was rejected, Kiranjit won her case on the grounds of diminished responsibility, based on psychiatric reports that indicated she was suffering from depression. She was released on time served in September 1992.[8]

Kiranjit's case was publicized through an immensely successful media campaign by Southall Black Sisters working in coalition with Justice for Women, a predominantly white feminist group. Justice for Women grew out of a campaign pressing for the release of Sara Thornton, a white woman serving a life sentence for killing her abusive husband. The two high-profile cases marked a turning point in antiviolence activism:

> There was a time, from 1990 onwards, that there was a momentum that grew around women that killed violent partners. Does it make sense for those women to be incarcerated for those kind of crimes when they were effectively going through a double punishment, having gone through domestic violence already, separated from their children? That didn't serve the public interest. We were asking for things like clemency as well as working on the legal cases to overturn their convictions. And it created a momentum in the country [for] a major debate on domestic violence. There were debates in the House of Commons, media talking about it constantly, the general ordinary public was talking about it in a way that they hadn't talked about domestic violence before. So it really did put domestic violence on the national agenda.[9]

Southall Black Sisters converted media interest in Kiranjit's case to support their appeal for leniency. While early stories in the local Crawley press described Kiranjit as a dangerous killer, the national media soon picked up on the image of a submissive woman facing constant oppression within a traditional South Asian community. The South Asian tradition of *izzat*, sometimes used as a defense for men accused of killing their female family members, was invoked to explain Kiranjit's failure to seek help outside the family before events escalated. Finally, she was viewed sympathetically because of her role as an exemplary mother, for her sacrificial decision to stay in an abusive situation in the interests of her two children, and her quiet and nonconfrontational demeanor.

In the end, public opinion swung in Kiranjit's favor not only because of a general rise in awareness about domestic violence and its brutal effects, but also because the case reinforced dominant tropes about South Asian immigrants. In the context of British colonial legacies, the South Asian community, comprised of predominantly rural Pakistanis, Bangladeshis, and Indians—who migrated after the Second World War—and their British-born children, is viewed as a site of outdated traditions, religious fundamentalisms, and political fanaticisms. Racist immigration legislation, such as the 1981 Commonwealth Immigrants Act, was justified in part by an appeal to defend "English values" of common sense, decency, and democracy from, in Margaret Thatcher's terms, being "swamped" by people of different cultures. Presenting South Asian cultures as alien and unfathomable is one way of erasing the colonial legacy of violence, exploitation, and cultural intermixing.

The dominant idea that South Asian cultures, symbolized by the veil and the arranged marriage, are particularly oppressive to women is one way they are marked as "other," and therefore outside of the realm of citizenship. The implication, then, is that South Asian women need to be protected by British law from brutal South Asian patriarchy. This myth that South Asian women need saving from "death by culture" is one prevailing belief that justified British colonial rule. In India, for example, the British Raj banned *sati*, the Hindu practice of widows immolating themselves on their husbands' funeral pyres. Outlawing *sati* subsequently led to the revival of this formerly marginal practice and its reinvention as a symbol of national integrity.[10] As the British assumed the role of "the white knight," the immense colonial violence against women, the rape of women by British colonial troops, and forced labor in tea plantations was therefore invisibilized. It is this narrative of colonial paternalism that generated support for Kiranjit in the media and subsequently led to her release.

The differential racialization of African Caribbean and South Asian communities in Britain also fed into the presentation of Kiranjit as "not belonging" in prison. The depiction of African Caribbean neighborhoods as sites of civil disorder, violence, and criminality has led to disproportionate rates of police surveillance and incarceration. South Asian communities, on the other hand, have been depicted as rigidly policed by internal religious and traditional rules. While African Caribbean women have been portrayed as matriarchal heads of households—thus "out of control" and in need of external policing—Asian women's subjection to patriarchal males has largely exempted them from official surveillance and control. South Asian women are, in fact, underrepresented in prison statistics, making up only 0.8% of women in prison compared to 3.5% in the general population.[11] Kiranjit was therefore racially marked as "out of place," in contrast to African Caribbean women whose disproportionate incarceration has been left unquestioned.

Violent Women: Creation of a Moral Panic

Kiranjit's case and the subsequent release of Sara Thornton were seen by feminists and legal scholars as turning points in the treatment of women who kill their batterers in Britain. Yet six years later, Zoora received little of the empathy offered to Kiranjit. The difference between the two cases can partly be seen as the result of a masculinist backlash after the earlier successful appeals. During Kiranjit's case, a number of editorials appeared in conservative newspapers suggesting that the floodgates might have been opened, and disgruntled women might be allowed to kill their husbands with impunity.[12] Furthermore, stories about violent women and girls were increasingly represented in the media by the early 1990s.[13] Women's liberation, it was argued, had shifted social and psychological constraints that had previously prevented women's aggression, and led to a violent female crime wave:

It is not unreasonable to wonder whether these women represent the vanguard of a new social phenomenon; women who are no longer willing to see themselves discarded or ill-treated without hitting back ... the tip of a post-feminist iceberg in which women who have learned to assert themselves in everyday life have also begun to take the law into their own hands.[14]

Many psychologists believe that the disturbing rise in violence by girls is an inevitable legacy of the women's movement. Women are seizing upon equality in crime too.[15]

Academic fodder was inadvertently provided by feminist scholars in Britain and the United States who produced a rash of books on violent women. These scholars were seeking to challenge the paternalistic notion promoted in mainstream criminology that women are inherently non-aggressive.[16] Yet their work was open to cooptation by a conservative law-and-order agenda fueling a moral panic about a dramatic rise in violent crimes by women. As Stuart Hall's work on the invention of the "Black mugger" in the 1970s has shown, moral panics about crime are self-fulfilling. Once a certain type of "offense" is defined as a problem, there is greater media coverage and state intervention, thus leading to increases in "offenses" tried and sentenced in the courts. This increase in sentencing in turn produces dramatic growth in "crime rates" which further fuels the moral panic and leads to public calls for harsher sentencing and increased policing.[17] In the 1990s, the panic over violent women followed a similar pattern. Once the notion of women as perpetrators of violence was seen to sell newspapers and push up TV ratings, there was a spate of articles about "girl gangs," "female muggers," and "violent women." "Experts," including psychologists, judges, and criminologists, were called on to explain why women and girls had become "more violent" and to make the connections between women's liberation, girl power, and women's crime. This focus, combined with a general backlash against feminism, led to hardened attitudes toward women by the police and judiciary who saw women's violence as evidence that women's liberation had gone too far.[18]

Anne Worrall argues that when women are not being disciplined by male family members, the state steps in, in the guise of social workers, psychiatrists, and the judiciary, to supervise and punish women who "offend" gendered norms.[19] But the debate about violent women is not only gendered. Articles about "girl gangs" and women involved in fights inevitably focused on either African Caribbean or white working=class girls from impoverished public housing estates. Behavior which deviated from gendered norms of passivity and self-sacrifice was therefore "explained" through racialized and class-based ideologies which depicted Black people and impoverished and unemployed women and men as aggressive, irrational, and alienated. Thus, paternalistic notions of femininity were mediated through prisms of race and class, creating the ideological space for the punishment and incarceration of Black and working-class women.

Karlene Faith points out that the backlash against feminism in the 1990s led to popular representations of women who appropriate power and force—traditionally seen as masculine characteristics—as pathologically manipulative and evil.[20] Against this backdrop of shifting perceptions of gender, violence, and culpability, Zoora Shah's life history was utilized to differentiate her from Kiranjit Ahluwalia. Where Kiranjit was seen as an abused and self-sacrificing wife and mother who was pushed to do something entirely out of character, Zoora fit the image of the new "criminal" woman:

> Poisoning is something that people find hard to take. So her image is very different from Kiranjit's. She's someone who's a bad character, and who is seen as very manipulative, the poisoning is seen as quite cold-blooded.[21]

The cultural defense that was used successfully in Kiranjit's case was ruled out in Zoora's:

> And they said that she has no honor to preserve, she's a prostitute basically. That was the implication. So basically what it means is that we can accept that Asian women feel shame and honor and that's the reason why Kiranjit couldn't leave her husband. But what does she mean she felt shame, she doesn't fit the stereotype. That's why she lost the appeal.[22]

While Kiranjit was a middle-class woman whose social circles did not take her into impoverished and criminalized communities, Zoora was tied into prostitution, drug dealing, and violence in Bradford's working-class Muslim community. Public reactions may also have been influenced by a rise of what has been termed "Islamophobia," or fear and hostility toward the Muslim presence in Britain and in the global arena.[23]

While much has been made of the "new" anti-Muslim racism post-9/11, Islamophobia has historical precedents dating back as far as the Crusades, and was a feature of British life prior to the September 11 attacks. In particular, it was whipped up during the Second Gulf War when mosques in Birmingham and London were attacked. The sight of Muslim youth demonstrating in protest of Salman Rushdie's *Satanic Verses* was also read by white commentators as an indication that Islam was undermining the "British way of life." So while Kiranjit's life leant itself to white fantasies of colonial paternalism, Zoora was clearly defined as part of a racialized religious threat to "law and order." Rather than rescue her, this threat was met with brutal repression by the criminal justice system. Kiranjit's freedom could be given on terms that did not seriously disrupt the racialized, gendered, and class ideologies of neocolonial Britain. Zoora's case, however, demands a rethinking of the criminalization of the racially marginalized, sexually abused, and financially exploited.

Taking off the Blinkers

While activist women of color working against domestic violence have made some impressive gains regarding recognition of the problem of violence in Black British communities, some activists are concerned that the limits of pragmatic politics have been reached. Presenting women who kill their batterers as different from other women prisoners —"victims" not "perpetrators," and therefore "not guilty" of a crime—won support for the argument that Kiranjit should not be incarcerated. But this argument is not effective if the accused woman, like Zoora, does not fit cleanly into the "innocent" category—meaning she is innocent of any other "offenses" besides the act of self-defense against the abuser. As Hannana Siddiqui of Southall Black Sisters reflects, "Zoora does not sit comfortably with the image of a passive Asian woman ... She is not 'squeaky clean,' but that is the reality of many Asian women's lives."[24] The majority of women who come into conflict with the law are not "squeaky clean," yet they too have a history of violence and abuse that in some way contributed to their incarceration.

For many poor women and women of color, sexual, emotional, and physical abuse early in life can lie at the root of an addiction that leads to a drug-related charge. In addition, male violence and coercion is often implicated in the lives of women incarcerated for a range of criminalized acts, from drug importation to prostitution. If feminist activists do not embrace a politics of prison abolitionism, their demands for exceptional treatment for a handful of cases do not speak to the majority of women prisoners who are also survivors of violence. In many cases, resources that are racialized or class-based determine whether a woman will deal with violence in "law-abiding" ways (for example, get a prescription for antidepressants or other legal pharmaceuticals, call the police, take out a restraining order, find a new home) or ways which come into conflict with the criminal justice system (for example, use illegal substances, be coerced into prostitution or drug dealing, use physical violence). Without a general campaign to release all women prisoners, speaking for this "innocent" minority limits the politics of antiviolence, cutting it off from its revolutionary potential.

The antiviolence movement has in many ways been complicit in the "law and order" agenda that has emerged as a response to globalization in Britain, Canada, the United States, and elsewhere. White feminist activists generally think of the 1970s as a triumphant period in which second wave feminism brought the personal into the political arena, raising awareness about domestic violence, incest, and rape. Yet the 1970s also marked immense shifts in global capital that were enabled by developments in new technology. As corporations began to relocate their production operations to the Global South, unemployment hit urban communities of color in the Global North, and steady union jobs were replaced by irregular, "feminized," minimum-wage jobs. Governments responded to the creation of increasingly unstable urban "ghettos" by deploying punitive victim-blaming rhetoric that justified a shift from welfare and social services to policing and incarceration.[25] This was facilitated by the growth of a transnational prison industry, first in the United States and then in Britain, Canada, and Australia.[26] Corporations such as Wackenhut and Corrections Corporation of America developed sophisticated lobbying techniques to promote the use of incarceration as a "panacea" for social problems. Racialized practices of punishment became central to the political economy and social order of Western nations.

Young men of color, in particular, were criminalized and channeled into prison, where they disappeared off the unemployment statistics and became a cheap and disciplined source of labor. Women of color, and in particular Black and immigrant women, were labeled as "dole scroungers" (welfare bums) and subjected to surveillance and punitive health and welfare cutbacks that, in turn, freed up funds for prison construction. This shift was most marked in the US, where states like California, New York, and Texas embarked on a prison-building explosion throughout the 1980s and 1990s.[27] But Black Canadian, Caribbean, and indigenous communities were increasingly channeled into prisons in Canada too. In Britain, African Caribbean boys and young men were demonized as troublemakers and "muggers" and put in "sin bins" (special educational units) or prison.

Unlike the white-led feminist movement, which at this time viewed coalitions with Black men as antifeminist, the Black Women's Movement, which emerged in Britain in the mid-1970s, was particularly concerned with the educational segregation and criminalization of African Caribbean boys and young men.[28] Groups like the Organization of Women of African and Asian Descent (OWAAD) and Brixton Black Women's Group led several campaigns against busing, "sin bins," and overzealous policing. The Black Women's Movement was also active in making visible and challenging domestic violence and rape in African Caribbean and South Asian communities. Some women pointed out the dilemma facing Black women who looked to the police for protection against male violence when "law enforcement" was a source of brutality toward both Black men and women.[29] Unfortunately, this contradiction was not analyzed at a collective level. Instead, Black women in antiviolence work gradually became a part of the Women's Aid Federation, a national coalition of women's refuges that advocates more police intervention and harsher sentencing for male perpetrators of violence.

By the early 1990s, there was no effective Black feminist activism against criminalization and incarceration. Instead, most Black women had adopted the logic of incarceration in dealing with perpetrators of male violence. This acquiescence to mainstream "law and order" rhetoric was mirrored in the antiracist movement's demand for harsher punishment and increased police protection against racist violence. Both demands were co-opted by New Labour's "tough on crime, tough on the causes of crime" platform after its election in 1996. Radical antiracist and Black feminist voices were therefore united in demanding that the state increase its use of force to "protect" women and communities of color, rather than in challenging the racially repressive role of the police, judiciary, and prisons.

The shift of focus from resisting to reforming the criminal justice system explains why there has been little response from Black British women activists to the significant increases in women's incarceration. Between 1992 and 2002, the number of women in prison increased from 1,577 to 4,299, representing a 173% increase in ten years, compared to a 50% increase in men's imprisonment. This has led to the conversion of seven male prisons to incorporate women prisoners and the construction of two new female prisons. And the numbers keep swelling. Prison Service projections estimate that by 2009, there will be 5,600 imprisoned women.[30] In common with the United States and Canada, racial disparities in the British prison population are startling. 26% of women prisoners are women of color, compared to 5% of the general population. 24% are African Caribbean compared to 1.5% of the general population.[31]

Activists who seek longer terms of incarceration for racist and sexist violence seldom recognize that additional resources for policing, surveillance, and prisons inevitably lead to increased repression of Black and working-class communities. Since the early 1990s, African Caribbean women have been incarcerated in ever-greater numbers for poverty and drug-related offenses. Yet the criminalization of poor women of color, and the associated violence of separation from young children, has not been addressed by either the mainstream antiviolence movement or by most Black women's organizations. And while there are a few organizations, such as Hibiscus and Women in Prison, campaigning for women prisoners' rights with an abolitionist platform, they are isolated from other Black women activists and the antiracist movement in general.

Lessons from a British Prison

Zoora's case presents women of color activists in Britain, the United States, Canada, and elsewhere with a number of challenges. Firstly, the criminalization of Zoora as a woman who experienced multiple forms of exploitation and abuse points to the failure of the "law and order" approach to violence against women of color. Women of color who experience male violence are more likely to be criminalized for the survival strategies that they develop than to be protected by the criminal justice system. Advocating for a strengthening of state agencies— such as the police and judiciary—without transforming the racial/class ideologies underpinning incarceration inevitably leads to increased surveillance and policing of poor communities and people of color. This, in turn, fuels prison expansion. Increasingly, private corporations are contracted to staff and manage prisons, and once they are built, private lobby groups, politicians, and prison unions demand a regular flow of incarcerable bodies from the courts. In growing numbers, the bodies of women of color, punished for poverty and drug-related crimes, form the raw material for the prison-industrial complex. If we redefine violence to include the brutality of isolation; deprivation of family ties; psychological, verbal, and physical harassment; and racial abuse associated with imprisonment, then the women of color antiviolence movement must rethink its belief in incarceration as a solution to the multiple forms of violence facing women.

Secondly, the differences between Kiranjit's successful campaign, and Zoora's continued abuse at the hands of the state, highlight complex issues facing antiracist activists. While the details of Kiranjit's personal history and her location within neocolonial discourse on South Asian women facilitated widespread support for her release, that support often did not challenge the racist, classist nature of the criminal justice system. Kiranjit was identified as exceptional and misplaced within a prison population, represented in the popular imagination as a dangerous underclass of racialized women. If campaigns to release battered women who kill their abusers are not located within a broader abolitionist discourse, they may accentuate artificial differences between "battered women" and "female offenders." This distinction obscures the histories of violence and abuse experienced by most women prisoners, reinforcing the legitimacy of incarcerating the silent prison majority.

In fact, Kiranjit's case is similar to other campaigns to release individual prisoners. Campaigns for the release of men and women who have been falsely accused, or who are political prisoners, implicitly suggest that the "correctly accused" or "non-political prisoners" exist. But, as Assata Shakur points out, all prisoners in capitalist societies are victims of a criminal justice system that is based on the oppression and exploitation of men and women of color.[32] Therefore, campaigns need to be located in, and informed by, a broader political analysis of, and opposition to, the prison-industrial complex.

In the United States, the successful case for clemency for Kemba Smith, who was released in 2000, can be seen as similar to Kiranjit's as exemplary of the impact of the war on drugs on women of color. Kemba was an African American college student and mother who was forced into involvement in drug dealing by an abusive boyfriend and sentenced to 24.5 years.[33] The brutality of the judicial system's treatment of Kemba as a battered woman is indeed shocking. However, like Kiranjit, Kemba was presented by such mainstream media sources as *Glamour* magazine as being "out of place" in prison because of her "innocence," and her exemplary life as a college student and mother. This analysis bypasses the central point: women don't belong in cages regardless of how they have tried to survive. Until we really embrace this abolitionist position, freedom for Kemba will not translate into freedom for all African American women, including those who are poor and lack formal education.[34]

A third lesson from Zoora's case is the danger of replacing the struggle for social justice with the demand for criminal justice reforms. In Britain, feminists involved in the cases of Kiranjit, Sara Thornton, and Emma Humphreys successfully demanded an increased awareness within the judiciary of the differences between violent men who kill their partners, and women who kill their abusive partners. Demands by prison reform groups have led to the establishment of a Women's Policy Group in the Prison Service with the mission of "transforming the care of women."[35] Criticisms by antiracist activists of racist abuse and discrimination in prisons have also led to the formation of RESPOND, a racial equality strategy for the prison service, and the establishment of a Prison Service Race Relations Group. Yet throughout this period when antiracist and feminist reforms were made, the number of women of color in prison has continued to spiral.

The British antiracist and Black women's movements of the 1970s and 1980s incorporated a strong analysis of state violence and repression. However, in the 1990s, as Black British communities have made a greater impact on mainstream political agendas, there has been a convergence between progressive movements and the state. Women of color activists have increasingly become invested in the illusion of an "antiracist/antisexist state," deploying the forces of law and order in defense of women and men of color. While the New Labour government has responded to feminist and anti-racist activism by incorporating some of the movements' demands into legislation, this has been at the price of a radical analysis of the role of state violence in the lives of women of color. As such, the state-corporate investment in mass incarceration has gone largely unchallenged by Black women's organizations.

These developments are mirrored in Canada, where penal reformers, such as the Canadian Association of Elizabeth Fry Societies (CAEFS), successfully demonstrated to the Correctional Service of Canada that the needs of women prisoners were not being met in a prison system designed around male imprisonment. After several years of consultation and negotiation, four new regional "women-centered" prisons and a "healing lodge" for aboriginal women were built, designed around the female prison population and staffed, at least in the early stages, by professionals experienced in working with women in refuges, social services, and prisons. Despite good intentions, women-centered prisons revictimize the Black, indigenous, and poor women they house, most of whom are survivors of multiple forms of violence, leading to extensive self-harm and suicide attempts. Continuing abuses indicate that even within the new women-centered framework, the traditional penal culture of racism and sexism has quickly re-emerged.[36] Most significantly, the investment of energy into women prisoners has not led to any decrease in the number of women in Canadian prisons and jails.

Reform-based demands risk absorption into the existing racial-class dynamics of state systems of repression and control. Furthermore, progressive activists involved in such demands are in danger of becoming incorporated into the very system that they initially opposed, as they are invited to sit on consultation and implementation committees of "antiracist" or "woman-centered" prisons.

Finally, Zoora's case requires us to develop an analysis of differential racisms affecting communities of color, and of the interactions between immigration and violence against women. The low numbers of South Asian women in the British prison system have led to little awareness within Black women's organizations of the impact of criminalization on South Asian women. However, as Islamophobia increases and traditionally paternalistic attitudes toward South Asians harden, Muslim young people in particular are becoming vulnerable to criminalization. In addition, Pakistan's role within the heroin trade means that some women risk long terms in prison for working as "mules." Therefore, activists must be aware of shifting patterns of racialization, and how they are shaped by public events. In Canada, for example, the conservative press whipped up a moral panic about the capture of several boatloads of undocumented Chinese refugees, which has led to a hardening of attitudes toward Chinese immigrants. Police in several Canadian cities now have units targeting Chinese gangs and smugglers.

In the United States, activism around criminalization and racial disparity in policing and sentencing has tended to focus on African Americans and Latinos. Native Americans are generally excluded, despite the fact that they also experience disproportionate policing, arrest, and imprisonment.[37] Moreover Asian American youth—especially Vietnamese and Laotians—who are increasingly being targeted for gang involvement, are made invisible by the black/white binary. Greater analysis of the intersection of immigration, colonization, and criminalization is necessary, and women of color activists should play a key role in building coalitions between groups traditionally targeted by the criminal justice system and newly criminalized and immigrant groups.

Like corporate agendas under global capital, practices of "law and order" do not develop within rigid national borders. The media, politicians, and penal administrators in Europe and North America form a transnational network of newspaper and magazine conglomerates, television and radio empires, and political and professional relationships. This network disseminates ideologies and strategies of control and punishment such as "three strikes," private prisons, mandatory minimums, and "women-centered" penal regimes. The experiences of women of color affected by state violence and incarceration are fundamentally shaped by these transnational connections. However, as activists, we seldom build transnational coalitions or seek to learn from the experiences and activism of women of color across the border, or across the Atlantic. In order to build an effective anti-violence movement, women of color in the United States, Canada, Britain, and elsewhere need to analyze critically the successes and failures of activists in multiple locations. When we develop the habit of thinking outside of national borders, we open ourselves to new challenges and critiques. These radical critiques bring us closer to building a movement that simultaneously resists male violence, state repression, and the mass incarceration of poor communities of color.

2

Disability in the New World Order

Nirmala Erevelles

When examining the relationship between the World Bank and issues related to disability in neocolonial contexts, it is essential to explore policy development and institutional power from a historical perspective, and to *always* interrogate whose interests are being served. If we examine these issues ahistorically, we elide social, political, and economic complexities that (re)constitute oppressive social relations, even as nation-states "liberalize" their economies in efforts to become viable participants in transnational capitalism. In particular, this exploration foregrounds the geopolitical power imbalances that exist between nation-states, and the roles that international organizations like the United Nations, the World Bank, and the International Monetary Fund (IMF)—the power brokers in the New World Order—have in continuing (neo)colonialism under the auspices of globalization, which represents a violent outcome for the world's poorest citizens.

In this chapter, I speak from the critical vantage point of two theoretical perspectives: Third World feminism(s) and disability studies. By deploying the term Third World feminism(s), I am referring to the political constituency of women of African, Caribbean, Asian, and Latin American descent, as well as Native peoples of the United States who constitute an oppositional alliance against the sexist, racist, imperialist, neocolonial structures that shape our lives (Mohanty, 1991). When defining Disability Studies, I refer particularly to the social, political, and economic conditions within the category of "disability" which is constituted as "deviant" difference, and the ideological effects that such constructions of "disability" have on the reproduction of racial, gendered, and class oppression (Russell, 1998; Charlton, 1998; Erevelles, 2002). At the same time, my discussion will address the actual conditions and experiences of Third world people's lives when mediated via the oppressive and often violent social relations of race, class, caste, gender, and disability.

The dialectical relationship between poverty and disability has been recognized for some time (Shirley, 1983, Russell, 1998; Elwan, 1999). Living with a disability adds to the risks of living in poverty, while at the same time, conditions of poverty increase the possibility of becoming disabled (Elwan, 1999). In this essay, I will elaborate on this relationship between poverty and disability in Third World contexts—with a special focus on India—in the wake of sweeping economic reforms implemented by state governments in deference to structural adjustment policies (SAPs) which have been recommended by the World Bank and the IMF. After briefly describing SAPs in their historical context, I focus specifically on how these policies impact women living in poverty, and how they contribute to the social construction of disability in Third World contexts. Then I explore the effects of SAPs on Third World disabled people, especially in contexts where there has been a decrease in social spending because of the economic reforms mandated by the World Bank and the IMF. Finally, I conclude this essay by reflecting on the epistemological assumptions that SAPs are based on—assumptions rooted in transnational capitalism's emphasis on productivity and efficiency defined within the narrow parameters of accumulation of profit for multinational corporations. In particular, I will discuss these epistemological assumptions in light of a measure designed to calculate the cost-effectiveness of health services called disability adjusted life years (DALYs). Foregrounding the ideological assumptions that undergird this measure, I expose the political commitments of such seemingly benevolent gestures that support the continued marginalization, exploitation, and dehumanization of, and therefore violence against, Third World people, especially Third World disabled people.

Historical Perspectives: Colonial Discontinuities
Colonial history has played a critical part in the economic crises experienced in the Third World. Colonialism supported the old International Division of Labor (IDL), where raw materials and labor were appropriated from the colonies and transported to the colonial metropolises for manufacturing and production, before being returned to the colonies and sold as consumer goods for large profits, once again appropriated by the metropolises. Clearly, as a result of the old IDL, the colonies were impoverished because they occupied the lowest rungs of this division of labor. The old IDL was disrupted when the former colonies began clamoring for independence and waged nationalist struggles against their colonial rulers. It was around the same time that Europe and Japan were ending and recovering from World War II. In 1944, the Bretton Woods Conference was convened by the United States and Europe to support the construction of three international economic institutions—the World Bank, the IMF, and the GATT (General Agreement on Trade and Tariffs)—that would help stabilize the world economy. These organizations were charged with the tasks of determining exchange rates for international currency; supporting the reconstruction of war-devastated Europe and Japan; and supporting free international trade across national boundaries. Once again, political and economic power remained under the control of the former colonial powers and the United States, which now emerged as the leading economic power in the world. Moreover, because colonization had already forced the former colonies to participate, albeit through coercion in the global economy, their economic stability and continued participation in the new global order was essential. It was for these reasons that the World Bank, along with the US and Britain, became the principal donors and lending institutions for the former colonies struggling to build a viable economic infrastructure after more than a century of economic exploitation.

Still locked in economic dependence on the former colonial powers, Third World economies spiraled into dangerous economic crises in the 1970s when the Organization of the Petroleum Exporting Countries (OPEC) raised the price of oil. Most of these Third World economies were dependent on oil exports for their industrial and economic development. As a result, many of these nation-states defaulted on their loan payments. At this point, the IMF and World Bank intervened with SAPs that were, on paper, intended to promote efficiency and sustained economic growth to enable these economies to meet their debt obligations. This stabilization was also seen as a critical precondition for Third World nations to qualify for loans needed in the future (Chang, 1997).

Clearly without any bargaining power, Third World nations were forced back into similar colonialist economic relations with their former colonial powers by adhering to SAPs that demanded radical transformations in the nation-state's economic life. As a result, they continue to provide raw materials to donor markets, and remain the primary consumers of goods manufactured in the donor nations. These unequal relations were justified through the SAPs requirements on deflation, devaluation, decontrol, and privatization (Elson, 1992). These requirements resulted in the following economic reforms in Third World nation-states: trade liberalization which required a more focused export policy on "cash crops" and other raw materials and import substitution for all other goods that were not manufactured in the nation-state's economy; increased dependence on international financial resources; cuts to public spending which included reduction in public sector employment, limitations on food and agricultural subsidies, denationalization of public sector enterprises, and decreased expenditures in the areas of health, education, and social welfare (Feldman 1992).

In addition to these austerity measures, borrowing countries were encouraged to promote private investment, support trade and tariff reforms that benefited the donor nations, and construct export processing zones (EPZs) for multinational companies to produce tax-free goods using cheap labor from the host country— employing mostly Third World women. In this way, the former colonial powers and the United States supported what can be called the new IDL (Mies, 1985): a continuation of the same power inequalities in the current (neo)colonialist New World Order of transnational capitalism.

Engendering Economic Reform: Implications for Disability

Third World feminists have documented how the effects of (neo)colonial institutions and policies have transformed indigenous patriarchies and consolidated hegemonic middle-class cultures in metropolitan and colonized areas in support of oppressive patriarchal structures, albeit in new forms (Mies, 1985; Mohanty, 1991; McClintock,1995). This has been especially true in the context of the SAPs, where women and children have become the most vulnerable populations. Critics of the World Bank and the IMF have pointed out that SAPs were instituted to prioritize the efficient management of debt, rather than to transform the abject conditions of poverty in contexts where women and children represent the disproportionate percentage of the world's poor (Feldman, 1992; Elson 1992; Chang 1997). Programs instituted by the World Bank and the IMF also supposedly sought to include women as active participants in wage labor markets to enable their emancipation from patriarchal oppression.

However, most of the labor activities offered to Third World women are for low- wage work, because these women are considered "cheap" and "pliable" labor in both factory production and the service industry (Beneria and Feldman, 1992). As a result, this new gendered labor shift has forced men out of jobs, and, as a result, poor Third World women are forced to balance wage labor along with subsistence and domestic production. Because of the sharp fall in the purchasing power of their incomes, Third World women, many of whom are single heads of households, are faced with the sole responsibility of meeting household reproduction costs. In the desperation for employment, poor women are forced to take jobs in the informal and other low-wage sectors while, at the same time, their unpaid labor escalates because they must stretch limited funds to cover the subsistence of their households. Additionally, their health is also affected because of reduced food consumption, stress, and domestic violence—experiences that affect fertility, infant mortality, and disabling conditions in both their children and themselves.

It is this economic context that sets the stage for the social construction of disability. According to Elwan (1999), UNICEF's list of major causes of disability among children in Third World countries includes inadequate nutrition of mothers and children, vitamin deficiencies, abnormal prenatal or perinatal events, infectious diseases, accidents, and various other factors including environmental pollution and lack of adequate sanitation—all of which occur as a result of poverty conditions. Notwithstanding the World Bank's claims that the SAPs would eventually lead to a reduction in poverty, according to UNICEF, there has been a drop of 10% to 25% in average incomes, a 25% reduction in spending per capita on health, and a 50% reduction in spending per capita on education in the poorest countries in the world. Though officials argue that they advise sound macroeconomic policies and strategies that favor investment in basic human capital—primary health care and universal primary education—the implementation of the SAP's belie this claim. Abbasi points out that even though World Bank lending for health services has increased over the years, low-income countries are unable to meet and maintain health service costs and at the same time pay their debts, and have therefore begun to levy a small fee also called a "user charge" to all clients using public health services. In already destitute communities, these user charges have resulted in a decline in access to health services with disastrous consequences to these populations. As a result, according to Andrew Creese, a health economist at the World Health Organization (WHO), increases in maternal mortality and the incidence of communicable diseases such as diphtheria and tuberculosis have been attributed to such policies (Abbasi, 1999).

India offers a good case study of these practices. Forced to implement the structural adjustment programs (SAPs) in the early 1990s to meet the deficit in its balance of payments, the Indian state was encouraged to liberalize its economy, which required that it perform three main functions: protect and sustain the functioning of markets; use all policy instruments available to entice foreign capital investment; and undertake certain minimal expenditures so as to ameliorate the excesses perpetrated by the market (Patnaik, 1994). The implementation of the SAPs has only exacerbated the relationship between poverty and disability in India. Thus, for example, nearly fifteen thousand children in India under the age of five go blind because of a vitamin A deficiency caused by malnutrition (Pandey and Advani, 1996). Additionally, limited access to clean water supplies as well as overcrowding in inadequate and unsanitary living conditions are responsible for the spread of intestinal, infectious, and vector-carrying diseases that also contribute to the onset of disability.

Even health policies actively supported by the international organizations barely address the crux of the problem. For example, the Indian state's investment in "Health for All by 2000," based on the Alma Ata Declaration of 1978, fostered only two major programs—oral rehydration therapy and immunization—instead of providing general health care for everyone. While such programs produced good statistics that claimed a lower rate of infant mortality, malnutrition and morbidity rates increased (Werner, 1995). And in the current context, as SAPs have mandated the increased privatization of health care and user financed health services, the transfer of resources from its poor clients to the wealthy investors of health care is the main outcome.

Additionally, even the rehabilitation projects, such as community based rehabilitation (CBR) programs (which are actively supported by the World Bank and other international organizations, such as ActionAid) also have served to accentuate inequalities along the axes of gender, class, caste, and disability. The dominant representation of the philosophy of CBR has been to integrate disabled people into the social mainstream (Thomas, 1992; Pandey and Advani, 1996). In a context where the resources allocated to rehabilitation programs are low and where there is a shortage of trained personnel to provide these services, CBR has become one of the most cost-efficient means to save on mounting staff costs, waste of labor, and the low efficiency of services (Thomas, 1992). Thus, in an attempt to ensure maximum cost-efficiency, policy makers assume that the primary support for these programs will come from the community, where parents and workers, supervised by health volunteers (a village rehabilitation worker, or VRW, and a multipurpose rehabilitation worker, or MRW) will provide more specialized services to disabled members of the community.

However, the very concept of inclusion becomes exploitative in such contexts. Like the health programs supported by SAPs, CBR only serves to transfer the costs of services to the community. Thus, for example, even one of its advocates, Maya Thomas, director of the disability division ActionAid International-India has admitted that "the trend of progressive impoverishment of rural dwellings and the growing abandonment of extended family systems leave little economic and manpower resources in families that continue to look after the needs of their disabled members." (Thomas, 1992). Further, in patriarchal contexts, the provision of rehabilitation services by the family predominantly implies the woman, and so this becomes another burden in the life of the rural housewife caught up in her struggle for day-to-day economic survival. At the same time, most of the rehabilitation aides, who are low down in the occupational hierarchy and who receive pitiably low wages, are once again predominantly poor women from the community. Therefore, what has happened is that these state-initiated policies that have been celebrated for their cost-effectiveness are actually geared to "[mobilize] people's resources for government programs," (Kalyanpur, 1996) where the additional costs of these services continue to be absorbed by both the paid and unpaid labor of women.

"In Whose Interests?": Thinking Beyond Survival
Perhaps the most controversial concept that the World Bank has contributed to this discussion of disability in a global context is the concept of the Disability-Adjusted Life Year (DALY). According to the World Bank, the DALY is

a unit used for measuring both the global burden of disease and the effectiveness of health interventions, as indicated by reductions in the disease burden. It is calculated as the present value of the future years of disability-free life that are lost as the result of the premature deaths or cases of disability occurring in a particular year.

Put more simply, using the DALY, the World Bank now prioritizes health interventions by calculating their relative cost-effectiveness. In other words, cost-effectiveness is measured by the number of DALYs saved through each intervention where the cost of each intervention is weighed against the person's potential "productivity" (i.e., contribution to economic growth) (Werner, 1995). Thus each disease, ailment, or disability is classified according to how many years of "productive" (disability free) life the individual loses as a result, and is weighed against age and work potential. Hence, children and the elderly have lower value than young adults, and presumably disabled persons who are unable to work are awarded zero value and therefore have little or no entitlement to health services at public expense.

From a disability rights perspective, such calculations can only be regarded as simply preposterous. In fact, scholars in the area of disability studies have already critiqued how ableist society has constructed disabled people as defective citizens incapable of contributing anything to society (Ferguson, 1987; Thomson, 1997; Russell, 1998; Charlton, 1998; Kittay, 2000). For example, Marta Russell has vividly exposed the brutal connection between capitalism and social Darwinism that is implicit in these arguments that construct disabled people as "defective" and unproductive in the economy (Russell, 1998). However, productivity is not a transhistorical category; instead, it is very much dependent on historical context, where the present demands of (global) capitalism depend on the ease with which the multinational companies can extract the maximum profits from its workers, and nation-states can extract low- wage and unpaid labor from its citizens (Ebert 1996). In such contexts, an individual's productivity is not measured by his/her skill to produce goods and services that would satisfy social and human needs; rather, her/his productivity is based solely on the capitalists' exploitative demands for increasing profits.

This logic under which capitalism operates has particularly deleterious effects on disabled individuals. Since most disabled individuals have physiological complications that prevent the easy and efficient extraction of surplus value from their labor power, their labor power is accorded little value within the competitive market place, and they are therefore constructed as unemployable. It is here then, that the DALY constitutes disabled people as a liability in state spending rather than a valued investment. Herein, lies the violence of this representation. By locating disabled people as unworthy of receiving necessary health resources so that they can actively participate in both the social and economic life of their communities, this characterization actively consigns them to institutional care or active neglect. Moreover, such policies provide further impetus for contemporary eugenic practices that are justified by conflating the value of human life with economic efficiency.

Conclusion

This chapter points very clearly to the hegemonic economic and political power imbalances that work against people of color and disabled people across the globe. If the World Bank, the IMF, and the UN were genuine in their expressed interests in supporting oppressed people, their policies would protect vulnerable populations from the excesses of capitalism ("adjustment with a human face") by applying political and economic pressures on both donor and debtor nations and by pushing for the transformation of the oppressive social relations supported by the power elite. Policies that presume to embody "adjustment with a human face" should be linked with people's struggles for human dignity, rather than merely enabling them to survive on the borders of a hostile world.

However, as many activists are aware, the World Bank and the IMF cannot be relied on to provide the impetus for such radical changes. I am therefore calling for critical alliances to be forged between a Third World feminist movement and the disability rights movement that will foreground the intersections of race, class, gender, and disability in our struggle against economic violence. Only a movement that is conscious of our differences and our commonalities will be able to mount a critical and concerted opposition against the economic violence that is an intrinsic part of our unique and diverse life experiences.

3

Federal Indian Law and Violent Crime
Native Women and Children at the Mercy of the State

Sarah Deer

> As you return to your homes, and as you talk with your people, please tell them that the time of dying is at its end. Tell your children that the time of shame and fear is over. Tell your young men and women to replace their anger with hope and love for their people. Together, we must wipe the tears of seven generations. Together, we must allow our broken hearts to mend.—*Kevin Gover, assistant secretary for Indian Affairs in the Department of the Interior, September 8, 2000*

> [O]ne public speech by a single mid-level government official—especially one who is a member of the oppressed minority—is unlikely to have much lasting impact without actual changes in government policies and citizen attitudes in the United States.—*Weston 2001, 1050*

> Our women are open game. So many are violated, and they tell us no one will do anything.—*Deborah Blossom, Western Shoshone, Tosawihii clan, acting director of the Great Basin Women's Coalition against Violence*

On the 175th anniversary of the establishment of the Bureau of Indian Affairs (BIA), Assistant Secretary Kevin Gover (Pawnee) issued a monumental apology to Native people on behalf of the bureau. In the apology, Gover acknowledged the failures of Indian policy and the atrocities committed by United States government officials against Native peoples (Gover, 2000). Many felt that the apology showed profound humility and accountability. However, in the aftermath of Gover's statement, Native persons continue to suffer the highest rates of poverty, unemployment, and violent victimization in the United States.

More recently, several US senators have proposed yet another apology—this one to take the form of a national apology, authored by Congress and signed by the president of the United States (Senate Joint Resolution 15, 2006). While the importance of public acknowledgments and apology cannot be underestimated (Bradford, 2003), such actions by the United States government do not go far enough in addressing the systemic violence experienced by women and children in Indian country today. For example, the resolution "apologizes on behalf of the people of the United States to all Native Peoples for the many instances of violence, maltreatment, and neglect inflicted on Native Peoples by citizens of the United States" (Senate Joint Resolution 15, 2006). But drafters and proponents of a national apology would do well to study and understand the complicated history of criminal justice in Indian country, and the impact on victims who fall through the wide gaps created by a system originally designed to destroy—not heal.

Addressing five hundred years of violence, maltreatment, and neglect requires more than apology; indeed, major changes and adjustments to the current structure of federal laws, policies, and regulations impacting tribal nations are needed. For example, decision-making authority and control over violent crime should be restored to indigenous nations to provide full accountability and justice to the victims. The status quo leaves the most vulnerable citizens of Indian nations without recourse for repeated abuses at the hands of government officials.

The federal government has systemically stripped power from tribal nations over the course of the last several hundred years. As a result, Native people residing in Indian country are largely dependent on federal agencies, such as the Indian Health Service, the Bureau of Indian Affairs, and the Department of Justice (including the Federal Bureau of Investigation) to provide for basic human needs such as health care, education, and protection from crime. Numerous reports have found these agencies to be underfunded, understaffed, and unable to meet the increasing needs of a growing indigenous population. In 2003, the United States Commission on Civil Rights issued a scathing report entitled "A Quiet Crisis: Federal Funding and Unmet Needs in Indian Country" which highlighted the insufficiency of federal funding to meet even the most basic needs of Native peoples.

This article will focus on the unique impact of federal Indian law on Native crime victims. Through an analysis of historical events, contemporary statistics, and federal laws, this article will demonstrate why the adjudication and response to victimization of Native women and children must be restored to tribal nations. While the federal system is currently tasked with primary control and power in cases where Native women and children are victimized in Indian country, true justice and healing will only be possible when the victims can seek accountability within their own judicial systems.

Federal Indian Law and Crime Victims

In order to understand why indigenous people have become so dependent upon federal agencies, it is necessary to review the federal laws and policies that have stripped tribal governments of their power to provide for the safety and well-being of indigenous people. For the purposes of this article, I will limit the discussion to the most significant federal actions that have an impact on the response to violent victimization of Native women and children.

First and foremost, it is critical to point out that tribal nations had full jurisdiction (legal authority) over all crimes and disputes prior to intrusion by European and American legal systems. Historical evidence indicates that most indigenous nations had extremely powerful and effective justice systems that provided strong deterrence to crimes against women and children. Crimes such as rape, domestic violence, and child abuse were extremely rare, but when they did occur, tribal systems of jurisprudence provided a powerful system of social checks and balances that held offenders accountable for their behavior (Poupart, 2003; Allen, 1986). Unlike the Anglo-American legal system, wherein victims of violent crime have historically had no voice in the criminal justice process (Beloof, 1999), most indigenous legal systems were victim-centered. The tribal governments strived to provide a sense of spiritual and emotional recovery from violent crime, as well as any compensation or restitution. While no system is perfect, it has been suggested that indigenous philosophies of justice generally provide more protection and healing to victims than does the Anglo-American system (Lee, 1996; Valencia-Weber and Zuni, 1995).

Over the past 125 years, policies of the United States government have weakened these indigenous justice systems and replaced them with the adversarial Anglo-American model (Porter, 1997). The results have been devastating: today, Native women are the most victimized population in the United States (Greenfeld and Smith, 1999). The rates of domestic violence and sexual assault within indigenous communities far exceed those of any other racial or ethnic group (Rennison, 2001; Tjaden and Thoennes, 2000), and it is estimated that over one-third of American Indian and Alaskan Native women will be victimized by sexual violence in their lifetime (Tjaden and Thoennes, 2000). The laws and policies of the United States play a significant role in the high rate of victimization, because they have inhibited the ability of tribal communities to respond to and address crime in a culturally appropriate way (Bigfoot, 2000). Andrea Smith has provided a thorough analysis of the relationship between colonization and sexual violence by linking rape to other forms of forced assimilation, such as missions and boarding schools. In addition to understanding the historical context, understanding the complicated calculus of contemporary criminal jurisdiction in Indian country helps to illuminate the legal structures that continue to make Native women particularly vulnerable to violence (Smith, 1999).

The Major Crimes Act

In 1885, Congress passed the Major Crimes Act (MCA), which marked the first significant federal intrusion on tribal justice systems. The inspiration for the MCA arose from the US Supreme Court case in *Ex Parte Crow Dog*, which originated in a Lakota murder case. In reviewing federal law, which amazingly still recognized tribal nations as independent sovereigns despite the long-standing effort to extinguish them, the US Supreme Court ruled that only Lakota justice systems had authority to adjudicate murder committed by one Lakota against another. The non-Indian population was outraged and demanded that Congress intervene in order to allow the Native defendant to be prosecuted in an Anglo legal system (Harring, 1994). In response to this public outcry, Congress passed the MCA—an attempt to address intratribal crime by imposing the federal prosecutorial framework.

The MCA allows federal prosecution of Native defendants in cases of serious felony cases. From its inception, the MCA has included the crime of rape in its list of offenses that trigger federal prosecution. Child sexual abuse was added in 1986 (EchoHawk, 2001). When victims of serious violence in Indian country report crime to authorities, they are often referred to federal investigators and prosecutors, who may have high caseloads including bank robberies, drug smuggling, and immigration matters.

An important and underdiscussed facet of the MCA is that the federal law itself never explicitly divested tribal nations of authority over the enumerated crimes (Clinton et al. 2003). *Therefore, tribal nations technically retain concurrent jurisdiction over crimes such as rape, and can prosecute them simultaneously with the federal government.* However, the development of contemporary tribal legal systems has been largely controlled by the federal government, and the concurrent jurisdiction over violent crimes has not been adequately exercised. Therefore, many tribes do not pursue cases against rapists and batterers, or will wait until a declination from a federal or state prosecutor before proceeding with an official tribal response.

Public Law 280

Approximately seventy years after Congress passed the MCA, jurisdiction over criminal matters was transferred to some state governments through a federal law known as Public Law 280, or PL 280 (Melton and Gardner, 2000). PL 280 was part of a larger federal effort to ultimately "terminate" and end recognition of tribal nations—an official government policy which has since been abandoned. For those tribal nations located within the boundaries of states affected by PL 280, criminal activity and violence fall under the authority of the state. However, many of the states have not responded with effective law enforcement, leaving tribal communities at the mercy of criminals who prey on the vulnerable.

Like the MCA, PL 280 did not specifically divest tribal governments of concurrent jurisdiction over crime (Song and Jiménez, 1998). However, the practical impact of PL 280 has included a weakening of tribal justice systems and a lack of response to criminal behavior, leaving many victims of crime without recourse in either the state or the tribal system. As Goldberg and Champagne note:

> The legislative history of Public Law 280 is laden with references to the problem of "lawlessness" on reservations. Traditional tribal justice systems were described as weakened and ineffectual, and federal mechanisms were considered too limited in their jurisdiction and too costly to expand. Reservations were described as places of rampant crime and disorder. Public Law 280 was supposed to provide the solution to this problem of "lawlessness" by empowering state civil and criminal courts to do what the tribal and federal systems supposedly could not. Ironically and tragically, however, Public Law 280 has itself become the source of lawlessness on reservations (Goldberg and Champagne 1996).

The Indian Civil Rights Act

The Indian Civil Rights Act of 1968 (ICRA) was passed in an era generally known for its progressive and liberating legislation. Unfortunately, the ICRA was largely a misnomer; the act was actually an imposition of Anglo-American conceptions of civil rights upon the ancient wisdom and ways of tribal justice systems. Instead of concentrating on the racial discrimination and political disenfranchisement suffered by Native people, Congress instead focused on alleged abuses by tribal court systems (Pevar, 2002). ICRA was a congressional response to fears that tribal courts were unburdened by US constitutional limitations, and required tribal governments to honor the language contained in the US Bill of Rights (with a few exceptions). In addition, ICRA imposed significant limitations on the ability of tribal courts to incarcerate and fine criminal defendants. From 1968 to 1986, tribal courts could not impose a sentence of greater than six months in jail and/or a fine of more than five hundred dollars. In 1986, as part of a "crackdown" on drug trafficking, ICRA was amended to allow tribal courts to sentence a criminal defendant to up to one year in jail and/or a five-thousand dollar fine. (Pevar, 2002).

Even though tribal governments did not traditionally rely on incarceration as a response to violence, many understood ICRA to limit a tribal court's ability to respond to serious violence. Since Anglo-American systems respond to violent crimes with long periods of imprisonment, ICRA has served to further the myth that tribal governments have no power to respond to felony-level crimes. Assimilated tribal justice systems will often resist prosecuting extremely violent crimes, having internalized the Anglo-American belief that incarceration or monetary sanctions are the *only* possible response to violence.

ICRA does not impact a tribal government's ability to impose alternate or traditional sentences, such as banishment, community service, probation, counseling, or public apology. Nonetheless, the limitation on the ability to incarcerate has had a disparate impact on victims of rape and other violent crimes. Native women and children who are victimized often discover that their tribal nation does not have strong contemporary laws or prosecutorial policies on felony-level criminal behavior. If the federal or state systems choose not to prosecute, the victim is left at the mercy of the perpetrator.

Oliphant v. Suquamish

Perhaps the most dangerous and damaging contemporary intrusion on tribal justice systems occurred in 1978 with the US Supreme Court decision *Oliphant v. Suquamish Indian Tribe.* This decision has created a vacuum of justice for crime victims who have the misfortune of being attacked by a non-Indian. Ever since the decision in *Oliphant,* tribal nations do not have the power or authority to prosecute crimes committed by non-Indians. This decision has created a crisis situation in some tribal communities, because non-Indian sexual predators, drug manufacturers, pimps, and other violent persons have become attracted to Indian country as a location where crimes can be committed without recourse (Fletcher, 2004). Indian country has become attractive to pedophiles and sexual predators, because of the vulnerability of the citizens and the jurisdictional gaps.

The combination of the MCA, PL 280, ICRA, and *Oliphant,* along with numerous other federal laws and policies, has created one of the most complicated jurisdictional frameworks in American law (Frickey, 1996). Criminal behavior can go unchecked in a system where law enforcement, prosecutors, and policy makers cannot discern the appropriate response. Moreover, tribal legal systems have been weakened and/or assimilated such that they may be ineffective at addressing violence against women and children.

Federal Agencies and Criminal Behavior

The entire nature of federal Indian law, in its gradual weakening and devaluing of tribal justice systems, has placed tribal citizens at a high risk for victimization and violence. However, the federal systems that have replaced the tribal systems have perpetuated the problem by failing to provide accountability on a number of levels. First, allegations exist that the federal system fails to adequately investigate and prosecute crime when it does occur (McColl, 2004; Yost, 2003; Million, 2000). Native people are an extremely vulnerable population. Moreover, they are often invisible and forgotten in public discourse regarding social and community issues (Poupart, 2002).

Second, federal agencies entrusted to provide safety and support to Native people in the United States continue to hire persons with a history of violence, sex offenses, and child endangerment (Hinkle, 2003; Kelley, 2002). These actions continue to put Native peoples at risk, with no accountability in sight. Abuse committed by federal employees is a continuation of the colonization process, with no adequate forum for accountability or healing. Here are a few examples of criminal conduct committed by people entrusted to the most personal and sensitive aspects of Native people's lives:

- In 1990, a Senate Special Committee on Investigations issued a report detailing widespread sexual abuse committed against Native children by non-Indian BIA teachers (Senate Report 101-60, 1990).
- In 1991, Thomas W. Michaelis, an obstetrician-gynecologist, was convicted for attempting to sexually assault four teenage girls. He was then hired by an Indian Health Service hospital in Arizona, where he worked for eight years before being fired in 2001 (*Associated Press*, March 5, 2002).
- In 1996, Phillip G. Daugherty was hired as a nurse by the Oklahoma City Indian Health Service, despite his 1982 conviction for a sex crime in the Marine Corps. After being accused of fondling a female patient in 1998, Daugherty's criminal record was discovered and he was removed from federal service in 1999 (*Daugherty v. Thompson*, 2003).
- In 1997, an Oklahoma state court convicted Dr. Richard Clay Hudson, who worked at the Creek Nation Community Hospital, of rape and sodomy of one of his patients. Dr. Hudson had previously worked for the United States Air Force, where he was also accused of assaulting patients (*Shawnee News-Star*, October 9, 1997).
- In 1998, a former family practice physician at the Navajo Area Indian Health Service Agency pleaded guilty to seven counts of shipping child pornography (*Albuquerque Journal*, May 15, 1998).
- In 2000, a jury found a Bureau of Indian Affairs employee guilty of aggravated sexual abuse (*Billings Gazette*, July 30, 2000).

- In late 2003, a sixteen-year-old girl died of alcohol poisoning at a Chemawa boarding School (a federal institution) after apparently being abandoned in a holding cell (Associated Press, December 26, 2003). The US Attorney's Office has declined to pursue criminal charges in the case. (Lawrence-Turner, 2004).

The demoralizing impact of these numerous accounts cannot be overstated. Native people, already vulnerable to criminal victimization, may choose to go without necessary health care rather than risk being victimized by a federal employee. Many tribal justice systems, having been weakened by federal policies, often do not have the capacity to respond to these incidents (and have no criminal authority over non-Indians). Furthermore, there is no indication that federal officials who perpetrate crimes against indigenous people (or those who fail to conduct appropriate background checks) will be held accountable for their behaviors. Existing federal laws fail to provide justice to victims of these federal perpetrators.

The 1991 Indian Child Protection and Family Violence Prevention Act was passed, partly in response to a Senate Oversight Committee's 1989 finding that the BIA failed to detect and report child molestation at schools. However, federal funds have never been appropriated to support the mandates in the act (Cross, 2003), and it is not clear that the federal laws have resulted in increased safety for Native children. A recent audit by the Department of the Interior's Office of the Inspector General revealed that the "current process does not prevent unsuitable individuals from having contact with Indian children at BIA schools" (Dept. of Interior, 2004). Hinkle (2003) reports that child sexual abuse continues to be widespread at BIA schools and dormitories.

Some victims of violence perpetrated by federal employees have attempted to sue the US government under the Federal Tort Claims Act (FTCA). In the past ten years, several federal lawsuits have been filed on behalf of Native people, alleging negligence by the federal government in hiring and supervision. However, some federal courts have barred suits by victims against the federal government when the primary charge is assault and/or battery, citing a narrow provision of the FTCA. As Jack W. Massey recently noted, "the courts have willfully blinded themselves to the harm their obeisance causes victims and the law…[a]nd people are shut out from being made whole by a perverse system" (Massey, 2004). Massey argues that the FTCA must be amended in order to allow the victims of federal employees to seek justice in the federal justice system.

The federal criminal and civil justice systems have not been a panacea for the resolution of criminal behavior in indigenous communities. US governmental policies toward indigenous crime victims focus on psychopathology and dysfunction rather than healing and empowerment (Waller et al. 1998). Most defendants in federal prosecutions for sex crimes, for example, are Native, and this has resulted in a high number of Native persons imprisoned for sex crimes in federal prisons, which do not provide intervention, treatment, or counseling for sex offenders (Butcher, 2000). Native victims of violent crimes are sometimes caught in a dilemma of reporting a fellow tribal member to a system that imposes harsh, non-rehabilitative punishments, or having no response to the crime at all (Coughenour, 1994).

For Native survivors of sexual assault, relying on the federal or state systems to respond can be painfully ironic. As Brave Heart and DeBruyn note, "For American Indians the United States is the perpetrator of our holocaust" (Brave Heart and DeBruyn, 1998) If the tribal legal system is not able to provide safety and accountability to victims, some may choose to forego justice altogether. Echo-Hawk writes that "many Indians distrust the legal and social authorities that could be most helpful to them because of past experiences of unjust treatment" (EchoHawk, 2001).

Accountability and Restoration of Tribal Authority

Criminal victimization and trauma have a profound impact on the future of indigenous nations. Without an adequate system for resolution and healing, psychological trauma and victimization create a cyclical sense of despair and desperation—indeed, a very continuation of the colonization process. As Burstow explains, addressing the root causes and sources of trauma requires an exploration of these significant historical and political acts:

> I would particularly call attention to the significance of under-
> standing the impact of various institutions that have traumatized
> or might traumatize clients and the importance of helping clients
> protect themselves and resist.
>
> It is a common but serious mistake to downplay the traumatic
> impact of the various institutions of the state, either limiting the fo-
> cus to a discreet traumatic event, extending the analysis only to the
> traumatic impact of family denial or minimization, or otherwise
> acting as if the state has no role. It is crucial that the traumatizing
> of the state and its institutions be explored and, indeed, insofar as
> possible, coexplored (Burstow, 2003).

It is clear that the current matrix of criminal authority does not provide Native women and children with the protection and response that they deserve, given the extremely high rates of violence they currently experience. However, simply identifying colonization, historical trauma, and jurisdiction problems as reasons for high rates of violence and victimization does not go far enough in providing victims with a sense of justice in the contemporary setting. The next question to be asked is how the scheme can be rectified.

First, accountability is needed from both the federal and state systems for their responsibility to Native victims of crime. The Senate Committee on Indian Affairs should hold hearings on the high rate of sexual and domestic violence experienced by Native women and children, as well as the continuation of abuse and sexual violence perpetrated by persons employed by the United States. A federal Executive Committee for Indian Country Law Enforcement Improvements

(1997) has already determined that "basic law enforcement protection and services are severely inadequate for most of Indian country." Additional hearings, if centered upon the voices and experiences of Native women, will provide clear victim-centered guidance for modification, amendment, or repeal of existing federal laws. Moreover, independent oversight of federal agencies charged with serving Native people is needed. Perhaps the best way to ensure safety for Native people and establish the accountability of federal agencies is to establish an oversight committee made up of Native leaders, victim advocates, and survivors of abuse by federal employees to review the hiring decisions and policies made by federal agencies. Such a policy would also be consistent with Executive Order 13175 (2000), which requires all federal agencies to engage in active consultation with tribal governments.

Second, state governments charged with investigating and prosecuting crimes in Indian country under PL 280 or other federal laws should be held accountable for their responsibilities and duties to tribal nations. Congress could consider requiring state governments to provide an accounting of cases investigated and prosecuted in Indian country—perhaps as a prerequisite for receiving federal crime control funding.

Third, and perhaps most important, tribal governments must have the power to respond to crimes against women and children restored to full capacity. In addition, tribal justice systems need additional resources and training in order to develop the infrastructure to respond to violent crime. Former US attorney general Janet Reno recognized this when she testified in front of the Senate Committee on Indian Affairs in 1998: "One of the most meaningful steps the Department of Justice can take to combat crime in Indian country is to help Indian tribes to strengthen their own justice systems." The Tribal Justice Act, passed in 1993, was supposed to provide over $50 million per year (from 1994 to 2000) for the development and strengthening of tribal justice systems. When the act expired in 2000, only $5 million had been appopriated (US Commission on Civil Rights, 2003). Along with a lack of promised resources, jurisdictional disputes, geographic isolation, and federal limitations keep tribal justice systems in a stranglehold. It is difficult to provide a comprehensive system of protection and deterrence without these fundamental components.

Porter writes that sovereignty can be defined by three elements: belief, ability, and recognition (Porter, 2002). Responding to crimes such as child abuse, rape, and domestic violence is linked to the ability to protect one's citizens, as well as the ability to support and honor women and children. As O'Brien notes, "Without a commitment to tribal sovereignty, social justice for Indians is nonexistent" (O'Brien, 1991). Tribal governments have invaluable cultural values and beliefs which will contribute to a comprehensive response to violent crime—if only provided with the necessary resources.

Restoring full authority over crimes of violence against women and children to tribal governments will not be a "quick fix" and will not happen overnight. The internalized oppression, historical trauma and grief, and forced assimilation have created dysfunction in many tribal justice systems. However, victims can ultimately find true justice within their local, indigenous systems of justice. Community healing can be a crucial aspect of recovering from sexual violence. Activities such as ceremonies, reclamation of clan identity, and reintegration into the community are some possibilities (McBride, 2003). For these reasons, and on general social justice principles, non-Native antiviolence advocates should honor and respect the fight for tribal sovereignty, and offer support in jurisdiction struggles.

Carey Vicenti writes, "We must insist that repose, finality, and closure each are laden with moral consequence given the manifest injustice of the predominant society's attitude toward Native America" (Vicenti, 2001). In the case of violent victimization, the United States must acknowledge, and tribal nations must reclaim, their rightful roles as protector and responder. A sincere and comprehensive apology will provide the reforms and resources necessary to put indigenous nations at the center of response to violent victimization.

4

Feminism, Race, and Adoption Policy

Dorothy Roberts

Most of the children awaiting adoption in the nation's public child welfare agencies are African American. This racial disparity reflects a general inequity in the US child welfare system. Although they represent less than one-fifth of the nation's children, Black children make up more than 35%—more than a third—of the foster care population.[1] The color of child welfare is most apparent in big cities where there are sizeable Black and foster care populations. In Chicago, for example, almost all of the children in foster care are Black.[2] The racial imbalance in New York City's foster care population is equally mind-boggling: out of 23,000 children in foster care or officially authorized independent homes in 2004, 99% were Black or Latino/a.[3] Black children in New York were ten times as likely as white children to be in state protective custody. Spend a day at any urban dependency court and you will see a starkly segregated operation. If you came with no preconceptions about the purpose of the child welfare system, you would have to conclude that it is an institution designed to monitor, regulate, and punish poor Black families.

Most commentary regarding race and adoption concerns transracial adoption—the politics and ethics of white adults adopting Black children. Too little attention has been paid to why so many Black children are available for adoption in the first place. State agencies treat child maltreatment in Black homes in an especially aggressive fashion. They are far more likely to place Black children who come to their attention in foster care instead of offering their families less traumatic assistance. According to federal statistics, Black children in the child welfare system are placed in foster care at twice the rate of white children.[4] A national study of child protective services by the US Department of Health and Human Services reported that "[m]inority children, and in particular African American children, are more likely to be in foster care placement than receive in-home services, *even when they have the same problems and characteristics as white children.*"[5]

Most white children who enter the system are permitted to stay with their families, avoiding the emotional damage and physical risks of foster care placement, while most Black children are taken away from theirs. Foster care is the main "service" state agencies provide to Black children brought to their attention. Once removed from their homes, Black children remain in foster care longer, are moved more often, receive fewer services, and are less likely to be either returned home or adopted than any other children.[6] Thus, the overrepresentation of Black

I presented an earlier version of this essay as a lecture in the Voices of Public Intellectuals series at Radcliffe Institute for Advanced Study, Cambridge, MA on February 11, 2002. I elaborate my arguments about race and the child welfare system in *Shattered Bonds: The Color of Child Welfare* (New York: Basic Books/Civitas 2000).

children in the adoption market stems largely from the child welfare system's inferior treatment of Black families.

The new politics of child welfare threatens to increase the racial imbalance in the population of children awaiting adoption. In the last decade, federal and state policies have shifted away from preserving families, and toward "freeing" children in foster care for adoption by terminating parental rights. For example, the Adoption and Safe Families Act (ASFA), passed by Congress in 1997, implements a preference for adoption through a set of mandates and incentives to state child welfare departments. The new law establishes swifter timetables for terminating the rights of biological parents with children in foster care and offers financial incentives to states to move more children from foster care into adoptive homes. It also weakens the chances of family preservation by encouraging agencies to make concurrent efforts to place foster children with adoptive parents while trying to reunite them with their families. Thus, federal child welfare policy places foster children on a "fast track" to adoption as a strategy for curing the ills of the child welfare system, especially reducing the enormous foster care population.

By throwing many families deeper into poverty, welfare reform heightens the risk that some children will be removed from struggling families and placed in foster care. The rejection of public aid to poor families in favor of private solutions to poverty—low-wage work, marriage, and child support—mirrors the appeal to adoption to "fix" the public foster care system. The overlap of ASFA and the Personal Responsibility and Work Opportunity Reconciliation Act of 1996 marked the first time in US history that "states have a federal mandate to protect children from abuse and neglect but no corresponding mandate to provide basic economic support to poor families."[7]

In addition, tougher treatment of juvenile offenders, imposed most harshly on African American youth, is increasing the numbers incarcerated in juvenile detention facilities and adult prisons. These political trends are converging to address the deprivation of poor Black children by placing them in one form of state custody or another—the "innocent" ones to be moved into more nurturing, adoptive homes; the "guilty" to be locked up in detention centers and prisons. Child welfare policy conforms to the current political climate, which embraces punitive responses to the seemingly intractable plight of America's isolated and impoverished inner cities.

Feminists should be alarmed and activated by the racial disparity in the child welfare system. Feminists should be concerned about the role of race in determining which families are subject to state interventions and, consequently, which children become available for adoption. Feminists should also direct our response to the disparity. Concern about the overrepresentation of Black children in foster care has generated very different solutions. Today's popular answer is to expedite termination of these children's ties to their mothers and to move them more swiftly into adoptive homes. Quite a different approach would be to devote more resources to supporting their families to reunite them more quickly with their parents or to avoid removing them from their homes—and the need for adoption—in the first place. Feminism's reinterpretation of private problems as political issues, its ambition to emancipate and improve the lives of all women, and its method of taking women's voices seriously—especially the voices of the most disadvantaged women—can shed critical light on these thorny questions of child welfare.

Feminism and Systemic Inequities

Feminist theory has highlighted the political dimension of intimate relationships and sought to restructure them in more just and equitable ways. So we should start out by recognizing that how we interpret child maltreatment is a political issue. Which harms to children are detected, identified as abuse or neglect, and punished are determined by inequities based on race, class, and gender, for the US child welfare system is, and always has been, designed to deal with the problems of poor families. This system conceals the larger systemic reasons for poor families' hardships by attributing them to parental deficits and pathologies that require therapeutic remedies rather than social change—while harms caused to children by uncaring, substance-abusing, mentally unstable, absentee parents in middle-class and affluent families usually go unheeded. Those privileged children might spend years in psychotherapy, but they won't spend a day in foster care.

Newspaper headlines about grievous child beatings, usually involving a tragic death, lead many people to believe that most of the children in the system are victims of serious physical abuse. But most cases of child maltreatment stem from parental neglect. Nationwide, there are twice as many neglected children as children who are physically abused.[8] When child protection agencies find that children have been neglected it usually has to do with being poor. Most neglect cases involve poor parents whose behavior is a consequence of economic desperation as much as lack of caring for their children.

Poverty itself creates dangers for children—poor nutrition, serious health problems, hazardous housing, inadequate heat and utilities, neighborhood crime. Children are often removed from poor parents when parental carelessness increases the likelihood that these hazards will result in actual harm.[9] Indigent parents do not have the resources wealthier parents have to avoid the harmful effects of their negligence, nor can they afford to pay professionals to cover up their mistakes. Affluent parents with a drug habit, for example, can check themselves into a fancy drug treatment center and hire a nanny to care for their children. No one suggests that their children should be taken away from them and placed for adoption.

Parental conduct or home conditions that appear innocent when the parents are middle class are often considered to be neglectful when the parents are poor. Several studies have found that mandatory reporters are more likely to label poor children "abused" than children from more affluent homes with similar injuries. An investigation of suspected cases of child abuse referred by Boston hospitals, for example, discovered that removal of the child from the family was associated with Medicaid eligibility, not the severity of abuse.[10] A recent study of missed cases of abusive head trauma found that doctors failed to diagnose the abuse twice as often when the child was white.[11] Another study of Philadelphia hospital records reported that African American and Latino toddlers hospitalized for fractures between 1994 and 2000 were over five times more likely to be evaluated for child abuse, and over three times more likely to be reported to child protective services, than Caucasian children with comparable injuries.[12]

Because Black children are disproportionately poor, we would expect a corresponding racial disparity in the child welfare caseload. The Illinois Department of Children and Family Services prepares a multicolored map that shows the distribution of abuse and neglect cases in Chicago. Neighborhoods with the highest concentration of cases form an L-shaped pattern colored in red. There is another map of Chicago with the same color coding that shows levels of poverty across the city. The poorest neighborhoods in the city form an identical red L-shaped pattern. A third map shows the distribution of ethnic groups in Chicago. The red-colored section marking the city's segregated Black neighborhoods is virtually a perfect match.[13] In Chicago, there is a geographical overlap of child maltreatment cases, poverty, and Black families.

There is a persistent and striking gap in the economic status of Blacks and whites that shows up in unemployment, poverty, and income.[14] The strength of the economy in the late 1990s didn't erase the racial gap in child poverty or improve the situation of Black children at the very bottom.[15] Despite recent declines, the US child poverty rate is still exceptionally high by international standards, extreme poverty is actually growing, and Black children still lag far behind. State disruption of Black families reflects this gulf between the material welfare of Black and white children in America.

But racial differences in child poverty rates don't tell the entire story. Race also influences child welfare decision-making through strong and deeply embedded stereotypes about Black family dysfunction. Some case workers and judges view Black parents as less reformable than white parents, and less willing and able to respond to the treatments child protection agencies prescribe. A popular mythology promoted over centuries portrays Black women as unfit to bear and raise children.[16] The sexually licentious Jezebel, the family-demolishing matriarch, the devious welfare queen, the depraved pregnant crack addict, accompanied by her equally monstrous crack baby—all paint a picture of a dangerous motherhood that must be regulated and punished. An unmarried Black woman represents the ultimate irresponsible mother—a woman who raises her children without the supervision of a man.

This is precisely how officials explained to Florida researchers Donna Bishop and Charles Frazier why they sent Black delinquents to juvenile detention while referring white delinquents to informal alternatives for the same offenses.[17] Many juvenile justice authorities think that Black children come from female-headed households ill-equipped to handle a troubled child. Because they perceive Black single mothers as incapable of providing adequate supervision of their children, they believe they are justified in placing these children under state control. "Inadequate family correlates with race and ethnicity. It makes sense to put delinquent kids from these circumstances in residential facilities," a juvenile court judge told Bishop and Frazier. "Detention decisions are decided on the basis of whether the home can control and supervise a child," explained a prosecutor. "So minorities don't go home because, unfortunately, their families are less able to control the kids." Another prosecutor's racial (and patriarchal) views were more blunt: "In Black families who the dad is, is unknown, while in white families—even when divorced—dad is married or something else. The choices are limited because the

Black family is a multigenerational non-fathered family. You can't send the kid off to live with dad."

The racial disparity in the child welfare system also reflects a political choice to address the startling rates of Black child poverty by punishing parents instead of tackling poverty's societal roots. It is no accident that child welfare philosophy became increasingly punitive as Black children made up a greater and greater share of the caseloads. In the past several decades, the number of children receiving child welfare services has declined dramatically, while the foster care population has skyrocketed.[18] As the child welfare system began to serve fewer white children and more Black children, state and federal governments spent more money on out-of-home care and less on in-home services. This mirrors perfectly the metamorphosis of welfare once the welfare rights movement succeeded in making Aid to Families with Dependent Children (AFDC) available to Black families in the 1960s. As welfare became increasingly associated with Black mothers, it became increasingly burdened with behavior modification rules and work requirements until the federal entitlement was abolished altogether in 1997. Both systems responded to their growing Black clientele by reducing their services to families while intensifying their punitive functions.

The child welfare system not only reflects an inequitable social order; it also helps to maintain it. It assumes a nuclear family norm that gives women the responsibility of caregiving, while denying them adequate government support and vilifying those who do not depend on husbands.[19] Mothers who are unable to rely on a male breadwinner or their own income to raise their children must pay a high price for state support. Feminist scholars have described how this model produces a welfare state that provides stingy benefits to poor mothers that are stigmatized and encumbered by behavioral regulations.[20] Less explored by feminist scholars is the role of the public child welfare system in caregiving by poor mothers. Like welfare, the child welfare system is a significant means of public support of poor children, especially poor Black children. The child welfare system also exacts an onerous price: it requires poor mothers to relinquish custody of their children in exchange for state support needed to care for them.[21] Involvement in the child welfare system entails intensive supervision by child protection agencies, which often includes losing legal custody of children to the state. This state intrusion is typically viewed as necessary to protect maltreated children from parental harm. But, as discussed above, the need for this intervention is usually linked to poverty and racial injustice. It is this systemic inequality, in the welfare of children and in the state's approach to caregiving, that produces the excessive supply of adoptable children in foster care.

The overrepresentation of Black children in this population represents massive state supervision and dissolution of families. This interference with families helps to maintain the disadvantaged status of Black people in the United States. The child welfare system not only inflicts general harms disproportionately on Black families, it inflicts a particular harm—a racial harm—on Black people as a group.

Excessive state interference in Black family life damages Black people's sense of personal and community identity. Family and community disintegration weakens Blacks' collective ability to overcome institutionalized discrimination and work toward greater political and economic strength. Family integrity is crucial to group welfare because of the role parents and other relatives play in transmitting survival skills, values, and self-esteem to the next generation. Families are a principal form of "oppositional enclaves" that are essential to democracy, to use Jane Mansbridge's term.[22] Placing large numbers of children in state custody—even if some are ultimately transferred to adoptive homes—interferes with the group's ability to form healthy connections among its members and to participate fully in the democratic process. The system's racial disparity also reinforces the quintessential racist stereotype: that Black people are incapable of governing themselves and need state supervision.

The impact of state disruption and supervision of families is intensified when it is concentrated in inner-city neighborhoods. In 1997, one in ten children in central Harlem had been taken from their parents and placed in foster care.[23] In Chicago, almost all child protection cases are clustered in two zip code areas, which are almost exclusively African American. The spatial concentration of child welfare supervision creates an environment in which state custody of children is a realistic expectation, if not the norm. Everyone in the neighborhood has either experienced state intrusion in their family or knows someone who has.[24] Parents are either being monitored by caseworkers or live with the fear that they may soon be investigated. Children have been traumatized by removal from their homes and placement in foster care or know that their parents are subject to the state's higher authority.

I don't think we have even started to imagine, much less measure, the extent of community damage caused by the child welfare system. Social scientists are just beginning to investigate the harm caused to Black communities by locking up the large portions of young Black men and women in the nation's prisons.[25] They have recently focused attention, for example, on the corrosive impact high Black incarceration rates have on Black communities' civic life. Excessive state supervision of families inflicts a similar collateral damage on Black communities.

Taking Women's Voices Seriously

Radical, engaged feminism takes the child welfare system's political impact seriously. It also takes women's voices seriously. Yet in the public debate about the ills of foster care and the cure, the voices that are noticeably absent are the mothers involved with child protective services. Newspaper stories mistakenly call all of the half million children in foster care "orphans of the living"—even though most still have ties to families who care for them. As he promoted his "Contract with America," the precursor to welfare reform, former Republican speaker of the house Newt Gingrich proposed opening orphanages to house the children of women who could no longer count on government aid. As *The Nation* columnist Katha Pollitt pointed out, calling children in foster care "orphans" teaches the public to view their parents "as being, in effect, dead."[26]

In a more equitable system, there would be fewer children in need of adoptive homes and policies promoting their adoption would be commendable. But the current campaign to increase adoptions makes devaluation of foster children's families and the rejection of family preservation efforts its central components. Adoption is no longer presented as a remedy for a minority of unsalvageable families but as a viable option—indeed, the preferred option—for all children in foster care. Black mothers' bonds with their children in particular are portrayed as a barrier to adoption, and extinguishing them is seen as the critical first step in the adoption process. Congressional and media discussion of ASFA linked family preservation policies to white middle-class couples' difficulties in adopting Black children in foster care. For example, a 1998 *US News and World Report* article titled "Adoption Gridlock" began with the story of a white North Carolina physician and his wife who resorted to adopting two Romanian orphans after several American agencies rejected their offer to adopt a Black child.[27] This article and others implied that the emphasis on reuniting Black children with their biological families unfairly prevented white couples from adopting American children. Terminating parental rights faster and abolishing race-matching policies were linked as a strategy for increasing adoptions of Black children by white families. Supporting this strategy is the myth that the foster care problem can be solved by moving more Black children from their families into white adoptive homes.

We are left with the impression that the parents involved in the foster care system have all abandoned their children. But I have heard from mothers across the country who defy this image. Far from abandoning their children, they devote every waking moment to winning them back. Many poor Black mothers fight desperately against a wealthy and powerful bureaucracy without resources and without adequate legal representation to regain custody of their children. If they give up, it is often because they are worn down by pointless and burdensome requirements and the constant assaults on their dignity.

Take for example, Jornell, the founder of Mothers Organizing Systems for Equal Services in Chicago, whose one-month-old baby was held at the hospital when she brought him there for stomach problems and was still in foster care four years later. Jornell was suspected of overmedicating her baby because she was a recovered addict who lived in public housing. Jornell not only devoted her energies to being reunited with her son, but she also began organizing other mothers in Chicago who felt that state authorities had unjustly separated them from their children. "I live for this now. I have no other life, I have no other purpose," Jornell told me at one of the group's meetings. "My life is an ongoing battle to hold on to my child."[28] Or Devon, who had cared for her four nieces and nephews since they were toddlers, until they were abruptly placed in a distant foster home because her apartment didn't meet the room requirements for licensed care. "Until my last dying breath, I'll continue to fight for my children," Devon told me. "All I can do is fight to let the kids know I didn't give up on them."[29]

Or the desperate voice mail message I received at my office from Michelle:

> I got your number from a friend. She said that you're a professor and can help me. I'm not sure really if you can help me or not. I've had a lot of people say they can and it has not helped. Please give me a call—if it's at night, if it's in the morning. I need to speak to you. My children are my life and it's been a year that they have been in

the system. And now they're trying to take my baby who's only five weeks old. And they don't really have a reason why except they have my other two. He has nothing to do with why I lost them. He wasn't even here. I really need somebody who can help me. Please call me.

We cannot dismiss these mothers' perspectives on the child welfare system. Rather these voices must play a significant part in feminist analysis of the systemic reasons for the racial disparity in foster care and in our proposals to eradicate it.

Battered Women and Adoption Policy

Does my argument about a feminist analysis of child welfare policy contradict the feminist analysis of intimate abuse against women? Harvard law professor Elizabeth Bartholet argues that the demand by the battered women's movement that the state "punish male perpetrators and liberat[e] their female victims" supports a similarly coercive approach to child abuse and neglect. An initial problem with this analogy is that there is a significant difference between the typical case of battery and the typical case of child maltreatment. As I have described, most children in foster care were removed from their homes because of neglect related to poverty. It is misleading to compare a wife batterer to a mother who leaves her children unattended or fails to feed them properly. Feminists don't advocate imprisoning husbands who fail to support their wives. I do not mean to discount the very serious harm that children can suffer as a result of parental neglect. But parental neglect that comes to the attention of child protective services is usually harder to extricate from poverty and other unequal social conditions than men's battery of their intimate partners.

More importantly, some feminist scholars have critiqued the political implications of both intimate violence and coercive state intervention. This kind of feminist analysis situates private violence within a broader context of inequitable social structures—including male domination but also barriers created by poverty, racism, and anti-immigrant policies—that trap many women in violent homes. Feminists of color especially have tied domestic violence to a continuum of social violence that, in the words of scholar-activist Angela Davis, "extends from the sweatshops through the prisons, to shelters, and into bedrooms at home."[30] We know that the state can inflict injuries on our bodies, families, and communities at least as damaging as the fists of any man. We are cautious about participating in a regime that is eager to incarcerate huge numbers of minority men, but won't allocate similar resources to programs and services that would make women less vulnerable to violence.[31]

A new wave of feminist researchers who have examined state interventions, such as mandatory arrest and no-drop policies, are now questioning the emphasis on criminal remedies for domestic violence. These aggressive measures have not only led to the arrest of a disproportionate number of low-income and minority men, but they have failed to protect low-income and minority women. One study shows that mandatory arrest in Milwaukee, while decreasing violence by employed, married, and white men, actually increased repeat violence by unemployed, unmarried, and African American men.[32] The author concluded that the policy prevented thousands of acts of violence against white women at the price of many more acts of violence against African American women.

Given the history of police brutality against Blacks, many Black women are reluctant to turn to law enforcement to protect them.[33] Some scholars point out that the criminal justice approach can intensify state control of women.[34] Mandatory arrest policies increase the arrest of women for domestic violence, usually because they acted in self-defense. Battered women have been forced to testify against their will. A judge held a battered woman in contempt of court because she violated a restraining order by contacting the abuser.[35] NYU professor Linda Mills warns, "Feminists should reflect on the abusive character of the state power they have unleashed upon the women they seek to protect."[36]

It makes no sense to split women into two camps for purposes of evaluating coercive state intervention—guilty women whose children are victims of maternal abuse versus innocent women who are victims of male abuse. The very same women who risk losing their children to child protective services are the ones who are hurt most by a unidimensional criminal approach to domestic violence. The most clearcut example of this overlap is the practice of some child welfare departments of taking custody of battered women's children on grounds that the mothers abused them by allowing them to witness violence or by allowing them to reside in a home where violence takes place.[37] The child welfare system blames and punishes battered mothers for exposing their children to violence, just as it blames and punishes mothers for other family problems that may be beyond their control. State intervention in battered women's lives often replicates the terror they suffered at the hands of their intimate partner and may make it harder for them to take steps to counter it.

More fundamentally, it is the public's mistrust of poor women, especially women of color, and its unwillingness to put money directly in their hands that underlie the emphasis on coercive state intervention to address both violence against women and child maltreatment. A social welfare system that improved women's economic status would enable them to discard violent partners and to take better care of their children. Feminists shouldn't be fighting for increased state separation of mothers and children as part of a campaign against domestic violence. We should be fighting for affordable housing and generous supports for struggling mothers as a more effective and just strategy to reduce both battery of women and neglect of children.

It is not my impression, however, that there is a vociferous women's movement rallying on behalf of poor Black mothers whose children are in state custody. If there is a contradiction at work, it isn't in women's opposition to violence against women but in their silence regarding violence against children. I see a greater contradiction in feminists' silence surrounding the massive state disruption of women's bonds with their children. Grappling with the racism in the child welfare system is difficult for many women, because it raises in a very personal way the power differences among women. Perhaps the most important development in contemporary feminist thought is its recognition that women are different in terms of race, ethnic background, class, religion, and sexual orientation; the critique of gender essentialism in mainstream feminist theory has inspired an ongoing reconstruction that includes this diversity of women's experiences. But facing the awful history and reality of racism that helps to create differences in power and privilege is much harder. This is especially true in the realm of child welfare where a privileged group of women stands to benefit from devastating state intrusion in the lives of the least privileged women. Let's face it: the continuing supply of adoptable children for middle-class women depends on the persistence of deplorable social conditions and requires severing the ties between the most vulnerable mothers and children.[38]

The scene that best illustrates this point in my mind is the playground in the Cambridge Common that I passed every day during a fellowship at Harvard University a number of years ago.[39] The diverse group of adults and children playing in the park appeared at first to represent an idyllic multicultural mix that one rarely finds outside a university community. But on closer inspection I discovered a disturbing pattern. It seemed as if all the minority children had white mothers—in many cases, the result of transracial adoptions. Many of the white children, on the other hand, were tended by minority women—not their mothers, but nannies hired by their white mothers. Despite the impression of racial harmony the scene conveyed, it really showed the clear demarcation between the status of white and minority women and their claims to children. Women have been complicit in silencing the voices of poor mothers with children in foster care—voices that are inconvenient to plans to create a new family, voices that complicate a simple picture of a benevolent government saving innocent children, voices that force us to deal with our own participation in an unjust system and that demand that we work to change it.

Conclusion

Some well-meaning feminists may think that the best way to help the thousands of Black children in foster care is to terminate their mothers' rights and place them in better adoptive homes. They do not see themselves as racists who are bent on destroying Black families; they may even endorse stronger programs to provide social supports for America's struggling families. But they believe child protective services must intervene immediately to save Black children from their current crisis. Bartholet, for example, recognizes that child welfare policy has a racially imbalanced effect, but sees family preservation as more damaging to Black children. "Keeping them in their families and their kinship and racial groups when they won't get decent care in situations may alleviate guilt," Bartholet argues, "but it isn't going to help groups who are at the bottom of the socioeconomic ladder to climb that ladder. It is simply going to victimize a new generation."[40]

Instead, Bartholet calls for intensified state intervention into poor Black families to protect children from parental harm as well as efforts to move these children from their communities to more privileged adoptive homes. This approach appears to whites only to pity Black mothers involved in the child welfare system but not to respect their autonomy, their claims of discrimination, or their bonds with their children. It demands an especially pernicious type of white benevolence toward Black people—a benevolence that depends on loss of Black family integrity in favor of white supervision of their children. It sets up adoption as the only realistic way to persuade whites to care for Black children, and an expectation that white Americans will not endorse programs that would improve the welfare of Black children living within their own families and communities. White compassion for Black children depends on Black children "belonging" to them, to use Bartholet's term. This, it seems to me, is a particularly selfish and—given the history of slavery in the United States—an especially toxic and ahistorical way to approach child welfare. It perpetuates, rather than challenges, America's racial hierarchy.

Feminism's political critique of private problems, its commitment to improving the lives of the most disadvantaged women, and its method of listening to their voices should yield a radically different response. Feminists should reject the emphasis on adoption to cure the ills of foster care and insist on fundamental change in our approach to child welfare. The racial disparities in the foster care population should prompt us to reconsider the state's current response to child maltreatment. The price of present policies which rely on child removal and adoption, rather than family support, falls unjustly on Black families. A policy that matches an individual child's need for a home and an individual woman's desire to be a mother, while ignoring the societal inequities and injustices that brought them together, is decidedly unfeminist. All feminists should acknowledge that the racial disparities in adoption are powerful reasons to radically transform the child welfare system, so that it generously and noncoercively supports families.

5

The Color of Choice
White Supremacy and Reproductive Justice

Loretta J. Ross[1]

> [T]he regulation of reproduction and the exploitation of women's bodies and labor is both a tool and a result of systems of oppression based on race, class, gender, sexuality, ability, age and immigration status.[2]

It is impossible to understand the resistance of women of color to the reproductive politics of both the Right and the Left without first comprehending how the system of white supremacy constructs different destinies for each ethnic population of the United States through targeted, yet diffuse, policies of population control. Even a cursory examination of the reproductive politics dominating today's headlines—such as debates on abortion and welfare—reveals that some women are encouraged to have more children while others are discouraged. Why are some women glorified as mothers while others have their motherhood rights contested? Why are there obstacles for women who seek abortions while our society neglects mothers and children already here? As we move toward "designer babies" made possible by advances in assisted reproductive technologies, does anyone truly believe that all women will have an equal right to benefit from these "new reproductive choices," that children of all races will be promoted, or that vulnerable women will not be exploited?

Women of color reproductive justice activists oppose all political rationales, social theories, and genetic justifications for reproductive oppression against communities of color, whether through blatant policies of sterilization abuse or through the coercive use of dangerous contraceptives. Instead, women of color activists demand "reproductive justice," which requires the protection of women's human rights to achieve the physical, mental, spiritual, political, economic and social well-being of women and girls.[3] Reproductive justice goes far beyond the demand to eliminate racial disparities in reproductive health services, and beyond the right-to-privacy-based claims to legal abortion made by the pro-choice movement and dictated and limited by the US Supreme Court. A reproductive justice analysis addresses the fact that progressive issues are divided, isolating advocacy for abortion from other social justice issues relevant to the lives of every woman. In the words of SisterSong president Toni Bond, "We have to reconnect women's health and bodies with the rest of their lives."[4] In short, reproductive justice can be described as reproductive rights embedded in a human rights and social justice framework used to counter all forms of population control that deny women's human rights.

White Supremacy and Population Control on the Right, and Left

> Population control is necessary to maintain the normal operation
> of US commercial interests around the world. Without our trying
> to help these countries with their economic and social develop-
> ment, the world would rebel against the strong US commercial
> presence.[5]

Although the United States does not currently have an explicit population control policy, population control ideologies march from the margins to the mainstream of reproductive politics and inform policies promoted by the Right and the Left. Fears of being numerically and politically overwhelmed by people of color bleach meaning from any alternative interpretations of the constellation of population control policies that restrict immigration by people of color, encourage sterilization and contraceptive abuse of people of color, and incarcerate upwards of 2 million people, the vast majority of whom are people of color.

The expanded definition of white supremacy as I use it in this essay is an interlocking system of racism, patriarchy, homophobia, ultranationalism, xenophobia, anti-Semitism, and religious fundamentalism that creates a complex matrix of oppressions faced by people of color in the United States. As a tenacious ideology in practice, it is evidenced on both the Right and the Left—in the Far Right, the Religious Right, paleoconservatives, neoconservatives, neoliberals, and liberals. Abby Ferber, a researcher on the intersection of race, gender, and white supremacy, writes that "defining white supremacy as extremist in its racism often has the result of absolving the mainstream population of its racism, portraying white supremacists as the racist fringe in contrast to some non-racist majority."[6]

White supremacy not only defines the character of debates on reproductive politics but it also explains and predicts the borders of the debate. In other words, what Americans think as a society about women of color and population control is determined and informed by their relationship to white supremacy as an ideology, and these beliefs affect the country's reproductive politics. Both conservatives and liberals enforce a reproductive hierarchy of privatization and punishment that targets the fertility, motherhood, and liberty of women of color.

Population control policies are externally imposed by governments, corporations, or private agencies to control—by increasing or limiting—population growth and behavior, usually by controlling women's reproduction and fertility. All national population policies, even those developed for purportedly benign reasons, put women's empowerment at risk. Forms of population control include immigration restrictions, selective population movement or dispersal, incarceration, and various forms of discrimination, as well as more blatant manifestations, such as cases in which pregnant illegal immigrants and incarcerated women are forced to have abortions. According to a 1996 study by Human Rights Watch, abuses of incarcerated women not only include denial of adequate health care, but pressure to seek an abortion, particularly if the woman is impregnated by a prison guard.[7]

Meanwhile, impediments are placed in the way of women who voluntarily choose to terminate their pregnancies. The only logic that explains this apparent moral inconsistency is one that examines precisely who is subjected to which treatment and who is affected by which reproductive policy at which time in history. Women of color have little trouble distinguishing between those who are encouraged to have more children and those who are not, and understanding which social, political, and economic forces influence these determinations.

Population control policies are by no means exclusively a twentieth-century phenomenon. During the Roman Empire, the state was concerned with a falling birthrate among married upper-class couples. As has been the case for elite classes throughout history, procreation was seen as a duty to society. Emperor Augustus consequently enacted laws containing positive and negative incentives to reproduction, promoting at least three children per couple and discouraging childlessness.[8] Augustus probably knew that the falling birthrate was not a result of abstention among Roman men and women, but rather of contraceptive and abortifacient use by Roman women to control their fertility. Through legislation, he asserted the state's interest in compelling citizens to have more children for the good of society.[9] Because no ancient Roman texts offer the perspectives of women on this issue, it is difficult to ascertain what women thought of this territorial assertion of male privilege over their private lives. However, the Roman birthrate continued to decline despite the emperor's orders, suggesting that Roman women probably did what most women have done throughout the ages: make the decisions that make sense for them and refuse to allow men to control their fertility. As historian Rickie Solinger points out, "The history of reproductive politics will always be in part a record of women controlling their reproductive capacity, no matter what the law says, and by those acts reshaping the law."[10]

Despite the Roman failure to impose the state's will on individual human reproductive behavior, many governments today have refused to recognize the virtual impossibility of regulating human reproductive behavior through national population policies. China and Romania have instituted population control measures with catastrophic results. Even governments seeking to achieve their population objectives through more benign policies, such as offering financial incentives for women to have children, can only report negligible results. Despite government and moralistic pronouncements, women perceive their reproductive decisions as private, like their periods and other health concerns. Even when the law, the church, or their partners oppose their decisions, they tend to make the decision about whether or not to use birth control or abortion, or to parent, for themselves.

This lived reality has not stopped lawmakers from trying to assert control over women's reproduction. Who gets targeted for positive, pronatalist policies encouraging childbirth versus negative, antinatalist policies that discourage childbirth is determined by powerful elites, informed by prejudices based on race, class, sexual identity, and immigration status. Policies that restrict abortion access, distort sex and sexuality education, impose parental notification requirements for minors, allow husbands to veto options for abortion, and limit use of emergency and regular contraception all conspire to limit access to fertility control to white women, especially young white women. Meanwhile, women of color face intimidating obstacles to making reproductive choices, including forced contraception, steril-ization abuse, and, in the case of poor women and women of color on social assis-tance, welfare family caps. These population control policies have both domestic and international dimensions, which are rarely linked in the minds of those who believe that the struggle is principally about abortion.

Internationally, the fertility rate of women of color is the primary preoccupa-tion of those determined to impose population controls on developing countries. According to the United Nations, in 2000, more than one hundred countries world-wide had large "youth bulges"—people aged fifteen to twenty-nine accounted for more than 40% of all adults. All of these extremely youthful countries are in the developing world, where fertility rates are highest, and most are in sub-Saharan Africa and the Middle East. Many of the young people who make up these "youth bulges" face dismal prospects because of deliberate underdevelopment. Over the past decade, youth unemployment rates have risen to more than double the over-all global unemployment rate. In the absence of a secure livelihood, many experts believe that discontented youth may resort to violence or turn to insurgent orga-nizations as sources of social mobility and self-esteem. Recent studies show that countries with large youth bulges were roughly two and a half times more likely to experience an outbreak of civil conflict than countries below this benchmark.[11]

To respond to these alarming trends, many on the Right and the Left want to restrict the growth of developing world populations, and in this context, "family planning" becomes a tool to fight terrorism and civil unrest. Some on the Left want to increase access to family planning, economic development, and education as a way to curb population growth, even if achieved through the coercive use of con-traceptives and sterilization. Some on the Right prefer military interventions and economic domination to achieve population control.

The Bush administration's family planning and HIV/AIDS policies are also having the impact of serving as tools of population control in the Global South. The US government's "ABC program" (A is for abstinence, B is for being faith-ful, and C for condom use) is purportedly designed to reduce the spread of HIV/AIDS. Critics of the policy point out that the ABC approach offers no option for girls or women coerced into sex, for married women who are trying to get preg-nant yet have unfaithful husbands, or for victims of rape and incest who have no control over when and under what conditions they will be forced to engage in sexual activity. As a result, instead of decreasing the spread of HIV/AIDS, some suspect the ABC policy of actually increasing the ravages of the disease. In combi-nation with the US government's failure to provide funding for and access to vital medications for individuals infected with HIV, the effects are deadly.

Meanwhile, right-wing policies that appear to be pronatalist—such as the Global Gag Rule which prohibits clinics in developing countries that receive USAID funds from discussing abortion—are, in fact, achieving the opposite result. Catering to its radical antiabortion base, the Bush administration has withdrawn funds from programs for family planning for women around the world, withhold-ing $136 million in funding for the United Nations Population Fund (UNFPA) since 2002. This money could have prevented at least 1.5 million induced abor-tions, 9,400 maternal deaths, and 154,000 infant and child deaths.[12] In September 2005, the US State Department announced that it was denying funding to UNFPA for the fourth year.

One might ask why staunch conservatives are opposed to family planning in developing countries when family planning so clearly limits population growth and reduces the need for abortions. One of the leading causes of death for women in developing countries is maternal mortality—death from childbirth. The UN estimated a worldwide total of 529,000 maternal deaths in the year 2000, with less than 1% of deaths occurring in developed nations.[13] Women of color cannot help but observe that family planning is not nearly as efficient in reducing populations of color as factors such as maternal mortality, infant mortality, and AIDS. We are also not oblivious to the wealth of natural resources like oil, gold, and diamonds in the lands where these populations are shrinking—after all, a depopulated land cannot protect itself.

Overt and covert population control polices are also at play on the domestic front. In October 2005, former secretary of education William Bennett declared on his radio talk show that if "you wanted to reduce crime...if that were your sole purpose, you could abort every Black baby in this country, and your crime rate would go down." While Bennett conceded that aborting all African American babies "would be an impossible, ridiculous, and morally reprehensible thing to do," he still maintained that "the crime rate would go down."

Bennett is merely echoing widespread perceptions by many radical and moderate conservatives in the United States who directly link social ills with the fertility of women of color. The Heritage Foundation, a right-wing think tank influential in the national debates on reproductive politics, offers the following analysis: "Far more important than residual material hardship is behavioral poverty: a breakdown in the values and conduct that lead to the formation of healthy families, stable personalities, and self-sufficiency. This includes eroded work ethic and dependency, lack of educational aspiration and achievement, inability or unwillingness to control one's children, *increased single parenthood and illegitimacy* [emphasis added], criminal activity, and drug and alcohol abuse."[14]

This mainstream white supremacist worldview is based on the notion that people are poor because of behaviors, not because they are born into poverty. In reality, according to Zillah Eisenstein, "poverty is tied to family structures in crisis. Poverty is tied to the unavailability of contraceptives and reproductive rights. Poverty is tied to teenage pregnancy. Poverty is tied to women's wages that are always statistically lower than men's. Poverty is tied to the lack of day care for women who must work. Poverty is tied to insufficient health care for women. Poverty is tied to the lack of access to job training and education."[15]

It would be logical to assume that people who claim to value all human life from the moment of conception would fiercely support programs that help disadvantaged children and parents. Sadly, this is not the case. Surveys show that, on average, people who are strongly opposed to abortion are also more likely to define themselves as political conservatives who do not support domestic programs for poor families, single mothers, people of color, and immigrants.[16] They are also opposed to overseas development assistance in general, and to specific programs for improving women's and children's health, reducing domestic violence, helping women become more economically self-sufficient, and lowering infant mortality.[17]

Perspectives from the Left are hardly more reassuring to women of color. Is Bennett, a member of the Heritage Foundation, any worse than an environmentalist who claims that the world is overpopulated and drastic measures must be taken to address this catastrophe? Betsy Hartmann writes about the "greening of hate," or blaming environmental degradation, urban sprawl, and diminishing natural resources on poor populations of color. This is a widely accepted set of racist myths promoted by many in the environmental movement, which is moving rather alarmingly to the right as it absorbs ideas and personnel from the white supremacist movement, including organizations such as the Aryan Women's League.[18]

The reality is that 20% of the world's population controls 80% of the global wealth. In other words, it is not the population growth of the developing world that is depleting the world's resources, but the overconsumption of these resources by the richest countries in the world. The real fear of many in the population control movement is that the developing world will become true competitors for the earth's resources and demand local control over their natural wealth of oil and minerals. Rather than perceiving overconsumption by Americans, agricultural mismanagement, and the military-industrial complex as the main sources of environmental degradation, many US environmentalists maintain that the fertility of poor women is the root of environmental evil, and cast women of color, immigrant women, and women of the Global South as the perpetrators, rather than the victims, of environmental degradation.[19] This myth promotes alarmist fears about overpopulation, and leads to genocidal conclusions such as those reached by writers for *Earth First! Journal* who said, "The AIDS virus may be Gaia's tailor-made answer to human overpopulation," and that famine should take its natural course to stem overpopulation.[20]

Population control groups on the Left will often claim that they are concerned with eliminating gender and economic inequalities, racism, and colonialism, but since these organizations address these issues through a problematic paradigm, inevitably their efforts are directed toward reducing population growth of all peoples in theory and of people of color in reality.[21] In fact, these efforts are embedded within the context of a dominant neoliberal agenda which trumps women's health and empowerment. And some prochoice feminists have supported the neoliberal projects of "privatization, commodification, and deregulation of public health services that…have led to diminished access and increasing mortality and morbidity of women who constitute the most vulnerable groups in both developing and developed countries."[22]

Similarly, the prochoice movement, largely directed by middle-class white women, is oblivious to the role of white supremacy in restricting reproductive options for all women, and, as a result, often inadvertently colludes with it. For instance, a study published in 2001 in the *Quarterly Journal of Economics* by John J. Donohue III, a professor of law at Stanford University, and Steven D. Levitt, a professor of economics at the University of Chicago, claimed that the 1973 legalization of abortion prevented the birth of unwanted children who were likely to have become criminals. Of course, the authors state that these children would have been born to poor women of color. They also disingenuously and incorrectly assert that "women who have abortions are those most at risk to give birth to children who would engage in criminal activity,"[23] and conclude that the drop in crime rates approximately eighteen years after the *Roe v. Wade* decision was a consequence of legal abortion. Despite the quickly revealed flaws in their research, some prochoice advocates continue to tout their findings as justification for keeping abortion legal, adopting a position similar to Mr. Bennett's.[24]

Indeed, the prochoice movement's failure to understand the intersection between race, class, and gender led leaders of the movement to try their own "Southern Strategy" in the 1980s. Central to this strategy was an appeal to conservative voters who did not share concerns about women's rights, but who were hostile to the federal government and its public encroachment on individual choice and privacy. Some voters with conservative sympathies were pruned from the antiabortion movement for a while, uneasily joining the ranks of the prochoice movement in an admittedly unstable alliance based on "states' rights" segregationist tendencies.[25] Not surprisingly, on questions of abortion policy—whether the government should spend tax money on abortions for poor women or whether teenagers should have to obtain parental consent for abortions—the alliance fell apart. And this appeal to conservative, libertarian Southern voters drove an even deeper wedge in the prochoice movement, divorcing it from its original base of progressive white women and alienating women of color.

Meanwhile, the Right pursued its population control policies targeting communities of color both overtly and indirectly. Family planning initiatives in the Deep South in the 1950s encouraged women of color (predominantly African American women) to use contraceptives and sterilizations to reduce the growth of our populations, while obstacles were simultaneously placed in the paths of white women seeking access to these same services. A Louisiana judge, Leander Perez, was quoted as saying, "The best way to hate a nigger is to hate him before he is born."[26] This astonishingly frank outburst represented the sentiments of many racists during this period, although the more temperate ones disavowed gutter epithets.

For example, conservative politicians like Strom Thurmond supported family planning in the 1960s when it was used as a racialized form of population control, aimed at limiting Black voter strength in African American communities.[27] When it was presented as a race-directed strategy to reduce their Black populations, North Carolina and South Carolina became the first states to include family planning in their state budgets in the 1950s. One center in Louisiana reported that in its first year of operation, 96% of its clients were Black. The proportion of white clients never rose above 15%.[28] Generally speaking, family planning associated with women of color was most frequently supported; but support quickly evaporated when it was associated with white women.

Increased federal spending on contraception coincided with the urban unrest and rise of a militant Civil Rights movement in the late 1960s. In 1969, President Nixon asked Congress to establish a five-year plan for providing family planning services to "all those who want them but cannot afford them."[29] However, the rationale behind the proposed policy was to prevent population increases among

Blacks—this would make governance of the world in general, and inner cities in particular, difficult. Reflecting concerns strikingly similar to those driving US population policies overseas, Nixon pointed to statistics that showed a "bulge" in the number of Black Americans between the ages of five and nine. This group of youngsters who would soon enter their teens—"an age group with problems that can create social turbulence"—was 25% larger than ten years before.[30] This scarcely disguised race- and class-based appeal for population control persuaded many Republicans to support family planning.

Today the US government's less obvious—but no less effective—approach of promoting policies overseas that contribute to high maternal mortality rates and devastation as a result of HIV/AIDS was also recently revealed to have a counterpart on the domestic front. Images of chaos and death as Hurricane Katrina's floodwaters engulfed Black neighborhoods shocked many Americans. But according to Jean Hardisty, a researcher on white supremacy in America, these pictures of poor New Orleans residents, many of them Black women and their children, revealed some essential truths:

> Much of the white public will never understand that those images were more than the result of neglected enforcement of civil rights laws, or the "failure" of the poor to rise above race and class. They were images of structural racism. In one of the poorest cities in the country (with 28% of New Orleanians living in poverty—over two times the national poverty rate), the poor were white as well as African American. But, the vast majority (84%) of the poor were Black. This is not an accident. It is the result of white supremacy that is so imbedded in US society that it has become part of the social structure. Structural racism is not only a failure to serve people equally across race, culture and ethnic origin within private and government entities (as well as "third sector" institutions, such as the print, radio and TV media and Hollywood). It is also the predictable consequence of legislation at the federal, state, and local level.[31]

This racial illiteracy on the part of white people is part of the hegemonic power of whiteness. Through a historical mythology, white supremacy has a vested interest in denying what is most obvious: the privileged position of whiteness. For most people who are described as white, since race is believed to be "something" that shapes the lives of people of color, they often fail to recognize the ways in which their own lives and our public policies are shaped by race. Structural or institutionalized racism is not merely a matter of individual attitudes, but the result of centuries of subordination and objectification that reinforce population control policies.

Politicians have continuously used policies of population control to conquer this land, produce an enslaved workforce, enshrine racial inequities, and preserve traditional power relations. For just as long, women of color have challenged race-based reproductive politics, including the forced removal of our children; the racialization and destruction of the welfare system; the callousness of the foster care system that breaks up our families; and the use of the state to criminalize our pregnancies and our children. These become an interlocked set of public policies which Dorothy Roberts calls 'reproductive punishment.' She observes that the "system's racial disparity also reinforces negative stereotypes about…people's incapacity to govern themselves and need for state supervision."[32]

Reproductive politics are about who decides "whether, when, and which woman can reproduce legitimately and *also* the struggles over which women have the right to be mothers of the children they bear."[33] Entire communities can be monitored and regulated by controlling how, when, and how many children a woman can have and keep. This is particularly true for women on Native American reservations, incarcerated women, immigrant women, and poor women across the board, whose reproductive behavior is policed by an adroit series of popular racist myths, fierce state regulation, and eugenicist control. The use of the "choice" framework in the arena of abortion, as Rhonda Copelon points outs, underwrites "the conservative idea that the personal is separate from the political, and that the larger social structure has no impact on [or responsibility for] private, individual choice."[34]

For the past thirty years, women of color have urged the mainstream movement to seriously and consistently support government funding for abortions for poor women. The 1977 Hyde Amendment prohibited the use of taxpayer funds to pay for abortions for women whose health care is dependent on the federal government, and it affects women on Medicaid, women in the military and the Peace Corps, and indigenous women who primarily rely on the Indian Health Service for their medical care. Yet despite its obvious targeting of poor women of color, prochoice groups have not made repealing the Hyde Amendment a priority because polling data has indicated that the majority of Americans do not want taxpayer money used to pay for abortions.

When the Freedom of Choice Act was proposed by prochoice groups in 1993, it retained the provisions of the Hyde Amendment. According to Andrea Smith, one NARAL Pro-Choice America (formerly known as the National Abortion Rights Action League) petition in favor of the act stated that, "the Freedom of Choice Act (FOCA) will secure the original vision of *Roe v. Wade*, giving *all* women reproductive freedom and securing that right for future generations [emphasis added].[35] As Smith wryly points out, apparently poor women and indigenous women did not qualify as "women" in the eyes of the writers of this petition.

In a 1973 editorial, the National Council of Negro Women pointed out the link between civil rights activism and reproductive oppression that mitigated the concept of choice for oppressed communities:

> The key words are "if she chooses." Bitter experience has taught the Black woman that the administration of justice in this country is not colorblind. Black women on welfare have been forced to accept sterilization in exchange for a continuation of relief benefits and others have been sterilized without their knowledge or consent. A young pregnant woman recently arrested for civil rights activities in North Carolina was convicted and told that her punishment

would be to have a forced abortion. We must be ever vigilant that what appears on the surface to be a step forward, does not in fact become yet another fetter or method of enslavement.[36]

Yet currently the hard-core Right has begun to demand the political disenfranchisement of people receiving public assistance. For example, in 2005 a law was proposed in Georgia that would have required voters to have driver's licenses or other forms of state identification to vote; right-wing proponents complained that the bill didn't go far enough, and that the vote should be taken away from welfare recipients.[37] And while linking political enfranchisement to population control is blatantly coercive and antidemocratic, it has not been unusual in United States. In 1960, when the city of New Orleans was ordered to desegregate its schools, local officials responded by criminalizing the second pregnancies of women on public assistance; after they were threatened with imprisonment and welfare fraud, many of these African American women and children disappeared from the welfare rolls.[38] The Right is often blatant in its determination to restrict the fertility of women of color, and thus control our communities. They endlessly proffer an array of schemes and justifications for intruding on the personal decisions of women of color and for witholding the social supports necessary to make healthy reproductive decisions.

On the other hand, in its singular focus on maintaining the legal right to abortion, the prochoice movement often ignores the intersectional matrix of race, gender, sovereignty, class and immigration status that complicates debates on reproductive politics in the United States for women of color. The movement is *not* the personal property of middle-class white women, but without a frank acknowledgement of white supremacist practices in the past and the present, women of color will not be convinced that mainstream prochoice activists and organizations are committed to empowering women of color to make decisions about our fertility, or to reorienting the movement to include the experiences of *all* women.

Mobilizing for Reproductive Justice

Prior to the 1980s, women of color reproductive health activists organized primarily against sterilization abuse and teen pregnancy, yet many were involved in early activities to legalize abortion because of the disparate impact illegal abortion had in African American, Puerto Rican, and Mexican communities. Most women of color refrained from joining mainstream pro-choice organizations, preferring instead to organize autonomous women of color organizations that were more directly responsive to the needs of their communities. The rapid growth of women of color reproductive health organizations in the 1980s and 1990s helped build the organizational strength (in relative terms) to generate an analysis and a new movement in the twenty-first century.

This was a period of explosive autonomous organizing.[39] Women of color searched for a conceptual framework that would convey our twinned values—the right to have and not to have a child—as well as the myriad ways our rights to be mothers and parent our children are constantly threatened. We believed these values and concerns separated us from the liberal pro-choice movement in the United

States, which was preoccupied with privacy rights and maintaining the legality of abortion. We were also skeptical about leaders in the pro-choice movement who seemed more interested in population restrictions than women's empowerment. Some promoted dangerous contraceptives and coercive sterilizations, and were mostly silent about economic inequalities and power imbalances between the developed and the developing worlds. Progressive women of color felt closest to the radical wing of the women's movement that articulated demands for abortion access and shared our class analysis, and even closer to radical feminists who demanded an end to sterilization and contraceptive abuse. Yet we lacked a framework that aligned reproductive rights with social justice in an intersectional way, bridging the multiple domestic and global movements to which we belonged.

We found an answer in the global women's health movement through the voices of women from the Global South. By forming small but significant delegations, women of color from the United States participated in all of the international conferences and significant events of the global feminist movement. A significant milestone was the International Conference on Population and Development in 1994 in Cairo, Egypt. In Cairo, women of color witnessed how women in other countries were successfully using a human rights framework in their advocacy for reproductive health and sexual rights.

Shortly after the Cairo conference, drawing on the perspectives of women of color engaged in both domestic and international activism, women of color in the United States coined the term "reproductive justice." In particular, we made the link between poverty and the denial of women's human rights, and critiqued how shared opposition to fundamentalists and misogynists strengthened a problematic alliance between feminists and the population control establishment.

The first step toward implementing a reproductive justice framework in our work was taken two months after the September Cairo conference. A group of African American women (some of whom became cofounders of the SisterSong Women of Color Reproductive Health Collective) spontaneously organized an informal Black Women's Caucus at a national pro-choice conference sponsored in 1994 by the Illinois Pro-Choice Alliance in Chicago. We were attempting to "Bring Cairo Home" by adapting agreements from the Cairo program of action to a US-specific context. In the immediate future, we were very concerned that the Clinton administration's health care reform proposals were ominously silent about abortion rights, which appeared to renege on the promises the Administration made at Cairo. Even without a structured organization, we mobilized for a national signature ad in the *Washington Post* to express our concerns, raising twenty-seven thousand dollars and collecting six hundred signatures from African American women to place the ad in the *Post*. After debating and rejecting the choice framework in our deliberations, we called ourselves Women of African Descent for Reproductive Justice. We defined reproductive justice, at that time, as "reproductive health integrated into social justice," bespeaking our perception that reproductive health is a social justice issue for women of color because health care reform without a reproductive health component would do more harm than good for women of color. Three years later, using human rights as a unifying framework and reproductive justice as a central organizing concept, the SisterSong Women of Color Reproductive Health Collective was formed in 1997 by autonomous women of color organizations.

SisterSong maintains that reproductive justice—the complete physical, mental, spiritual, political, economic, and social well-being of women and girls—will be achieved when women and girls have the economic, social, and political power and resources to make healthy decisions about our bodies, sexuality, and reproduction for ourselves, our families, and our communities in all areas of our lives. For this to become a reality, we need to make change on the individual, community, institutional, and societal levels to end all forms of oppression, including forces that deprive us of self-determination and control over our bodies, and limit our reproductive choices to achieve undivided justice.[40]

An instructive example of how the reproductive justice framework employed by SisterSong has influenced the mainstream movement is the organizing story behind the March for Women's Lives in Washington, D.C., on April 25, 2004. The march, which mobilized 1.15 million participants, was the largest demonstration in US history. Originally organized to protest antiwoman policies (such as the badly named Partial Birth Abortion Ban Act) and to call attention to the delicate pro-choice majority on the Supreme Court, it also exposed fissures in the pro-choice movement that have not been fully analyzed.

Mobilizing for the march uncovered cleavages on the Left. The event's original title, the "March for Freedom of Choice," reflected a traditional focus on a privacy-based abortion rights framework established by the Supreme Court. At the same time, the dominant issue on the American Left was the illegal war against Iraq, not abortion politics. Tens of millions of people had marched around the globe to protest Bush's invasion in February 2003. As the initial organizing for the march progressed in 2003, it became clear that targeted supporters would not turn out in sufficient numbers if the march focused solely on the right to legal abortion and the need to protect the Supreme Court. Abortion isolated from other social justice issues would not work.

Ultimately, in order to broaden the appeal of the march and mobilize the entire spectrum of social justice activists in the United States, organizers sought a strategic framework that could connect various sectors of US social justice movements. They approached SisterSong in the fall of 2003, asking for endorsement of and participation in the march. SisterSong pushed back, expressing problems with the march title and the then all-white decision-makers on the steering committee. SisterSong demanded that women of color organizations be added to the highest decision-making body, and counteroffered with its own "reproductive justice" framework. (The original March organizers were the Feminist Majority Foundation, the National Organization for Women, Planned Parenthood Federation of America, and NARAL Pro-Choice America. Eventually, the National Latina Institute for Reproductive Health, the Black Women's Health Imperative and the American Civil Liberties Union were added to the march steering committee.) Reproductive justice was a viable way to mobilize broader support for the march. It also had the potential to revitalize an admittedly disheartened pro-choice movement. The central question was: were pro-choice leaders ready and willing to finally respect the leadership and vision of women of color?

Through the leadership of Alice Cohan, the march director, the March for Freedom of Choice was renamed in the fall of 2003, and women of color organizations were added to the steering committee. Using the intersectional, multi-issue approach fundamental to the reproductive justice framework, march organizers reached out to women of color, civil rights organizations, labor, youth, antiwar groups, anti-globalization activists, environmentalists, immigrants' rights organizations, and many, many others.

The success of the march was a testament to the power of reproductive justice as a framework to mobilize and unite diverse sectors of the social justice movement to support women's human rights in the United States and abroad. Just as importantly, it also showed how women of color have to take on the Right and the Left when asserting control over our bodies, our communities, and our destinies.

> I am not wrong: Wrong is not my name
> My name is my own my own my own
> and I can't tell you who in the hell set things up like this
> but I can tell you that from now on my resistance
> my simple and daily and nightly self-determination
> may very well cost you your life.
>
> —June Jordan

6

Heteropatriarchy and the Three Pillars of White Supremacy
Rethinking Women of Color Organizing

Andrea Smith

Scenario #1

A group of women of color come together to organize. An argument ensues about whether or not Arab women should be included. Some argue that Arab women are "white" since they have been classified as such in the US census. Another argument erupts over whether or not Latinas qualify as "women of color," since some may be classified as "white" in their Latin American countries of origin and/or "pass" as white in the United States.

Scenario #2

In a discussion on racism, some people argue that Native peoples suffer from less racism than other people of color because they generally do not reside in segregated neighborhoods within the United States. In addition, some argue that since tribes now have gaming, Native peoples are no longer "oppressed."

Scenario #3

A multiracial campaign develops involving diverse communities of color in which some participants charge that we must stop the black/white binary, and end Black hegemony over people of color politics to develop a more "multicultural" framework. However, this campaign continues to rely on strategies and cultural motifs developed by the Black Civil Rights struggle in the United States.

These incidents, which happen quite frequently in "women of color" or "people of color" political organizing struggles, are often explained as a consequence of "oppression olympics." That is to say, one problem we have is that we are too busy fighting over who is more oppressed. In this essay, I want to argue that these incidents are not so much the result of "oppression olympics" but are more about how we have inadequately framed "women of color" or "people of color" politics. That is, the premise behind much "women of color" organizing is that women from communities victimized by white supremacy should unite together around their shared oppression. This framework might be represented by a diagram of five overlapping circles, each marked Native women, Black women, Arab/Muslim women, Latinas, and Asian American women, overlapping like a Venn diagram.

This framework has proven to be limited for women of color and people of color organizing. First, it tends to presume that our communities have been impacted by white supremacy in the same way. Consequently, we often assume that all of our communities will share similar strategies for liberation. In fact, however, our strategies often run into conflict. For example, one strategy that many people in US-born communities of color adopt, in order to advance economically out of impoverished communities, is to join the military. We then become complicit in oppressing and colonizing communities from other countries. Meanwhile, people from other countries often adopt the strategy of moving to the United States to advance economically, without considering their complicity in settling on the lands of indigenous peoples that are being colonized by the United States.

Consequently, it may be more helpful to adopt an alternative framework for women of color and people of color organizing. I call one such framework the "Three Pillars of White Supremacy." This framework does not assume that racism and white supremacy is enacted in a singular fashion; rather, white supremacy is constituted by separate and distinct, but still interrelated, logics. Envision three pillars, one labeled Slavery/Capitalism, another labeled Genocide/Capitalism, and the last one labeled Orientalism/War, as well as arrows connecting each of the pillars together.

Slavery/Capitalism

One pillar of white supremacy is the logic of slavery. As Sora Han, Jared Sexton, and Angela P. Harris note, this logic renders Black people as inherently slave-able—as nothing more than property.[1] That is, in this logic of white supremacy, Blackness becomes equated with slaveability. The forms of slavery may change—whether it is through the formal system of slavery, sharecropping, or through the current prison-industrial complex—but the logic itself has remained consistent.

This logic is the anchor of capitalism. That is, the capitalist system ultimately commodifies all workers—one's own person becomes a commodity that one must sell in the labor market while the profits of one's work are taken by someone else. To keep this capitalist system in place—which ultimately commodifies most people—the logic of slavery applies a racial hierarchy to this system. This racial hierarchy tells people that as long as you are not Black, you have the opportunity to escape the commodification of capitalism. This helps people who are not Black to accept their lot in life, because they can feel that at least they are not at the very bottom of the racial hierarchy—at least they are not property; at least they are not slaveable.

The logic of slavery can be seen clearly in the current prison industrial complex (PIC). While the PIC generally incarcerates communities of color, it seems to be structured primarily on an anti-Black racism. That is, prior to the Civil War, most people in prison where white. However, after the thirteenth amendment wsa passed—which banned slavery, except for those in prison—Black people previously enslaved through the slavery system were reenslaved through the prison system. Black people who had been the property of slave owners became state property, through the conflict leasing system. Thus, we can actually look at the criminalization of Blackness as a logical extension of Blackness as property.

Genocide/Colonialism

A second pillar of white supremacy is the logic of genocide. This logic holds that indigenous peoples must disappear. In fact, they must *always* be disappearing, in order to allow non-indigenous peoples rightful claim over this land. Through this logic of genocide, non-Native peoples then become the rightful inheritors of all that was indigenous—land, resources, indigenous spirituality, or culture. As Kate Shanley notes, Native peoples are a permanent "present absence" in the US colonial imagination, an "absence" that reinforces, at every turn, the conviction that Native peoples are indeed vanishing and that the conquest of Native lands is justified. Ella Shoat and Robert Stam describe this absence as "an ambivalently repressive mechanism [which] dispels the anxiety in the face of the Indian, whose very presence is a reminder of the initially precarious grounding of the American nation-state itself.... In a temporal paradox, living Indians were induced to 'play dead,' as it were, in order to perform a narrative of manifest destiny in which their role, ultimately, was to disappear."[2]

Rayna Green further elaborates that the current Indian "wannabe" phenomenon is based on a logic of genocide: non-Native peoples imagine themselves as the rightful inheritors of all that previously belonged to "vanished" Indians, thus entitling them to ownership of this land. "The living performance of 'playing Indian' by non-Indian peoples depends upon the physical and psychological removal, even the death, of real Indians. In that sense, the performance, purportedly often done out of a stated and implicit love for Indians, is really the obverse of another well-known cultural phenomenon, 'Indian hating,' as most often expressed in another, deadly performance genre called 'genocide.'"[3] After all, why would non-Native peoples need to play Indian— which often includes acts of spiritual appropriation and land theft—if they thought Indians were still alive and perfectly capable of being Indian themselves? The pillar of genocide serves as the anchor for colonialism—it is what allows non-Native peoples to feel they can rightfully own indigenous peoples' land. It is okay to take land from indigenous peoples, because indigenous peoples have disappeared.

Orientalism/War

A third pillar of white supremacy is the logic of Orientalism. Orientalism was defined by Edward Said as the process of the West defining itself as a superior civilization by constructing itself in opposition to an "exotic" but inferior "Orient." (Here I am using the term "Orientalism" more broadly than to solely signify what has been historically named as the Orient or Asia.) The logic of Orientalism marks certain peoples or nations as inferior and as posing a constant threat to the well-being of empire. These peoples are still seen as "civilizations"—they are not property or "disappeared"—however, they will always be imaged as permanent foreign threats to empire. This logic is evident in the anti-immigration movements within the United States that target immigrants of color. It does not matter how long immigrants of color reside in the United States, they generally become targeted as foreign threats, particularly during war time. Consequently, orientalism serves as the anchor for war, because it allows the United States to justify being in a constant state of war to protect itself from its enemies.

For example, the United States feels entitled to use Orientalist logic to justify racial profiling of Arab Americans so that it can be strong enough to fight the "war on terror." Orientalism also allows the United States to defend the logics of slavery and genocide, as these practices enable the United States to stay "strong enough" to fight these constant wars. What becomes clear then is what Sora Han states— the United States is not at war; the United States *is* war.[4] For the system of white supremacy to stay in place, the United States must always be at war.

Because we are situated within different logics of white supremacy, we may misunderstand a racial dynamic if we simplistically try to explain one logic of white supremacy with another logic. For instance, think about the first scenario that opens this essay: if we simply dismiss Latino/as or Arab peoples as "white," we fail to understand how a racial logic of Orientalism is in operation. That is, Latino/as and Arabs are often situated in a racial hierarchy that privileges them over Black people. However, while Orientalist logic may bestow them some racial privilege, they are still cast as inferior yet threatening "civilizations" in the United States. Their privilege is not a signal that they will be assimilated, but that they will be marked as perpetual foreign threats to the US world order.

Organizing Implications

Under the old but still potent and dominant model, people of color organizing was based on the notion of organizing around shared victimhood. In this model, however, we see that we are victims of white supremacy, but complicit in it as well. Our survival strategies and resistance to white supremacy are set by the system of white supremacy itself. What keeps us trapped within our particular pillars of white supremacy is that we are seduced with the prospect of being able to participate in the other pillars. For example, all non-Native peoples are promised the ability to join in the colonial project of settling indigenous lands. All non-Black peoples are promised that if they comply, they will not be at the bottom of the racial hierarchy. And Black, Native, Latino, and Asian peoples are promised that they will economically and politically advance if they join US wars to spread "democracy." Thus, people of color organizing must be premised on making strategic alliances with each other, based on where we are situated within the larger political economy. Thus, for example, Native peoples who are organizing against the colonial and genocidal practices committed by the US government will be more effective in their struggle if they also organize against US militarism, particularly the military recruitment of indigenous peoples to support US imperial wars. If we try to end US colonial practices at home, but support US empire by joining the military, we are strengthening the state's ability to carry out genocidal policies against people of color here and all over the world.

This way, our alliances would not be solely based on shared victimization, but where we are complicit in the victimization of others. These approaches might help us to develop resistance strategies that do not inadvertently keep the system in place for all of us, and keep all of us accountable. In all of these cases, we would check our aspirations against the aspirations of other communities to ensure that our model of liberation does not become the model of oppression for others.

These practices require us to be more viligant in how we may have internalized some of these logics in our own organizing practice. For instance, much racial justice organizing within the United States has rested on a civil rights framework that fights for equality under the law. An assumption behind this organizing is that the United States is a democracy with some flaws, but is otherwise admirable. Despite the fact that it rendered slaves three-fifths of a person, the US Constitution is presented as the model document from which to build a flourishing democracy. However, as Luana Ross notes, it has never been against US law to commit genocide against indigenous peoples—in fact, genocide *is* the law of the country. The United States could not exist without it. In the United States, democracy is actually the alibi for genocide—it is the practice that covers up United States colonial control over indigenous lands.

Our organizing can also reflect anti-Black racism. Recently, with the outgrowth of "multiculturalism" there have been calls to "go beyond the black/white binary" and include other communities of color in our analysis, as presented in the third scenario. There are a number of flaws with this analysis. First, it replaces an analysis of white supremacy with a politics of multicultural representation; if we just *include* more people, then our practice will be less racist. Not true. This model does not address the nuanced structure of white supremacy, such as through these distinct logics of slavery, genocide, and Orientalism. Second, it obscures the centrality of the slavery logic in the system of white supremacy, which is *based on a black/white binary*. The black/white binary is not the *only* binary which characterizes white supremacy, but it is still a central one that we cannot "go beyond" in our racial justice organizing efforts.

If we do not look at how the logic of slaveability inflects our society and our thinking, it will be evident in our work as well. For example, other communities of color often appropriate the cultural work and organizing strategies of African American civil rights or Black Power movements without corresponding assumptions that we should also be in solidarity with Black communities. We assume that this work is the common "property" of all oppressed groups, and we can appropriate it without being accountable.

Angela P. Harris and Juan Perea debate the usefulness of the black/white binary in the book, *Critical Race Theory*. Perea complains that the black/white binary fails to *include* the experiences of other people of color. However, he fails to identify alternative racializing logics to the black/white paradigm.[5] Meanwhile, Angela P. Harris argues that "the story of 'race' itself is that of the construction of Blackness and whiteness. In this story, Indians, Asian Americans, and Latinos/as do exist. But their roles are subsidiary to the fundamental binary national drama. As a political claim, Black exceptionalism exposes the deep mistrust and tensions among American ethnic groups racialized as nonwhite."[6]

Let's examine these statements in conversation with each other. Simply saying we need to move beyond the black/white binary (or perhaps, the "black/nonblack" binary) in US racism obfuscates the racializing logic of slavery, and prevents us from seeing that this binary constitutes Blackness as the bottom of a color hierarchy. However, this is not the *only* binary that fundamentally constitutes white supremacy. There is also an indigenous/settler binary, where Native genocide is central to the logic of white supremacy and other non-indigenous people of color also form "a subsidiary" role. We also face another Orientalist logic that fundamentally constitutes Asians, Arabs, and Latino/as as foreign threats, requiring the United States to be at permanent war with these peoples. In this construction, Black and Native peoples play subsidiary roles.

Clearly the black/white binary is central to racial and political thought and practice in the United States, and any understanding of white supremacy must take it into consideration. However, if we look at only this binary, we may misread the dynamics of white supremacy in different contexts. For example, critical race theorist Cheryl Harris's analysis of whiteness as property reveals this weakness. In *Critical Race Theory,* Harris contends that whites have a property interest in the preservation of whiteness, and seek to deprive those who are "tainted" by Black or Indian blood from these same white property interests. Harris simply assumes that the positions of African Americans and American Indians are the same, failing to consider US policies of forced assimilation and forced whiteness on American Indians. These policies have become so entrenched that when Native peoples make political claims, they have been accused of being white. When Andrew Jackson removed the Cherokee along the Trail of Tears, he argued that those who did not want removal were really white.[7] In contemporary times, when I was a non-violent witness for the Chippewa spearfishers in the late 1980s, one of the more frequent slurs whites hurled when the Chippewa attempted to exercise their treaty-protected right to fish was that they had white parents, or they were really white.

Status differences between Blacks and Natives are informed by the different economic positions African Americans and American Indians have in US society. African Americans have been traditionally valued for their labor, hence it is in the interest of the dominant society to have as many people marked "Black," as possible, thereby maintaining a cheap labor pool; by contrast, American Indians have been valued for the land base they occupy, so it is in the interest of dominant society to have as few people marked "Indian" as possible, facilitating access to Native lands. "Whiteness" operates differently under a logic of genocide than it does from a logic of slavery.

Another failure of US-based people of color in organizing is that we often fall back on a "US-centrism," believing that what is happening "over there" is less important than what is happening here. We fail to see how the United States maintains the system of oppression here precisely by tying our allegiances to the interests of US empire "over there."

Heteropatriarchy and White Supremacy

Heteropatriarchy is the building block of US empire. In fact, it is the building block of the nation-state form of governance. Christian Right authors make these links in their analysis of imperialism and empire. For example, Christian Right activist and founder of Prison Fellowship Charles Colson makes the connection between homosexuality and the nation-state in his analysis of the war on terror, explaining that one of the causes of terrorism is same-sex marriage:

> Marriage is the traditional building block of human society, intend-
> ed both to unite couples and bring children into the world … There

is a natural moral order for the family ... the family, led by a married mother and father, is the best available structure for both child-rearing and cultural health. Marriage is not a private institution designed solely for the individual gratification of its participants. If we fail to enact a Federal Marriage Amendment, we can expect not just more family breakdown, but also more criminals behind bars and more chaos in our streets.[8]

Colson is linking the well-being of US empire to the well-being of the heteropatriarchal family. He continues:

When radical Islamists see American women abusing Muslim men, as they did in the Abu Ghraib prison, and when they see news coverage of same-sex couples being "married" in US towns, we make this kind of freedom abhorrent—the kind they see as a blot on Allah's creation. We must preserve traditional marriage in order to protect the United States from those who would use our depravity to destroy us.[9]

As Ann Burlein argues in *Lift High the Cross*, it may be a mistake to argue that the goal of Christian Right politics is to create a theocracy in the United States. Rather, Christian Right politics work through the private family (which is coded as white, patriarchal, and middle class) to create a "Christian America." She notes that the investment in the private family makes it difficult for people to invest in more public forms of social connection. In addition, investment in the suburban private family serves to mask the public disinvestment in urban areas that makes the suburban lifestyle possible. The social decay in urban areas that results from this disinvestment is then construed as the result of deviance from the Christian family ideal rather than as the result of political and economic forces. As former head of the Christian Coalition, Ralph Reed, states: "'The only true solution to crime is to restore the family,'"[10] and "Family break-up causes poverty."[11] Concludes Burlein, "'The family' is no mere metaphor but a crucial technology by which modern power is produced and exercised."[12]

As I have argued elsewhere, in order to colonize peoples whose societies are not based on social hierarchy, colonizers must first naturalize hierarchy through instituting patriarchy.[13] In turn, patriarchy rests on a gender binary system in which only two genders exist, one dominating the other. Consequently, Charles Colson *is* correct when he says that the colonial world order depends on heteronormativity. Just as the patriarchs rule the family, the elites of the nation-state rule their citizens. Any liberation struggle that does not challenge heteronormativity cannot substantially challenge colonialism or white supremacy. Rather, as Cathy Cohen contends, such struggles will maintain colonialism based on a politics of secondary marginalization where the most elite class of these groups will further their aspirations on the backs of those most marginalized within the community.[14]

Through this process of secondary marginalization, the national or racial justice struggle takes on either implicitly or explicitly a nation-state model as the end point of its struggle—a model of governance in which the elites govern the rest through violence and domination, as well as exclude those who are not members of "the nation." Thus, national liberation politics become less vulnerable to being coopted by the Right when we base them on a model of liberation that fundamentally challenges right-wing conceptions of the nation. We need a model based on community relationships and on mutual respect.

Conclusion

Women of color–centered organizing points to the centrality of gender politics within antiracist, anticolonial struggles. Unfortunately, in our efforts to organize against white, Christian America, racial justice struggles often articulate an equally heteropatriarchal racial nationalism. This model of organizing either hopes to assimilate into white America, or to replicate it within an equally hierarchical and oppressive racial nationalism in which the elites of the community rule everyone else. Such struggles often call on the importance of preserving the "Black family" or the "Native family" as the bulwark of this nationalist project, the family being conceived of in capitalist and heteropatriarchal terms. The response is often increased homophobia, with lesbian and gay community members construed as "threats" to the family. But, perhaps we should challenge the "concept" of the family itself. Perhaps, instead, we can reconstitute alternative ways of living together in which "families" are not seen as islands on their own. Certainly, indigenous communities were not ordered on the basis of a nuclear family structure—is the result of colonialism, not the antidote to it.

In proposing this model, I am speaking from my particular position in indigenous struggles. Other peoples might flesh out these logics more fully from different vantage points. Others might also argue that there are other logics of white supremacy are missing. Still others might complicate how they relate to each other. But I see this as a starting point for women of color organizers that will allow us to reenvision a politics of solidarity that goes beyond multiculturalism, and develop more complicated strategies that can really transform the political and economic status quo.

7

A Call for Consistency
Palestinian Resistance and Radical US Women of Color

Nadine Naber

On January 27, 2002, the racialized marker of the "irrationally violent Muslim extremist" was feminized when the media announced the emergence of the "first female suicide bomber," Wafa Idris. As the world had recently been reduced by George Bush to "those who are with us versus those who are with terrorism," the US media painted Wafa Idris as an irrationally violent terrorist brainwashed by Islam and on the side of evil. Now the question is: will radical women of color shift the dominant discourse from focusing on whether we agree with Palestinian methods of resistance to a recognition and understanding of historical conditions that produce female-led martyr operations? We have learned—from African slavery and the colonization of the Americas—that when women are faced with no options, they will continue to resist.

Consider Wafa's everyday life experiences. She worked as a volunteer for the Palestinian Red Crescent Society (PRCS). She carried children on stretchers, witnessed brutal deaths and injuries, and evacuated bodies daily that were, quite literally, in pieces. A friend of Wafa's, who also worked as a volunteer for the PRCS, had fiven first aid to a boy who had been shot in the head by an Israeli soldier, and found herself holding his brain in her hands. Today, children's games in Palestine mean making victory signs while playing on a stretcher carried by playmates, or playing dead in an alley several yards away from where older children are clashing with Israeli soldiers.

For most Palestinians, the violence Wafa experienced daily is standard operating procedure. In spring 2002, journalists from the Egyptian newspaper *Al Ahram Weekly* interviewed international photographers who had been in Palestine to develop an art exhibit about children. The journalists quoted the photographers saying, "The streets looked like a football match between kids and soldiers but the kids were being shot…it was surreal…the rules of the game: get shot or don't get shot." The photographers added, "Kids stand up and curse Israeli soldiers or they go in front of them and lift their shirt to bare their chest as they are shot. One kid had two bullets in him…he lifts his shirt and then points to the center of the chest calling, 'Give the third…come on…give me the third!'" The photographers were there taking pictures and they said that they would see kids dropping and being shot at with no sound.

One photographer showed *Al Ahram* writers a photograph of children who appeared to be smiling, holding hands in their school uniforms next to graffiti on a wall that read, "Israel means killing children." Looking at the photo of the children, the reporter asked, "They were laughing?" The photographer replied, "They were dying."

Between the first *intifada* and March 2005, more than four thousand Palestinians civilian were killed and thirty thousand more were injured. Palestinians have also been locked up in ghettos controlled by the Israeli army, who use US-supplied "Apache" helicopters, tanks, and other supplies. F-16s mow down people, houses, olive groves, and fields every day. Babies die at birth at civilian checkpoints as Israelis regularly shoot and kill ambulance drivers and target paramedics saving the injured. In Palestine, many of the elites have left; many are suicidal; those who have stayed behind are throwing themselves out in the streets to die. Israelis are using fighter jets, helicopters, and tanks to attack refugee camps—including Balata, Jabaliya, and Dheisha—and to occupy Ramallah, so the list goes on and on.

Israeli massacres cannot be viewed as accidents of history. They are systematized and an integral policy of the military. Israel was created by a process of war, by pillaging the very fabric that held the indigenous Palestinian population together: Palestinian land, Palestinian national identity, and Palestinian interpretations of respectability. For example, mothers and daughters have been violated in front of their fathers, brothers, and husbands. When we examine the dominant Israeli historical narrative, it is difficult to ignore the massacres that facilitated the process of "nation building" and the use of fear to encourage Palestinian displacement from historical Palestine.

Moshe Dayan, the former prime minister and ex-Israeli general, admitted that every Israeli town in every Israeli neighborhood was built on the remains of a Palestinian village with an Arab name, Arab people, and an Arab history associated with it. For example, Beir Shiva was Bier Al Saba'a; Tel Aviv was Tel Abib; and Acco was Acca. Currently we are witnessing the transformation of El Khalil to Hebron. Yitzhak Rabin, the Nobel Peace Prize Laureate and revered martyr for peace, massacred civilians in villages surrounding Jerusalem when he led the Israeli army into the city during the 1967 wars. And Ariel Sharon, whom the Israeli public elected in order to "send a message to" Palestinians, engaged in many massacres, including Kibya in 1953, Sabra and Shatilla in 1982, and Jenin in 2002.

Israeli massacres are often accompanied by sexual assault, particularly of pregnant women, as a symbolic way of uprooting the child from the mother, or the Palestinian from the land. Today, another strategy to disrupt childbearing is the prevention of pregnant women in labor from crossing borders for medical care. In 2005, a report submitted to the UN General Assembly from UN agencies operating in Palestine exposed the detrimental effects of Israeli checkpoints and the apartheid wall on Palestinian women's health, such as the denial of obstetric care to 61 Palestinian women who were forced against their will to give birth at one of Israel's illegal checkpoints. The report stated that from the beginning of the second *intifada* to March 2004, a number of unsafe deliveries in which both mothers and infants have died have occurred at checkpoints. 55 Palestinian women have been forced to give birth at checkpoints, and thirty-three newborns were stillborn at checkpoints, owing to delays or denial of permission to reach medical facilities.

Palestinians are made aware of the message behind Israeli massacres because the Israeli army advertises it on bullhorns to trigger panic and fear. In a series of air raids, the calls would often sound like, "If you surrender yourselves and leave your homes, you will not be hurt. If you don't, remember what happened in Deir

Yassin." In Deir Yassin, approximately 460 Palestinians, most of them women and children, were executed en masse. Some of them were tortured, some of them were beaten to death, and some of them who survived recounted the mutilation and the torture of their own family members while they were held back to watch.

As we look at the prospects for the future, we cannot forget the women and children executed en masse in 1982 at the Sabra and Shatilla refugee camps in Lebanon—some of them killed using glass bottles instead of bullets so the pain could be felt for hours. Meanwhile, most of us in the United States are subsidizing this at the rate of $6 billion of our tax dollars per year. We also cannot separate all of this from histories of European colonialism and expansion and US colonization of the Americas; indeed, US democracy was founded on the theft from and genocide of African Americans, Native Americans, Mexicans, and Puerto Ricans.

Contrary to US media propaganda, there is a real and massive disparity in the balance of power between Israel and the Palestinians. Israel is a settler colonial state and as it stands today, in order for this colonial project to succeed, Palestinian people cannot exist within the dominant Israeli national consciousness. For Israel to consolidate its regional military and economic power, it must continue to assert itself as indigenous within the region. And in order to pull off this feat, Israel has recreated its entire history, which, in turn, entails the displacement of the Palestinian population. According to the vision behind this project, at best, the "Palestinian people" are destined to become a relic, incorporated within a new Israeli construct as a minority—despite the fact that Israeli cultural consciousness is a recreation of everything that is indigenous to the land of Palestine.

The ongoing colonization of Palestine has entailed a process of cultural appropriation in which Palestinian dance, food, clothing, and arts have been refashioned through European cultural forms, redefined as "Israeli" and denied for the Palestinians to enjoy in their homeland. Today, 70% of the Palestinian population has been forced into exile. Despite United Nations Resolution 194, which defines the right to return as an inalienable human right, the Israeli government continues to deny and violate the right of return, each time it confiscates land, each time it displaces a Palestinian family, each time it demolishes a home, each time it harasses civilians at checkpoints, each time it holds up workers on the way to work, and each time it imposes closure upon the occupied territories. For those of you who wonder about the peace process initiated by the Oslo agreement in 1993, more land has been confiscated since 1993 than between 1967 and 1993.

Many Palestinians remain landless, but the Palestinian struggle to demand the right to exist as a unified people with the opportunity to return home persists. There are similarities between the Palestinian context and Vieques, Puerto Rico, Makua Valley in Hawai'i, and indigenous struggles all over the world, where the destruction of land and the uprooting of people has erased spiritual and sacred indigenous spaces and blocked access to food and other elements of sustainability; but many of us have not yet made these connections. Palestine is often isolated as an anomaly that stands outside of history. As a significant partner of US imperialism on a global scale, Israel has been an executor of discrimination and racism internationally. It has provided military expertise and hardware to other abusive undemocratic regimes, and Israeli intelligence training has been central to the development of oppressive regimes throughout the Global South, including South Africa, Uganda, Argentina, El Salvador, Guatemala, and Indonesia. As we move forward, I hope radical women of color will begin to recognize the transformative possibilities of our shared histories for movement building. And I hope that today, we will be consistent in our critiques of colonialism by linking the Palestinian struggle to indigenous struggles internationally, as well as all struggles against imperialism from a radical women of color perspective.

Allow me to return to Wafa Idris and where, at this historical juncture, do radical women of color, with our focus on intersections of race, class, gender, sexism, homophobia, colonialism, and imperialism, locate her? Will we explore the impact of colonization on Wafa's family? Palestinian families? Palestinian communities? What about increases in domestic violence? Shifts in women's labor? Will we take interest in Palestinian feminists' analysis of women's resistance? Where do we locate her in the context of feminist heroine metaphors that highlight women's transformations from passivity to agency? And how might feminist theorizations of the body grapple with a woman who deploys the body as a weapon against an unstoppable military machine?

Radical women of color movements provide useful frameworks for historicizing Wafa Idris' power-laden realities. Yet as long as we buy into the dominant corporate media propaganda that devalues Palestinian lives, blames the victim, and victimizes the oppressor, we will fail to recognize her struggle against the intersecting axes of colonialism, racism, classism, and sexism, and we will fail to see her humanity. Today, I would like to know if Wafa Idris would ever be positioned among us? We must explore more closely why progressive women of color have not called Zionism out, to the same extent that other colonialist projects are ferociously called out?

Typically, progressives in the US value integration, so sites on the left often exclude those seeking national liberation. Arab women activists have contributed a great deal of work to the task of exposing the Palestinian struggle as a legitimate anti-colonialist cause. Still, I have repeatedly heard my Palestinian sisters make the following claim to other activists: "I am not asking to 'become American' and I'm not asking you to redefine me as a US 'person of color' or a 'woman of color.' I'm asking you to recognize our struggle for liberation and support our struggle to return home."

Despite the media blackout on the Palestinian struggle, coalitions between radical people of color and the Palestinian struggle have existed for decades. Recently, women of color organizations such as INCITE! Women of Color against Violence and the Women of Color Resource Center have highlighted links between Palestinian women's struggles and indigenous women's struggles. These organizations have also opened up spaces for coalition between US women of color; immigrant, refugee, and displaced women; and women struggling with their communities against US imperialism globally.

In the last several years, we have seen our struggles intensify. Our communities have been polarized along the lines of those who say that the "war on terror" has nothing to do with us, and those who refuse to be silent about the backlash; the detentions; the surveillance; the use of Arab, Iranian, and Afghan women's bodies as symbols for justifying war; the Bush administration's theft of resources from poor communities of color into the US military budget; the use of people of color as canon fodder for Bush's war; and the rape and sexual harassment of women of color in the US military. As Israel continues its slaughter of Palestinians and the rest of the world sits back and watches, let us assert that Palestinians exist. Let us continue this struggle. All Palestinians are granted the right to return to their original homes or towns of origin. Let us mount our resistance! Let us make history! Almost 2 million dead in Iraq, and we continue to fight! Over five hundred years of uprooting Native America, and we continue to fight! Over half of the Palestinian population expelled and we continue to demand Palestinians' right to exist! Let us demand that the United States and Israel end their colonization of Arab land! If we continue to rise up—Zionism, colonialism, racism, sexism, classism, and homophobia will cease to exist! This is the only just solution.

II
FORMS OF VIOLENCE

8

The Color of Violence

Haunani-Kay Trask

At one time, the land upon where the University of California–Santa Cruz sits was home—as was all land in California—to an untold number of Native tribes who had occupied the area for more than twenty thousand years.

Who were these indigenous peoples? Of the Native nations we do know of, there were Tolowa, Yurok, Chilula, Karok, Shasta, Wiyot, Whilkut, Yana, Waintu, Maidu, Washo, Konkow, Patwin, Wappo, Pomo, Paiute, Ohlone, and many, many others in an area from the Northern California border down to the Golden Gate Bridge in the west and Yosemite National Park in the east, an area of 250 miles by 200 miles.[1]

Few of these tribes remain today. From the eighteenth century onwards, California Indians were rounded up in Jesuit and Franciscan missions which were, in historian David Stannard's words, "furnaces of death." Mission Indians died as a result of European-introduced diseases, malnutrition, brutal enslavement, fatal forms of punishment, and sexual abuses.[2]

An official policy of genocide was enunciated by California governor Peter Burnett in his 1851 message to the California legislature, in which he argued that the ongoing wars against Native peoples "must continue to be waged between the races until the Indian becomes extinct."[3]

The situation in South America was no different. During the course of four centuries—from the 1490s to the 1890s—Europeans and white Americans engaged in what Stannard calls, "the worst human holocaust the world has ever witnessed." At contact, there was an estimated population on two American continents of some seventy-five million Native people; five million remained at the end of the nineteenth century .[4] Colonization was the historical process, and genocide was the official policy.

The United Nations definition of genocide is:

> any act committed with the intent to destroy, in whole or in part, national, ethnic, racial or religious groups, including killing members of the group; causing serious bodily or mental harm to members of the group; inflicting conditions of life calculated to bring about physical destruction of the group in whole or in part; imposing measures intended to prevent births within the group; and forcibly transferring children of one group to another group."[5]

Therefore, the European conquest of the Americas can be defined as genocide. Colonialism is the historical process of conquest and exploitation. And the United States of America is a country created out of genocide and colonialism.

Today, the United States is the most powerful country in the world, a violent country created out of the bloody extermination of Native peoples, the enslavement of forcibly transported peoples, and the continuing oppression of dark-skinned peoples.

The color of violence, then, is the color of white over Black, white over brown, white over red, white over yellow. It is the violence of north over south, of continents over archipelagoes, of settlers over natives and slaves. Shaping this color scheme are the labyrinths of class and gender, of geography and industry, of metropolises and peripheries, of sexual definitions and confinements.

There is not just one binary opposition, but many oppositions. Within colonialism, such as now practiced in my own country of Hawai'i, violence against women of color, especially our Native women, is both the economic and cultural violence of tourism, and of militarism. It is the violence of our imprisonments: reservations, incarcerations, diasporas. It is the violence of military bases, of the largest porting of nuclear submarines in the world, of the inundation of our exquisite islands by eager settlers and tourists from the American and Asian continents.

These settlers have no interest in, or concern about, our Native people. Settlers of all colors come to Hawai'i for refuge, for relaxation. They do not know, nor do they care, that our Native government was overthrown by white sugar planters in 1893 with the willing aid of the American troops; that our islands were annexed in 1898 against the expressed wishes of our Native people; that our political status as Hawaiian citizens was made impossible by forced annexation to the United States. Many non-Natives have said that we should be grateful for the alleged opportunity of American citizenship even if this has meant termination as an independent country.[6]

How do we, as a terminated people, understand the color of violence? We look at all the non-Native settlers and tourists around us and know we are subjugated in our own land, suffering landlessness and poverty, consigned by the American government to the periphery of our own country, to its prisons and shanties, to its welfare rolls, hospital wards, and graveyards.

We exist in a violent and violated world, a world characterized by "peaceful violence," as Frantz Fanon so astutely observed.[7] This is the peaceful violence of historical dispossession, of racial, cultural, and economic subjugation and stigmatization. Our psychological suffering and our physical impairments are a direct result of this peaceful violence, of the ordered realities of confinement, degradation, ill health, and early death.

Allow me to shock you with a profile of our health statistics. Below one year of age, the Hawaiian death rate is more than double the overall US average. Between one and four years of age, it is triple the US figure, and so on through early adulthood. And in every age category up to age thirty, the Hawaiian death rate is never less than double, and is often triple, the non-Hawaiian mortality rate in our islands. With just under 20% of the state's population, Hawaiians account for nearly 75% of the state's deaths for persons less than eighteen years of age. And while the mortality rate for non-Hawaiians decreased significantly between 1980 and 1990, for both full and part-Hawaiians, it actually increased.[8]

This state of ill health is, of course, Fanon's "peaceful violence" that kills without a sound, without a passing notice. Indeed, most of the oppression and violence people of color experience is hidden from view. In our case, more Hawaiians live below the poverty level than any other ethnic group in Hawai'i. More of our people are in prison, are homeless, are undereducated. Is this a violent situation? Of course. Is this a result of American colonization? Of course.

Colonialism began with conquest and is today maintained by a settler administration created out of the doctrine of cultural hierarchy, a hierarchy in which European Americans and whiteness dominate non-European Americans and darkness. As a result, we live in a country where race prejudice, in the words of Fanon, obeys a flawless logic. For, after all, if inferior peoples must be exterminated, their cultures and habits of life, their languages and customs, their economies, indeed, every difference about them must be assaulted, confined, and obliterated. There must be a dominant culture and therefore a dominant people, a dominant religion, a dominant language, a dominant legal system, a dominant educational system, and so on, and so on. In other words, there must be dominance and subordination.

In a colonial country such as the United States, white hegemony delineates this hierarchy. Thus, white people are the dominant group, Christianity is the dominant religion, capitalism is the dominant economy, militarism is the dominant form of diplomacy and the force underlying international relations. Violence is thus normal, and race prejudice, like race violence, is as American as apple pie.

In a racist society, there is no need to justify white racist behavior. The naturalness of segregation and hierarchy is the naturalness of hearing English on the street, or seeing a McDonald's on every other corner, or assuming the American dollar and United Airlines will enable a vacation in Hawai'i, my native country. Indeed, the natural, everyday presence of "the way things are" explains the strength and resilience of racism. Racism envelops us, intoxicating our thoughts, permeating our brains and skins, determining the shape of our growth and the longevity of our lives.

It is normal that hierarchy by color exists, that mistreatment by color exists, that income by color exists, that life expectancy by color exists, that opportunity by color exists, and all the other observable hierarchies documented by scholars over the years exist. The sheer normalcy of white dominance underpins the racist assertion that white people and culture are superior, for if they were not, how else can we explain their overwhelming dominance in the United States.[9]

Dominance is the cause and engine of racism. Power over peoples and land and economies. Power to take and consume. Power to define and confine. Power to maintain power.

There is no escape from origins; colonial countries are racist countries. The United States of America exists because centuries of extermination campaigns were waged to rid the continent of millions and millions of Native peoples. Some estimate that 100 million were killed.

And after taking the continent, the United States took Hawai'i and Guam and Puerto Rico and the Philippines. Born in conquest, the United States continues in conquest.

Let me tell you about my own country. Like most Native peoples, Hawaiians

lived in our mother's keeping until the fateful coming of the *haole*—Western foreigners—in 1778. Then our world collapsed from the violence of contact: disease,
mass death, and land dispossession; evangelical Christianity; plantation capitalism; cultural destruction including language-banning; and finally, American military invasion in 1893, and forced annexation in 1898. During the course of little
more than a century, the *haole* onslaught had taken from us 95% of our Hawaiian
people, 99% of our lands and waters, and the entirety of our political sovereignty.
As the twentieth century dawned, we were but a remnant of the great and ancient
people we had once been.[10]

During the long suppression of our territorial period (1900–1959), Hawaiians
lived under martial law for seven years. We suffered increased land confiscations
for military bases, and fearfully watched as the vicious process of Americanization
created racist political, educational, and economic institutions. By the time of my
birth in 1949, being Hawaiian was a racial and cultural disadvantage rather than a
national definition. The federal American government had officially classified our
people by blood quantum in 1921: those of us of 50% Hawaiian blood quantum
were Native; those of us of less than 50% were not Native. "Fifty %ers," as they
have come to be known today, have some small claims to live on what amounts to
reservation land; "less than fifties" do not have such rights. In this way, our nation
is divided by race, a concept and reality foreign to our way of thinking. Thus was I
born into captivity, a Native person in a racist, anti-Native world.

And so it is for people of color on this continent. We are non-white in a
white universe. We are different, and therefore inferior, categorically. And we are
marked by captivity: economic, political, and cultural captivity.

Indeed, "captivity" is the condition of all the peoples of the Pacific region.
Covering half the earth's surface, the Pacific is home to thirty-two countries and
many nations. We are the largest nuclearized region in the world. And we know one
thing for certain: until the Pacific is decolonized, it cannot be demilitarized.[11]

Let me frighten you with some statistics.

On O'ahu, the capital of our state and the most densely populated island, the
military controls 25% of the land area. Statewide, the combined American armed
forces have 21 installations, 26 housing complexes, 8 training areas, and 19 miscella-
neous bases and operating sites. Beyond O'ahu, Hawai'i is the linchpin of the American military strategy in the Asia-Pacific region. It is home to the largest portage of
nuclear-fueled ships and submarines in the world. These ships are received, cleaned,
and refashioned at Pearl Harbor, where workers are called "sponges" because they
absorb so much radiation during cleaning.

Regionally, in military terminology, Hawai'i is "the forward basing point" for
the American military in the Pacific. The Seventh Fleet, which patrols the world
from the Pacific to the African coast, is stationed at Pearl Harbor. Planes and ships
which test nuclear weapons in the Pacific leave from Pearl Harbor or other military installations in Hawai'i.[12]

This kind of "peaceful violence" results in land confiscations, contamination
of our plants and animals and our peoples, and the transformation of our archipelago into a poisonous war zone. Additionally, many of the lands taken by the
military are legally reserved lands for Hawaiians.

In the southern and eastern Pacific, American military violence has taken the form of nuclear testing in the Marshall Islands, nuclear waste dumping on Christmas Island, siting of electronic facilities vital to nuclear war, and construction of air bases with nuclear capabilities including airborne delivery of weapons. To the east of Hawai'i, in the Marianas Islands and Guam, there are airbases with nuclear capabilities.

The violence of nuclearization and militarization has included nuclear testing in the Marshall Islands, where more than sixty bombs have been detonated. We must all remember that the world's first hydrogen bomb was tested on Bikini Island. The force of this weapon of destruction was one thousand times stronger than the Hiroshima bomb. Marshall Islanders were used as guinea pigs to test the effects of contamination. They were not told of the bomb's effects nor were they removed before testing .[13]

Predictably, cancer is now widespread among the Marshallese. They have one of the highest rates of severely deformed children, including "jellyfish babies" who have no heads, arms, legs, or human shape. Native women from these islands have given birth to babies they describe as "octopuses," "turtles," and "apples." Such babies are born not only on islands declared radioactive by the Americans, but on all atolls and five major islands in the Marshall's archipelago.[14]

Before such tests, Marshallese people enjoyed incredible longevity, with many of their people living more than one hundred years. Today, young women have a life expectancy of forty years. The United States tested twenty-three bombs on Bikini Island and forty-three on Enewetak. Now the Marshallese know that their nation has been damaged forever as a result of the United States of America.[15]

In our part of the world, the color of violence has been the color of white countries, the United States and France, testing nuclear weapons, deploying nuclear ships, and basing military forces in every part of the north and south Pacific.

Nuclearization is a unique kind of racism. The kind that produced famous Nazi doctors and forced sterilization of Indian women in America. The kind that produced centuries of genocidal campaigns against the rest of the Third and Fourth Worlds. The kind that continues to produce and reproduce a psychology of subjugation.

Racism is not only history and sociology, economics and politics. Racism is also the psychology of subjugation. The inferior must be made to feel inferior every day, to suffer their subjugation, to be dehumanized in accordance with the colonizer's rules. Thus, as Frantz Fanon so eloquently argued, colonized people, like colonized cultures, are no longer open, dynamic, and fertile. Once colonized they become moribund, oppressed, segregated, closed, or apathetic. They must negotiate a hostile world and a menacing daily reality with great care lest they suffer increased injury. Is it any wonder that white Americans, on the whole, live longer than Black people, and Native people? For the colonized, the colonizer is a killer; literally, a killer.[16]

Like the physical attributes of killers, the culture of killers becomes bloated, disfigured, and vulgar. Such cultures celebrate their vulgarity, as American culture celebrates Christopher Columbus. And these celebrations follow from the center to the periphery, so that the whole is permeated with the thrill of cruelty.

Is it possible to rid the United States of racism? In light of the history of Native people in this country, I would say no. In light of the history of Black people, I would say no. In light of the current fight in the United States regarding affirmative action, I would say no. Racism has never ended in the United States. And it never *will* end.

Only the dismantling of the United States as we know it could begin the process of ending racism. Look to history. After the genocidal campaigns against American Indians came the confinements of reservations, and the slow attrition by early death, by starvation, by infant mortality, by FBI infiltration and murder.

After the freeing of slaves came lynching campaigns, segregation, ghettoization, discrimination, and now police wars and vicious imprisonments. After belated and half-hearted federal attempts at ameliorative programs in the sixties and seventies, Black people in this country still die younger, make less money, and suffer poor housing, inferior community services, low educational attainments, tremendous police brutality, and, of course, the everyday injuries of race. What better evidence do we need to illustrate that America is a white country for white people. As Malcolm X repeatedly said, America is irretrievably racist.

Given this, what can be done, what should be done? Fanon believed that revolutionary action was the only answer in Algeria, and in Africa as a continent. Malcolm X said that separation of Black people from white people was the only answer in the United States. I believe that my own people need separation in Hawai'i. A separate land base, economy, educational system, language base, and on and on.

Sovereignty is what we call this in Hawai'i. And what the Maori call it in Aotearoa, otherwise known by the West as New Zealand, and what African people call it. And what Indians call it here on the continent. Sovereignty on *our* land base, with *our* rules, in *our* language, for *our* people.

Who could dare deny that sovereignty is preferable to the white racism we now suffer? After all, we are separated and segregated under white rules now. Why not acknowledge the falsity of alleged American democracy, equality, and liberty? Why fight to get into white society when it so imprisons us now? Why not create our own base of power rather than be ghettoized according to white power?

How much more honest and historically accurate to acknowledge that racism prevents us as people of color from living together with white people as equals. Under the current violent hierarchy, there is only daily pain and fear. Fear because violence breeds hatred which, in turn, breeds more violence. Not the revolutionary violence that cleanses victims, as Fanon so honestly argued, but the violence of racism.

Can America afford violence, revolutionary or otherwise? For it is everywhere now. The violence of a police state protecting itself, and its white citizens. The violence of a political system dependent on mass exploitation. Looking into the heart of whiteness, I do not see a willingness to change, only a ferocious determination to keep the Black masses at bay.

So be it. If we must be kept at bay, then let it be in our own place, on our own land, with our own people. And let white people—their police, tourists, and segregated schools—stay away. Let us return to the political status of many nations. Not one sovereignty, but many sovereignties. Not one path, but many paths.

You may ask, but how can we do this? How can we be separate? Let me answer that first: we are separate now, separate and hostile and unequal. We are ghettoized by a hierarchy where people of color, and particularly indigenous people, occupy the bottom strata and where white people occupy the top.

Secondly, it is not separatism that white people oppose but the dissolution of their intimate and raw power over our lives. To have our own nations is what the white powers oppose simply because they don't want to give up their dominance over us and our resources, especially our labor and lands. *Separate sovereignties is what white people oppose, not separatism per se.*

As Native peoples all over the world know—as the Irish and the Kurds and the Palestinians and the Maori know—it is a never-ending struggle to be both separate and sovereign. Because of millennia of resistance, the Irish people remain, and the Kurdish people remain, and the Palestinian people remain, and the Maori people remain. Resistance and the legacy of resistance to incorporation, to disinheritance, to disappearance is what has kept these nations alive.

Women's leadership has been formative in this resistance. Let me just mention some of our indigenous women leaders in the Pacific Basin: Lijon Ekniland of the Marshall Islands who has represented her people all over the world in testifying to the effects of nuclear testing and radioactivity; Tamara Bopp du Pont, member of the Polynesian Liberation Front of Tahiti and an outspoken critic of French nuclear testing in the Pacific; Isabella Sumang, fierce defender of the world's first nuclear-free constitution in Belau and a constant critic of American military imperialism in the Pacific; my sister, Mililani Trask, who created our largest sovereignty initiative, Ka Lahui Hawai'i, including our Native Constitution and master plan; Jacqui Katona, of the Gundgehmi Aboriginal Association, who has opposed Australian uranium mining in the Marrar peoples' lands; Josephine Kauona Sirivi, of Bougainville, who founded and became the first president of the Bougainvillean Women for Peace and Freedom and is still a combatant in the war for Bougainvillean independence from Papua New Guinea.

These women leaders, and many more unknown, continue to carry the burden of indigenous resistance against imperialism.[17]

So I leave you with a message of remembrance and resistance: we are not one people, and it is racist to believe that we *are* one people. I join with Toni Morrison, one of the finest writers of our age, in asserting that I am not American. Nor, I might add, do I want to be American. Those who believe as I do, especially those who did not become part of the United States voluntarily, will surely nod in agreement.

For in the ugly and violent history of the United States, indeed, of the Americas, you will find that many peoples and many nations occupy these lands, not under the Christian God or the United States Constitution, but in the diverse humanity of peoples, in the many-colored family of nations.

9

Four Generations in Resistance

Dana Erekat

Between 1967 and 1986, Ariel Sharon, the former Israeli prime minister who acted as Israeli defense minister from 1981 to 1983, spearheaded a colonial philosophy called "Fighting Terrorism" which paved the way for the confiscation of all of historic Palestine and justified genocide. In 1977, Sharon was appointed minister of agriculture and settlements and made the expansion of Israeli settlements in the West Bank and Gaza his priority. He proposed the Sharon Plan, which called for the annexation of more Palestinian land, bisecting the Palestinian areas, and the building of more settlements. The Israeli government of that time adopted the plan and began carrying it through. In 1981, Sharon brought about the first strategic cooperation agreement with the United States, and in 1982 he was the architect of both the war in Lebanon and the massacre of Sabra and Shatila. Some twenty years later, the war against Palestinians and the efforts to take our land are largely funded and supported by the US government. The number of Israeli settlers in the West Bank has jumped from 5,023 in 1977 to an estimated 400,000 today.

Words cannot convey the terror and harassment faced daily by Palestinians, but perhaps this multigenerational testimonial shall permit us, if only for a moment, to experience what it is like to be a Palestinian woman living under the occupation. This story is knitted with the daily realities of Palestinian women; they are all true stories intertwined as one.

January 1, 2003. Khan Younis and Raffah Refugee Camps, Gaza.

I have never been to such a place before—throughout my twenty-four years of going home, not once have I set foot in Gaza. Concrete skeletons half standing with bare windows and closed doors, every façade on the border with Egypt is a mosaic of missile holes and bullet wounds. Rubble and toxic waste fill the streets. Here are hopes hijacked prior to their flight. Children stomping their bare feet onto broken Jerusalem stone and shattered glass, hungry and begging with spotted faces revealing their diet, yelling the one English word they know: "MONEY!" Angry and frustrated, cursing their birth in exile and occupation. I take out ten pieces of chocolate and one hundred children surround me, and I wonder, where are their mothers?

You are a mother.

Imagine, just for a moment, that you are a Palestinian momma living in a refugee camp. You were born thirty years ago to parents grieving over a land kidnapped twenty-eight years prior. As a child, you had no sense of stability, since a camp can never replace a home uprooted in 1948. But you yearned for a place to nurture and claim as your own. You are married and dream of a space of love, ties, and strength that would embrace your eight children, future grandchildren, and in-laws. You begin building a dream, saving every drop with your palms, your partner exhausting every waking hour to achieve your goal. Except a couple of years into the work, he falls ill, unable to move or speak, a living death. You are left with defeated aspirations, but you refuse misery. You continue raising your children, educating them, feeding them, attending to your husband. You are the anchor of the home. You stand in the space between barriers of occupation and occupation-inspired fundamentalism. Working in farming and cleaning, in pursuit of a dream you demur to put on the shelf, it takes you twenty painstaking years to stack three stories of family into a built home. The physical structure is now tied into your sense of self, every drop of sweat you have collected rests in between the layers of cement. The family has now grown to thirty. You live in pursuit of stability, and your home is your source of strength. You are proud.

And then one night, in the middle of the night, you hear banging on the door. Eighteen-year-old soldiers, sons of colonizers, telling you to pack up and leave within two hours. But why? Orders for your home to be demolished. They give you some excuse about the illegality of a permit or a fighter passing through your home, or some lame excuse, you care less to hear. You cannot even hear. This is twenty years of your blood down the drain. How can you possibly pack twenty years in a suitcase? Wait, you don't even own a suitcase, movement was never an option. Your right of return will not pass. You insist on staying but you are told, and you know it true, that they will kill you in this home, and no one in the world is going to hear your cry. You shed tears and sweat onto the ground as you watch, with your twenty-nine family members as your home is levelled. You shed tears and sweat onto the ground.

You take refuge in an abandoned storefront. You make a kitchen in the storage area, your grandchildren around you looking at you for a smile of reassurance. Your twenty-five-year-old daughter-in-law with her three fatherless children, for your son was martyred six months prior to the killing of your home. You relive the day the young men came to give you the news of his entry into heaven. You turn to his wife. You lost your husband to illness, she lost hers to the land. The tribe surrounds the two of you, waiting for the moment of ululation expected of you. You wonder how she feels.

You are now your daughter-in-law.

Your clan is waiting for the sound of twirling tongue to bounce off your fingers, onto the ceiling, and echo into the skies announcing your husband, a bird flying beyond a horizon you once dreamt of reaching. Your tears mingle with your vibrating lips, sending a shiver of confused pain hiding itself amidst the noise of the room. You are the wife of a martyr, expected to honor a death for land. You are left alone with the mere memory of his perfect olive-skin face, with full lips and eyes; you can still feel his touch in them. You awaken on the seventh day wondering why he has not returned home for lunch. You awaken on the eighth day surprised to not have found him in bed. You awaken a year later in a storefront-turned-home to the sound of shelling so near to your ears, worried why he is out so late in the night. You refuse to accept his never coming back and ask your frightened six-year-old daughter if she has seen him. Her father's eyes stare back at you with astonishment.

You look to the skies for prayer. God cries for you, sending tears through cracks in the ceiling, dripping onto the sheets, artifacts from beds under rubble. The shelling stops in time for your six-year-old daughter to go to school, but her body refuses to awake from exhaustion, her face still twitching from nightmares. But you have to wake her up. As a Palestinian you know education is a vital weapon for the fight in the struggle, this is why the Israelis close the school every other day and enter the school every other day. Your daughter runs home in fear but you keep sending her back knowing that education is the only way. Knowing that interference with education is a colonizer's tactic of preventing the growth of society, you don't need a diploma to understand that: it is your lived reality. But you sympathize with your daughter, and imagine what it is like to be her. In your head you walk with her to the school yard, you merge into her body.

You are now your daughter.
Outside the school wall, Israeli soldiers watch you, carrying machine guns taller than your four-foot body. You look to the ground to protect your soul from the hate in their glances. In the school yard your classmates talk about the attack of the prior night. You shrug your shoulders—death has become more normalized than play. In the hallway, you lean against the window and begin counting the number of broken stone blocks of demolished homes on the street. The bell rings when you reach 235.

The next period you have an exam, but you cannot remember the lesson. All you remember is the shelling thunder over your storefront-turned-home sending drops of rain onto your sleeping face. The teacher passes the exams. You begin twirling the pencil, wondering whether your baba's alive or dead, for your momma's question about him is still disturbing you. Does she really think he is alive? Maybe that is why the shelling happened, maybe the Israelis found him running and wanted to kill him. But no! I saw his dead body with the sweater grandma had knitted for him, except it had a hole where the flower once laid and it was purple instead of blue. So maybe it wasn't really him! You awaken to the ringing of the bell, staring at the blank exam.

You run home in tears to your mother's open arms unable to comprehend your failure, but she understands. You admire her strength.

It is seven o'clock at night and your momma and your aunt are worried about your eighteen-year-old cousin who has not returned home from the university yet. It is just past seven thirty when your cousin enters through the door. You watch her with admiration, a bit of a crush perhaps. She begins telling her story and your imagination makes you believe you are her.

You are your cousin.
You left the house at four thirty in the morning to make it to university by nine. Although the distance is only about a forty minute drive, you had to take into account the checkpoints. On the bus, you lay your head on the seat, staring at

the stretch of land between the two checkpoints you are crossing. A year ago, this land was prosperous with citrus trees tended by the hands of a Palestinian farmer; today it is deserted and infertile. The Israelis stripped the land of its roots to plant their barricades. A few miles prior to your university, another checkpoint is posted. You walk with your five female friends; you are all veiled. The veil gives you mobility, it imparts you freedom within tradition. The soldiers stop and ask you to form two lines, one for the ugly women, another for the pretty ones. You look at each other in disbelief. Your legs lock when you feel a soldier's arm shoving you to pass and hear him say something about your privilege of beauty. You look behind you, your friends have not passed. Thirty minutes later they are let go, except for one. You see a female soldier and a male soldier taking her aside. The female soldier puts a machine gun to your friend's head and you hear something about eyes open. You are not able to register what is happening. You have never felt such disgust in your life. The male soldier unzips his pants and pulls out his organ and begins masturbating. You turn your face away and wonder why your friend's eyes are wide open—has she no shame? Then you see the the machine gun against her head. Fifteen minutes seem like eternity, when your friend runs to you with a muted scream. She collapses on the ground at your feet. It has been two months since the rape, and she is still mute. On the way home the bus reaches a mile-long stretch of cars lined up at humiliation barricades—you've stopped calling them checkpoints.

It takes the bus seven hours to make the forty-minute ride. You are outraged: when will you have time to eat, study, and clean, and be up again at the crack of dawn? What use is college to you anyhow. You wonder what it would be like if you just got married and led a normal family life like your grandmother, but what is normal when you're under siege? You can read the sadness of your grandmother in her wrinkles. You realize it is your sadness she holds.

You leave school and marry. Your husband cannot cross the barricades to get to work, he is made to belly dance at checkpoints; he returns home and sheds his powerless rage onto you, asserting his suffocated masculinity. You live the link of state violence and domestic violence. You keep on living with hopes of a free Palestine in the next generations. You give birth to a daughter, knowing she will continue the fight. New generations of Palestinian women are born resisting with their bodies, with their pens, and with their lives. Motherhood is an act of defiance in the midst of colonization.

10

The War to Be Human / Becoming Human in a Time of War

Neferti Tadiar

In 1990, a Filipina writer, Joi Barrios, wrote a poem entitled, "Ang Pagiging Babae Ay Pamumuhay sa Panahon ng Digma—To Be a Woman Is to Live in a Time of War." (Or, more closely translated, "Becoming Woman is a Living in a Time of War.") The poem refers to a time in the Philippines, from the 1970s until the turn of the millennium, when the trafficking of Filipina women and the sale of other national resources—our people, our land, and our organic wealth—were conducted with impunity under the sponsorship and management of a repressive, authoritarian regime and its successors. This time of war, which has lasted for more than thirty years, has seen the imprisonment, torture, and killing of thousands of persons opposed to the regimes that instituted it, regimes backed by the financial, political, and military prowess of the United States, the World Bank and the International Monetary Fund (IMF). Barrios writes,

> "No moment / Is without danger. / In one's own home, / To speak, to defy / Is to court pain. / In the street, to walk at night / is to invite injury. / In my society, / to protest against oppression / is to lay oneself open to even greater violence." And she continues, "How long I have studied / the depth and length / of war. / In the end I have come to understand / that to be a woman / is a never-ending struggle / to live and to be free."

What does it mean, now, to live in a time of war? I want to talk today about the present war against terrorism launched by the US government and its industrial patrons, and about what—for the vast peoples of this world who continue to be the unspoken objects of this war—can be viewed as the challenge of being human in this time. To its ardent supporters, the purported war against terrorism is no less than a war to be human. As the United States and the UK continue to bomb Afghanistan in an ever-increasing escalation of the violence of the attacks on the World Trade Center on September 11, it would seem there is no way to remain human. And yet, the war against terrorism promises to be precisely that: a way to secure humanity for those who would support the universal patriotic cause of America. As the US president and those around him say, "If you are not with us, you are against us."

What is the purported objective of this war? That is to say, what is this

This was a public address given at the symposium organized by INCITE! Women of Color Against Violence, called "Race, Gender, and the War," on November 6, 2001, at the University of California–Santa Cruz. Translated into Portuguese for *Revista Estudos Feministas*, 9, no. 2 (December 2001): 360–366.

enemy—terrorism—that this war aims to defeat? To my mind, terrorism is the rule and deployment of terror for the purposes of gaining and securing power over the living. It doesn't matter if this rule and deployment is carried out in the name of "anti-terrorism." At this moment, with daily announcements of life-threatening menaces issuing from all sides, and warnings about vague but nevertheless imminent explosive, bioterrorist, and nuclear attacks, terror reigns. And as it does, anti-terrorist measures, which provide ever-greater powers to the state that can and will be used against the people, are passed: measures such as the practical suspension of habeas corpus for foreigners—that is, the state's assumption of the license to detain without lawful charges—and the expanded application of search warrants; the license to tap and monitor private communication lines and obtain personal history and information records; and so on and so forth.

More and more measures are proposed, not because domestic and international intelligence and security forces can not yet exercise these powers they propose, but because they already have and they want to be guaranteed impunity. Since 9/11, 1,147 foreigners, largely Middle Eastern and South Asian men, have been indefinitely detained in prisons all over the country contracted by the Immigration and Naturalization Service (INS). Only 185 of these detainees are being held on minor immigration charges and—except for the story of one man who died in a New Jersey jail, a few reports of the physical and psychological abuse inflicted on some and the systematic denial of legal representation and communication for nearly all—almost nothing of the rest of the detainees and how they are being treated is reported. They, of course, have joined the rest of the permanent numbers of people of color already in confinement. In this way, domestic security meets international security, and the prison-industrial complex allies with the military-industrial complex.

In the meantime, the CIA is recovering their "right" to conduct and contract political assassinations of US "enemies" in the world at large. The US military is sending advisors and arms to repressive regimes elsewhere, including the Philippines, in support of redefined "counterterrorist" campaigns that attempt to extinguish indigenous peoples' struggles for the right to life and self-determination, social resistance movements against oppression, anti-state movements for social justice, and poor people's claims to subsistence, safe shelter, and other resources for a better life. And finally, George Bush issues an executive order that seals in secrecy past, and presumably future, presidential papers even after the twelve-year wait currently required by law. We will, it is planned, never learn what Bush, Cheney, and the rest of them are doing now.

But all of this happens almost silently, because the reign of terror has taken hold. We are taxed through fear, a fear generated precisely by those who have everything to gain from it—the wielders, makers, and regulators of the weapons of terror and the instruments of defense. In the meantime, millions of Afghan women, children, and men are on the brink of starvation and a freezing winter without adequate shelter, mercilessly shut off from humanitarian assistance and political asylum, while their families and friends continue to be bombed to death, with explosives, peanut butter crackers, and pamphlets from airplanes flying overhead. With the deaths of two US postal workers from Anthrax poisoning, a state official announced, "The lesson we're learning is that you can bomb the wrong place in Afghanistan and not take much heat for it. But don't mess up at the post office." That heat—the daily emotional, physical, and psychological toll exacted from people in this country—is used to create the organs of homeland security, the ideological might and right of the US military and police forces, and the unimpeachable moral high ground on which they stand. Supreme power—that is the yield of this war on terror.

What are the wages of this war? The money allocated to perform this war includes: whatever amount of the $40 billion has been spent on relief for those affected by 9/11 (very little of which, if any, was spent on the relief of the working classes in hurting industries, and much more directed toward the relief of stockholders); billions of dollars on new weaponry including missiles; a $200 billion account granted to Lockheed Martin to design and build nearly three thousand Joint Strike Fighter warplanes for the Air Force, Navy, Marines and the British Royal Navy; and billions of dollars allocated to pharmaceutical companies in the hypothetical defense against all kinds of bioterrorism. And we have not even touched the rich, opportunistic bloodline that makes kin of George W. Bush and Osama bin Laden, the United States and Saudi Arabia, and gives us an entirely different and staggering picture of world events, tracing the transnational tracks left by pipelines and shipment routes of barrels of oil. Other countries are cashing in as well. The payoff to Egypt for joining the US-led coalition before the Gulf War was $60 billion forgiven debts, debts that the forgivers had helped to set up. There are other currencies of payoff: arms, military and intelligence technology "assistance," economic deals, political latitude, and so forth.

So you see, power and wealth go hand in hand. And the war against terrorism will see that this continues. The state of emergency that now reigns is not a "crisis," in the sense of the breakdown of a prevailing order, but rather an extension and intensification of a logic of that order in the very historical moment that this order has been called into question by all the social struggles for change all over the world. These social struggles are the historical condition of possibility for the real concern and doubt about the world as it currently exists, a concern and doubt that, in the aftermath of the attacks, surfaced in the form of one constantly repeated word: Why? War has become the practical answer to that question. War today is the act by which the suspects are tried and judged. Their defeat will be the proving definition of "terrorism" (in defeat, suspects become fixed as the definitive enemy, the figures of terrorism), conveniently distanced from the state that carries out this exorcist production of the absent evidence of its moral basis. War is the trial that vindicates the US nation-state and its unilateral right to rule the earth. Rather than propaganda in the service of war, then, the present war has been placed in the service of propaganda. By this I mean war is the means for propagating a longstanding international and domestic order that the struggles of peoples everywhere trying to live and be free have placed in crisis. And as we have seen, in this age of information, such propaganda—the media production of spectacle after spectacle of affluence and power—itself produces instant profit. But immediate profits lag far behind in comparison to the long-term gains to be had, when a global police force will be established as the main security force for the new political and economic alliances consolidated through war.

By claiming that the present war is an intensification and protection of a worldwide organization of power and wealth, I am not saying that things are the same. We are in a new situation whereby the US state has come to adopt the coercive, repressive techniques of self-preservation and self-aggrandizement of the very tyrannical postcolonial states it has sponsored and continues to sponsor. Psyops, the main strategy of low-intensity warfare developed by the CIA, and used against Third World peasant and guerilla movements, for example, have been put to work against broader and broader sectors of its own population. This is the situation with which we must now contend, a situation that those who experienced the repressive regimes of CIA-backed postcolonial states surely have much to say about. In claiming the continuity, however, I am trying to demonstrate the perpetual lie on which the so-called peace before 9/11 was predicated. The war is a major effort to bolster the structure of a lie. This lie is not only the achievement of a mass media that caters to the interests of its ruling elite, it is also a consequence of a system of production. Capitalism hides and contains its contradictions in places and peoples who, by virtue of an endemic class colonialism, are deemed inhuman and secondary to those privileged enough to be regarded as human. Needless to say, This worldwide system of exploitation has race and gender as central principles of its organization.

This brings us finally to the costs of this war. It is in the face of the "already human" at the helm of this war—the humanitarian face lent to cluster bombs by trivial food packages in identical yellow cans—that the immense challenge of living on the part of those who are deemed not yet human becomes most acute. The already human among us—those long privileged by histories of colonialism and racism as exemplars of humanity—wrap themselves in the very terror they wish to put to an end. But they will never see the end of that terror so long as they hold it around their hearts like a pledge, while they wait for the state, which they have allowed to speak in their name and to act in their interests, to annihilate those they imagine to be the source, the very being and expression of terror. When a Palestinian detainee asked the officers what he had done (he overstayed his visa), he was told: "You did nothing; your people did." My body for my people.

The already huma" want to defend their freedoms. And yet they so readily hand it over to a police state that can, without compunction, carry out the stark meaning of that freedom: the freedom to be indifferent to and violate the lives of others, the very lives that support theirs, the very lives that now, with the help of the war, they will as fate, condemned to be at the mercy of "Operation Enduring Freedom." The "already human" do this because they are held hostage to a pain that, in the fast grip of a patriotic grievance, admits little or no empathy for the deaths and suffering of others. And the ransom? The infinite bodies of others. The incommensurability of people's loss becomes translated into the incommensurable human value of some people over others. The price of US sanctions—one million Iraqis, half a million who were children under five—was worth it, according to former Secretary of State Madeleine Albright. And more and more, in other places, before and after. Collateral damage. Whether the object of hate crimes, or the target of bombs and food embargoes, or niche markets for the international traffic in drugs, people of color are that collateral from the outset. As excess people, they may be used, as the women of Afghanistan and Iraq have been used, as token signs, mere symbolic means, in the contest of virile powers and patriarchal states. Is it any wonder that they should be totally excluded from the plans and negotiations now taking place over the determination of their future?

Let me just end by saying that there is a real crisis at the heart of the permanent state of emergency monstrously looming before us. Far from being passive victims, the social costs of this war are also the causes of a real global crisis. That real global crisis lies in the demands everywhere being made for better lives, for open presents and open futures, for clean air, sovereign lands, food, shelter, creative work and education, claims to difference and freedom; not "freedom" issued from murderous hands, and not "difference" we are forced to inhabit—but rather, difference to the world as we make it. There are many examples of the ways that, collectively, people's struggles have caused great trouble for the US superstate and its military-industrial, petro-chemical, and pharmaceutical capitalist patrons, challenging their power and legitimacy. That challenge is evident in the rulings of the World Court, and in resolutions of the UN Security Council against US violations of international law, as was in the case of Nicaragua, as well as the UN General Assembly's 1987 resolution against terrorism, both of which the United States vetoed or voted against, just as it walked out of the UN World Conference on Racism and reneged on the Kyoto Protocol.

And there are the struggles to guarantee medical care for the sick poor in countries like India, South Africa, and Brazil, which are producing cheaper generic versions of patented and costly AIDS drugs, as well as other vital medicines currently under the monopoly of multinational pharmaceutical companies—the same corporations that, incidentally, constitute the biggest industrial lobby in the US Congress. These are struggles on the part of life, not death. Life has no country, has no flag, has no proper name. It has no measure to which it can forever or for everyone be held. That is life's great power, and yet, in the face of the ruling potency of death, also its fragility. For the potency of death's subject lies in its capacity to permanently place the dead with a mark of its choosing, to drive the stake of a flag, a sign, in a body as if that flag were the sole meaning of the life that took leave of it. Just as we should bolster our dissent against this war, we should hold fast to our unremitting refusal to be used as fuel or signs for it, or as beneficiaries of its gains.

In this deathly time of war, becoming human is the struggle of life practices, the struggle for the living. We need to strengthen those practices and our capacities to create, not destroy. To do that, rather than the kind of memorials and eulogies that seal, in the intent to heal, the gaping wounds before us, we need living memories, living histories, as openings into other futures.

11

The Forgotten "–ism"

An Arab American Women's Perspective on Zionism, Racism, and Sexism

Nadine Naber, Eman Desouky, and Lina Baroudi

Preface

Four months had passed since the beginning of the Al-Aqsa Intifada (the second Palestinian uprising) when board members of the San Francisco chapter of the Arab Women's Solidarity Association gathered for an event-planning meeting in early 2001. The strain of the previous months was apparent amongst us. As Arab women activists, we had been calling for Palestinians' right to self-determination, and resisting the censorship of Arab voices on multiple fronts: in the media, in public lectures, in our classrooms, in our workplaces, and among our friends and colleagues. Each of us had been harassed, intimidated, and sabotaged by supporters of Zionism who have been committed to silencing our resistance.[1] We realized that while on many occasions, each of us felt unsupported in our daily claims for Arab rights and human dignity, we were not alone. The policing and silencing of Arab and Arab American women activists was an all too common experience, shared by Arab and Arab American women activists throughout the United States, particularly those who are critical of Israeli state violence, racism, and sexism, and the US state's unconditional support of Israel.

We agreed that very few analyses providing perspectives on Zionism and racism by Arab women living in the US existed, and we came together to break the silence. Building on the history of Arab women activists in the United States, such as members of the Union of Palestinian Women's Associations in North America, who have been exposing links between Zionism, racism, and sexism for decades, we agreed that we must continue naming our oppressors. Otherwise, we would remain isolated and invisible among contemporary peoples' struggles for social justice locally and globally. We decided to write a paper to distribute to activists and academics worldwide as to how Zionist racism and sexism affect our lives in the United States. We agreed that it would be a collective, grassroots effort, a weaving together of our collective ideas and experiences. In continuity with women of color efforts to produce collective thinking, research, and analysis, we formed a team of researchers and an advisory committee, including Dena Al Adeeb, Lillian Boctor, Renda Dabit, Noura Erakat, Sema Dudum, Nada Elia, Heba Nimr, and Fadwa Rashid. Researchers conducted interviews among thirty Arab American women activists across the United States on their experiences of "racism and discrimination." These women are from various national, religious, social, professional, and generational backgrounds. Their history of activism links them together with US feminist and other progressive political movements.

We also interviewed ten diverse non-Arab Bay Area activists on the issue of Zionist racism in various spheres of US society, including the media, education, religious institutions, labor, and progressive politics. Additional research took place in libraries, universities, and within activists' homes.

After organizing the collected experiences and literature, analyzing the data, searching for patterns and making observations, we began the writing process. In addition to endless pages of transcribed interview material, we had dozens of articles and nearly a hundred books on Zionism written from every perspective—including leaders of the Zionist movement, right wing Israelis, Israeli feminists, radical Israeli historians, revolutionary Palestinian nationalists, and Arab American intellectuals. We had two writing teams and an editorial team. We completed the paper in two months after every member of the committee read the paper and contributed their revisions.

This paper has two parts. In part one, we provide an historical background to the Zionist project in the Arab world and the United States. In part two, we explore the ways that Zionism contributes to the interconnected structures of racism and sexism and to the positioning of Arab and Arab American women as the "most invisible of the invisibles" within progressive US politics.[2] Our argument is not that all Arab women have always been excluded from all progressive politics in the United States as a consequence of Zionist racism and sexism. It is that most progressive political spaces in the United States (that claim to be critical of colonialism, racism, and sexism) allow Zionism (a colonialist, racist, and sexist project) and the consequent exclusion of Arab voices, to go unquestioned. While we acknowledge Arab and Arab American women's histories of participation within progressive US politics (including Arab women who are critical of Zionism), the purpose of this paper is to illustrate that Zionism is alive and well, even in some of the most self-proclaimed radical or progressive political spaces in the United States. It also illustrates that Zionism, an inherently racist ideology, also reinforces anti-Arab racism and sexism in the United States. Thus, an understanding of Zionism is central to understanding racism directed against Arab and Arab American women. In conclusion, we will address Arab and Arab American women activists' contributions to transnational, radical women of color politics.[3]

Introduction
This paper was originally written for the United Nations World Conference against Racism in Durban, South Africa, in August 2001. Our research sheds light on how efforts to quell critiques of Zionism and Israel contribute to the silencing and *racialized* exclusion of the voices of Arab and Arab American women activists who are critical of Israel. Ironically, we distributed this paper as the US government was complaining about proposed language in the conference declaration equating Zionism with racism. Even though the word "Zionism" was removed from the official conference documents, a few days into the conference, the United States and Israel pulled their official delegations out in protest of anti-Zionist activists who refused to be intimidated. In the aftermath of the attacks against the World Trade Center and the Pentagon on September 11, 2001, the Bush administration has utilized the repressive climate to help justify its increased support of Israel as necessary towards

the fight against "terrorism." The colonization of Afghanistan and Iraq and the
threats against Syria and Iran at the time of this writing are carried out with careful input from, and collaboration with, Israeli officials. The United States has mod-
eled its propaganda war after Israel's campaign of ideological warfare against the
Palestinian people through a program of hyper-militarized patriotism. Moreover,
dominant Israeli state discourses have celebrated soldiers who provide "security"
through a policy that brutally murders Palestinians, while the Bush administration
celebrates New York City policemen who receive their training in Israel. Meanwhile, the Bush administration has provided Israel with the rhetoric of the "war on
terrorism" to support its intensified ethnic cleansing of the Palestinian people. Israel's growing apartheid wall is but one example of how the US and Israel have used
the "war on terror" to legitimize the ongoing colonization of Palestine.

In the aftermath of 9/11, Arab women activists and their allies have witnessed
the Ford Foundation back down on its promise to fund the organization Incite!
Women of Color against Violence because Incite! published a statement in solidarity with Palestinians. We have also seen vehement citywide threats against
the thirty year old advocacy organization San Francisco Women Against Rape
(SFWAR), including threats to defund the organization (the city actually pulled
their funding), after they integrated a critique of Zionism into their analysis of
racism and sexism.

We define Zionism as a settler-colonial political movement that seeks to ethnically cleanse historical Palestine of the indigenous population and populate it as
a Jewish-only state. While other Zionist narratives exist, this paper refers specifically to the dominant form of Zionism that shapes the world Zionist movement
and governs official Zionist policy. Among the claims that underlie hegemonic
Zionism is that Jews have the right to possess all of the land between the Nile and
the Euphrates rivers, thus threatening the stability of the entire region—beyond
the borders of Palestine. (We have already seen the decades-long Israeli occupation
of Southern Lebanon, Syria's Golan Heights, Egypt's Sinai Desert, and current
plans to annex the Jordan valley.)

This Zionist narrative is given credibility through the biblical notion that the
Jewish people are entitled to the land because it was given to them by God. The
Zionist movement has not only supported the creation of the state of Israel on
Palestinian land, but has supported the creation of a Jewish-only state in that historically diverse land. Within this paradigm, Zionism constructs Jews as a race (or
distinct ethnic group) and the state of Israel as a Jewish-only state, with non-Jews
considered a "demographic threat." This exclusionary logic has produced the conditions for torture, home demolitions, restriction of movement, unemployment,
poverty, apartheid, and ethnic cleansing in Palestine. Any state that officially and
legally privileges members of one "race" or "ethnicity" over another, and establishes national identity on the basis of race or ethnicity, is inherently racist.[4] Therefore, Israel is a racist state that is founded upon a racist ideology that protects and
preserves the rights of Jews only. That racist ideology is Zionism.[5]

A dominant trend in US progressive politics is to avoid building solidarity
with Arab activists and our allies who are critical of Zionism or Israel, out of
fear of being targeted by Zionist organizations (which could entail risks such as

losing funding or being targeted by smear campaigns). By naming Zionism the "Forgotten '–ism,'" we call on progressive activists to be more consistent in their alliances with struggles against imperialism, colonialism, and racism. Our work demands that social justice and human rights activists critique all cases of ethnic supremacy and settler-colonial aggression, be they in South Africa, Central America, Indonesia, the United States, or Palestine.

Historical Background: Zionism and Colonialism

Zionism was born through the writings of Theodore Herzl in Germany in the late 1880s. As outlined by Herzl, Zionism was to be a secular political project that defined "the Jews" as a people, a nation, and a race, rather than as a religious group. In the context of the fervent European anti-Jewish discrimination of the time, Herzl argued for the need to create an independent Jewish state for "the Jewish people" who, he argued, could never possibly assimilate in the countries they inhabited.[6] Although multiple locations were suggested, the Zionist movement proposed Palestine as the site for a Jewish state, in a strategic move that would allow them to use the religious history of Palestine to justify their political goal of colonization.[7] At every point of its genesis, the Zionist movement was informed and reinforced by nineteenth-century European colonialism and its white supremacist ideology.

Britain recognized the potential of the Zionist project in Palestine to further its own colonial economic and political goals. During the first part of the twentieth century, Britain assisted the Zionists in exporting 610,000 Jews from various parts of the world to Palestine to make way for the eventual establishment of Israel on indigenous Palestinian land. In 1917, the Balfour Declaration of Britain legitimized the establishment of "a national homeland for Jews in Palestine."[8] The genocide of World War II created a new impetus for immigration; in 1947, further mass immigration projects ensued. After they were refused entry to countries such as Britain and the United States, Jews from all over the world were sent to settle a land where they had no prior territorial affiliation—Palestine. It is important to point out that, although Judaism as a religion did originate in Palestine, not all Jews today are the descendents of the original Semitic people. Indeed, Judaism was a successful proselytizing religion in Europe until the fifteenth century, and many of today's Jews are ethnically European. In 1948, the Zionists occupied Palestine by force through massacre and war, destroying more than four hundred villages, taking over nearly three-fourths of Palestine and uprooting more than 750,000 native Palestinians from their homes. In 1967, Israel continued uprooting Palestinians and took over the remainder of Palestine.

Palestine is a unique colonial situation because its colonizer, Israel, is a Jewish-only nation-state imposed on Arab Palestinian land.[9] Israel was not constructed to colonize the natives, per se, but to remove them entirely from their land and to construct Israeli Jews as the authentic people of the land. Several historical state documents illustrate the centrality of ethnic cleansing to the Zionist project. In Herzl's diaries, for example, he writes, "We shall try to spirit the penniless population across the border by procuring employment for it in the transit countries, while denying it any employment in our own country ... expropriation and the removal of the poor must be carried out discreetly and circumspectly."[10] Though the contemporary Zionist consensus argues that Israel is not a colonial state, Herzl, in fact, argued to the contrary: "To go further than any colonialist has gone in Africa ... where involuntary expropriation of land will temporarily alienate civilized opinion. By the time the reshaping of world opinion in our favor has been completed, we shall be firmly established in our country, no longer fearing the influx of foreigners, and receiving our visitors with aristocratic benevolence."[11] In short, Zionism was constructed as a colonial project to ethnically cleanse the indigenous population and assert European Jewish hegemony.

Britain furthered its own early twentieth century colonial political goals in the Middle East through Zionism and the establishment of Israel. By the second half of the twentieth century, however, primary financial and military support for the Zionist project was transferred from the hands of Britain to the hands of the US government. Since the 1967 completion of the Zionist takeover of Palestine, no country has received more US foreign aid than Israel.

Britain and the United States have provided Israel with the military machinery, strategy and funding necessary to illegally move over four million Jews to Palestine, uprooting Palestinians from their native homeland.[12] Since the inception of the Zionist state, thousands of Palestinians have been killed and five million Palestinians have been displaced from their homes.[13] In pursuit of their own geopolitical goals of dominance in the region, Britain and the United States have collaborated in dispossessing Palestinians. While the Zionist narrative of history argues that the creation of the state of Israel was necessary to the cause of fighting anti-Jewish oppression,[14] the forces of Western imperialism allied with the Zionist project of Israel as a means to maintain Israel's position as a Western ally within the Arab region.[15] Israel has become a conduit of globalization, militarization, and imperialism.[16] The United States has supported Israel as a Western ally in the center of the Arab region as part of its commitment to maintaining its geopolitical power, including access to oil, in this region. The Zionist movement is currently dependent on unconditional US government support, whether Democrat or Republican.

For years, Israel has shared its military expertise with other abusive, undemocratic regimes across the globe, and Israeli intelligence training has been central to the development of oppressive regimes throughout much of the Global South, including apartheid South Africa, Uganda, Argentina, El Salvador, Guatemala, Chile, and Indonesia.[17] Israel has aligned itself politically with other racist, colonial projects such as Apartheid South Africa, and has, through organizations such as the Anti-Defamation League (ADL), waged campaigns to silence antiracist and anticolonialist social justice movements.

Several scholars and activists, such as Nada Elia, Elham Bayour, Penny Johnson, Rema Hammami, and Eileen Kuttab, have argued that violence against Palestinian women permeates the Zionist project. Living under Israeli colonization, Palestinian women have experienced the denial of basic human resources, including education, health, and employment; violence, including sexual assault and violence against pregnant women at checkpoints; gendered forms of torture against women prisoners; intensified forms of masculinity among Palestinian men within families as a response to the emasculation of Palestinian men by the Israeli state;

and intensified material and psychological pressure and responsibilities as a consequence of the loss of their men and children who have been jailed or killed by the
Israeli military or forced to live and work away from home due to poverty induced
by Israeli colonization.

Historical Background: Zionism in the United States

Israel defies international law and hundreds of United Nations human rights resolutions in its occupation of Palestine, yet the US government continues to fun-
nel over five billion tax dollars per year to the state of Israel. In nearly every sector
of US politics, this contradiction remains unchallenged. In the United States,
Zionism is highly influential in the shaping of public opinion.[18] Many self-iden-
tified Zionists, both Jews and non-Jews, belong to the organized body referred
to as the World Zionist Organization. Other Zionist organizations in the United
States include American Israel Public Affairs Committee (AIPAC), the American Jewish Congress, the Anti-Defamation League (ADL), the Jewish Community Relations Council, Hillel, and the Jewish Student Committee. Whether
it is in labor, education, media, or politics, the Zionist movement's strategy is
to maintain a unified pro-Israel position and to silence any and all criticism of
Israeli policy while demonizing its critics. A central myth promoted by the Zionist movement is that criticism of Israel or Zionism is anti-Semitic.

As Noam Chomsky puts it, the ADL sets out "to use any technique however
dishonest and disgraceful in order to defame and silence and destroy anybody
who dares to criticize the holy state (Israel)."[19] One example of a context in which
Zionists practiced such tactics took place during one period in the history of the
Palestine liberation movement in the late 1980s and early 1990s, when major
pro-Israeli, anti-Palestinian organizations established espionage rings, and published books and kits to help their members discredit Palestinian justice struggles and revive the deteriorating public image of Israel.[20] The San Francisco spy
scandal that broke out in the early 1990s,[21] just as the Oslo agreements were
being orchestrated, revealed that the ADL was engaged in spying on the Arab
American community, as well as numerous peace and anti-apartheid activists
and organizations. The ADL operation used paid informers, police officers, student recruits, and a full-time staff to meet its goal of discrediting Palestinian and
other liberation struggles. The ADL was exposed as one of many examples where
devoutly anti-Palestinian sentiment and covert Israeli intelligence activity are
hidden behind a seemingly benign civil rights organization.[22]

According to the ADL, "anti-Zionism is anti-Semitism, period.[23] The ADL further contends that the interests of the United States, including its interest in targeting so-called "Arab terrorists" or peace activists, are so identical to those of Israel
that any disagreement with the Israeli government and its policies is a betrayal of the
United States. The ADL and its affiliate organizations, such as Hillel and AIPAC,
have utilized intimidation, scare tactics, the infiltration of organizations, the violation of civil rights and sabotage to achieve their goals.[24] In the United States, organized Zionist forces enforce censorship in nearly every sphere of society, including
the media, work and labor, public policy, political arenas, and religious and educational institutions.[25] In the aftermath of September 11, alongside the "war on

terror" and increased government repression, college campuses have increasingly become sites for the proliferation of such tactics. This systematic attempt to silence and exclude Arabs and Arab Americans from the political process is one example of what Helen Samhan refers to as *political racism*. While Zionism is a politically organized racial project that directly and systematically targets Arabs and Arab Americans[26] and their allies, through a network of organizations with shared objectives, the terrain of Zionism extends much broader than the practices of particular organizations. In the US context, Zionism has become hegemonic, or common sense—"a way of comprehending, explaining, and acting in the world"[27] that goes completely unquestioned and unchallenged.

Zionism, Racism, and Sexism

Consistent with racist colonial invasions throughout the world, including the Americas, Africa, and Asia, Zionism justifies colonization by promoting the racist myth that the natives are a backward, violent people who are not civilized, and that native women are extremely oppressed by "native culture" and require Western liberation. The dual goals underpinning this racist mythology are to construct a homogenous colonial society, not in national origin, but in its exclusion of the indigenous people, while manufacturing the cultural and historical facets necessary to project an organic rooting to the land. As the United States has become the Israeli state's number one ally,[28] racist, sexist Zionist narratives about Arab women and men have shaped anti-Arab racism in the US. Such contemporary propaganda shapes Zionist narratives that produce the distinction between "Arab terrorists" and "peaceful Israeli victims" in order to justify the colonization of Palestine. These Zionist discourses portray Palestinian women as both agents of violence and terror and victims of misogynist, excessively patriarchal, violent Arab men.

Like Zionist ideology, the Bush administration deployed myths about Arab and Muslim women such as these in justifying the US wars on Afghanistan and Iraq, justifying war and murder through the rhetoric of "saving the women." Zionist myths that distinguish between "backwards Arabs" and "modern, civilized Israelis," "oppressed Arab women" and "liberated Israeli women," "homophobic Arab society" and "queer-friendly Israeli societies" serve to legitimate the idea that Palestine is in need of Westernization/colonization. They also reinforce colonialist, racist approaches to feminism and queer politics that assume that allying with Arab women and queers entails supporting the invasion of their homelands. The proliferation of Zionist ideology impacts persons from every racial and ethnic community in the United States, particularly those who are perceived to be potential allies to the Palestinian struggle for national liberation and self-determination.[29] Yet, as long as progressive movements continue to omit a social justice stance on this issue, Zionism will remain the "Forgotten '-ism,'" an unquestioned, unchallenged rationalization for colonialism, imperialism, racism, and sexism. Our research indicated that Arab and Arab American women who are active in the US feminist movement tend to agree that Zionism is a forgotten -ism that contributes to anti-Arab racism in the United States and the colonialist racist view that Arab and Arab-American women are the most oppressed women in the world, who need to be saved and/or spoken for by their Western or white feminist "sisters." Those who speak up about Palestinian rights agreed that they are often excluded, silenced, censored, and/or erased from progressive politics by the systematic, institutionalized attempts to exclude and delegitimize critiques of Israel.

Part Two: The Demonization of Arab American Women

We situate our analysis of Arab American women's engagements with Zionism in the context of the ways that US-led imperialism in Arab homelands, including support of Israel, takes on local form within the everyday lives of Arab American women and men. We argue that the "racial formation" of Arab American women emerges in the context of an ongoing relationship between US racism and the Zionist project in the United States.[30] We use the term "racial formation" to refer to the process by which US imperial and colonial interests in the Arab world shape the processes by which the US state and media mark "Arabs" as different and inferior to Americans. Representing Arabs as uncivilized and backwards and Arab women as the most oppressed women in the world justifies war, murder, and domination. Zionism contributes to the racial formation of Arab Americans because it promotes similar racist ideas about Arab women and men, and promotes the exclusion and censorship of Arab American political critique.

The demonization of Arab women within Western academic and cultural traditions has deep historical roots,[31] and is often blamed on Islam. Kahf writes that, ever since the eighteenth century, Western discourse on Islam has been shaped by the idea that "Islam is innately and immutably oppressive to women, that the veil and segregation epitomized that oppression, and that these customs were the fundamental reasons for the general and comprehensive backwardness of Islamic societies."[32] In different historical moments within European and US colonization of the Arab world, this image has been refashioned and has taken on different forms. Contemporary US state and media discourses conflate the categories Arab and Muslim even though not all Arabs are Muslim and not all Muslims are Arab.

Our research participants' narratives illustrate that three key images have contributed to racist portrayals of Arab and Muslim women in the United States. They are the images of the "inadequate Palestinian mother,"[33] the "super-oppressed Arab woman," and the "nameless veiled woman." Salam, a young Palestinian American woman, summarizes her engagements with this problem as follows: "All of the images that I see of myself everywhere tell me that Arab women are subhuman, lower on the evolutionary scale compared to other women in the world...[t]his imagery serves to justify Israel's continued violence against Arab people."[34]

The Inadequate Palestinian Mother

Tala, an Arab American scholar and activist, she explains:

> Negative images of Arab women are linked to Zionism, even though Zionism has done it to the whole Arab community. The media has portrayed Palestinian women as either victims of sexist Arab men or murderous mothers who bring up terrorists, as if their pride and joy is to have their kid killed. The mere thought that the image is actually credible to people … it just shows how powerfully

> Zionism has portrayed the Palestinian culture as backwards and
> the Palestinian woman as nonhuman—as if Palestinian women
> have no problem bringing up kids that die!

This image of the "inadequate Palestinian mother" is one example of how women
become targets of the Zionist project. To justify colonization, Zionist propaganda
represents Arab women as either violent agents of terror (who are brainwashed by
Arab men or Islam) or victims of Arab men and Arab culture. Representations
of women are essential to the racialization of Arabs as backwards, violent, and
uncivilized.

The Super-Oppressed Arab Woman

The most powerful image that nearly all of our research participants have
been referred to is that of the "super-oppressed" Arab woman. For example, Iman
remembers that when she introduced herself as an Arab to a college peer, her peer
remarked, "And your father let you go to college?" Sawsan, a senior Arab American
college student adds:

> Within feminist circles, as soon as people find out that I am Arab,
> they bring up the issue of Arab women and how badly they are
> treated. It is very frustrating to me, since I have been maltreated by
> American and European coworkers! I find myself in a place where
> I have to defend Arab women and the Arab world and the entire
> Middle East all the time.

In the words of Zein, who refers to herself as a feminist activist:

> Racist stereotypes about us force me to deny what I am not—i.e., a
> terrorist or a victim—before I can even begin to assert what I am—
> an Arab American. So I find myself constantly defending myself
> and constantly explaining myself to make people understand that
> what they think about us isn't true.

Nehad, a graduate student and activist, says,

> I was studying in a café in Berkeley. A woman sitting next to me
> asked me what I was reading. I said, "a book about Arab immigra-
> tion to the US." She said, "Are you from that part of the world?" I
> said, "Yes." She said, "You sure are lucky to be here. They treat wom-
> en really bad over there, don't they?" I said, "The US has its positive
> sides, but it also has its negative sides for Arabs who live here." She
> said, "Like what?" I said, "Like as we speak the US government is
> funding Israel to murder and maim our children by the thousands."
> She said, "That's not the US fault and you know what I think? I
> think you should go back home if you don't like it here."

Confronted with the image of the "super-oppressed Arab woman," our research participants explained that they tended to be marginalized, and needed to justify their existences as Arab and Arab American women. Hala, a Muslim woman activist, depicts how people see her through the image of "the nameless veiled woman." She says that "even within progressive feminist groups, I am accused of not being feminist enough because I wear a veil."

While we were conducting interviews on college campuses, one student told us about a student who approached the Muslim students' table on campus. Her first question to them was about the veil. She said, "I thought that the reason women wear the veil is to cover up the bruises they have on their face from when their husbands beat them."

The Nameless Veiled Woman

Within mainstream US media, the "nameless veiled woman" is either crying and screaming, or passively accepting her oppression. These images mark Arab and Muslim women as either "out of control" or "having no control"—there is no space in between for them to assert their identities or power as agents of social change. Yet as our research participants explain, the demonization of Arab women does not only obstruct the ways that they are perceived, but it obstructs Arab American women's activism by adding to their agenda the additional task of challenging myths and breaking stereotypes.

Within contemporary US popular culture, the images of the "inadequate Palestinian mother," "the super-oppressed Arab woman," and the "nameless veiled woman" entail a consolidation of Zionist and US racist discourses on Arab women. They also contribute to dominant US and Israeli narratives that Israel is the civilized anomaly amidst a sea of violent Arabs with their pathological sexism and their culturally-sanctioned misogyny.

The Consolidation of Zionism and Racism: Censoring Arab American Women's Critiques

In addition to demonizing Arab American women and men, our research also illustrates that the consolidation of Zionism and racism also contributes to the censorship of Arab American women activists' critiques. These patterns can be summarized in the words of our research participants:

1) "Our issues are ignored and excluded wherever we go, even among human rights activists, feminists, people of color, and progressives."— *Nadia, Lebanese American*
2) "We are viewed as anti-Semitic and that's what silences our voices of resistance against Israeli occupation. Every time we speak about Zionism as a political project, we are silenced. We are trying to fight Israeli state power and our words are twisted around as if we were making statements about Jewish people."—*Suha, Palestinian American*
3) "We are even isolated from other people of color when it comes to our issues because the Zionists got to them first."—*Emily, Jordanian American*

The Zionist movement and its allies within the United States create confusion about the Israeli occupation of Palestine. This strategy renders the issue entirely incomprehensible and subverts social justice critiques of Israel by producing responses among progressive activists such as, "The Palestine/Israel conflict is just too confusing," or "It's so complicated, I'm just not going to get involved." One of the ways by which the Zionist project propagating confusion is by generating myths that cloud any attempt to understand Arab people and their struggles. These myths manifest in nearly every sphere of US society and include the ideas that: "All Arabs are Muslim" and "All Muslims are Arab;" the categories Arab and Jew are mutually exclusive (in other words, Arab Jews do not exist); Arabs and Jews have been fighting one another for centuries; and it's a religious war. These myths are consistently repeated in the US news media, TV shows, and Hollywood films.

Attributing the colonization of Palestine to an abstract religious conflict that is completely separated from politics and material realities is central to Zionist mythology. The argument that "it is a religious war" obscures racism, discrimination, and colonization, renders the entire "Middle East" an incomprehensible, homogenous mass, and leads to the exclusion of the issue of justice for Palestinians and Arabs from political debates. In particular, it erases the modern history of Israel as a colonial settler state formed in the context of European colonization/expansion.

All of our research participants agree that a lack of credible information about Arab peoples and their struggles contributes to Arab American women's invisibility within progressive and feminist circles in the United States. This lack of credible information leads to ongoing experiences where our research participants find themselves misrepresented, misperceived, and misunderstood. Amira is a professor and a writer. She explains:

> I wish I had forty-eight hours a day to deal with the ignorance. As a direct consequence of Zionism, it's become my responsibility, my duty, to make Palestine visible. Now, instead of advancing my scholarly future, I am explaining about Palestine.

Bisan, an NGO activist recalls:

> I was working in a human rights organization on the issue of Palestine when at a meeting, even when my colleague was trying to support me, she said, "Bisan should attend the UN conference on racism. It be would be important for Bisan to go because of her work on Pakistan.

Bisan's experience exemplifies the ways that nearly all of our research participants are forced to contend with or position themselves in response to a lack of information, ignorance, and confusion regarding both the issues and the geographic regions of the Arab world.

Suha provides additional examples of the systematic process through which

Arab American women activists are rendered invisible and voiceless:

> As a participant in many national and international meetings ad-
> dressing human rights, the Arab woman's perspective is consistent-
> ly left out. We're either excluded entirely, or minimized by being
> blended into other categories. In the United Nations meetings I at-
> tend, the category "Arab" is often mixed into the category "Asian"
> or "African." There is hardly anything out there for us that allows us
> to specifically deal with Arab issues, and this leads to a lack in Arab
> women's representation at these meetings. Arab women are rarely
> represented in decision-making on national and international levels,
> especially in the area of human rights advocacy. So the remedies that
> are created in these settings are not relevant to the needs of Arab
> communities. And if you're not at the table, how can you create solu-
> tions relevant to your community? That's the problem with invisibil-
> ity. It's much deeper than just not being at the table. It's about how
> not being included impacts our communities in policy making.

The Zionist project also strategically confuses the issue by portraying the Palestinian struggle as "exceptionally too political," and therefore too sensitive, too
loaded, and untouchable in the world of daily social justice critique, debate, and
movement-building. In the words of Farah:

> Hanan Ashrawi once noted that when she identifies herself as a
> Palestinian, it is as though she is automatically perceived by others
> to be making a political statement, rather than conveying a simple
> fact about herself. Perhaps the single most pervasive and insidious
> effect of Zionism on my daily life is that it automatically places
> me in a contentious relationship with those around me as soon as
> I voluntarily link myself to my Palestinian origins. The Zionist
> influence on the US media, educational system, political institu-
> tions, and national psyche has made it nearly impossible for me to
> view my Arab-ness and my Palestinian-ness apart from the macro
> political debates that inform the Arab-Zionist conflict as it is seen
> through Western eyes. As a result, I find myself on the defensive,
> having to explain myself, before I am able to properly situate myself
> within the surroundings into which I have been thrust.

Farah's experience speaks to the debilitating effects of Zionist propaganda, which
often marks the Arab American woman as "contentious," and never fully allowed
to claim her space within progressive movements for social justice and political
change.

The Anti-Semitic Charge: A Silencing Strategy

Equating Zionism to Judaism plays a large part in antagonizing Arab American
women activists' potential allies. One example of this deliberate conflation is that

the Oxford English Dictionary defines anti-Semitism as opposition to the state of Israel. While anti-Semitism is real and continues to exist, the Zionist movement has produced a default sympathy for Jewish people in the United States regardless of the conflict in which they are embroiled, especially in the case of Palestine, where the Jewish state is the victimizer and not the victim. As a result, Jewish colonial aims in occupied Palestine are rarely judged by the same measures as other colonialist aims on a global scale. Not only does the Zionist project use the experience of the Holocaust to legitimate the creation of an exclusionary state at the expense of the displaced indigenous Arab population,[35] it also attempts to foreclose the possibility of other peoples—whether in Rwanda, former Yugoslavia, Turkey, Afghanistan, or Palestine—from calling attention to genocidal practices which in many ways mirror the atrocities that took place in World War II, even if not on the same scale. The constant effort on the part of Zionists to isolate the suffering of the Jewish people as the only "authentic" suffering and to render inappropriate any rightful recognition of non-Jewish genocide serves to paint a picture of Palestinian terror, intransigence, irrational extremism, and a penchant for violence on the one hand, and Jewish suffering, besiegement, generosity, self-defense,and victimization on the other. Within this asymmetric and historically inaccurate model, support for Palestinians is often thought to be aggressive, unsympathetic, and anti-Semitic. Laila, a law student and activist, explains:

It's difficult in the classroom, in a dinner time conversation, or even in a well thought-out presentation, to critique Israel and its colonialist existence given that it is perceived to be a haven for persecuted Jewish people surrounded by a sea of vicious misogynistic, anti-democratic Muslim Arab states. Before I open my mouth, I feel that I have to refashion Americans' historical and political unconditional sympathetic sensibilities for Jews so that I can properly make my case—a case which stands quite apart from the Holocaust since Israel's creation was principally a colonial project in predominantly Arab-Islamic land for the benefit of white Europeans.

Naila, a university professor and activist further adds:

In my university, there are blinders that equate anti-Zionism with anti-Semitism. People assume that because I'm Palestinian, I am anti-Semitic and racist. Why not accuse me of anti-Zionism? The failure to distinguish a political stance from a racist stance makes it very easy to say someone is a racist or an anti-Semite if they talk about justice for Palestinians. If I'm going to try and get a job and I am criticizing the Israeli state and Zionism, the hiring committee thinks, "We're not going to hire someone who's racist." This is part of the Zionist discourse that presents Arabs and Palestinians as always anti-Semitic. How can we, as Semites, be anti-Semitic? We're trying to get rid of an outside occupier. Blacks were not against whites as a people, they wanted freedom. But when Palestinians want to fight for their freedom, they have to fight the charge of racism.[36]

Naila's experience illustrates that even before she can express herself, the Arab American woman is positioned by Zionist myths as a racist and an anti-Semite solely based on her identity as an Arab.

Compounding the previous three dynamics that contribute to Arab American women's invisibility is the Zionist project's deliberate attempt to sabotage coalition-building between Arab Americans and other communities of color. As Dina puts it, "My audience is always … afraid of allying with me because they think they will be perceived as unsympathetic to what happened to the Jews at the hands of the Nazis."

This strategy is part of a broader Zionist strategy in the United States that strategically uses the discourse of "civil rights" to promote Zionism among US people of color (Blacks and Latino/as in particular), while promoting extremely right-wing, white supremacist viewpoints in relationship to the Arab world in general and Palestine in particular. For example, the websites of Zionist organizations such as AIPAC simultaneously promote alliances with Latinos and Blacks in support of civil rights in the United States, while promoting solidarity with right-wing politicians such as Bush and Vice President Dick Cheney when it comes to their policies in Palestine. This strategy not only impacts relationships between communities, it also impacts every community's access to resources in that individuals, organizations, or communities of color who oppose Zionism risk defunding or slander. Soraya explains:

> Since Zionists have a long history in progressive circles in the US even though their stance on Palestine contradicts their stance on other political issues, they play a role in the funding of non-governmental organizations. Many activists fear publicly supporting Palestine because a precedent has already been set that you will lose your funding or you will not be funded at all if you support Palestinian liberation.

The following story succinctly captures a common challenge that most of our research participants address. Here, Sara's experience illustrates how the Zionist narrative shifts the discourses of oppression, so that Arab voices are systematically excluded, while Zionist voices that uphold and reinforce colonialism and racism remain unchallenged even in the most radical feminist circles. Sara, a university professor and activist, says:

> In this country, progressive circles are Zionist circles. That's why I'm extremely alienated. Feminist circles are completely alienating. You might be able to say Palestinians are victims, but you can't say they're victims of Jews. There's just no room. When I say Jews, I'm aware that I'm saying it. Israel claims to be the Jewish state, the Home for all Jews. You can't name Jews as your oppressor, but it's

the Jewish state. So it's a thin line.

I contributed an essay to a book that is the follow-up to the groundbreaking anthology by radical women of color published over twenty years ago. One of the two coeditors established an e-mail list for the contributors. This was not "middle-class white feminism." This was supposed to be an anthology of radical women of color. On the list, one of the other Arab contributors brought up the Palestinian issue, and the atmosphere on the list suddenly turned extremely ugly as a Jewish contributor accused the Arab contributor of being racist and anti-Semitic. The hostility escalated, as every pro-Palestinian voice was met with a barrage of accusations by the Jewish contributors (who identified themselves as such), accusations ranging from our being blind to the continuing oppression of Jews, and to having zero tolerance for any Jewish voices.

Despite extremely articulate arguments by the Arab contributors, the supposed "radical women of color" on the list failed to comprehend that the Palestinian denunciation of the Zionist policy of occupation did not stem from anti-Semitism. The anti-Arab rhetoric was virulent, vile, and kept coming, unprovoked. I contacted the editor, urging her to put an end to it, but she repeatedly told me she couldn't see how this discussion had turned racist. I explained to her that it was obvious that there was zero-degree tolerance of Arab voices, but the editor refused to address the matter. As the entire book project was threatened by this issue, the editor finally shut down the e-mail list, making it impossible for contributors to post messages.

The dynamics of silencing were fascinating: every time a pro-Arab message was posted, we were reminded that the list was not a political forum but was a place to communicate about the book project. Yet every time an anti-Arab message was posted, it was followed by a half dozen messages supporting whatever ugly accusations had been made. In one message, the pro-Arab contributors were accused of being so racist that they were said to be in league with the KKK. This is what finally made the contributors who had been silent until then realize that the woman who was criticizing us was really out of touch.

The Arab voices were silenced again and again and we were not given a chance to respond and our complaint was not addressed by the editor. The book is now coming out without a mention of how politics played out among the contributors, and a panel is planned at a major conference later this year which does not feature any of the silenced voices, and where it is unlikely that the editor, who still refuses to address the issue, is going to bring it up. That was my experience among "radical women of color."[37]

Conclusion: Censored, but not Silenced

In exploring the ways that our research participants resist Zionism, racism, and sexism, we found that, while varied, three common themes shape their resistance. First, they agree on expanding the scope of "oppression" by demanding the integration of a critique of Zionism within progressive critiques of racism, class exploitation, and sexism. Second, they prioritize making Arab American women's voices audible within multiracial movements for social justice, particularly in terms of highlighting the ways that US-led imperialism in the lands the United States is invading impacts the experiences of peoples from those lands living in the United States. Third, they insist on linking Arab and Arab American struggles to the struggles against all forms of oppression based on race, sex, gender, and sexuality.

Within their families and their communities, Arab American women activists have engaged in the struggle for self-determination as heads of households, workers, writers, activists, teachers, and community organizers. We have developed feminist critiques for challenging sexism within our communities, nations, and the neocolonial societies that seek to oppress us based on masculinist, racialized terms; as well as understanding the impact of multiple forms of oppression on our lives. Some of our research participants, for example, actively participate in the struggle against neighborhood gentrification in their communities, while simultaneously making the link to gender oppression and the uprooting and displacement of Palestinians. Others are active in strengthening alliances between Arab and Arab American communities and our anti-Zionist Jewish allies. Others link Israel's criminalization of Palestinians to the struggle against the criminalization of people of color and the poor in the United States, and the consequent growth of the prison-industrial complex. Others participate in multiracial coalitions around issues of increased militarization in the United States and internationally. As evident in the stories of our research participants, we are consistently highlighting the issue of indigenous peoples' rights, whether in Palestine, Mexico, the Philippines, Hawai'i, or the United States, engaging in coalition building with various indigenous people struggles throughout the world.

As politicized, progressive Arab American feminist activists and organizers, we view multiracial coalitions as essential foundations in the struggle for social change, yet we cannot fully participate within movements that are inconsistent in their critiques of colonialism and racism. By insisting on consistency among progressive activists in general and our women of color allies in particular, we are asserting our voices in transnational women of color movements and racial justice struggles. We refuse to be silenced by the powerful attempts on the part of the US administration and supporters of Zionism to quell our critiques and erase our narratives, and call on all our allies to join us in this movement. We are affirming the histories of those who have paved the way before us in the struggle for self-determination. And we invite our allies to learn our histories as we learn theirs, together demanding an end to all forms of oppression.

12

Reflections in a Time of War
A Letter to My Sisters

Dena Al-Adeeb

Sitting in my Cairo apartment, I look at the sun setting over the bluest part of the Nile. It reminds me of the passing of time, of hopes, dreams, loss, and solitude cast like reflections. The past lingers, spilling over the waters I now call home and I remember it all.

"Deported" from Iraq in 1980, my family and I escaped to Kuwait. Our new abode served as a shelter until the Iraqi invasion of Kuwait in 1990. I was able to return to Iraq three times during that period: 1988, 1989, and 1990. In response to the Iraqi invasion of Kuwait and the Gulf War, we were forced to relocate to San Francisco, California, where we waited for the situation to settle down. As I sit and reflect this evening, I remember our arrival—and our unanticipated mandatory stay—in the Bay Area, with its own set of violent and tumultuous realities. I went back to Iraq in 1999 and 2004. Each time, the return becomes a distorted mirage. The deportations, assassinations, round-ups, mass exterminations, secret police, poison gas, Iraq-Iran War, Gulf War, bombings, sanctions, uprisings, quelling, deadly sanctions, more bombings, Second Gulf War, and now, a full-scale invasion and neocolonial occupation, are changing Iraq forever.

Shades of Colonization

Colonization today has many different colors, shades, and hues. It has been more than three years since Iraq was invaded by American, English, Polish, Italian, Spanish, Danish, Bulgarian, Mexican, Ukrainian, Thai, Estonian, Salvadoran, Slovak, Latvian, Kazakh, Hungarian, and Dutch armies, among others. Of course the red, white, and blue banner stands atop the heap of the war profiteers, since it has grabbed the biggest share of the pie, followed by the UK and other Western European countries reaping the benefit of this neocolonial project.

Unfortunately, some Third World countries with forces in Iraq have been forced into accepting forms of financial assistance (like structural adjustment programs) by the World Bank and International Monetary Fund (IMF), leaving them with little bargaining power to resist quotidian demands. Conditions have been imposed on them, including participation in "Operation Enduring Freedom" and the "War on Terrorism." While occupying Iraq, these countries are simultaneously attacked and undermined by this "assistance," other Western powerhouses (including the United States) and the same multinational and transnational corporations that have invaded Iraq, including Halliburton, Bechtel, Boeing, Lockheed Martin, Northrop Grumman, General Dynamics, Raytheon, MCI WorldCom, Flour Corporation, Perini Corporation, United Technologies, General Electric, Science Applications International Corporation., CSC/DynCorp, among others.[1]

The invasion/occupation of Iraq has been driven by forces with vested interests in overseeing and controlling the largest oil reserves, and the second-largest oil-producing country in the world. This invasion/occupation is also about dominating and securing the region's energy resources, which make up the main source of reserves, production, and distribution internationally. But ultimately, it is about a neocolonial and modern imperial project orchestrated by the United States to set the stage for the New World Order. This New World Order is about establishing the United States as the hegemonic world leader to dominate the global economy through a hypercapitalist system by military force. Iraq became the theatrical stage, testing ground, and setting of an example to anyone who might stand in its way. The invasion/occupation of Iraq is only the beginning of a series of interventions by the United States in one of the most geostrategic regions in the world, with the examples of Iran, Syria, Lebanon, Afghanistan and Palestine. These US interventions are a part of its larger "Middle East Project."

This "Middle East Project" is a long-term vision and strategy towards reconstructing and controlling this geo-politically strategic region. Since the "Middle East" is situated at the crossroads of three continents—Asia, Africa, and Europe—and it intersects the passageways from the Indian Ocean, (Persian/Arabian) Gulf, Mediterranean Sea, and the Atlantic Ocean, dominating its rich energy resources is essential to controlling the world economy. Thus, this need to secure, manage, and organize oil production and distribution internationally is linked to control over the political, economic, ideological, and geostrategic future of the region. This also secures the United States' role by keeping its fiercest competitors—China, Russia, and Europe—in check politically, economically, and militarily. This occupation safeguards Israel's role as a colonial settler state and facilitates its presence, expansion, and domination into Palestinian territories. This is also an attempt to eliminate the Palestinian liberation struggle, which is the main struggle that has unequivocal support and presence inside and outside of Palestine, and links the region, from to Lebanon to Syria to Iran.

Lastly, under the guise of the "War on Terrorism," the United States, Israel, and the "coalition of the willing" are also setting out to eliminate any ideological threats to their dominance. In their pursuit of paving the road for a hypercapitalist "democracy," the US empire, like many empires prior to it, must establish the flourishing ideological opposition in the region as a threat to "freedom and the American way of life." As a result, this region must be constructed as fertile ground for producing, organizing, and transmitting some of the most "extremist" ideologies to the rest of the world: "Islamic Terrorism."

Wrapped in Red, Black, and Green

A red, black, and green dragonfly lands on my windowsill, spurring me to recall the days when I, together with many Arab and WANA (West African/North African)[2] sisters, brothers, and allies, in solidarity wrapped myself in these colors. We marched down Market Street toward the UN Plaza in San Francisco, chanting for liberation, self-determination, justice, and an end to the wars against Iraqi, Palestinian, and Afghani peoples, and others under attack. It was an incredibly intense time. As Arab women activists we struggled at different levels and on multiple fronts to insert a vision of justice and liberation that included linking US imperialism, Zionism, and racism.[3] We critiqued US imperialism and its ties to Zionism, and the racist policies of both, that manifest not only in Palestine, but throughout the region and globally. We also demanded that our potential allies in the United States be consistent in their politics and practices. This proved once again to be dangerous terrain, and we were systematically marginalized and silenced. At the same time, we were able to build strong foundational solidarities with some women of color institutions, organization, coalitions, activists, artists, and others who have proved to be supportive allies in struggle.

Right now, I take a moment and check in with my body. It is this struggle I carry in my back, and it is from this struggle that I attempt to constructively share my experiences as an Iraqi-born, Iranian-deported, diasporas-lived, and American-naturalized woman who spent fourteen years of her life in the Bay Area. It is from this struggle that I share my experiences organizing within progressive and radical spaces attempting to shed light upon Arab women's struggles in the United States and abroad, against the US-backed dictatorships they are forced to live under, and against US empire and Zionism.

For example I wonder what happened to the antiwar, social, and racial justice movements? Where has our momentum gone? Our thrust kicked in after September 11, 2001, and continued to peak until the Second Gulf War in 2003—at that time, it seemed nothing could stop our fervor, commitment, and strength. Now it seems we've been steadily declining.

I recall lengthy hours, exhausted in meetings, conferences, and gatherings mainly in the Bay Area, at the height of organizing after September 11, 2001. I remember feeling a sense of marginalization and angst around discussions on the war on Iraq because the frameworks, language, and organizing efforts focused first on the "war at home," and then on the "war abroad." "The war at home" consisted of the impact the war has/had on people and women of color in the United States and how our organizing efforts should address these communities' needs and interest. There was a general tendency to equalize the war on people of color, immigrants, and Third World peoples as victims of the same systems of oppression: colonialism, racism, sexism, and classism. No one can deny that people of color in the United States, especially women of color, are and have been the targets and victims of colonialism, slavery, poverty, police brutality, the prison-industrial complex, domestic violence, sterilization, and other forms of violence. Women of color bear the brunt of the cutbacks that are being made in social spending on health care, welfare, housing, education, and child care as the war budget climbs. These are real issues, and for women of color the possibility of living just and free lives in the United States is made more remote every day.

However, when we frame the way systems of oppression in the United States operate as a "war" and then equate this to the war on Iraqis, Afghanis, Palestinians, and other Third World peoples, this prevents us from understanding the intensity and complexity of these military invasions, as well as our complicity in these violations. Instead, we choose to fall back on a focus on our own oppressions in the United States, and "take care of our backyard." For some people of color, this position offers security and frees us from our responsibility as "First Worlders" and from examining the attendant privileges we've accrued due to our nationality and our class positions.

Instead, we need to examine our classist, racist, and sexist views towards women from the Third World, especially "Arab" and "Muslim" women (a reductionist term used to name women from countries ranging from Morocco to Indonesia). We also need to accept and understand that we are charged with speaking against all oppressions within the context of US empire. As women of color, we must hold ourselves accountable and understand our implicit roles in this colonization project.

For example, people of color comprise the majority of the US armed forces and carry the burden of fighting this war. "During the Gulf War, over 50 percent of frontline troops were people of color."[4] Undeniably, people of color in the military are victims of the system of oppression; as such, they are on the frontlines of the battlefields. But they are still the bodies which are advancing the colonization of Iraq. I've had different discussions with women of color about this, and the conversations repeatedly arrived at the voicing of a personal dilemma. Some women said, "My brother/sister/cousin in the military is paying the price as much as any Iraqi, and they did not choose to go to war." But there is a difference here that cannot be elided. Indeed, empire-building projects have historically employed and used other colonized peoples to fight their wars for them. For example, during British colonial expansion and the colonial wars in Africa and Asia (including West Asia), the British used Indian soldiers. When not engaging in combat, the Indian Army was used to police and suppress uprisings. Despite the coercive conditions of participation, the participant army should not be absolved from self-reflection and accountability for its role in furthering and engaging in colonial violence. Therefore, since communities of color, and especially youth of color, are targeted for recruitment into the military, we have the power to challenge the military-industrial complex. We are the ones charged with ending this war. The myths of military opportunities, the poverty draft, Junior ROTC—all need to be contested. For example, we can start challenging the military by educating youth of color about the dangerous and horrific, oppressive, racist, sexist, and homophobic facts about joining and serving in the military. We can also urge our sisters and brothers in the military to end this war by becoming conscientious objectors; this was one of the strategies that worked during the Vietnam War.

The United States' history of colonialism, land theft, slavery, violence, and racialization of people of color has imposed such violent victimization on us that we don't always stop to assess how we become complicit and active in furthering racist and colonialist attacks against our own and each other's communities. This history is also framed by repeated attempts to separate us from each other through strategies of divide and conquer. Unfortunately, these strategies continue to be played out in the antiwar, racial, and social justice movements' frameworks, as well as in the construction and struggle of people of color in the United States—for example, the oppression of people of color in the United States is privileged or framed in opposition to the oppression of people of color throughout the world.

Conclusion

I do not want to attack or dismiss the reality, work, efforts, and organizing that we engage in, but hold a mirror to our positions in an attempt to hold ourselves accountable. Hopefully, this will force us to engage in more radical work that will have a ripple effect on all of our communities, and prompt us to always situate our activism in an internationalist framework. This would radically reorient our efforts, strategies, and visions. An internationalist framework deepens and strengthens our analysis, strategies, tactics, and organizing. In a time when the United States' imperialist ascent increasingly wants those in the United States to be kept separate and unaware of the havoc it wreaks throughout the Third World, it is increasingly important to build movements that are deeply aware of realities outside the United States and are committed to centering those realities in their organizing work. Building transnational relations that are aware and conscious of the United States' status as an imperialist nation can work to defy the US imperialist borders that keep its privilege, and instead connect communities of color and movements throughout the world. This move will nurture our accountability to all nations and peoples and all of our communities throughout the world, especially those under severe attack.

Of course, concerns about limited resources, such as capacity, time, and building rank, may emerge from such reorientation. Also, questions about how to structure and create solid movements with an internationalist framework will emerge. These are legitimate and important questions and realities, and we must take the time to deal with them in practice, because unless we incorporate an internationalist framework at the beginning of our organizing and theorizing efforts, we are not fully engaging with the struggle for justice and peace, and we are not being consistent in our politics. We need to learn from our brothers and sisters in various Third World movements: how have they managed to create and sustain social movements and instigate change with fewer resources, and less time, capacity, and structure?

I glance outside my window, and notice the sun setting in the west. In this essay, I have been attempting to reorient myself away from US-centered work, and carve a space for myself that represents my diasporic or transnationalist reality and orientation. I've explored an internationalist framework for organizing in solidarity with Arab and WANA peoples that challenges assumptions made by progressives in the United States, and potentially offers an opportunity for us to do urgent and radical work together.

I also want to continue working with my sisters in the United States, and come together to find better ways to understand, listen, and organize, and I think the biggest challenge we face is to truly hear each other. From my new home in Cairo, I want to join hands with my sisters in the United States, and encourage them to open their hearts and minds to their Arab and WANA sisters living in the United States, and to be receptive to learning lessons from outside of the United States. We all have expertise and resources to share with each other that will allow us to build strong, foundational, long-lasting solidarity movements, and organizations which speak to, and are inclusive of, all our oppressions. This includes tackling the connectedness of imperialism, Zionism, racism, classism, sexism, and homophobia in our work and implementing it in our movements and organizations.

13

Don't Liberate Me

S. R.—*an Iraqi living in the United States*

June 30, 2005

"Do you absolutely *have* to go everywhere looking like that?" asked a friend when the war on Iraq started two years ago. She was asking about what had almost become my uniform: a *hijab* on my hair, a *kuffiya*[1] on my shoulders, a white T-shirt stained with theatre blood, and a peace sign drawn on my forehead with an eyeliner pencil. "Of course I do," I responded. "I wouldn't bother if my homeland and my very identity weren't under attack."

While I have grown less adamant about publicizing my people's cause as a walking billboard, I occasionally find myself reflecting on how the accident of my birth and the politics of my identity have been impacted by recent world events. For example, when the war on Iraq began in March 2003, I felt I was suddenly in the limelight. Few seemed to be paying attention when hundreds of thousands of people fell on both sides of the Iraq-Iran War in the 1980s. Few were concerned about the additional hundreds of thousands who fell prey to the sanctions in the 1990s. But now, all of a sudden, many people across the world, chanting a myriad of reasons, rushed to my aid. On one hand, the American and British governments wanted to liberate me from my dictator. On the other hand, people led gigantic demonstrations to liberate me from foreign invasion. Liberators on my right, antiwar activists on my left, fighting each other to make me happy and serve my best interests. How flattering! I joined my Afghani sisters in occupying the world's public eye. My tyrant became as pressing an issue as Afghani women's *burqas* were.

However, all liberators forgot something profoundly important: that my yearning for freedom is my own instinct. I do not need to be rescued by anyone, whether their underlying motive is driven by oil or feminism. As such, I have only one unequivocal demand of all "liberators": Leave me alone. The only solidarity I am interested in seeing is the kind that throws a wrench in the war machine which occupies my homeland. That is the most I expect of an American or British citizen. Otherwise, please spare me lectures on how oppressive you think my *hijab* is, or how I should follow your lead in fighting patriarchy, or how I should work for achieving democracy in my country. And for your own horizons' sake, do read the history of Iraqi women's contributions to civilization. You may end up finding yourself inspired to follow our example.

14

"National Security" and the Violation of Women

Militarized Border Rape at the US-Mexico Border

Sylvanna Falcón

The US-Mexico border represents an uneasy "union" of the First and Third Worlds. Due to disparaging levels of nation-state power, it is a contentious region that has been militarized to violently reinforce the territory of the United States. In this region, daily attacks occur against border crossers in the form of brutal beatings and assaults—including rape and harassment—by the state and by racist vigilantes. Due to the hypermasculine nature of war and militarism, the use of rape as a tactic against women is well documented.

In this article, I explore documented rape cases involving Immigration and Naturalization Service (INS) officials or Border Patrol agents[1] at the US-Mexico border by accessing data from nongovernmental organizations, government committees, and US newspapers.[2] Each of the women in the case studies took some action against the INS;[3] with some of them using an advocate to move their cases forward through an investigation. (Data indicate that some men report being raped at the border, but the vast majority of rapes involve women victims/survivors, at this border and throughout the world.)[4] In this article, I argue that rape is routinely and systematically used by the state in militarization efforts at the US-Mexico border, and provoked by certain factors and dynamics in the region, such as the influence of military culture on Border Patrol agents.

US-Mexico border militarization rests on two key elements: the introduction and integration of military units in the border region (the war on drugs and national security concerns provide primary justification for involving military units); and the modification of the Border Patrol to resemble the military via its equipment, structure, and tactics. At one time, domestic duties were not part of the US military's mandate. But this regulation changed with the approval of numerous Department of Defense (DOD) authorization acts which facilitated the integration of military units in the border region and loosened restrictions placed on the military for domestic duties.

The 1982 DOD Authorization Act nullified a one-hundred year statute prohibiting cooperation between the army and civilian law enforcement, and changing the role of the military in domestic affairs. This act encouraged an alliance between civilian law enforcement and the military, and subsequent DOD Authorization Acts advanced and expanded this cooperation. Ideological and institutional shifts have also had a role in border militarization. Transferring the INS from the Department of Labor to the jurisdiction of the Department of Justice in 1940,[5] altered the classification of immigration as an issue of labor to one of national security. And more recently, by moving the INS to the Department of Homeland Security (the INS has been renamed "US Citizenship and Immigration Services"), the link between immigration and national security issues has intensified.

Sociologist Timothy Dunn draws on low-intensity conflict (LIC) military doctrine to contextualize the militarization of the US-Mexico border. LIC doctrine advocates for "unconventional, multifaceted, and relatively subtle forms of militarization" and emphasizes "controlling targeted civilian populations." The US military-security establishment drafted this doctrine to target Third World uprisings and revolutions, particularly in Central America. LIC doctrine is characterized by the following:

> an emphasis on the internal defense of a nation; an emphasis on controlling targeted civilian populations rather than territory; and the assumption by the military of police-like and other unconventional, typically nonmilitary roles, along with the adoption by the police of military characteristics.[6]

Dunn's study demonstrates that these aspects of LIC doctrine have been actualized in the border region, indicating that a form of "war" exists there. And in every war, in every military conflict, rapes occur because sexual assault is in the arsenal of military strategies; it is a weapon of war, used to dominate women and psychologically debilitate people viewed as the "enemy."

In the context of mass war rape in the former Yugoslavia, Susan Brownmiller likens female bodies to territory.[7] "Rape of a doubly dehumanized object—as woman, as enemy—carries its own terrible logic. In one act of aggression, the collective spirit of women *and* of the nation is broken, leaving a reminder long after the troops depart." Beverly Allen extends this analogy to the imperialist practice of colonization.[8]

Acts of sexual violence which target undocumented (primarily Mexican) women at the US-Mexico border are certainly informed by a legacy of colonialism, which dates back to the forced imposition of a border in 1848.[9] More than 150 years later, migrant women's bodies continue to denote an "alien" or "threatening" presence subject to colonial domination by US officials. Many women who cross the border report that being rape was the "price" of not being apprehended, deported, or of having their confiscated documents returned. This price is unique to border regions in general; while militarized rapes are part of a continuum of violence against women, I call these violations militarized *border* rapes because of the "power" associated with the border itself. In this setting, even legal documentation can provide a false sense of security, because militarization efforts have socially constructed an "enemy" and Mexican women and other migrants fit that particular profile.

My goal in this article is to make visible a form of military rape which has not been previously considered in the range of military rapes by feminist scholars. Militarized border rape is overlooked because many of the world's border regions are not considered war zones. For example, the US-Mexico border conflict is not typically thought of as a "war," because opposing military forces (or insurgents) are not trying to kill each other. But a war is underway at the US-Mexico border, facilitated by cooperating military and civilian units, and the adoption of a militaristic identity in border patrolling efforts. Furthermore, the stance of the US government on immigration suggests that the United States views itself in some form of war with undocumented migrants. Calls to "shut down" the border, or to build an entire wall along the two-thousand mile border, are frequently reported in the news and supported by members of Congress as a way to "protect" the United States.[10] And when engaged in any form of war, women are always disproportionately affected.

Feminist scholar Cynthia Enloe explores three conditions under which rape has been militarized. Observes Enloe, "'recreational rape' is the alleged outcome of not supplying male soldiers with 'adequately accessible' militarized prostitution; "national security rape' as an instrument for bolstering a nervous state; and 'systematic mass rape' as an instrument of open warfare."[11] She also contends that certain conditions which allow militarized rapes are in place on the US-Mexico border:

> A regime is preoccupied with national security; a majority of civilians believe that security is best understood as a military problem; national security policy making is left to a largely masculinized policy elite; and the police and military security apparatuses are male-dominated.[12]

In my view, a variation of national security rape and systematic rape characterize the reality in this border region. First, national security entails the control of labor, migration, and women. In the 1990s, the US government expanded the definition of national security to include "domestic political concerns and perceived threats to culture, social stability, environmental degradation, and population growth."[13] During this time, immigrants and refugees became top national security issues.[14] And in the aftermath of 9/11, the US-Mexico border was completely shut down for several days due to national security reasons, reifying the classification of the US-Mexico border as an area of national security.[15] With a masculinized elite emphasizing the normalcy and role of militarism with regards to "national security," broader definitions of security have become marginalized. For example, the provision of basic necessities—such as shelter, health care, and food—is not seen as a "security issue" by the US government, though international human rights standards and laws do characterize the meeting of basic human needs in this way.

The cases of militarized border rape discussed here can be categorized as a form of "national security rape" for two reasons: first, the absence of legal documents positions undocumented women as "illegal" and as having committed a crime. Thus, law-abiding citizens need "protection" from these criminals; the existence of undocumented women causes national *in*security, and they are so criminalized that their bodily integrity does not matter to the state. Second, national security rape privileges certain interests; in other words, Arizona ranchers who pick up arms to "protect" their property, or recently formed "Minutemen patrols" along the US-Mexico border (specifically in Arizona and California) are seen as legitimate because they are protecting their property, land, and families. Their actions are supported by the state because they are literally taking the issue of national security into their own hands.[16]

Occurrences of rape are systematic if they fall into a pattern, suggesting that they have not been left to chance, according to Enloe. "They have been the subject of prior planning. Systematic rapes are *administered* rapes."[17] In the cases highlighted here, the planning involved is palpable. These were not random acts of violence against women; they were violent crimes which involved planning and efforts to avoid being caught. Additionally, the rapists capitalized on their institutional power over undocumented women. and each man followed their own "script" in attacking these women. These individual patterns became clear during court testimonials by victims/survivors.

Notably, because of the prevalence of sexual violence at the border, a Mexican immigrant woman told the National Network for Immigrant and Refugee Rights in Oakland, California that women heading north routinely use birth-control pills because they anticipate possible sexual assaults. This suggests border rapes are neither random, nor isolated.

Militarized Border Rape at the US-Mexico Border

If they decide to prosecute, women who have been sexually assaulted in the US-Mexico border region confront not only an individual, but directly challenge several powerful institutions—the INS (INS officials tend to conduct these investigations), the US government, the US legal system. And even in more "fair courts," proving rape is extremely difficult.[19] Undocumented women are further disadvantaged because of unfamiliarity with the US judicial process and language or communication barriers.

The rape cases detailed below occurred between 1989 and 1996, and all involved INS or Border Patrol officials.

Juanita's Story

Juanita Gómez and a female cousin crossed through the hole in the border fence between Nogales, Sonora, and Nogales, Arizona, on September 3, 1993.[20] They were on their way to meet two male friends at a nearby McDonald's to go shopping. Larry Selders, a Border Patrol agent, stopped all four people, but only detained Gómez and her cousin in his Border Patrol vehicle. According to both women, Selders told them that he would not take them to the Border Patrol station for processing and deportation to Mexico if they would have sex with him. Both women refused. He eventually asked Gómez's cousin to step outside of his vehicle. When he drove off alone with Gómez, Selders raped her.

Gómez and her cousin eventually found each other at the Mexican consulate in Nogales, Arizona, and informed officials at the Mexican consulate. The consulate immediately contacted the Nogales Police Department and Border Patrol to inform them of the situation. But one of the Nogales detectives did not believe the women's statements, asked them if they were prostitutes, and threatened them with jail time if they failed to pass a lie detector test. However, after this questioning, Gómez and her cousin identified Selders in a photo lineup. Despite their identification, the incompetence of the police led to the loss of other important evidence such as Selders's clothes. In addition, the police seized the wrong Border Patrol vehicle and realized the error a week and a half later.

Selders eventually entered a "no contest" plea on a reduced charge on July 25, 1994. The county attorney decided to reduce the original charge of "rape and kidnapping" to "attempted transporting of persons for immoral purposes...while married." This crime is the lowest felony class, and the charge upset many immigrant rights advocates. Selders received a one-year prison sentence on October 7, 1994, and served only six months of the sentence. But he resigned from the Border Patrol in August 1994.[21]

Selders also attempted to secure immunity from prosecution on federal charges, but he was unable to plea-bargain with the US attorney in Arizona because investigators found Gómez's story to be credible. In April 1995, a federal grand jury in Tucson, Arizona, indicted Selders for Gómez's rape.[22] He plead guilty in federal court to violating Gómez's civil rights, and received a fourteen month sentence in the federal trial, receiving credit for time served.

Despite the unfairness of his sentence, on October 13, 1999 Gómez received a $753,045 settlement.[23] Her attorney successfully argued the rape could have been prevented if Selders had been held accountable for previous acts of violence against women; three other women testified at Gómez's trial that Selders attacked them as well.[24] Unlike Gómez, these women had been afraid to file charges, and the statute of limitations in their cases expired by the time of her trial. Since Selders was a government employee at the time of the incident, the US government paid the monetary award to Gómez.

Edilma, Maria, and Rosa

On October 6, 1989, Edilma Cadilla, a US citizen, was driving her car on the highway in Imperial County, California, and was stopped at a checkpoint in the area. Border Patrol agent Luis Santiago Esteves began to question her during this routine stop, but allowed her to continue driving. Further down the road, Esteves pulled her over, asked her additional questions, and then talked about himself, eventually getting her phone number. Edilma believed these questions were official.

Edilma's boyfriend called Esteves's supervisor in El Centro to report the suspicious stop, and the supervisor told him that she should notify the office if Esteves attempted to call her. Three days later, on October 9, Esteves called and purportedly requested a date for the weekend. When she turned him down,

> Esteves told her that was "too bad" because he wanted to take her
> out dancing, get drunk, and have her "sexually abuse his body." She
> told him she had a boyfriend and he then asked if she could fix him
> up with one of her friends.[25]

After Edilma reported the phone call to Esteves's supervisor, the Border Patrol relocated Esteves to the Calexico, California, border crossing point. But Esteves received no disciplinary action for his inappropriate behavior towards Edilma.[26] and he remained as a Border Patrol employee where his new position enabled him to continue having contact with women.

On December 16, 1989, Esteves had problems in Calexico. He stopped Maria, a young woman from the area, and asked to see her immigration papers. While on duty, he asked for her phone number and for a date later that evening. She initially agreed to the date, but called him later to say she could not go out with him. Esteves looked for her at her workplace and then pursued her at a shopping center. Maria agreed to the date on the condition that they first stop at her house to get her mother's approval. He agreed to the request, but indicated he wished to stop at his place to change out of his Border Patrol uniform before going to her house.

According to the court records,

> Esteves told her he wanted her to "be with him." At this point, Maria describes him "changing" his attitude and he became angry. He told her she had to have sex with him. He told her to take a shower. Esteves positioned a gun on each side of the bed on two nightstands...[27]

Fearful for her life, Maria complied with Esteves's sexual orders. According to Maria's testimony at the trial, Esteves "force[d] an object into her vagina, placed his hands into various parts of her body, orally copulated her and forced her to have intercourse with him."[28] She testified that none of these sexual acts were consensual. She escaped from his apartment when he left the room after the rape. Maria received assistance from people passing in a car. The police were immediately notified, and Esteves was subsequently arrested. But Maria did not show up to the preliminary hearing in court, and the charges against Esteves were dropped. He resumed active duty as an agent.

The third incident in June 1991 involved Rosa, a minor. Rosa was talking to family members at the US-Mexico border fence. She and her mother were on the US side, and family members were on the Mexico side. Esteves approached them for documentation. During the conversation, Esteves learned from Rosa's mother that Rosa had an upcoming deportation hearing. Esteves informed them he could be of assistance to Rosa in that hearing.

He reportedly took Rosa out a few times after meeting her at the border. On June 28, 1991, he took Rosa out around 10:45 p.m. and bought her alcoholic drinks before taking her to the vacant apartment of a coworker. At this time, Esteves apparently instructed her to take off her clothes. She stated in her testimony that Esteves "ordered her to masturbate." At first she refused, but eventually complied when "he placed his hand on his gun." She testified that throughout the encounter Esteves assaulted her.

> [Esteves] repeatedly slapped her and at one point, he punched her. Rosa contends that Esteves then sodomized her. At one point he told her, "I know what I'm doing. And I am capable of everything and if I want I can rape your mother." According to Rosa's testimony, Esteves

then told her that he wanted to sell Rosa to his friends. Finally, he told her that he wanted to have sex with her and another woman.[29]

The police arrested Esteves again in July 1991 and prosecuted him for the rapes of Maria and Rosa. He was acquitted for Rosa's rape, but convicted in Maria's case, and Rosa's testimony likely played a role in securing this conviction. In July 1992, Esteves received a twenty-four year prison sentence for the felony rape charge. However, he was released on December 22, 1994.[30]

Like Selders and Riley, Esteves used the threat of revealing the lack of legal documents to gain the upper hand with these women, even suggesting he could be of assistance in a deportation hearing. Legal documents quite literally control the lives of immigrants, so when a US official "seems" helpful regarding matters which may determine your future, it adds another layer of vulnerability. Esteves manipulated this reality to his advantage. Edilma's story also reflects Esteves's violent past with women; he allegedly beat his first wife, raped his second wife, and threatened to rape the second wife's ten-year-old daughter.[31] Esteves continued to target young women; he understood how his official position provided him with sufficient discretion and authority.

Luz and Norma

Luz López and Norma Contreras filed an INS complaint against an El Paso Border Patrol agent who sexually assaulted them on March 7, 1996. The agent arrested them near the Rio Grande River and detained them in his vehicle. López and Contreras, both from Guatemala, were each twenty-three years old at the time of the assault. According to the complaint the women filed against the agent:

> [The agent] lifted up Contreras' dress, pushed her legs open, pulled aside her underwear and stuck his fingers in her vagina. The other woman, López, was told to undo the buttons on her jumpsuit and the agent put his hands inside her top and felt her breasts. The two women said they stared at each other, paralyzed by terror.[32]

López said: "We feared the worse. We didn't know where he was going to take us. Just the sight of him with a badge and a gun was enough to intimidate anyone." The agent briefly left the women in the car. He spoke to another agent, who was alone in a different vehicle nearby. Both men returned to the car. At this time, "in full view of the second agent, the arresting agent assaulted both women again." The women were then taken to the Border Patrol office. At the office, the same agent allegedly committed a third sexual assault by the same agent "in a detention cell and in a bathroom." After torturing them for several hours, "the agent gave the women one dollar each and released them" into the United States.[33]

Following the ordeal, López and Contreras filed a formal complaint against both agents. The women stayed in El Paso in order to cooperate with the investigation. They recounted the attacks to male Office of Inspector General (OIG) investigators, identified the agent from photographs, and received rape counseling. The OIG began an investigation, but did not pursue the complaints, accusing

López and Contreras of "lying and threatened to prosecute them."[34] The women then filed a lawsuit, which is still pending, against the Border Patrol. As in all cases of rape, the women were severely traumatized from the ordeal, and Contreras attempted to commit suicide later that same year.

This case demonstrates the systematic nature of militarized border rape; the officer reportedly raped López and Contreras in different locations, indicating some prior planning. Furthermore, the agent was protected during an OIG investigation which retraumatized the women; officials questioned the women's credibility, and attempted to discredit their story. Contreras attempted suicide in 1996 largely due to this insensitive investigation.

While documenting rape cases in the former Yugoslavia, UN officials described the risks of subjecting women to repeated interviews about their sexual assaults:

> Health care providers are concerned about the effects on women of repeatedly recounting their experiences without adequate psychological and social support systems in place. The danger of subjecting women to additional emotional hardship in the course of interviews is a real one. There have been reports of women attempting suicide after being interviewed by the media and well-meaning delegations.[35]

Factors Associated with Militarized Border Rape

With the integration of aspects of LIC doctrine in its border enforcement efforts, for example, the occurrence of militarized border rapes is not surprising because systematic rapes occurred in the war zones throughout the Central American region where this doctrine was initially implemented. The access to wide, discretionary (and unaccountable) power and an ineffective complaints protocol are factors that perpetuate militarized border rape. And the hiring of military personnel and the "code of silence" ensure that militarized border rapes continue and remain central to border enforcement.

- The level of militarization produces warlike characteristics that make rape and other human rights violations an inevitable consequence of border militarization efforts

Several aspects of LIC doctrine apply to the militarization efforts at the US-Mexico border.[36] UN monitors have documented the systematic rape of women during war, and have categorized rape as a war crime, a weapon of war, and a form of torture. War-like conditions at the border reinforce a climate in which rape and the systematic degradation of women are fundamental strategies. Furthermore, agent impunity and the absence of institutional accountability have created a border climate in which rape occurs with little consequence.

- The recruitment of former military personnel to join the border enforcement staff reinforces the militarization of the border.

The 1996 federal immigration policy increased the presence of agents at the border and the INS hired individuals at an unprecedented rate. In addition to hiring "agents with dubious pasts, including criminal records and checkered careers with police agencies and the military."[37] the INS engaged in an effort to recruit former military officers. San Diego's INS is among the most successful in hiring former military officers.[38] A high concentration of former military agents in the Border Patrol tends to make border enforcement more compatible with the maintenance of a war zone.

- The "code of silence" found in law enforcement and military culture prevents agents from reporting on each other.

Law enforcement and military cultural norms obfuscate human rights violations because agents do not report one another during or after incidents of wrongdoing. The "code of silence" is integral to the militarized border system because it maintains the system's legitimacy. The code is difficult to penetrate and if an individual breaks it, they will likely experience negative consequences.

- Border enforcement agents have wide discretionary power while on the job.

Since "much of their work is unsupervised," border enforcement agents have a great deal of discretion on the job.[39] It is impossible to micro-manage the agents' work and conduct when in the field. This unaccountability can produce an environment of impunity.

For example, since 1989, the INS has reported "only one registered complaint for every 17,000 arrests."[40] Furthermore, Human Rights Watch, Amnesty International, the Citizens' Advisory Panel (organized by the INS), and the state advisory committees to the US Commission on Civil Rights all concluded no effective or useful mechanisms exist to enable victims of human rights violations to file formal complaints against border enforcement agents.[41] According to the Citizens' Advisory Panel, "in 1996, 99% of the complaints received by the Justice Department's Civil Rights Division were not prosecuted. Furthermore, most cases investigated by the Federal Bureau of Investigations do not result in criminal charges or presentation to a grand jury."[42]

The nonexistence of a standardized complaints form and appeals process are systematic and structural shortcomings that allow the INS to minimize the situation at the border. Moreover, the lack of a standardized process and the option of reporting incidents to duty supervisors of the local Border Patrol offices lead to underreporting of abuses. The existing format presents overwhelming obstacles in getting complaints properly investigated.[43] In addition, an increase in border enforcement agents is never met with a proportionate increase of investigative staff.[44]

According to the INS-organized Citizens' Advisory Panel, the INS complaint protocol is completely inadequate for what it is meant to do—investigate allegations of civil rights abuses.[45] Since complaints must be provable beyond a reasonable doubt before proceeding with an investigation, the likelihood of achieving this standard is difficult, leading to a low number of thorough investigations. (Thus, the evidence against the border enforcement agents or INS officials in the rape cases included here was clearly convincing, or they would not have been investigated at all.)

Human Rights and US Accountability

Women all over the world migrate for several reasons: to reunite with family members, to seek economic opportunities via employment, to flee domestic violence,[46] or to escape political strife and instability in their homelands.[47] Human rights treaties seek to ensure basic security and protection—including the right to be free from the threat of sexual violence—in border regions. Yet, the US-Mexico border system supports, protects, and reinforces an environment where militarized border rape routinely occurs.

Human rights establish international standards and "allow groups to hold the US government accountable for its acts of commission and omission with regard to the violation of the human rights of women."[48] Given the actors involved in this region—undocumented people, US officials, and, in some cases, US citizens or residents "mistaken" as undocumented people by US officials—these standards may challenge the system at the US-Mexico border because they provide "a counter-hegemonic language through which the self-justifications of the rich and powerful can be discredited, and the system's legitimacy contested."[49]

Indeed, the desire to protect national (capitalist) interests, institutions, and structures is integral to the legitimacy of the US-Mexico border system. And the strategies employed by the US government to protect state military institutions from international laws and standards are brazen examples of US exceptionalism.[50] Not surprisingly, the US government has grown increasingly dismissive and undermining of international laws and treaties which support human rights. Nevertheless, a human rights framework has great potential for facilitating cross-border alliances and for placing the border situation in its rightful context; the border crisis is clearly an international matter because of who is involved, as well as the factors—trade, militarism, violence, and political instability—which spur migration.

Conclusion

> Rape is among the most underreported crimes in peacetime throughout the world. Shame and secrecy often silence the victims because of the stigma attached to rape. Rape continues to be underreported during wartime...Many women will not talk about their experience of rape for fear of reprisals. Some were reluctant to tell the experts the names of the perpetrators because of fear for their own and their family's safety.[51]

This UN report addressed the specific situation in the former Yugoslavia, but many of its arguments are relevant to all forms of rape.[52] As Beverly Allen argues, rape occurs when fear and insecurity are joined with power and immunity from prosecution in a sexist social system. All rape is related in that "it derives from a system of dominance and subjugation that allows, and in fact often encourages, precisely the violent crime of rape as a way of maintaining that system."[53]

Militarization requires militarized border rape. My goal in highlighting actual cases of militarized border rape is to highlight the humanity of migrant women; rape statistics can be useful in conveying the crisis' severity, but they can also create a sense of detachment from the victims/survivors themselves. The women in these cases displayed courage and agency, and their bold acts revealed some realities about how rape is used as a weapon at the US-Mexico border. Their stories represent an urgent call to hold the United States accountable for human rights violations.

My warmest thanks and appreciation to Clarissa Rojas for her support, encouragement, and feedback on this piece. Mil gracias hermana. Thanks also to Jill Petty and to South End Press for their dedication and assistance, as well as Matthew and Aracely Lehman for their love and support.

15

The Complexities of "Feminicide" on the Border

Rosa Linda Fregoso

The campaign to end the killing of women in Ciudad Juárez took the name "Ni una más." *Ni una más en Ciudad Juárez.* Not one more murdered woman in Ciudad Juárez. Mothers and grandmothers, women's rights and human rights groups, and friends from both sides of the border joined in a movement of denunciation, demanding an end to the most sordid and barbarous series of gender killings in Mexico's history. By mid-2002, there were 282 victims of feminicide[1] in this city across the border from El Paso, Texas, and 450 disappeared women.[2] Between 1985 and 1992, by contrast, 37 women were murdered in Ciudad Juárez. "Ni una más" stages women's visibility and invisibility in the nation as well as a confrontation with the historical and social trauma in the region.

The politics of gender extermination in this region took the form of the apparently random yet seemingly systematic appearance of brutally murdered women's bodies and the equally horrific disappearance of many more. What is now understood as various forms of feminicide started in 1993, a year after the signing of NAFTA. As the numbers grew, the state continued to turn a blind eye to the violence afflicting women.

Records of the identities of the assassinated and disappeared women are kept by the nongovernmental organization Grupo 8 de Marzo of Ciudad Juárez.[3] They were poor women, most were dark, and many of them had been mutilated, tortured, and sexually violated.[4] Although there have been random appearances of dead bodies in public places throughout the city, most of the bodies were found near the outskirts of Juárez, in the desert, near poor *colonias* (shantytowns) like Anapra, Valle de Juárez, Lomas de Poleo, and Lote Bravo. Ranging in age from eleven to fifty, the murdered and disappeared women shared humble origins and, in many instances, their migratory experience to these borderlands.

In a highly perceptive study, Julia Estela Monárrez suggests that the murder and disappearance of women in Juárez cannot be considered simply as the work of psychopaths. Rather than the aberration of a single individual or group, the murders of women are "politically motivated sexual violence" rooted in a system of patriarchy. In fact the various feminicides in Mexico make evident the exercise of power across the social spectrum: the power of the state over civil society; the rich over the poor; the white elite over racialized people; the old over the young; men over women. It is a novel kind of "dirty war," one waged by multiple forces against disposable female bodies. According to Franco, the women targeted in these unprecedented border feminicides represent the "stigmatized bodies," those "marked for death in drug wars and urban violence." Feminicide in Juárez makes evident the reality of overlapping power relations on gendered and racialized bodies as much as it clarifies the degree to which violence against women has been naturalized as a method of social control.

From Negation to Disaggregation

The state's early response, negation, involved at first a denial that the killings were systematic. Then, when the state could no longer deny this reality, officials shifted the blame onto the victims, committing further sacrilege against already violated bodies.[5] In many instances the state emphasized women's nonnormative behaviors, accusing them of transgressing sexual norms, either of lesbianism or of leading a *doble vida* (double life)—that is, engaging in respectable work by day and sex work by night—as though nontraditional sexual behavior justified their killings.[f]

The discourse of negation thus tended to discredit the murdered women by emphasizing their alleged transgressive sexual behavior: "She visited a place where homosexuals and lesbians gathered"; "she liked dating different men and was an avid patron of dance halls."[6] Such expressions of nonnormative sexuality have been so relentless that the mother of murder victim Adriana Torres Márquez responded indignantly: "Don't they have anything else to invent? They have said the same in every case: that it's the way women dressed or their alleged double life."[7] Nonnormative sexuality is central to the causal chain that goes from the transgression of patriarchal norms to murder.

The patriarchal state's initial preoccupation with women's morality and decency is a form of institutional violence that makes women primarily responsible for the violence directed against them. Thus, those women who do not conform to the mother/wife model of womanhood (lesbians, working women, women who express sexual desire, and so forth) are deemed "immoral" and suitably punished. In effect women are transformed into subjects of surveillance; their decency and morality become the object of social control. What's more, shifting the blame toward the victims' moral character in effect naturalizes violence against women.

Negating the reality of widespread violence against poor and dark women proved to be not just a transparent, but an obscene, interpretive strategy. To counter the growing national and international movement of outrage and denunciation, the state transformed its narrative of interpretation from outright denial to disaggregation.

The state shifted the discussion away from broader social issues by isolating each "case" from the more general and systemic phenomenon of violence against women. In other words, the state now conceded the fact of the murders, but it refused to accept their interconnection.

Globalism on the Borderlands

It is important to recognize how under current conditions of capitalist expansion, Chomsky observes that transnational corporations function as "the masters of a 'new imperial age' ... spreading an inhumane model of development ... with islands of enormous privilege in a sea of misery and despair." Antiglobalization perspectives provide valuable insight into how Juárez figures as the "local" embodiment of the wave of global neoliberalism (market-based development) under the coordination and direction of the G-8, the IMF, the WTO, and the

World Bank; of the concentration of economic power in transnational corporations; of the internationalization of social divisions; and of the subordination of
national economies to global forces. There is no doubt that global and transnational dynamics implode into the geography of Ciudad Juárez.

This newly constituted global economic order impacts the most vulnerable
communities—the bodies of the poor and Third World women, who are its disposable targets of labor exploitation.[8] And critical globalization theories have rightly
noted the unevenness of development in Ciudad Juárez, the further exploitation of
the poor, and the lack of infrastructural development—housing, sewage, electric-
ity, health, and other basic services—to accommodate the many poor immigrants
recruited from southern Mexico and Central America by the maquiladora industry. However, conflating the exploitation of gendered bodies with their extermination does not offer us the nuanced account of violence that feminicide demands.

Attributing the murders of women to processes of globalization has created
the enduring myth of "maquiladora killings," where the killers allegedly target
maquiladora workers.[9] Rather than targeting "actual" maquiladora workers, it is
much more accurate to say that the misogynist and racist killers are targeting
members of the urban reserve of wage labor of the maquiladora industry, namely
a pool of female workers migrating from southern Mexico and Central America
and living in the poor surrounding *colonias* of Juárez.

Rethinking State Terrorism
Much of the problem with the discourse of globalism stems from its portrayal
of sexual violence as primarily an effect of global capitalism without accounting for the ways in which global manifestations of power differ and also intensify
earlier and more traditional forms of patriarchy within the nation-state. A more
nuanced understanding of sexual violence in Juárez identifies the multiple sites
where women experience violence, within domestic and public spaces that are
local and national as well as global/transnational.

It is important to recognize how violence—not only in Ciudad Juárez, but
also in Mexico City—is not simply a problem *for* the state but is in fact endemic
to it, a "state of exception" produced by an authoritarian government that has
cultivated extreme forms of violence, corruption, and yes, even death, in order to
cripple people's capacity to resist, to smother effective counterdiscourse and over-
power the revitalized democratic opposition.

As the uprising of the Zapatistas in Chiapas has reminded us, the Mexican
government has been waging a "dirty war" of terror, violence, and extermination
against all forms of dissidence, including poor women and indigenous communities. We should consider feminicide in Ciudad Juárez a part of the scenario of
state-sponsored terrorism because it is situated in what Taussig calls the "space
of death," which "is important in the creation of meaning and consciousness
nowhere more so than in societies where torture is endemic and where the culture
of terror flourishes."

The fact that all of the victims were members of the most vulnerable and
oppressed group in Mexican society—dark-skinned women—underscores the
extent to which in Mexico women's relationship to the state is racialized and eth-

nicized. One way to politicize violence against women of intersecting identities is by highlighting the role of the patriarchal state in creating the conditions of possibility for the proliferation of gender violence.

Another way to politicize violence is to think about it in broader terms, not just as isolated or personal in nature, but as a form of state-sanctioned terrorism, a tool of political repression sanctioned by an undemocratic patriarchal state in its crusade against poor and racialized citizens. In the words of a 1995 Human Rights Watch report, "the choice of particular women as targets of rape is almost inevitably determined by their identities…[as] members of an ethnic group, race or class."

The murders of poor and dark women in Ciudad Juárez, situated as they are in a nexus of violence that spans from the state to the home, are thus connected to broader questions of power and gender inequality within a patriarchal state.

Transnational Activism on the Border

In March 1999, the crosses started appearing. Black crosses on pink backgrounds, painted in protest on electrical poles throughout Juárez, by *Voces sin Eco* (Voices without Echo), a grassroots group of families of the murdered women. Eerily barren crosses, silent witnesses to symbolic and experiential instances of violence, suggestive of what local poet Micaela Solís calls "the language of the abyss: the cries for help we never heard/the screams of their voices."[10] The fusion of traditional secular and religious iconography—pink for women; cross for mourning—contravenes against epistemic and real violence. Women are the protagonists of this grassroots movement.[11] Crosses speaking for justice for eyes that cannot see, for women who can no longer speak, crosses marking the threshold of existence. In painting the crosses in public spaces, Voces sin Eco forged a new public identity for women, claiming public space for them as citizens of the nation.

Although the women have been targeted for their gender, perhaps even more significant are the racial and class hierarchies that constituted their identities as women. As one of the mothers, Mrs. González, so aptly phrased it: "For the poor there's no justice. If they'd murder a rich person's girl, they'd kill half the world to find the murderer. But since they've only murdered poor people, they treat us like dirt."[12]

By early 2002, a new coalition of feminist activists from hundreds of organizations came together under the campaign Ni Una Más. In December 2001, thirty thousand protesters from both sides of the border gathered in Juárez. And in March 2002, hundreds of women dressed in black (elderly women, *campesinas*, housewives, factory workers, students, and professionals) marched for 370 kilometers, from Chihuahua City to the Juárez-El Paso border, in the Exodus for Life campaign.

Horrific forms of violence against women have had an unintended and spiraling effect. In the wake of feminicide in Juárez, this emerging formation of feminist and cross-border activism is part of the movement for global justice, of the challenges to global capitalism, neoliberal state policies, and the rise of the global police state. This transnational borderlands movement for women's rights poses unique challenges. For example, is it possible to locate women's oppression within the human rights framework developed by feminists in the First World? Is it possible to evoke a transnational subject identity within a planetary civil society? The writings of Third World feminists provide a cautionary tale.

Claiming a singular transnational identity for women ignores the profound differences among women across the globe, but especially within specific national localities. Grassroots activists in Juárez are well aware of the limitations of basing a human rights framework on a singular transnational identity. For as Mrs. González reminds us, it is their intersectional identities as specific class, race, and gender subjects which makes women in Mexico particularly vulnerable to feminicide and state terrorism.

At the national level, the state continues to produce the very "state of exception" it aims to police, combining rhetoric with inaction and nonintervention in eliminating violence against women.[13] As of this writing, the cultural elaboration of fear continues in Chihuahua. So too does the struggle to eradicate all forms of violence in the lives of excluded citizens, disenfranchised subjects of the patriarchal state, women, indigenous people, dark and poor women, gays, the urban and rural poor, and children. Human rights activists on the borderlands hold onto a vision of a future in which no person can "rape or kill a woman without fear of retribution."

16

INS Raids and How Immigrant Women Are Fighting Back

Renee Saucedo

I can't tell you how proud I feel to be at this conference put on by, and for, women of color. I think for many of us it is like coming home. It is very affirming, inspiring, it is that breath of fresh air we all need in our day-to-day work. What I've been asked to address today is how immigrant women are faced with INS enforcement. I'm not going to focus so much on the border, because I could go on and on about what happens at the Mexico-US border. Instead, I'm going to focus on what INS enforcement looks like inland and how it impacts women.

I'd like to describe to you what INS raids look like because they're secret. And then most importantly I would like to talk about how immigrant women are organizing to resist the repression by the INS.

Generally, INS raids, arrests, and detentions are characterized by abuse, physical violence, and humiliation. These are all the things that immigrant women have to face and are terrorized by almost every day. Even if they are not personally victimized by INS raids, thousands and thousands of immigrant women wake up every day, wondering, is today the day when I will be caught by the INS, is today the day when I walk my children to school, or take my kids to the health center, or go talk to my social worker, is today the day when someone will betray me and I will be reported, and, ultimately, deported?

So let me tell you what happens to those women who unfortunately do see the claws of the INS. The first way the INS raids happen are at people's homes. INS enforcement officers, generally arrive at people's homes without warrants, without the necessary probable cause or suspicion that people living inside are undocumented. They usually arrive at four or five in the morning, pounding on the door. Typically it is an official who speaks perfect Spanish in plain clothes. And the families open the door; why shouldn't we? We're not committing anything illegal. But that's not how we're treated.

Take what happened at 305 Chestnut in Redwood City, California, in the fall of 1999. Redwood City police officers, collaborating with INS agents, stormed about six apartments where families were sleeping and paraded them in the hallway before they were sequestered in one family's apartment. They would not allow

Speech delivered at Color of Violence at UC–Santa Cruz, April 17, 2000. Editor's note: Since this speech was delivered significant changes have taken place with regard to the INS (Immigration and Naturalization Services). The "War on Terrorism" has unleashed increased attacks, including raids, against immigrants and created the new Department of Homeland Security where the entity formerly known as the INS, now the US Citizenship and Immigration Services is housed. For additional analysis on the danger these changes pose for immigrants, please refer to the National Network for Immigrant Rights' report "Human Rights and Human Security at Risk: The Consequences of Placing Immigration Enforcement and Services in the Department of Homeland Security" at www.nnirr.org.

the family members to dress even though many of them were in their underwear since they were shaken out of their beds. Two of the women were forced to raise their blouses, exposing their breasts to the INS agents, the police officers, and fellow family members. About half of the people caught in this raid were arrested by INS agents, and weren't allowed to even put their shoes on. Afterwards, one INS agent yelled at them, "What are all you Mexicans doing here? Don't you know you belong in LA?"

What is significant about this case is who called the INS: the landlord of the building they were living in. And do you know why the landlord called the INS? Because the immigrant families, most of them undocumented, were complaining about the slummy conditions of their building; the rotting rugs, the broken windows, the urine smell in the staircase, the cockroaches falling down into people's food when the oven was being used, and steam would creep up the walls and ceiling.

Many times when the INS shows up at people's homes, INS agents tell the women, "If you don't sign these voluntary departure forms, you will never see your children again." And where I work, we've seen cases involving women who've told us about children who have been left behind after their mother and father have been arrested and deported.

INS raids also happen in the workplace; even the threat of an INS raid is especially dangerous to immigrant women workers. Why? Let me tell you about the case of Guadalupe Sanchez, who I have had the honor of knowing for many years. She was working for a janitorial company in San Francisco, and she was raped twice by her employer, the head of the janitorial company. A lot of people asked, "Renee, do you really believe her? Why didn't she leave the first time she was threatened by this guy?" Well, Ms. Sanchez was the sole breadwinner in her family; her husband had a bullet in his head and was bedridden. She not only had to support her three children, but found it extremely difficult to find another job because of Employer Sanction, a law on the books since 1986. As a result, it is not easy for people without immigration status to get a job, or at least a job that pays over four dollars an hour. Besides, Guadalupe Sanchez's employer told her if she ever complained or left her job, he would report her to the INS. She would be deported. That was enough information for her to decide to endure the abuse.

It is very common for women workers, when they are unionizing their workplace, to be told by their employers, "If you lift a finger in the direction of unionizing, I'm going to have not only you, but also your coworkers, reported and deported." Undocumented women still have the right to organize themselves into unions, knock on wood. Let's hope a bad law doesn't pass in the next few years. But employers, just like the landlord in Redwood City, California, use the threat of the INS and deportation as a way to intimidate women.

INS raids also happen in collaboration with local law enforcement and with the criminal justice system. I have been doing immigrant rights work for over ten years, and I can't tell you how many immigrant women suffer from domestic violence and never report their batterers to the cops because most of the time the police ask the batterer *and* the woman about their immigration status.

I've been working on a case in Contra Costa County, where a probation officer in the juvenile court system there had such a very close relationship with the INS. Apparently, the INS would come check in with him every so often to ask, "Who are your gang members? Who's on your caseload, and which of them are gang members?" So, this probation officer reported Jadine, who is a 15-year-old. She had a tattoo on her face, but it was never proven that she was a gang member. Now she's in the system, and you know what the INS found? She has no papers. Jadine has been living in the United States all her life because she was brought over by her mother from Tijuana, Mexico, when she was less than a year old, she's never been to Mexico. But the INS goes to Jadine's home, arrests her, and puts her in a detention center. And they put a ten-thousand dollar bond on her, so that she can't get out. Why? Because of her so-called gang affiliation.

The INS right now is very tricky. They say, "We're conducting raids, but we're not arresting the women that you're talking about. Of course not, we don't want to interfere with union organizing, and we don't want to deal with sleazy landlords, we just want to arrest those 'criminal aliens.' We are helping you US citizens, because we are getting rid of the 'criminal aliens' among us." Criminal aliens! Jadine was charged in juvenile court for petty theft, went to juvenile hall for two days, and was put on probation. Then she was put in INS detention, and that's who they use as a justification to terrorize an entire community?

So, INS raids are being used to subjugate immigrant women into submission, or they attempt to, anyway. INS raids intimidate immigrant women so they won't ask for the services they're entitled to, morally and legally. They use intimidating tactics so that immigrant women will be afraid to complain and assert their rights. They are trying to subjugate women into submission so they won't fight back.

But immigrant women are fighting back! Forced through political pressure, the police chief of Redwood City has established a no-collaboration policy between his police department and the INS, meaning that after this campaign, spearheaded by the women who had to lift their blouses and expose their breasts, no Redwood City police officer is legally allowed to collaborate with INS agents in any way. These immigrant women know that they're not going to be able to legislatively get rid of the INS by next year, but what they do know is that they have the right to do everything in their power to make sure that the INS doesn't come back.

We have also pressured the city of San Francisco to declare itself an INS raid-free zone. And for the first time in the country, the papers and the radio and television said, an elected official from the county met with the INS to convey the message that INS raids are wrong. And the stories of the immigrants I talked about came out in full force! Immigrant women are fighting back because INS raids are wrong. They try to terrorize women into submission, but immigrant women, along with our allies, are fighting back!

17

Law Enforcement Violence Against Women of Color

Andrea J. Ritchie

Cau Bich Tran, a twenty-five-year-old Vietnamese woman, shot to death by police responding to a call for help at her San Jose home.[1]

Malaika Brooks, a Black woman who was eight months pregnant, shot by a police officer in November 2004 with a fifty-thousand volt Taser gun outside the African American Academy in Seattle, where she was dropping her son off for school.[2]

Mrs. Afaf Saudi, a sixty-eight-year-old Egyptian permanent US resident, forcibly removed from a store in Greensboro, South Carolina, "hog-tied" and tossed into a police cruiser, suffering a broken shoulder, a broken rib, and a mild heart attack in November 2004.[3]

Jaisha Akins, African American, five, handcuffed and forcibly removed from her St. Petersburg, Florida, school by police.[4]

Margarita Acosta, a sixty-two-year-old Puerto Rican grandmother, slapped and beaten by police officers before being shoved into a police van without her shirt or shoes.[5]

Ms. H., an undocumented Latina woman sexually assaulted by a Los Angeles police officer responding to her 911 call for help when a man was beating her in her home.[6]

Frankie Perkins, a Black woman choked to death by Chicago police officers who believed she had swallowed drugs.[7]

Jalea Lamot, a Latina woman sexually harassed by officers responding to a call for emergency medical assistance, who, along with her family, was beaten and pepper-sprayed once the officers realized she is transsexual.[8]

An African American woman who plays on the D.C .women's football team arrested after using the women's bathroom at a local restaurant.[9]

In workshops on law enforcement violence against women I often ask participants to jot down the first name or image that comes to mind when I say "police brutality." None of these women's names or experiences come up. The same is true when I ask them to note the first image that comes to mind when I say "violence against women." Yet, clearly, these experiences are manifestations of both.

To date, public debate, grassroots organizing, litigation strategies, civilian oversight, and legislative initiatives addressing police violence and misconduct have been almost exclusively informed by a paradigm centering on the young Black or Latino heterosexual man as the quintessential subject, victim, or survivor of police brutality.[10] To cite just one example of how pervasive this paradigm is, one need look no further than a 2002 call-to-action from the Black Radical Congress, an organization which embraces a gender analysis in its Principles of Unity. In seeking support for a boycott of the City of St. Louis in response to several incidents of police brutality, the call states:

> [r]egardless of the city, the scenarios of police violence are the same; only the names and faces change. A handcuffed black male shot to death because he allegedly lunged at an officer; a black youth running from an officer and posing no threat is shot in the back; car chases by police that kill innocent bystanders; a black man shot to death because police thought he had a weapon; and the scenarios go on.[11]

Not much has changed in this regard in recent years, although our understanding of racial profiling and arbitrary detentions has broadened to include the experiences of Arab, Middle Eastern, South Asian, and Muslim men. These narratives of racial profiling and police brutality, as well as prevalent quantitative comparisons of the frequency and nature of traffic stops experienced by "African Americans," "Hispanics," and "whites" which fail to analyze data along gender *and* racial lines, dominate discourse and debate around race-based policing and police violence to the exclusion of the experiences of women of color.

Yet women and girls, and particularly women of color, are sexually assaulted, raped, brutally strip-searched, beaten, shot, and killed by law enforcement agents with alarming frequency, experiencing many of the same forms of law enforcement violence as men of color, as well as gender- and race-specific forms of police misconduct and abuse. Dramatic increases in the number of African American and Latina women incarcerated pursuant to "law and order" agendas and "war on drugs" policies over the past two decades suggest that police interactions with women of color are increasing in frequency and intensity.[12] The "war on terror" continues to reach into the lives of women of color across the United States as well as abroad in the form of harassment, violence, and sexual abuse at the hands of military and law enforcement agents, including federal immigration and "homeland security" officers. "Zero tolerance" and "quality of life" policing practices have particular impacts on young women in schools and on the streets, women street vendors, and women engaged in sex work which are rarely addressed in our assessment of or resistance to these policies. It is long past time that law enforcement accountability and organizing integrate and address the experiences of women of color—not just as mothers, partners, and children of men of color targeted by systemic state violence and the criminal legal system, but as both targets of law enforcement violence and agents of resistance in our own right.

Similarly, women's experiences of police brutality—rather than police protection—in the context of domestic violence interventions, implementation of mandatory arrest policies, and policing of racist, homophobic, and transphobic violence ("hate crimes") have not generally been addressed in service provision or in challenging violence against women, lesbian, gay, bisexual, and transgender (LGBT) individuals, and people of color. Rather, mainstream organizations advocating on behalf of and providing services to survivors of intimate violence, sexual assault, and racist, homophobic, and transphobic violence continue to rely almost exclusively on law enforcement agencies as the primary, if not exclusive, response to interpersonal violence.

The proliferation of mandatory arrest policies across the country is leading to increased arrests of domestic violence survivors, who then become subject to further violence in the criminal justice system, including use of force during arrest, threats to remove and removal of children into state custody, abusive strip searches, and other violent and degrading conditions of confinement. The impacts of our almost exclusive reliance on such law enforcement–based responses to violence in our homes and communities fall disproportionately on women of color, poor and low-income women, and lesbians. For instance, a New York City–based study found that a significant majority (66%) of domestic violence survivors arrested along with their abusers (dual arrest cases) or arrested as a result of a complaint lodged by their abuser (retaliatory arrest cases), were African American or Latina.[13] 43% were living below the poverty line, and 19% were receiving public assistance at the time of their arrest.[14] Lesbian survivors of domestic violence are frequently arrested along with their abusive partners by law enforcement officers who frame abuse in same-sex relationships as "mutual combat."[15] Alternatively, police base their decisions regarding who is the abuser in lesbian relationships on raced and gendered presumptions and stereotypes—the abuser must be the "bigger" partner, the more "butch" partner, the woman of color, or the person who is less fluent in English. Similarly, survivors of homophobic and transphobic violence have also been subject to arrest, as well as frequent verbal abuse and blame, by officers acting on similar stereotypes, or on a belief that survivors of such crimes "brought it on themselves" by simply being who they are.[16]

Until we challenge mainstream police accountability and antiviolence organizing to take up the challenge of integrating and addressing these realities, women of color survivors of law enforcement violence will continue to find that their experiences are not reflected in the dominant paradigms of police brutality and violence against women, leaving their voices largely unheard and their rights unvindicated.

This is not to say that women of color's experiences with law enforcement violence have never been the subject of discourse or organizing. In an essay entitled "Violence Against Women and the Ongoing Challenge to Racism," Angela Y. Davis commented on police violence against Black women involved in struggles for Black liberation in the sixties and seventies.[17] Indeed, the FBI's recent increase of the bounty on Black freedom fighter Assata Shakur's head serves as a potent reminder of the day she was shot three times by New Jersey state troopers during a traffic stop as she stood with her hands in the air by the side of the road.[18] Angela Davis has also described a personal experience of finding a woman by the side of a highway who had been raped, first by a group of strangers, and then by police officers who stopped to "investigate."[19] In a chapter of *Resisting State Violence,* Joy James cites a report entitled "Black Women under Siege by New York City Police," published by the Center for Law and Social Justice at Medgar Evers College four years before the Rodney King incident brought police violence to the forefront of the national consciousness.[20] The report documents incidents of police brutality against Black women which garnered virtually no national attention, including, among others, cases in which a police officer intentionally drove a patrol car into a woman, officers severely beat a woman who had witnessed a police assault on a Black man, and an officer maced a handcuffed woman in the eyes.

In 1984, when Eleanor Bumpurs, an elderly and disabled African American grandmother, was killed by a shotgun blast to the chest fired by officers who had come to assist in her eviction from public housing (because she was less than ninety dollars behind in her rent), Black communities in New York City rose up in outrage.[21] In 1998, when Tyisha Miller was shot twenty-four times by police officers who, responding to a distress call, found her in the midst of an epileptic seizure in her car, yet claimed she pulled a gun—which was never found— Black communities in Riverside, California, took to the streets.[22] When Margaret Mitchell, "a frail, mentally ill, homeless African American woman in her 50s," was stopped, harassed, and then shot by San Francisco police officers in 1999, Earl Ofari Hutchinson argued that controlling images of Black women as "menacing" inform police brutality against African American women in much the same way as do similar controlling images of Black men.[23] When US Customs authorities' practice of racially profiling and strip-searching Black women at airports on the presumption that Black women are "drug mules" was challenged in the nation's courts and on the floor of Congress, national mainstream civil rights organizations began to recognize, albeit only in that limited context, that Black women are also targets of law enforcement abuses. In 2002, Sista II Sista, a New York City–based organization of young African American and Latina women, made a video about sexual harassment of young women in their neighborhood by local police officers, and successfully organized their community to speak out against this form of law enforcement violence.

However, the few incidents of police violence against women of color which have commanded national attention continue to be viewed as isolated, anomalous deviations from the police brutality "norm." Perhaps the overwhelming silences are yet another manifestation of the ongoing sublimation of women of color's experiences to those of men in struggles for racial justice. Perhaps police violence against women of color is experienced as merely one strand in a seamless web of daily gendered/racialized assaults by both state and private actors, unworthy of the focused attention commanded by police brutality against men of color perceived as a "direct" form of state violence. Violence by law enforcement officers is also seen as beyond the explicit scope of mainstream conceptions of gender-based violence, which, in the United States, focus on the "private sphere," failing to imagine women as subjects of state violence in public spaces. Perhaps women's experiences of such violence have not been integrated into the dominant discourse surrounding violence against women because they are dissonant to a society which has invested considerable energy in framing law enforcement agents as protectors rather than as perpetrators of violence against women.

The challenge, then, is to bring these experiences to the center of our organizing against both state and interpersonal violence against women of color and our communities. Doing so will not only give voice to survivors of law enforcement violence, who, more often than not, are women who are also vulnerable to other forms of state, community, and interpersonal violence. It will also challenge us to move beyond law enforcement–based responses to violence and toward community-based responses which truly promote safety for women of color.

Policing Gender, Policing Sex

> Systems act as though they have a stake in keeping gender lines clear. If you step over them, you are treated as a suspicious character. [24]

> You want to act like a man, I'll treat you like a man.—*Statement made by a police officer immediately before punching an African American lesbian in the chest.*[25]

> In 2002, DC police officers grabbed an African American woman by the neck and smashed her face into a door, and then proceeded to force her to unzip her pants. Upon seeing that she was wearing men's underwear, they demanded "Why are you wearing boys' underwear? Are you a dyke? Do you eat pussy?"[26]

As the Audre Lorde Project, the first center for lesbian, gay, bisexual, Two Sprit,[27] and transgender (LGBTST) people of color in the United States, emphasizes, law enforcement agencies uphold and enforce society's raced, gendered, and class structures, conventional notions of "morality," and social norms established by dominant groups.[28] Accordingly, individuals whose existence, expression, or conduct defies these structures are, at best, objects of suspicion, heightened attention, and harassment by law enforcement officers, and, at worst, disposable people turned over to police to punish or ignore as they please.

Enforcement of racialized gender boundaries and regulation of sexual conduct are two cornerstones of police interactions with women of color. From enforcement of historical laws prohibiting people from wearing apparel associated with a different gender,[29] to present day enforcement of social expectations regarding use of gender-segregated facilities such as restrooms,[30] law enforcement agents have explicitly policed the borders of the binary gender system. Additionally, police officers engage in subconscious gender policing: departure from socially constructed norms of "appropriate" gender expression is perceived as grounds for suspicion and securing submission to gender roles.[31] Such perceptions are further complicated by presumptions of criminality based on race or class. Moreover, law enforcement agents have historically acted and continue to act on racialized gender stereotypes which reinforce existing systemic gendered and raced power relations. And, through historic laws making it an offense for a woman to be found in the streets unaccompanied at night[32] and current prostitution laws, morals regulations such as "lewd conduct" statutes, and, until recently, sodomy laws, police have been charged with enforcing dominant sexualities and punishing sexual "deviance."

Individuals perceived to be transgressing racialized gender norms or who are framed within gendered racial stereotypes are more frequently subjected to verbal abuse, invasive searches, and use of excessive force during encounters with police; are more likely to suffer abuse while in police custody; and are often denied protection by law enforcement when crimes are committed against them. The interactions of transgender women, often perceived as the "ultimate" gender transgressors, with law enforcement are generally marked by insistence on gender conformity and punishment for failure to "comply," including harassment, verbal abuse, and physical violence at the hands of police, often based on perceptions that they are fraudulent, deceitful, violent, or mentally unstable because of their perceived gender disjuncture.[33] Women framed as "masculine"—including African American women, who are routinely "masculinized" through systemic racial stereotypes[34]— are consistently treated by police as potentially violent, predatory, or noncompliant regardless of their actual conduct or circumstances, no matter how old, young, disabled, small, or ill.[35] As a result, they are subjected to verbal abuse in interactions with law enforcement officers, their handcuffs are tightened excessively, they are called "fucking dyke" while being beaten, and generally treated with greater physical harshness by law enforcement officers.[36] Working-class or low-income women are also perceived as more "masculine" than middle- or upper-class women, and therefore subject to greater violence by law enforcement officers.[37] Young women wearing "thuggish attire," as current hip-hop fashions are sometimes described, have also been reported to attract greater police attention than other women.[38]

Similarly, lesbians are often "defeminized" and "dehumanized" by the criminal justice system, and therefore subjected to considerable abuse by law enforcement agents.[39] Women perceived to be lesbians—often based on gender nonconforming appearance or conduct—are regularly called "dyke," "bulldagger," and "wannabe man," and subject to violence during interactions with law enforcement. For instance, an attorney in Chicago reports that one of her clients, whom she describes as very "butch," is subjected to constant harassment by police, and is frequently "slammed up against a wall, patted down, and verbally assaulted."[40] One sixty-five-year-old African American lesbian who lives in senior public housing in San Francisco is so frequently beaten by police officers responding to complaints by homophobic neighbors that she now says, "If I need help, I call the fire department. If they show up, at least it's not with guns drawn."[41] One advocate reports knowing an African American lesbian sex worker who is hit and "roughed up" by police officers so frequently that she is inured to the abuse.[42]

Violation of gender norms through public sexual conduct deemed inappropriate—be it engaging in sex work or expressions of affection between women—also gives rise to heightened police surveillance, harassment, and abuse. Two ground-breaking reports by the Sex Workers' Project in New York City document significant rates of violence experienced by sex workers at the hands of police: 30% of street-based sex workers and 14% of indoor sex workers interviewed reported violence by police officers.[43] "Reported incidents included officers physically grabbing and kicking prostitutes, as well as beating them; one incident of rape; one woman was stalked by a police officer; and throwing food. Sexual harassment included fondling of body parts; giving women cigarettes in exchange for sex; and police offering not to arrest a prostitute in exchange for sexual services."[44] 16% of indoor sex workers reported sexual assault or rape by police.[45]

Sexual harassment and abuse of lesbians aimed at securing sexual conformity is also prevalent. For instance, a South Asian lesbian reports that, in Los Angeles, when two women walking down the street are visibly a couple, officers driving or walking by will laugh and throw kisses.[46] Lesbians also report being regularly asked by police officers if they "would like to know how it felt with a man."[47] According to one researcher, women perceived as lesbian are also the subject of increased attention by law enforcement because they are perceived to be taking something that is not theirs to take, intruding on male territory and undermining male privilege by having sexual relationships with other women.[48] As a result, officers "get a kick out of breaking down their self-esteem, they feel that they need to be broken."[49]

Transgender women are framed by law enforcement agents as not only the ultimate gender transgressors, but also as overly sexualized, as indicated by the fact that they are pervasively profiled as sex workers and routinely subject to sexual abuse by police officers.[50] They are also frequently subject to sexualized verbal abuse—officers regularly call transgender women of color "fags," "whores," "sluts," "bitches," and "prostitutes" when they encounter them on the street.[51]

While the degree to which police are enforcing gender lines or acting on racialized gender stereotypes varies between law enforcement interactions with women of color, it is clear that the role played by gender in law enforcement violence has received insufficient attention in our analysis and organizing. What follows is the beginnings of development of an analysis of both "conventional" and more "gender specific" forms of law enforcement violence which centers gender along with race and class.

Racial Profiling and Use of Force

In February of 1996, Dr. Mae Jemison, the first Black woman astronaut, was stopped by a Texas police officer who alleged she made an illegal turn in her hometown. Upon discovering that Jemison had an outstanding traffic ticket, the officer cuffed her, pushed her face down into the pavement, and forced her to remove her shoes and walk barefoot from the patrol car to the police station. Commentators opined that, because she was wearing a low-cut afro hairstyle, she was mistaken for a man by police officers.[52]

In early 1996, Sandra Antor, a 26-year-old African American nursing student from Miami, was traveling along Interstate 95 to visit friends in North Carolina when she was pulled over by an unmarked car driven by a state trooper. A video camera on the dashboard previously recorded Officer Beckwith making approximately 15 traffic stops over the course of the day. Rather than approaching Ms. Antor's car with a friendly, "How ya' doin'?" as he had previously done with white motorists, the trooper charged out of the patrol car, gun drawn, screaming repeatedly at the top of his lungs "Roll your window down NOW! Roll your [expletive deleted] window down NOW!" Approaching the car swiftly until his gun was pointed directly at Ms. Antor's head, he proceeded to violently yank the driver side door open and tear at Ms. Antor's clothes, screaming "Out of the car NOW! Out of the damn car NOW!" Ms. Antor is heard explaining that she's having trouble getting out of the car because she has her seat belt on. Beckwith continues to pull violently on Ms. Antor's clothing and scream at her until she finally manages to disengage herself and begins exiting the car slowly. Beckwith then yanks her out of the car, throws her down to the ground on her hands and knees, shoves her into a prone position, face down on the asphalt in the right lane of the fast-moving highway, shoves his knee into her back, and proceeds to sit on her.

Although the videotape clearly shows that Antor put up absolutely no resistance to the officer's abuse, Beckwith is heard screaming "Quit fighting me!" and seen striking her as he handcuffs her. Once Ms. Antor is cuffed, Beckwith rises quickly and screams, "Stand your ass up lady, NOW! You're fixin' to taste liquid hell in just a minute," threatening to use pepper spray on the completely subdued woman. Once she manages to rise, the officer drags Ms. Antor to the patrol car, yelling "Get in the fucking car!" Ms. Antor's perception of the incident as motivated by both her race and gender is unwavering. When asked what she believed the patrolman was thinking when he was hitting her, she immediately responds "Damn Black bitch." She goes on to say "He was pissed…he couldn't believe this bitch didn't stop for him. Who the hell do I think I am? Don't I know where I am? This is his neck of the woods," adopting a white southern accent for the last sentence. "That is how I interpret it," she says, summarizing in a single statement the historical context in which she perceived her experience, as well as the inseparable role played by her race and gender identity in the officer's conduct.[53]

A Latina from Douglas, Arizona, says, "I have been pulled over so many times I can't even count them, sometimes with no reason at all. Once or twice the Border Patrol told me they received an anonymous tip about someone driving a car similar to mine. I've been told that my car looked weighted down, so it looked suspicious! I've heard of a lot of rapes and killings by the Border Patrol. It seems like the Border Patrol feels that they have the power to do whatever they want."

Going forward, our efforts to combat racial profiling and police brutality must recognize and reflect that women of color have been and continue to be subject to racial profiling and the use of force on streets and highways across the United States. For instance, Amnesty International's 1998 *Rights for All* report on police misconduct and abuse in the United States suggests that a pattern and practice of assaulting African American women developed among the all-male, all-white police force in Riverdale, a Chicago suburb which saw a dramatic increase in the number of Black residents in the mid-1990's:

> Linda Billups was stopped by police while driving home from church with her four young children in September 1993; she was… manhandled, arrested and charged with several offenses including assaulting an officer. All charges were later dropped, except for driving without child restraints. Dianne Overstreet was reportedly kicked, thrown to the ground and subjected to racial slurs after an officer stopped her for allegedly going through a red light in February 1994. At least eight [B]lack women were assaulted in separate incidents in two years.[55]

Similarly, at an October 2003 Amnesty International hearing on racial profiling held in Tulsa, Oklahoma, Native women reported frequent traffic stops, during which no citations would be written, of cars with tribal license plates.[56]

Women of color's experiences of traffic and street stops are often uniquely gendered. For instance, in 2001, a rash of traffic stops of Latina women took place in a low-income community in Suffolk County, Long Island, during which women would be forced to perform sexual acts and/or strip in public.[57] In one case, instead of being issued a traffic citation, a woman was forced to walk home in her underwear.[58] In two others, officers were alleged to have forced women to have sex with them after pulling them over for traffic infractions.[59] More recently, two New York City police officers followed a 35-year-old woman home after stopping her for a traffic offense, and subsequently forced her to perform oral sex on them in her apartment while her three children slept nearby.[60]

Women of color, and particularly African American and Latina transgender women, are also routinely profiled on the streets as sex workers by police, regardless of whether they are actually engaging in sex work at the time, or whether they are involved in the trade at all, and subjected to stops, strip searches, and arbitrary arrest and detention on this basis. Additionally, racial profiling of women of color has branched out from streets and airport lounges to more gender-specific contexts, including delivery rooms across the nation, where drug-testing of pregnant women fitting the "profile" of drug users—young, poor, and Black—has given rise to a new race-based policing phenomenon: "giving birth while Black."[61] Similarly, as demonstrated by professor Dorothy Roberts in her 2003 book, *Shattered Bonds: The Color of Child Welfare*, "mothering while Black" gives rise to more frequent allegations of child abuse and neglect against Black women, be it for perceived neglect resulting from poverty or for alleged failure to protect their children from witnessing abuse against them in the home.[62]

Use of force against women of color is also uniquely informed by racialized and gendered stereotypes—officers often appear to be acting based on perceptions of Black women as "animalistic" women possessing superhuman force, Latina women as "hot-tempered mamas," Asian women as "devious," knife-wielding martial arts experts, and so on. The operation of one such stereotype is apparent in the case of Cau Bich Tran, 25-year-old Vietnamese mother of two, who was shot to death by police responding to a call for help at her San Jose home in 2003. She had locked herself out of her bedroom and had called 911 for help getting back in. When police arrived at her home, she was sitting in the kitchen holding a vegetable peeler which she had been using to try to jimmy the door open. When she began explaining what had happened, using the vegetable peeler to point at the bedroom door, a police officer standing six to seven feet away from her immediately shot the woman, who was four feet eleven inches tall and weighed ninety pounds, in the heart.[63] She was dead within three minutes of police responding to her call for assistance.

These stereotypes are also apparent in the shooting death on August 15, 1998, of Ms. Cora Jones, a 79-year-old Black woman who suffered from Alzheimer's disease, who was partially blind and deaf, and used a wheelchair.[64] Ms. Jones was in her home when a drive-by shooting occurred nearby. Twenty police officers subsequently stormed the house, and began beating Ms. Jones's great-grandson, who allegedly came down the stairs with a gun to protect his family in the wake of the drive-by.[65] Ms. Jones yelled at the intruders, whom she may not have known were police officers, to stop beating her great-grandson.[66] When the officers maced her, her great-grandson begged them to let him calm her down.[67] Instead, the officers proceeded to shoot Ms. Jones in the chest at point-blank range as she sat in her wheelchair.[68] The officers later claimed that she had a knife, and the Detroit police force ruled the shooting a "proper use of force," coldly stating "a shot was fired and it went where it was directed."[69] It stretches the bounds of credulity to believe that a nearly 80-year-old woman who could neither see, hear, nor walk, and was the victim of a dangerous crime, posed such a danger to twenty armed police officers that she needed to be shot at point-blank range as she sat in a wheelchair, regardless of whether she held a knife.

Presumptions about Black motherhood also inform police violence. In December 1993, Los Angeles police shot twenty-seven-year-old Sonji Taylor after they cornered her and her three-year-old son in a rooftop parking lot where she had parked her car to go Christmas shopping. According to her family, the police officers surrounded Ms. Taylor for half an hour before she was killed. The officers claimed that Ms. Taylor was holding her son hostage with a kitchen knife while repeating "the blood of Jesus." Ms. Taylor's family maintains that the knife was a Christmas present, Ms. Taylor never harmed her son, and that "the blood of Jesus" was a phrase

Ms. Taylor repeated when in danger, a product of her Pentacostal upbringing. The scene is easy to imagine—a terrified Black woman, holding a Christmas present, trying to protect her child, surrounded by strange men in a lonely parking lot, seeking protection from her god. At some point, the officers charged Ms. Taylor, maced her, and tore her son from her. The officers say they shot Ms. Taylor after she "lunged" after them, as no doubt any mother would to protect her child, alleging that they had no choice but to act in self-defense. The autopsy revealed that Ms. Taylor was shot twice in the chest, and then seven times in the back. The fact that several shots had "mushrooms" indicated that she was also shot while lying face-down on the ground. This incident clearly reveals the operation of gender-specific controlling images informing police responses to Black women: as a Black mother, Sonji Taylor was presumed to be harming and holding her own child hostage, and this predominant stereotype of Black motherhood cost her her life.

These incidents illustrate the fact that, while racial profiling and the use of force against women of color take many of the same forms as they do with men of color, there are clearly gendered dynamics at play which require a more compli-cated analysis of racial profiling and a more complex approach to police brutality organizing and advocacy. Moreover, racial profiling takes place in gender-spe-cific contexts—such as implementation of mandatory arrest policies, in which women of color are disproportionately perceived to be perpetrators of domestic violence rather than survivors—and takes gender-specific forms—such as sexual harassment and assaults of motorists—which are unlikely to be uncovered by conventional cop-watches and monitoring of existing traffic stop statistics. These examples therefore bolster the need to center women of color's experiences within police accountability organizing and advocacy in order to ensure maximum effec-tiveness for all members of communities of color.

Rape, Sexual Assault, and Sexual Harassment

> 19-year-old Clementine Applewhite was walking down the street in her hometown of Baton Rouge, Louisiana, with two friends at ten o'clock in the evening when they were approached by a uniformed, on-duty officer traveling in a police K-9 unit. The officer told the three women that they would be arrested for vagrancy if they did not get off the street. The young women explained to the officer that they were walking to a friend's house several blocks away, and began to hurry along as they attempted to comply with his order. After the women traveled a few more blocks, they were again stopped by the officer and his companion, a uniformed corrections officer, and told that the officer would flip a coin to determine who went to jail. Losing the coin toss, Ms. Applewhite was ordered into the patrol car and told to keep her head down. The officer then drove to the Memorial Stadium, where he forced Ms. Applewhite to have oral sex with him at gunpoint. Both officers then proceeded to rape her. During this time, another officer came upon them, but turned around and left the area at the request of the first two.[70]

An African American lesbian reports being raped by a police officer who forced his way into her apartment at gunpoint and told her prior to assaulting her that he was "teaching her a lesson" because the world needed "one less dyke."[71]

An Immigration and Naturalization Service (INS) officer in Pomona, California, was convicted in 2004 of demanding sex and cash from two Chinese women seeking asylum.[72]

Rape, sexual assault, and sexual harassment by on-duty law enforcement officers are foremost among gender-specific forms of police brutality directed at women of color. Sex workers in particular report endemic extortion of sexual favors by police officers in exchange for leniency or to avoid routine police violence against them, as well as frequent rapes and sexual assaults. As described by fellow contributor Sylvanna Falcón, immigrant Latina women, both documented and undocumented, are routinely raped by local law enforcement and Border Patrol agents in the borderlands between Mexico and the United States.[73] Officers are also reported to regularly sexually harass young Latina women perceived to be gang members, in one instance telling them "give me a piece of your ass and I'll let you go." In some cases, sexual harassment takes place in the context of police response to domestic violence. In July 2005, a police officer working in a Chicago suburb was charged with "official misconduct" for making women strip naked when he responded to domestic violence calls.[74] In a number of domestic violence cases involving lesbians, officers have made comments to the effect that "this wouldn't happen if you were with a man, you need to try a man," and suggested that they, in fact, might be the man for the job.

The city of Eugene, Oregon, recently paid $667,000 to a woman who was sexually assaulted by officer Roger Magaña, who was recently convicted of sexually abusing more than a dozen women over a period of eight years and against whom eleven other suits are pending. His case, while unique in that it resulted in a criminal conviction and substantial penalty, is common in other respects. Officer Magaña preyed on domestic violence survivors, women involved in the sex trade, others who use controlled substances, and women who are labeled as mentally ill, first threatening arrest and then offering leniency in exchange for sexual acts. In some cases, he was conducting "welfare checks"—which allow officers to enter residents' homes by simply stating that they believe a person's well-being is at risk—at the time he raped and sexually assaulted women. He frequently conducted inappropriate and abusive searches of women on the side of the road. Many of the women who eventually came forward said they did not initially report the abuse because they were afraid of police retaliation and feared they would not be believed. One woman told of Magaña putting his service weapon up against her genitals and saying he would "blow her insides out" if she told anyone. Nevertheless, police files indicate that at least half a dozen officers and supervisors heard complaints from women that they had been raped or sexually assaulted by Officer Magaña and one of his fellow officers before either one was arrested.[75]

Some community organizing around sexual harassment by law enforcement officers has taken place. As described in their piece in this anthology, Sista II Sista, a Brooklyn-based collective of working-class young and adult Black and Latina women, began organizing against sexual harassment and violence by law enforcement officers in their neighborhood after two young women from the community were killed by police officers.[76] One was killed during a dispute with her mother on their stoop when a police officer stopped to intervene, and ended up shooting the young woman in the chest, claiming self-defense, while the second was killed by her boyfriend, who was an auxiliary cop. As they were organizing around these incidents, young women's experiences of daily sexual harassment by police officers began to come to light, and they decided to use video to document sexual harassment by officers from New York City's 83rd Precinct. They subsequently screened the video and performed skits depicting sexual harassment by police during a neighborhood block party outside the precinct house. The event was a success, leading the community to take up the issue in their ongoing police accountability work. Sista II Sista's work in this area serves as an important example of developing joint antiviolence and police accountability organizing strategies that link state and interpersonal violence in the ways they manifest in our every day lives.

Responses to Domestic Violence and Sexual Assault

> On September 28, 1999, 39-year-old African American Bronx resident Cherae Williams called 911 for help because her boyfriend was beating her.[77] Frustrated by responding officers' refusal to even get out of their patrol car to assist her or take her complaint, she asked for their names and badge numbers.[78] The two white officers responded by handcuffing Ms. Williams and driving her to a deserted parking lot. During the drive to the parking lot, a terrified Ms. Williams managed to get one hand out of her handcuffs only to be pepper sprayed by the officers. When they arrived at the lot, the officers pulled Ms. Williams out of the patrol car by her hair, repeatedly shook her and struck her head against the car, and beat her so badly she suffered a broken nose and a broken jaw which had to be wired shut.[79] Ms. Williams appeared before a New York City Council hearing on police responses to domestic violence complaints in October of 1999, testifying that "[the officers] beat me until I was bloody ... they left me there dazed and with a warning. They told me if they saw me on the street, that they would kill me ... I called the police to prevent a serious incident, and they brutalized me."[80]

Society's reliance on law enforcement–based responses to violence against women has had a number of unintended consequences, not the least of which is increased vulnerability of survivors to violence—at the hands of both their abusers and law enforcement officers. Often, police brutality against women of color and their families occurs when they seek assistance in the context of domestic violence or sexual assault. As a result, "law and order" agendas and "tough on crime" policies have not necessarily increased women of color's safety from violence—instead, fear of police violence or of inappropriate responses to interpersonal violence by law enforcement agents, combined with the lack of alternative responses, often leaves women of color with nowhere to turn when we face violence in our homes and communities. Moreover, in the current anti-immigrant climate, the absence of societal responses to violence that do not rely on law enforcement agencies, increasingly more concerned with detecting and deporting undocumented women than protecting them, increases immigrant women's vulnerability to violence.

Police interactions are very much informed by racialized notions of gender which dictate who is a legitimate survivor of domestic violence and sexual assault, and who is likely to be a perpetrator of violence. For instance, one African American woman testified at a 1999 Amnesty International hearing on police brutality in Los Angeles that on one occasion police officers responding to a "family quarrel" at her home beat her as her children were locked outside, powerless to answer their mother's cries for help. She reported that she was subsequently gagged with a rag by officers, and beaten again until she fainted, at which point officers dragged her across her yard to their police car.[81] In June 1994, Rebecca Miller, a twenty-two-year-old Black woman was shot and killed at close range in the hallway of her apartment, with her two-year-old son at her side, after police were called to intervene in a fight with her boyfriend.[82] On September 10, 1997, Oakland police responding to a neighbor's domestic disturbance call, proceeded to shoot Venus Renee Baird in the chest in front of her family, alleging that she attacked the police officers with a butcher knife.[83]

These incidents highlight the pervasive nature of the archetypes governing the manner in which women of color are perceived. At their most vulnerable, subjected to physical abuse in their own homes, women called on law enforcement officers for help. Rather than "serve and protect," officers brutalized them, either for daring to challenge or seek protection from violence, or simply because they were acting on stereotypes that framed women of color as violent and requiring submission by physical force regardless of the context. These women's experiences undermine the women's movement's purported success in increasing women's safety by exposing violence in the "private sphere" of the home and sensitizing law enforcement officers to take domestic violence seriously. Rather, they expose one of the failures of the mainstream domestic violence movement, which has been to contribute to perceptions of victims of domestic violence as almost exclusively white and middle class, excluding women of color from the "battered woman" narrative and, therefore, the right to protection by law enforcement. They also illustrate the isolation women of color survivors of both interpersonal and law enforcement violence face in light of the mainstream antiviolence movement's failure to integrate their experiences into their analysis, strategies, and advocacy.

The "War on Drugs"

> Frankie Perkins, mother of three daughters, aged four, six, and sixteen, was on her way home one evening, crossing an empty lot, when she was stopped by police, who later claimed that they had

seen her swallowing drugs, and tried to get her to spit them up.
Witnesses state that the officers simply killed her, strangling her
to death. Autopsy photos reveal bruises on her face and rib cage,
and show her eyes swollen shut, and the hospital listed the cause of
death as strangulation.[84]

Lori Penner, a Native woman living in Oklahoma, testified at a 2003
Amnesty International hearing on racial profiling that her house
was raided in August of that year by law enforcement officers claiming to be searching for drugs. During the raid, she stated that her
fifteen-year-old daughter "was jerked out of the shower and forced
to stand naked in front of three male officers. She was taken to her
room to put some clothes on where she had to get dressed in front of
three officers…the police laughed and smirked at us when no drugs
were found. One police officer had the audacity to tell my daughter
she cleaned up nice and looks good for a fifteen-year-old girl."[85]

Myths and stereotypes implicating women of color in the drug trade have also
proven deadly when acted upon by police officers. In South Seattle, Washington,
in October 1997, Theresa Henderson, like Frankie Perkins, was choked to death
by police who alleged that she tried to swallow a small amount of cocaine and
claimed that they were merely attempting to recover "evidence."[86] Danette Daniels, a pregnant Black woman arrested for dealing drugs in June of 1997 by New
Jersey police officers, was shot to death by officers as she sat in the squad car, after
an alleged "scuffle."[87] Witnesses deny that Ms. Daniels was involved in any drug
transaction at the time of her death.[88]

Additionally, the "war on drugs" and the potential consequences of a drug
conviction—which, as discussed in greater detail in this volume by Patricia Allard,
can include long mandatory prison sentences; loss of child custody; loss of access
to public housing, food stamps, and cash assistance; loss of professional licenses;
and denial of access to government loans for higher education—have given law
enforcement officers increased power, and have therefore increased the likelihood
of police abuse of women of color. From arbitrary stops, strip searches, and detentions based on perceptions of women of color as "drug mules" to increased lever-
age for police extortion schemes such as those in which officers routinely demand
sexual acts in exchange for leniency, it seems beyond question that the "war on
drugs" has increased the prevalence of law enforcement violence against women.
For instance, a Milwaukee police officer was recently charged with dropping drug
charges against a South Dakota woman in exchange for sex.[89] In another case
recently before the federal Ninth Circuit of Appeals court, Darla Motley was
allowed to proceed with her suit against the LAPD based on a March 1999 drug
raid. During the raid, Motley was shoved against a wall, and a police officer entered
her baby's room pointed a gun at the child while others rifled through her belong-
ings.[90] However, beyond documentation of rising incarceration rates of women of
color, the nature and quality of police interactions with women of color in the context of the "war on drugs" has yet to be systematically examined or addressed.[91]

The "War on Terror"

In early March 2003, F., a former high school teacher who describes herself as "hapa" (mixed race) and genderqueer, was walking in downtown Los Angeles around midnight with two friends when two men wearing purple shirts and black pants approached them, telling them, "You have to stop, you have to stop." Although the two men did not identify themselves as law enforcement or security officers until later, they immediately grabbed the three friends by the arms. An unmarked police car pulled up, and two men jumped out, guns drawn, also failing to identify themselves as police officers at the time. One of the men placed a gun to F.'s friend, G.'s head. Although F. was the smallest of the three, she was grabbed by three of the men. The officers then began questioning F. regarding the contents of her backpack, which, in addition to several antiwar buttons, had one button with two joined women's symbols on it and another which said, "We're here, we're queer, get used to it." The officers then grabbed her and threw her up against a wall with enough force to "bust" a cell phone in her back pocket, and held her there with her feet barely touching the ground as they questioned her.

One of the men wearing a purple shirt, whom F. believes, based on information she later obtained, was assigned to patrol the business district as part of a "homeland security" initiative, told her that they had received reports of people engaged in "un-American stuff" in the area. The officers repeated their questions regarding what was in F.'s bag, and then began demanding to know what was under F.'s sweatshirt. The officers next asked if F. was a boy or a girl, and tried to unzip her sweatshirt, asking what she had on underneath. Despite her protests that she did not consent to a search, the officers grabbed F.'s arms and held her down while another officer pulled up her sweatshirt and T-shirt and groped her chest area while asking her repeatedly, "What are you, are you a boy or a girl?," and grabbing her inappropriately. According to F., one of the officers had his gun drawn during the entire search, while another was telling her, "You need to calm down and cooperate." When describing the incident, F. wryly commented—"It was not pretty."[92]

One of the officers then grabbed F. by the hair, pulling her face up to allow him to take her photograph. One of the officers asked her, "Why do you dress this way?" while another was heard saying under his breath, "What is it, is it a he or a she?" F. was then placed in handcuffs so tight they cut F.'s wrists and interfered with circulation to her hands. When F. asked the officers to loosen them, they refused. When a marked police car arrived on the scene, the three

friends repeatedly asked why they were being detained. The officers
threatened several times to call the INS, asked them, "Why don't
you go back where you came from?" called them "towel head lov-
ers," and told them "If you are against war, you are for terrorism."
At one point, F. said something to G. in German. The officers,
assuming she was speaking Arabic, reportedly said, "You're one of
them." Later on, at the police station, when F. removed the hat
she had been wearing as she sat handcuffed to a bench, revealing
long hair, one of the arresting officers walked by and said "Oh,
maybe it is a girl." Another officer reportedly walked by and asked
a third, "Is that the one that's a he-she? It must be a girl, look at her
hair." Charges against F. were eventually dismissed. Her complaint
against the arresting officers is still pending.

The voices and experiences of Arab, Middle Eastern, South Asian, and Muslim women—and women perceived to be members of these groups—have been
noticeably absent from discourse regarding the impacts of the "war on terror" on
communities of color in the United States. This does not mean, by any stretch of
the imagination, that they have escaped its grasp. Rather, dominant anti-Arab/anti-
Muslim racism represents Arab, Muslim, and South Asian women as passive victims
of their violent, misogynist men, without agency and in desperate need of "liberation" by Western militaries and feminists alike, thereby eliminating the possibility
in the popular mind that they would be targets of state violence in the context of
this very "liberation."

However, images of Arab, Muslim, and South Asian women as potential suicide bombers are increasingly gaining currency, as evidenced by the case of six-
teen-year- old Tashnuba Hayder, a South Asian Muslim living in Queens, New
York, who was recently the subject of the first terrorism investigation involving a
minor. FBI agents who had monitored her visits to an Internet chat room where
sermons by an Islamic cleric in London were posted showed up at her home one
day, pretending to follow up on a missing persons report filed five months earlier
when Tashnuba briefly left home with a friend. The agents immediately began
going through her diary, papers, and home schooling materials, focusing on one
essay discussing the positions taken on suicide by various religions and another
about the Department of Homeland Security, in which she stated that she felt
that Muslims were being targeted and "outcasted" by the state since 9/11. Three
weeks later, based on a "secret" declaration, a dozen federal agents raided her
home at dawn, citing the expiration of her mother's immigration papers as justification for taking the daughter into custody. Without providing her parents with
any information as to her whereabouts for two weeks, Tashnuba was transferred
to a juvenile detention center in Pennsylvania where she was interrogated, without a parent or a lawyer present, by the members of the FBI Joint Terrorism Task
Force, and released only upon her mother's agreement to a "voluntary departure"
to Bangladesh. Another Muslim girl, Adama Bah, was also detained as part of the
investigation.[93]

Since 9/11, Arab, Middle Eastern, and Muslim women have also been routinely subject to street and airport profiling. Women who wear the *hijab* are disproportionately targeted by law enforcement. For instance, in December 2001, a Muslim woman wearing a veil was stopped by police for driving with suspended plates. Rather than simply write her a ticket upon production of a valid driver's license and registration, the officer arrested her, shoved her into the patrol car, and made inappropriate comments about her religion and her veil.[94] In November 2001, a Muslim woman was asked to remove her headscarf at an airport—even though the metal detector had not gone off when she went through it—and taken to a room for a full body search.[95] Transgender women also report increased profiling as potential terrorists based on assumptions that they are "disguised" as women. These cases, and countless others which have not yet come to light, must also guide our analysis and our antiviolence and law enforcement accountability organizing efforts in the post-9/11 world.

"Quality of Life" and "Gang" Policing

While the "war on drugs" and the "war on terror" have played significant roles in driving law enforcement policies and practices over the past decade, two additional trends in law enforcement have also influenced and contributed to police interactions with women of color. In an effort to address what are often described as "quality of life" crimes, many local governments have either passed or increased enforcement of legislation establishing juvenile curfews and prohibiting activities such as loitering, panhandling, unlicensed street vending, public drunkenness, urination in public places, graffiti, and sleeping on public benches or parks.[96] These provisions lead to criminalization of normally noncriminal behavior, and are often discriminatorily enforced.

Provisions targeted at those congregating in and using public spaces or living on the streets disproportionately impact homeless, precariously housed, and low-income women of color and youth who have limited access to private spaces, as well as individuals providing vital outreach services to those communities. "Gang policing" initiatives have been intricately intertwined with "quality of life" policies, and often serve as a pretext for profiling and harassment of groups of young people of color in schools and neighborhoods. Latina lesbians are reportedly profiled by police as gang members under these policies, at times based on gender-nonconforming appearance, behavior, and attire, such as wearing baggy pants.[97] Asian girls have also been subject to "gang" profiling based on stereotypes regarding criminal activity among recent East Asian immigrants.[98] School safety officers and school police charged with enforcing "zero tolerance" policies are reported to routinely harass and abuse youth, particularly youth of color, engaging in profiling, as well as arbitrary stops and searches, based on race, ethnicity, religion, gender, gender identity, sexual orientation, or style of clothing.[99] Sexual harassment and abuse of young women of color has also been reported, as well as violent arrests and detentions of young women of color—once again revealing the operation of gender policing and racialized gender-based stereotypes in current police practices.

Conclusion

Gender, sex, and race policing, as informed by stereotypical and archetypal representations of women of color, clearly underlie law enforcement interactions with women of color. Brutal physical and psychological assaults on women of color by police officers appear to be informed by beliefs that deviations from socially constructed norms of gender and sexual expression are legitimate bases for suspicion. Consequently, use of force on the part of state agents becomes necessary, as women of color, by their very existence, are seen as threats who must be met with brutal force; are sexually available and subject to sexual subjugation at the hands of police officers; are vessels for drugs swallowed or concealed; and/or are instruments of "terror." Yet the complexity of the interaction of structural oppressions in police encounters with women of color is not reflected within analytical and organizing frameworks which allow for consideration of only one axis of oppression—such as race-based police brutality against men of color or gender-based interpersonal violence against white women.

A reformulation of our struggles against police brutality to integrate an analysis of state violence based on gender *and* race, as well as other structural oppressions such as class, national origin, occupation, gender identity and expression, sexual orientation, age, and disability is clearly required. Similarly, a revisioning of our struggles to end violence against women is required to integrate women of color's experiences of state violence, as well as its intersections with interpersonal and community violence. The experiences of the women whose stories are recounted in this piece and countless others counsel strongly in favor of a critical examination of current approaches to violence against women, and the development and support of alternative, community-based accountability strategies which prioritize safety for survivors, community responsibility for creating and enabling the conditions which permit violence to take place, and transformation of private and public gender relations. These experiences not only challenge the effectiveness of law enforcement–based responses to domestic and sexual violence against women, but also serve as a basis for pursuing collaborations between antiviolence and anti–police brutality organizers to develop such community-based responses to violence against women which do not involve the criminal legal system.

Through such coalitions, all of our movements will be better able to integrate women of color's lived experiences into our organizing and advocacy strategies— after all, a woman's gender, race, immigration status, economic status, and gender identity can all converge in a single interaction with a law enforcement agent committing or responding to violence against a woman of color. Indeed, until the role of law enforcement agents in perpetrating and facilitating violence against women of color and their communities is examined and addressed, we cannot claim to be working toward safety for all women.

18

Crime, Punishment, and Economic Violence

Patricia Allard

"Tough on crime" policies, particularly those associated with the "war on drugs," are the primary engines driving mass incarceration in the United States. The current preoccupation with punishment rather than prevention and rehabilitation has resulted in the increasing dehumanization of women, especially women of color, through arrest, prosecution, and incarceration without regard for the circumstances that lead to women's contact with the criminal punishment system. Adding insult to injury, following a criminal conviction, through post-conviction penalties, the state further strips women of access to the very antipoverty tools—housing, financial assistance, food stamps, and educational supports—they need to survive. Limited thought is given to the destabilizing impact that incarcerating and disenfranchising growing numbers of mothers, workers, sisters, students, grandmothers, taxpayers, survivors of violence, educators, and young and old women, will have on our families and communities.

This essay examines the impact of three specific post-conviction penalties—the lifetime ban on receipt of welfare benefits, the federal ban on receipt of post-secondary financial aid, and the public housing ban—on women of color with drug convictions. The existence and persistence of these penalties is linked not only to an extension of criminal punishment beyond prison walls, but also to the state's interest in providing greater tax cuts to already wealthy Americans, and the consequent claimed need to cut social spending. The implementation of these penalties also reflect the Bush administration's commitment to increasing the role of faith-based communities in social reform, and to diverting funding from individual entitlements to marriage promotion and abstinence programs, advancing the latter as the solution to poverty in the United States. These punitive policies amount to economic violence against women, and disproportionately affect poor and low-income women of color.

The number of women in federal and state prisons has increased dramatically since the 1980s—there were 12,300 women behind bars in 1980, compared to over 105,000 in 2004.[1] The "war on drugs" is the most significant contributing factor to growth of the women's prison population in the United States. Latinas and African American women are most likely to be incarcerated for drug offenses: according to Bureau of Justice Statistics (BJS), in 1997, 44% of Latinas and 39% of African American women incarcerated in state prisons had been convicted of a drug offense, whereas only 23% of white women, 24% of Black men, 26% of Latinos, and 11% of white men were incarcerated for drug offenses.[2]

Women convicted of criminal offenses are further punished after serving their prison terms through a complex web of civil penalties. This essay addresses only three types of post-conviction penalties, but women leaving prison face many more statutorily imposed penalties. While employment and voting bars for people with felony convictions have a long history, the past decade has seen a significant expansion of post-conviction penalties into new areas of social policy. For example, in addition to a criminal sentence, a drug conviction can lead to a lifetime ban on the receipt of cash assistance and food stamps, denial of federal financial aid for postsecondary education and public housing, and preclusion from becoming a foster or adoptive parent.

The Personal Responsibility and Work Opportunity Reconciliation Act (PRWORA) [3]

In 1996, under a Democrat-controlled Congress and the Clinton administration's watch, the nation embarked on welfare "reform." The resultant Personal Responsibility and Work Opportunity Reconciliation Act (PWRORA) was hailed as the means by which people would transition from welfare to work and move out of poverty. One of the most significant features of the new law placed a five-year time limit on the receipt of cash assistance. But perhaps the most punitive provision of the 1996 welfare reform law was the lifetime welfare ban imposed on people convicted of felony drug offenses. Yet this provision was the subject of only two minutes of congressional debate during its passage. Under this provision, women with a felony drug conviction are not even entitled to a grace period of five years to enable them to overcome the socioeconomic barriers that brought them in contact with the criminal punishment system in the first place. Ineligibility for cash assistance and food stamps is immediate and lifelong, and results in limited access to, and in many cases outright denial of, education and job training programs, childcare support, and drug treatment programs linked to receipt of welfare benefits. It is estimated that between 1996 and 1999, over 96,000 women, 48% of whom were African American or Latina, were subject to the ban, affecting the well-being of 250,000 children.[4]

PRWORA authorizes states to modify or opt out of the ban, and, at the time of writing, thirty-four states and the District of Columbia had elected to do so. Eleven states and the District had entirely opted out of the ban; eleven states limited its applicability either by type of offense (such as, possession or trafficking) or type of benefit (e.g., cash assistance or food stamps), and twelve states maintained eligibility to benefits conditional on participation in a state-certified drug treatment program and/or submission to random drug testing. Only 16 states imposed a blanket lifetime ban on receipt of welfare benefits for women convicted of drug offenses.[5]

Several members of Congress have tried to repeal the ban in the context of the reauthorization of PWRORA. Since 2002, the House of Representatives and Senate have attempted to reconcile their respective welfare reform bills, but have been unable to reach an agreement. At the time of writing, Congress had passed its tenth extension of time for PWRORA, allowing other matters such as tax cuts and the war in Iraq to take precedence over women's social and economic needs. The fate of the ban, and the women impacted by it, continue to hang in the balance.

1998 Amendment to the Higher Education Act of 1965 [6]

Another federally mandated post-conviction penalty is enshrined in the 1998

Amendment to the Higher Education Act of 1965, which suspends eligibility, in some cases for life, for federal postsecondary financial aid—grants, loans, or work assistance—for women convicted of a drug-related misdemeanor or felony offense while attending a postsecondary institution.[7] Under the act, a young woman in college convicted of possession of a controlled substance will face a one-year suspension of federal aid following the first offense, a two-year suspension for the second offense, and a lifetime ban for a third offense.[8] Students for Sensible Drug Policy estimates that the law affects more than 175,000 students.

There are four distinguishing features to the education ban. First, unlike the lifetime welfare ban, states cannot modify or opt out of this federal law. Second, the education ban applies to both felony and misdemeanor drug offenses. Third, there is not an immediate lifetime ban after the first drug conviction. Finally, under the education ban, eligibility may be restored provided the university student satisfactorily completes a drug rehabilitation program. Unfortunately, eligibility requirements for public entitlements that are contingent on drug treatment remain problematic, given that not all women convicted of drug offenses are in need of such treatment. In addition, there are insufficient drug treatment slots available for low-income women, and particularly for mothers with children.

1996 Public Housing Ban: "One Strike and You're Out"[9]

In 1996, the federal government implemented the "One Strike and You're Out" policy, authorizing local public housing authorities (PHAs) to deny admission to or evict tenants from subsidized housing—public housing, Section 8 voucher programs, and project-based Section 8 housing—based on a felony or misdemeanor conviction, including those based on drug-related offenses. Unlike the education and welfare bans, suspicion of illegal activity can suffice to meet eviction or inadmissibility criteria. PHAs are authorized to conduct criminal background checks on adult applicants before approving their applications. PHAs can also evict entire families when one member of the family unit, or even a guest of a family member, is believed to have engaged in criminal activity, regardless of whether the person has actually been arrested or convicted of such activity. As with the education ban, a public housing tenant or applicant who satisfactorily completes a drug rehabilitation program may restore her eligibility. However, a woman's inadmissibility to, or eviction from, public housing could effectively constitute a lifetime ban given the serious shortage of public housing and resultant extremely long waiting lists.

Typically, PHAs exclude people convicted of any type of felony offense for a period of five years. Human Rights Watch estimates that at least 3.5 million men and women are currently ineligible for public housing because of the "One Strike" policy.[10] This constitutes an extremely conservative estimate as it does not include people convicted of misdemeanor offenses, or those excluded on mere suspicion of involvement in illegal activities.

In 2002, the United States Supreme Court heard the case of *Department of Housing and Urban Development v. Rucker*,[11] deciding the issue of whether, under the "One Strike and You're Out" policy, the Oakland Housing Authority (OHA) was authorized to evict a grandmother whose grandson was believed by OHA to be engaged in drug-related activity near or on the grounds of their housing complex. The court ruled that the law's "plain language unambiguously requires lease terms that give local public housing authorities the discretion to terminate the lease of a tenant when a member of the household or a guest engages in drug-related activity, regardless of whether the tenant knew, or should have known, of the drug-related activity."[12] In light of the court's expansive interpretation of the policy, renewed efforts to convince Congress to repeal or modify the law, or pressure the Department of Housing and Urban Development (HUD) and PHAs to limit its application, are clearly necessary.

Impact of Post-Conviction Penalties on Women of Color

Low-income women, and particularly low-income Native American women, Latinas, and African American women caught in the web of the prison-industrial complex, face incredible odds when attempting to become self-sufficient upon release from prison. As a result of race and gender-based socioeconomic inequities, Native American and African American women and Latinas are highly susceptible to poverty both before and after prison. In order to permanently escape the prison-industrial complex, low-income women need access to antipoverty tools: education, housing, jobs paying a living wage or temporary financial assistance, and child care. A disproportionate number of low-income and poor women, and especially low-income women of color, who come in contact with the prison-industrial complex did not have access to these antipoverty tools before their arrests, and in many cases this led to a lack of economic agency "compelling them to crime" in order to survive, and inhibiting their exercise of self-determination.[13]

Of women in state prisons in 1997,[14] African American and Latina women were twice as likely as white women to not have graduated from high school or received a GED. 36% of African American women and 31% of Latinas in state prison were welfare recipients prior to their arrest, compared to 20% of white women. Over 50% of Latinas and 49% of African American women in state prisons had incomes under six hundred dollars per month prior to their arrests, while only 39% of white women had similar incomes. Raced and gendered barriers to employment, which are further exacerbated by criminal convictions, also disproportionately affect women of color, increasing the likelihood of being underemployed or unemployed. In 1997, 65% of white men, 48% of African American men, and 57% of Latinos were employed full-time in the month prior to their arrests compared to 47% of white women, 36% of African American women and 30% of Latinas.[15] (Unfortunately, more recent statistics are not currently available—these are from a national BJS survey conducted every five to seven years.)

Without support to complete high school and postsecondary education, many women, and especially African American women and Latinas, are likely to continue to experience extreme poverty upon returning to their communities following incarceration. The ban on receipt of educational supports imposed on women convicted of drug-related offenses is likely to further inflict socioeconomic harm on women attempting to reintegrate into their communities by inhibiting their ability to attain economic agency through educational advancement. As African American women and Latinas are most likely to be convicted of drug offenses, and, due to the economic impact of systemic discrimination, most in need of financial support to get a college degree, the education ban disproportionately affects them. Limited educational attainment reduces their likelihood of finding full employment with living wages which would enable them to eventually reach self-sufficiency.

Many women unable to find work paying a living wage after a criminal conviction are likely to face a life sentence of poverty and hardship. The lifetime welfare ban essentially removes women's last hope for a second chance, and limits their ability to effectively reintegrate into their communities and, in some cases, provide for their children upon release from prison. Moreover, many residential treatment programs rely on women's welfare benefits to cover the cost of their stay. As a result, for many women, reentry options are limited to returning to or getting involved in abusive relationships. Others are often once again "compelled to crime"—the drug trade, prostitution, and property offenses.

One of the most important factors enabling women to move out of poverty and reach self-sufficiency is having a safe place to call home. The "One Strike" policy threatens this important building block, undermining women's ability to escape the prison-industrial complex. For women living in public housing at the time of their conviction, the "One Strike" policy increases the possibility of eviction, while for those seeking public housing upon release, their chances of obtaining such housing may be diminished, depending on the manner in which PHAs enforce the policy. Many women released from prison turn to relatives and friends for help upon release. As a disproportionate number of incarcerated women come from low-income communities of color, there is a strong possibility that their friends and relatives live in public housing, thus closing off this avenue of housing support.

These post-conviction penalties mean that many women return to their communities after prison destitute, potentially exposing them to further harmful social and economic conditions, including those likely to facilitate violence against them. Moreover, such economic violence is not limited to formerly incarcerated women. Women with criminal convictions represent only one of the many groups deemed "undeserving" of state support. The state justifies its economic violence against women in the name of cutting government spending to reduce the deficit, while simultaneously increasing spending and reducing revenues in order to advance other agendas.

"To Spend or Not to Spend?" Is Not the Question

Many of the most critical entitlement programs for low-income women, and particularly formerly incarcerated women, are consistently on the chopping block in the name of deficit reduction. For instance, proposed cuts to student loan programs contained in the 2006 House and Senate Budget Resolutions send a clear message about the likelihood of repealing the ban on receipt of educational assistance for women convicted of drug-related offenses. For formerly incarcerated mothers fortunate enough to find employment after their release, proposed cuts to child care represent a stark reality: their chances of receiving child care subsidies will be diminished and the quality of care they can afford may be questionable, thereby affecting their ability to keep their jobs or pursue employment.

With respect to welfare benefits, the Bush administration's plan proposed to tighten eligibility criteria for cash assistance, and to cut $57 million in 2006 and $507 million over a five-year period. The Center for Budget and Policy Priorities estimates that this cut will result in denial of benefits to between two hundred thousand and three hundred thousand people.[16] In this slash-and-burn political climate, it would be quite difficult to convince the administration to repeal the lifetime welfare ban, which could limit the cash assistance eligibility of at least one hundred thousand women convicted of drug offenses. The "One Strike" policy is also unlikely to be repealed given the current shortage of public housing, and the obvious commitment of the Administration to limiting its investment in housing maintenance and development.

Yet, even as the US government passes budget-trimming legislation, including laws imposing post-conviction penalties which have the effect of further limiting women's access to socioeconomic entitlements, it allows for increased expenditures in other areas and cuts to revenue-generating programs. For instance, tax cuts are likely to continue over the next five years—the House and Senate recommend $106 billion and $129 billion, respectively, in tax cuts over this time frame.[17] "Data from the Urban Institute-Brookings Tax Policy Center show that more than half of the benefits from extending these tax cuts will go to taxpayers with incomes over $500,000. About three-quarters of the benefits would go to taxpayers with incomes over $200,000."[18]

Formerly incarcerated women who are denied entitlements as a result of either post-conviction penalties or cuts to essential government programs to subsidize tax cuts for the wealthy are being forced through government spending patterns to turn to faith-based initiatives to meet their economic needs. The administration has committed billions of dollars in social service grants and contracts to faith-based organizations, and has asked Congress to codify this initiative into law.[19] A reentry grant application from the Florida Department of Corrections (FLDOC) illustrates the prominent role that faith-based organizations will play in the Bush administration's reentry initiatives: "[f]aith-based providers will provide housing as well as the majority of services."[20] It is clear from the proposal that faith-based organizations will act as the conduit through which the state will dole out what limited resources it is willing to make available to formerly incarcerated women. Such faith-based initiatives not only inhibit women's self-determination, they will likely also lead to denial of access to benefits altogether for many women, including lesbian, bisexual, and transgender women, as well as Muslim and other non-Christian women.

In addition to shifting spending from entitlement programs to faith-based initiatives, the Bush administration is also shifting funding from economic entitlements to marriage promotion programs.[21] The "administration has proposed to spend up to several hundred million dollars a year for the next five years on marriage, fatherhood and sexual-abstinence initiatives."[22] These funds are aimed at supporting initiatives like the Oklahoma Marriage Initiative, begun in 2001, which provides workshops to high school students on dating, maintaining relationships, and getting married, as well as marriage-skills classes for adults. More recently, this initiative has been expanded to Oklahoma prisons. "1,364 people like preachers and county agricultural extension agents have had training to teach marriage-skills classes...[a]nd 1,447 of the state's religious leaders have signed a covenant that commits them to encourage premarital counseling."[23] Such spending priorities not only clearly undermine women's economic self-sufficiency and self-determination, they also cement trends away from social and economic entitlements toward benefits conditioned on compliance with moral codes.

Conclusion

The criminalization of women's acts of survival, combined with the imposition of an ever-growing number of post-conviction penalties, enables the state to slash entitlement program spending and allocate funds to war efforts and tax cuts for the wealthy few. Additionally, formerly incarcerated women, along with low-income and poor women, are being driven into faith-based programs designed to force them to conform to the socially "acceptable" roles of "wife" and "virgin" in order to meet basic needs. While dire, these conditions present opportunities for coalitions to form around criminal justice reform or abolition. Additionally, economic justice movements should mobilize to resist economic violence against women of color, and fight for social, economic, and criminal justice policies which promote self-sufficiency and self-determination.

19

Pomo Woman, Ex-Prisoner, Speaks Out

Stormy Ogden

I am a recognized member of the Tule River Yokuts, Kashaya Pomo, and Lake County Pomo Nations, and a former prisoner. I was housed at the California Rehabilitation Center (CRC) located in Riverside County, in Norco. While imprisoned, I was influential in forming the prison's first American Indian women's support group and in having the first women's sweat lodge built at a state prison in California. Since my release, I have allied myself with many American Indian support groups. My focus and commitment has always been to include support for American Indian women imprisoned within the "white man's" criminal justice system.

In the past, when I have been a conference participant where the focus was on women or people of color, the lack of representation by tribal people of this land amazed me. I often wonder, where are the Indian people? Where are our tribal people? Why are they not here speaking? Over the years I have come to realize that the reason is because Indian people are continuously overlooked and forgotten. Let me remind all of you to remember where you are and remember whose tribal lands you walk upon; remember us when you begin the planning of your conferences, and remember to show respect to the land and to the people of these lands. Our voices are strong and they must be heard.

This essay focuses on American Indian women within the prison system. I will draw on my experiences while I was housed at CRC as prisoner W-20170/OTHER, and from the activist work I have been part of since my release.

Like the military industrial complex, the prison industrial complex is an interweaving of private business and government interests. It holds a twofold purpose, which can only be described as profit and social control. Like any industry, the prison economy needs raw materials. In this case, the raw materials are people/prisoners. The one thing that prisons do—and does well—is punish prisoners. Prisons strip prisoners of their dignity, their health, and whatever self-esteem they once had. Prisons also punish the children and families of prisoners. Regarding American Indians, the tribes are also punished.

Indian tribes traditionally had strict codes of conduct that were adhered to by their members, so there was seldom a need for sanctions to be placed against them for misconduct. In Indian societies, rules, laws, and ritualized observances associated with such laws were imbedded in the memories of the people. As noted by Sidney Harring in his book *Crow Dog's Case.* "The Indian tribes had their own laws, which evolved through generations of living together. This legal tradition is very rich, reflecting the great diversity of the Indian peoples in North America" (Harring, 1994).

But in some tribes these traditional rules and conduct are no longer part of our lives. The most brutal methods of social control are directed at a society's most oppressed groups; in this case, the ones that are most likely sent to jail (and prison) are the poor and/or women of color. In North America, Indians are overrepresented in the criminal justice system. On any given day, one in twenty-five American Indians is under the jurisdiction of the criminal justice system, a rate 2.4 times that of whites. Just as alcoholism has touched the life of every Indian person, so has the American criminal justice system, in particular the prison system. According to Native sociologist Luana Ross, "It is common for Native people either to have been incarcerated or to have relatives who have been imprisoned. Because we are a colonized people, the experiences of imprisonment are exceedingly familiar" (Ross, 1998).

Since the beginning of colonization, the people of these lands were imprisoned as a form of social control, which can only be described as deliberate genocide against the Indian people. As stated in Ross's book *Inventing the Savage*, "From the onset of colonization by the European powers Indian people have been imprisoned in many different ways. They were confined in military forts, reservations, boarding schools, orphanages, jails, mental hospitals, and prisons" (Ross, 1998). I will briefly examine two of these systems of control that were used against the American Indian people.

The Boarding School System

In 1878, the federal government established the first boarding school in Carlisle, Pennsylvania. Over the years, the Bureau of Indian Affairs (BIA) founded other such schools. From 1870 through 1929, the federal courts forcibly removed Indian children from their reservation lands and shipped them to boarding schools. The late Little Rock Reed, activist and former prisoner, explained that Americanization was the main goal of the federal government. He argued that , "'Americanization' of the Indian children was…most effective if they were removed from all tribal influence" (Reed, 1993).

Absolutely everything that was even remotely identifiable as being Indian was prohibited at the boarding schools. Upon entering these foreign institutions, Indian children were relieved of their personal effects, stripped of their tribal clothing, bathed in front of unfamiliar people, scrubbed down with harsh lye soap, and then issued standardized uniforms. To make matters worse, as if that was possible, their hair was cut off, their Indian names were exchanged for "proper" Christian names, they were forbidden from having any contact with their families, and their Native languages and religions were forbidden. These children were stripped of their traditional ways. As quoted from a boarding school survivor in Little Rock Reed's book, *The American Indian in the White Man's Prisons*: "They stripped us of our language, they stripped us of our religious beliefs, and they stripped us of our family life, our family values. They stripped us from our culture." (Reed, 1993).

Even as late as the 1970s, horror stories still emerged from boarding schools survivors. In their book, *On the Road to Wounded Knee*, Burnette and Koster reported that at Intermountian Boarding School near Brigham City, Utah, children were given Thorazine. The authors stated that the "boarding school authorities maintain that Thorazine is used only when the student is a danger to himself, usually because of drunkenness." (Reed, 1993).

From 1769 through 1823, twenty-one Spanish missions were established in Alta, California. These Spanish outposts were authoritarian institutions. Once inside the mission system the neophytes, as the Indian converts were called, were not free to leave. The conditions in which these Native people forcibly lived can only be compared to a prison. According to Native scholar Rupert Costo, "they were incarcerated in unhealthy and crowded mission barracks," (Costo, 1995) and whipping with a barbed lash was customary in case of failure to observe the rules. The Spanish, and later the Mexicans, used solitary confinement and mutilation for violation of rules. California Indians comprised the vast majority of the labor work force in the missions. Constantly under the absolute control of the Franciscans and soldiers, the Indians were forced to observe a rigid discipline—which was composed of intensive labor and a regimented personal life including dress, marriage, and social and family contacts.

The Prison System

The prison environment is not too different than boarding schools and the mission system established early on in California. When people first enter prison, they are stripped of their identity. Their names are replaced with numbers; they must give up their street clothes for state-issued uniforms; the inmate is showered, deloused, and searched for any type of contraband, which usually means a cavity search. To the humiliation of the inmate, prison personnel conducts these searches in front of male and female correctional officers. In addition to the dehumanizing searches, it is now reported in local Bay Area newspapers that the California Department of Corrections enforces the cutting of men's hair, even though some American Indian men wear their hair long, in observance of their religions and sense of cultural pride.

"To add insult to injury, tribal law has been decentered/replaced/undermined by the prison industrial complex." Long before non-Indians came to these lands, Indian tribes had their own systems of criminal justice. Using oral tradition, Native people passed rules and laws from generation to generation. The laws became customs, and as customs they were ingrained in the very lifeblood of the people.

Until 1855, while enforcing removal from lands and other violences on Indian people, the federal government did not interfere with traditional tribal systems. But in 1855, Congress passed the Major Crimes Act (MCA), which infringed on the tribe's traditional powers to punish its own members for crime. Congress rejected the application of tribal sovereignty to reservation Indians and imposed a policy of forced assimilation, backed by the extension of federal law to tribal Indians for serious offenses under this act. This authorized federal officials to prosecute reservation Indians who committed felony offenses, which in turn, has diminished tribal sovereignty.

In the 1930s, the BIA passed a law called the Indian Offenses Act. In short, this law prohibited the practices of Indian religions. English names were assigned to replace Indian names, and the federal government forbade Indian hairstyles under the penalty of criminal law. According to Reed, "Those Indians who resisted this colonial rule were labeled as 'hostile' and were subjected to arbitrary criminal punishment...[m]ass arrests of 'hostile' leaders were ordered and many served lengthy sentences at the US prison at Alcatraz and elsewhere" (Reed, 1993).

Because of the infringements on tribal law and inconsistencies from state to state, the American criminal justice system in Indian Country is highly complex and difficult to understand, let alone explain. Its governing principles are contained in hundreds of statutes and court decisions that have been issued during the past two hundred years. Consequently, Federal Indian law is just a continuation of colonialism. When Indians are charged with serious criminal offenses involving the prospect of imprisonment or the imposition of a death sentence, they usually find themselves within the federal criminal system or a state criminal justice system. And because of federal criminal jurisdiction over Indian lands, Indian offenders are often incarcerated mainly in federal prisons instead of state or local facilities.

Presently, prisons are populated by Indians and Alaska Natives who have been convicted in the white man's courts for a variety of offenses, including hunting, fishing, and subsistence gathering in accordance with their customs. These laws violate the treaties and aboriginal rights. Furthermore, some Indians have been targeted and sent to prison because of their political activism.

My Experiences in Prison

Based on my experiences, I know that a major problem for all female prisoners is accessing reliable health care. Many are afraid that incompetent medical attention, more than illness, will lead to death. Nevertheless, many walk around like zombies from all the "medication"; high dosages of Thorazine are given to "calm us down." Most of the women I knew in county jail and prison were medicated. Some prison staff may believe that women are more vulnerable to emotional upsets and are in need of medical treatment, but the stark reality of psychiatry in prison is that it has everything to do with control and management, and nothing to do with effective treatment or healing.

For example, during my time in county jail, before I was sentenced, the doctor prescribed 100 mg of Elavil (an antidepressant) twice daily and 100 mg of Meleril (an antipsychotic) three times daily for me. These pharmaceuticals made me sleep most of the day and night; I would wake only to go to chow hall and to take a shower. Undoubtedly, this kind of treatment made things easier on the staff, as the conditions for the prisoners were terrible. Since this was county jail we never were allowed any yard time, and the only daylight we saw was when we were being transported back and forth to court. I received these medicines for the entire nine months that I was incarcerated, and by the time I left for prison the pills had affected my speech—I had a hard time speaking; the thoughts were there but I had a difficult time getting the words out. My mouth and skin were dry and I was weak from constant sleep.

Immediately after I was sentenced to five years at the California Institution for Women (CIW), I returned to the county jail and I was given a med packet with a small pill inside. "What is this for?" I asked the guard as she locked my cell door. She replied, "It came from the doctor this morning when he found out that you were being sentenced. Take it Stormy; it's just to calm you down." The next thing I remember was my cellee shaking me as I was sitting on the floor watching my cigarette burn a hole into my nightgown. She said, "What did they give you Storm?" "I am not sure what it was," I said to her with slurred speech. "All I know is that it was small." "Must have been Thorazine," was her reply. "The doctor gives that to all of us women, especially the sisters that get sentenced to prison." When I finally arrived at the prison, Thorazine and chlorohydate were given to me interchangeably for two weeks at a time, and I became one of the "walking zombies." As I talked with other Indian women, I discovered that many of them were also given high doses of these "medications."

These abuses make us afraid to seek out the kind of supports that might help us. For example, my younger sister is incarcerated in Stockton, California at Northern California Women's Facility. She writes of her fear of going to counseling, even though she knows that she needs it because she does not want to be a zombie, especially when her kids come to see her.

Most American Indian prisoners are incarcerated because of alcoholism-related problems. Other factors related to high rates of incarceration for American Indians include inadequate legal representation, racism, poverty, and the mounting social and cultural stresses that result in the living of two worlds. In these conditions, without cultural or psychological relief, incarceration leads to anger, rage, and bitterness for many American Indian prisoners.

Conclusion

According to Amnesty International, there are more than 190,000 women in prisons and jails in the US—this number represents an increase of more than 100% since 2001. An African American woman is eight times more likely than a white woman is to be imprisoned, and Latinas experience nearly four times the rates of incarceration. (Amnesty International, 2006). And, according to the Prison Activist Resource Center article "Women in Prison," California has the distinction of having the most women prisoners in the nation, as well as the world's largest women's prison.

But recent information on American Indian women in prison is nonexistent. To quote American Indian activist Little Rock Reed, "The American Indian segment of the population of people…is the forgotten segment; the segment that is so small compared to other racial and ethnic groups warehoused in America's prison that it is [deemed] insignificant" (Reed, 1993). One reason we are not represented is because of the classification system that exists in the majority of the prisons: prisoners are *still* classified as white, Black, Hispanic, or other. I found that not much has changed since I was in prison.

I tried to fight this racist classification system while I was incarcerated. Located outside the door to my prison cell was a small white index card that listed my last name, Ogden, my state number, W-20170, and my ethnic classification, Other. Every morning as I left for my state job, I would erase the word "Other" and replace it with "AI" for American Indian. And each afternoon when I returned from count, the AI was replaced with Other. This continued for close to a week before the commanding officer approached me and said, "Next time, Ogden, you will receive a write-up and it could cost you sixty days of good time." The next morning in bold black letters was the word "OTHER." That morning I was late for my job. It took me some time to track down a black laundry marker. I removed the card from the wall and in its place wrote "AMERICAN INDIAN." Did I get a write-up and lose sixty days? Yes. But it was well worth it.

Despite the resistance to acknowledging our presence within the prison industrial complex, one agency—the Department of Justice (DOJ)—does keep track of our numbers. In February 1999, the DOJ estimated that 1,244,555 American Indians are in state or federal prisons. (These numbers are probably not accurate since so many American Indians are routinely misidentified and are classified as "other" in prison records). Also, American Indians caught up in the criminal justice system are much more likely than other populations to be in prison or jail (instead of on parole or probation); about half of American Indians in the criminal justice system are in prison while only one-third of the general population in the criminal justice system are in prison or jail (Greenfield and Smith, 1999).

But the numbers only tell part of the story. These incarcerated American Indians represent important human and cultural resources to their tribes and families. When they are released, it is important to the cultural survival of Indian Nations and Native communities that the returning offenders be contributing, culturally viable members, rather than further alienated by their experiences in the white man's prison. Therefore, virtually every American Indian and Indian Nation is directly and vitally impacted by prison policies, which affects the rights, rehabilitation, and well-being of these people.

The outcome of this high rate of imprisonment can only be described as genocidal. The Native world has been devastated by foreign laws that were forced upon us, and the number of jailed Natives is a chilling reminder of this fact. Native people are being locked up at alarming numbers in their own ancestral homeland. For the indigenous women of North America, sexual assault and imprisonment are two interlocking violent colonial mechanisms, the criminalization and imprisonment of Native women can be interpreted as yet another attempt to control indigenous lands and as part of the ongoing effort to dent Native sovereignty.

> What was my crime? Why did I do 5 years in state prison?
> Less than $200 in welfare fraud.
> My crime?
> Being addicted to alcohol and drugs.
> My crime?
> Being a survivor of domestic violence.
> My crime?
> Being a survivor of incest, the first time at the age of 5.
> My crime?
> Being an American Indian woman.
>   —Stormy Odgen

20

The War Against Black Women, and the Making of *NO!*

Aishah Simmons

I am a Black[1] woman who is a survivor of incest and rape. I write this because there are too many Black women who are unable to write, much less speak, these words. I write this because I do not want to be ashamed that my body was violated against my will on several occasions. I write this because victims and survivors of rape and other forms of sexual violence shouldn't ever have to carry the burden of shame and guilt. I write this with the hope and the belief that by breaking my silence, more and more Black women will break their silences about the atrocities that have been forced on them.

There is a silent war going on in the Black community. This war is being waged by Black men and boys on Black women and girls, and it takes the form of the rape and sexual assault of Black women and girls. Up until recently, this war had not been publicly acknowledged by the Black community, because it wasn't viewed as important. During the Mike Tyson rape trial in 1992, I watched and listened to many "so-called" Black male leaders—the same ones who defended Tawana Brawley, when she alleged that she had been raped and sodomized by four white men in 1989—accuse Desiree Washington of betraying the Black community. Then I began thinking about intraracial violence in the African American community.

At this time, I was fortunate and blessed to have Toni Cade Bambara,[2] an award-winning Black feminist writer, filmmaker, teacher, activist, and visionary, in my life as my teacher and as my older sistah-friend. Toni consistently challenged me and so many other aspiring cultural workers to create work that makes revolutionary social change irresistible. Largely as a result of her guidance and tutelage, my appreciation of the critical need to shed light on controversial and ignored subjects within Black communities has deepened profoundly.

Through Toni, the camera lens became my activist tool to make visible that which has been invisible for too long. In 1994, while working at a full time "day" job, I received a psychic, spiritual, emotional, psychological, and physical "calling" by my blood and spirit ancestors to embark on a project, which has since evolved into *NO!: The Rape Documentary*, a feature-length documentary which unveils the realities of rape, other forms of sexual violence, *and* healing in African-American communities. In one of the last scriptwriting courses I took with her at Scribe Video Center[3] in Philadelphia, PA, Toni created a space in which I was challenged to write "A State of Rage," a choreopoem which has served as the road map to *NO!*. At that time, in 1994, I had no idea that following that road map would be one of the most challenging experiences I would have, or that it would span eleven years. All I knew was that, in spite of all of the obstacles constantly thrown in my path, I had to answer this "calling."

In the extremely initial stages of this journey, I was fortunate enough to find another extraordinary woman who enabled this project. My sistah-survivor-cultural worker, Tamara L. Xavier, a Haitian-American feminist choreographer, dancer, scholar, and activist expressed an interest in "helping" me with *NO!*. Tamara's "helping" me has evolved into her becoming a co-producer and the director of choreography for *NO!*. Many women can't talk about their experiences of rape at all—much less in front of a camera—but many have written performance poetry, and choreographed movements about them. Tamara has taught me the importance of movement as a way to express oneself and to communicate effectively about the trauma of rape, incest and sexual assault. More importantly, she has shown me how dance and movement can aid in the spiritual and physical healing and transformation so necessary for the rape, incest and sexual assault victim-survivor to heal from trauma. I credit Tamara with the incorporation of dance into *NO!*. Through Tamara, I learned that movement and other artistic expressions are just as effective as speech, perhaps more so, in conveying the horror of being raped. Dance can also serve as a metaphor of the healing process as Black women move through the trauma of sexual violence and find wholeness and wellness of body, mind, and spirit.

The Vision

Rape and sexual assault are taboo subjects in every community. As a result of the impact of racism on the lives of Black people in the United States, many Black men and women think that exposing and addressing intra-racial sexual violence against Black women divides the Black community, and that we should only work to expose and address racism since that is the "real" problem facing our community. Additionally, American society frames the Black identity as male and the category woman as white—as in the expression "Blacks and women" implying that these categories are mutually exclusive. As a consequence, Black women are made invisible.[4] In *NO!*, Black identity is defined as woman, woman identity is defined as Black, and rape and sexual assault are central.

What does it look like to visually make central that which has been placed on the margins and on the periphery? Beginning with the enslavement of African people in the United States right up until present day, *NO!* moves from rage/trauma/emotional and physical pain to meditation to action to healing where the consciousness of the featured women, who have been raped or sexually assaulted, transforms from victim to survivor to educator, activist, and healer.

In *NO!*, I feminize Black history while simultaneously addressing the rape and sexual assault of Black women and girls. I consciously use the first-person testimonies of Black women victim-survivors, who range in age, geographic location, and sexual orientation. I integrate their experiences with commentary, scholarship, and artistic performances. Because I understand that violence against women will end when all men, regardless of race, culture, ethnicity, religion, age, sexual orientation, class, and/or physical ability, make ending this international atrocity a priority in their lives, the commentary and performance of five Black men activists and cultural workers addressing intra-racial rape and sexual assault in the African-

American community and by extension the larger American community are also integrated with the Black women's voices[5].

The reason I consciously use the voices of Black women scholar-activists as experts who both expose and address the issue of intra-racial rape and sexual assault in the Black community is because in the United States (and I would argue the entire 'Western' world) Black women are not viewed as experts. How often do viewers have the opportunities to see and hear Black women's perspectives as the authoritative voice on celluloid? Since *NO!*'s inception, making Black women's voices and experiences central—not on the sidelines, not on the periphery, but in the center of the work without any excuses or apologies, has always been a part of the vision of the documentary.

Additionally, *NO!* addresses the classist notion that rape, sexual assault and other forms of gender-based violence are only perpetrated at the hands of working class Black men who live in the "hood" or in the "ghetto." The majority of the victim-survivor testimonies featured in *NO!* challenge the classist stereotype that Black men with academic degrees, high profiles, and/or men who are on the front lines fighting for racial liberation are incapable of being sexist, misogynist, and/or rapists.

NO! also takes on the notion that, as freedom fighters, Black women must "choose" between race and gender. Gwendolyn Zoharah Simmons—PhD,[6] former SNCC (Student Non-Violent Coordinating Committee) organizer, Islamic scholar, and my mother—speaks in *NO!* about how Black women knew—and spoke amongst themselves—about rape and sexual assault within the Civil Rights Movement. However, at that time (for many of them felt that the principal issue was racism), rape, sexual assault, and sexual harassment were considered minor problems in comparison to the State-sanctioned racial violence that countless Black people across the United States were experiencing. But in 1964, my mother, one of the anonymous heroines in SNCC, became the Director of a COFO (Council of Federated Organizations)[7] project in Laurel, Mississippi. And during this time, based on what she both experienced and witnessed, she created a sexual harassment policy to protect the women volunteers on the project—one of the first policies ever established within SNCC. As a result, she gained the reputation of being an "Amazon," which meant "Gwen didn't take any shit from men." The Laurel project also became known as the "Amazon project," and as a result many men refused to work there.

NO! takes on the critical task of publicly uncovering Black women's herstories through testimonies of women such as my mother and sistah Elaine Brown, the only woman to lead the Black Panther Party. In her *NO!* interview, sistah Elaine also talks about the sexual violence she witnessed during the time of the Black Panthers. Too often in the United States, when we think about the Civil Rights movement or the Black Panther Party, we don't think about the countless Black women who were on the front lines of these revolutionary struggles. We forget that women were faced with death threats by the white establishment while simultaneously having to live with threats of rape and sexual assault by their Black male comrades. We do not consider how ironic, and how painful, it was for our mothers and sistahs to have to resist sexual assault and harassment by Black male comrades while having to fight with them against racial injustice, under the threat of death.

The Making of *NO!*

I may be the backbone of *NO!*, however the making of *NO!* has been a collaborative effort on the part of many women and some men behind the camera,[8] and men and women in front of the camera. Too often, documentaries are made by people who are not a part of the community they are documenting. Unfortunately in some instances, this has resulted in a distorted view of the documented communities. I believe it was important that the women behind the *NO!* camera were representative of the women featured in front of the *NO!* camera.

Since its very beginning in 1994, the creative production and advisory team has been inclusive of lesbians, young and older women, most of whom are of African descent. This conscious configuration of the production and advisory team resulted in my creating women only production sets, where the featured survivors felt safe to publicly disclose and psychically revisit, on camera, the horror, trauma, and victimization that they experienced during their rapes and sexual assaults. The filmmaking dynamic was a predominantly Black feminist space where everyone's voice and perspective was heard. As the director, I interviewed all of the survivors, scholars, and activists. However, after my interviews, there was always an opportunity for all members of the production and advisory team to ask follow up questions of all of the interviewees. I believe this Black feminist process of valuing everyone's perspective, regardless of their title, changed the dynamic of filmmaking, which is historically a 'top-down' process. This process also strengthened *NO!* because the production and advisory team helped me to take the documentary to a level that I wouldn't have been able to without the collective expertise of the team. It has been an absolute honor and a privilege to work with some of the most talented, technically proficient, intellectually sound, fiercely dedicated and committed women that I know.

In the beginning of my journey through the making of *NO!* very few people wanted to touch the documentary with a ten-mile pole. After all, African American (as well as Native American, Latina, Arab American, Asian American, and Pacific Islander) women are not valued in America (and in most parts of the world)—to quote Elaine Brown, the feeling is "what difference does it make? It's only some Black woman [who's been raped]." As a result, the number one obstacle in making of the documentary was funding. And unlike many other art forms, filmmaking can be very expensive. This has to do with the fact that more often than not, it's a collaborative undertaking, which means that director and producer are not only responsible for their expenses, they're also responsible for the salaries and expenses of the members of the production team. While it is very true that the digital video revolution has reduced the costs of resources needed to make a documentary, filmmaking is still an expensive collaborative art form.

Major progressive and mainstream foundations and funds, as well as major cable networks, consistently said "No" to funding the making of *NO!*. Some of the verbal and written responses I've received to funding requests include:

- "Why are you *only* focusing on the rape of Black women?"
- "Strong point of view and the concept is good; however, the example of Mike Tyson's case and the indifference from the [Black] community might be due, in part, to the moral point of view that one does not go to a man's room in the early morning; that opinion cannot be ignored."
- "Given that you are a lesbian, what's your axe to grind with making '*NO!?*'"
- "Let's face it, very unfortunately, most people don't care about the rape of Black women and girls, and therefore we're concerned that there won't be many viewers who will tune in to watch *NO!*, we were to air it on our network."

In the face of this racist, sexist and misogynist economic censorship, I developed an international grassroots Black feminist lesbian-led educational fundraising campaign that would raise awareness about intra-racial rape and sexual assault in African American communities while raising funds for the making of *NO!*. Through this network, I had the opportunity to speak about heterosexual intra-racial rape and sexual assault in African American communities across the United States, as well as throughout Italy, in Toronto, Paris and Marseilles, London and Birmingham, Amsterdam, Budapest, and in Dubrovnik and Stubicke Toplice, Croatia. During this eleven year journey, I have worked full time on *NO!*. for seven years. I also screened various versions, ranging from 8 to 75 minutes, of *NO!: A Work-in-Progress.* There have been audiences as small as two people and as large as five hundred. These events created a space for me to engage in dialogue with diverse audiences and receive feedback about *NO!* years before it was completed.

This enabled me to both resume production and to return to the editing room to aurally and visually address questions and concerns that weren't addressed in the work in progress. Initially *NO!* was going to be a short documentary, which only featured the testimonies of Black women survivors. Men weren't going to be involved and there weren't going to be any scholars or activists featured in the documentary. Based on the questions that I constantly received during the screenings of the work in progress, I realized that I could not address contemporary intra-racial rape and sexual assault in African-American communities without examining Black women's herstory in the United States. This decision resulted in *NO!* becoming a feature-length documentary. These experiences also helped me to understand that it was extremely important to include the perspectives, commentaries, and expertise of scholars, activists, and community leaders to not only contextualize the testimonies of the featured Black women survivors but also to create a historical, political, and cultural framework from which viewers will hopefully challenge their own beliefs about rape and other forms of sexual violence. Equally important, I came to fully understand and appreciate the fact that men can stop heterosexual rape. Therefore, I made the decision to include the activism and cultural work of Black men who are involved in the anti-sexual violence movement in *NO!*.

If one were to view the educational fundraising screenings as "test screenings" to see if a film/documentary works with audiences before it is officially released, I don't know of any film or documentary that has had as many test screenings as *NO!*, prior to its completion. Even in its work-in-progress forms, *NO!* has already been translated into both French and Italian. This translation work was done on a volunteer basis by grassroots European and diasporic African and Arab feminists and/or lesbians, queers, and transgender men based in France and Italy because they wanted *NO!* to be accessible to European-based women and men who did not speak English. In many instances, these people used their vacation time, ranging from a few days to three weeks, to travel with me in their countries and serve as my interpreters, while simultaneously translating the documentary during screenings.

NO! is unique in that it was already doing educational and healing work around sexual violence issues before its completion. To date, at every screening there has been at least one woman or girl who has disclosed to me personally or to the entire viewing audience that she has been raped, battered, sexually assaulted and/or molested.

It was not only my sistahs and their communities who welcomed me who made *NO!* a reality. In January 2003, noted hip-hop historian, author, and political activist Kevin Powell wrote an open letter, via email, to Black men urging them to come together to support *NO!*: *"Given the level of violence against women in this country, we owe it to ourselves and to future generations not to turn our backs on NO!. For in ignoring this documentary we would be once again ignoring the voices of [Black] women."* As a result of this email, a national intergenerational coalition of Black men came together to form "Black Men in Support of the Film *NO!*."[9] In March 2003, this coalition, in conjunction with Hiphop Speaks[10] and the Schomburg Center for Research in Black Culture in New York City, hosted a screening of the seventy-four minute version of *NO!* and a public discussion on intra-racial heterosexual rape and sexual assault in the Black community. The response was overwhelming. When Kevin Powell and I initially envisioned the event, we never in our wildest imaginations thought that it would generate the response it did—from women *and* men. On that cold and rainy/snowy evening, we had to turn away *at least* 200 women and men, many of whom were under the age of 30, who stood in line for at least an hour to attend the screening and public discussion. Even after being told that the auditorium was filled to capacity, many Black women *and* men still hung around in the lobby to see if they could get in for part of the screening and all of the public discussion that followed.

In this day and age of the glorification of sexism, misogyny, homophobia, and a "pimp culture" through mainstream hip-hop, there are many justifiable critiques of the hip-hop generation. However, it was the hip-hop generation that brought *NO!* to Harlem in 2003. Hands down, it was the hip-hop generation who promoted the event through emails, listservs, and print and audio media. It was the hip-hop generation that created the space, in Harlem, for an intergenerational (from as young as seven to over sixty-five years old) male/female dialogue exposing and addressing heterosexual intraracial rape and sexual assault in the non-monolithic Black community in the United States.

My maternal and paternal grandmothers used to always say "Aishah, what doesn't kill you makes you stronger." Through the making of *NO!*, I grew as a grassroots activist because I had to resort to forms of fundraising other than the traditional route. I was able to develop connections and alliances with a diverse group of people based in the United States and internationally who I might not have ever met had I received the funding I needed in one or two major grants.

Equally important, receiving the clinical support of Dr. Clara Whaley-Perkins, a Black feminist clinical psychologist and author, during the making of *NO!* journey has educated me, and this journey has definitely put a healing balm on my incest and rape wounds. Through my self-work and my cinematic activism, I developed much more compassion and empathy for myself as a survivor of incest and rape, and by extension for all women who are survivors, regardless of the circumstances in which their assault(s) occurred.

The Final Cut

As a thirty-seven-year-old woman, I have gained power, strength, and vision from these pioneers—Black women whose writings, activism, and cultural work has preceded and inspired my activist cultural work. Through *NO!*, I am putting on the screen that which has been written in books, journals, magazines, periodicals, notebooks, pieces of paper; talked and whispered about at conferences, in community centers and organizations, in schools, colleges, and universities, in churches, mosques, and temples, in beauty parlors and laundromats.

While *NO!* explores how the collective silence about acts of sexual assault adversely affects African Americans, it also encourages dialogue to bring about healing and reconciliation between all men and women. Because too many women, regardless of differences in national origin, culture, ethnicity, language, religion, race, sexual orientation, age, class, and physical ability experience rape and sexual assault, I believe *NO!* is a documentary that women from across the racial and class spectrum will connect with. This was apparent during the screenings of *NO!: A Work-In-Progress*—at colleges and universities, schools, conferences, film festivals, rape crisis centers, community centers, and correctional facilities, both grassroots- and government-sponsored, in the United States and internationally—that took place over the past eleven years.

While I work hard at not being a conspiracy theorist, it's clear to me that there is a reason why I had to struggle for years to raise funds to make *NO!*. Through all of my extremely diverse screening opportunities, I have come to understand that *NO!* is a powerful activist tool. I believe this is both a testament to the power of African American women's *herstory* and contemporary reality as well as a profound commentary on the unfortunate, sobering reality of the universality of rape and other forms of sexual violence. In all of its forms, *NO!* has required viewers to confront rape and other forms of sexual violence through the testimonies, scholarship, activism, and cultural work of predominantly African American women.

Were it not for the invaluable in-kind institutional support received from Solutions for Progress, a public policy firm founded by Robert J. Brand, as well as the ongoing international financial support[11] received from countless individual women and their grassroots organizations, a growing number of men who oppose violence against women, as well as women's, feminist, and/or lesbian foundations and funds, and community-based foundations and funds, *NO!* would still be an idea in my head as opposed to a completed documentary. Thanks to all of the people who were a part of the making of *NO!*, I believe that once *NO!* is properly distributed, it has the potential to play an integral role in international movements to end all forms of sexual violence against women and girls.

Finally, in response to the charge that Black women who publicly expose intraracial sexual violence in the Black community through the spoken and written word are traitors to the race, I offer the following thoughts. Yes, it is true that Black men in the United States are victims of racism, expressed in the forms of police brutality, racial profiling, incarceration, unemployment, and lack of access to decent education and jobs for which they are qualified, to name just a few. However, Black women not only experience the same harsh realities of racism every day of our lives, we also experience the horrific realities of sexism, misogyny, and patriarchy every day of our lives. In a system governed by racism, patriarchy, and sexism, Black men can be both victim and perpetrator simultaneously.

What I find most interesting is that too many Black men, male-identified Black women, and progressive, antiracist white people, are unable to step outside the awful reality of many Black men's lives to see and hear the physical, emotional, psychological, and psychic pain that Black women experience at both the hands of institutional white racism and at the hands of Black men, who are their fathers, brothers, uncles, cousins, husbands, boyfriends, comrades, and friends. Fortunately, I've never been beaten by the police, and I've never been incarcerated. However, whenever I hear a story about a Black man being beat or murdered by the police or about a Black man unjustly incarcerated, I am not only enraged, I am called to action. There isn't a day that goes by when, on a personal level, I don't worry about whether my brother, my father, my grandfather and my male friends will be unjustly stopped by the police for the crime of being a Black man. In my ongoing conversations with many of my Diasporic African, Arab, South Asian, Latina, Indigenous, feminist/womanist sistah-friends living in the United States, in Canada, and in Europe, I know I'm not alone with these feelings and fears.

And yet, very unfortunately, when it comes to rape, sexual assault, misogyny, sexual harassment, and other forms of violence perpetuated against women of color at the hands of men of color, men of color are too often silent. Instead of taking responsibility, more often than not, men of color want to spend time and energy focusing the blame on women of color for the sexual violence that they experience. These are the usual refrains: "*What were you doing out late at night? Most women say 'No.' when they really mean 'Yes.' You should've been properly dressed. etc.*"

When I was in South Africa in 1994 to monitor the first "free and fair" racial elections, I met with many Black South African women activists. One of these sistah-activists gave me a poster that reads "One of the most violent social settings in South Africa is in the home." In 1994, Black South African women were rejoicing about the end of legal apartheid while expressing serious concern about sexism and misogyny. Today, South Africa has one of the highest rape rates in the world. Black South African men are raping Black South African women. Where is the international outcry against these savage acts as there was against apartheid?

Black South African women, like Black South African men, fought and died for their freedom. And the highest rape rate in the world for women is their reward. Algerian women fought and died along with Algerian men and won the end of French colonization of Algeria in 1962. And in 2006, the forty-fourth anniversary of Algerian Independence from France, Algerian women are fighting and dying for their rights as women in Algeria.

If racism, in all of its violent manifestations, ended right this second, African and African American women, Arab women, Asian women, Pacific Islander women, Latinas, South Asian women, and indigenous women would not be safe. Until African and African American men, Arab men, Asian men, Pacific Islander men, Latinos, South Asian men, and indigenous men take up the issues of rape, sexual assault, misogyny, sexual harassment and other forms of gender based violence that happen every second of every day, with the same vigilance with which racism, xenophobia, colonialism, enslavement, police brutality, state-sanctioned violence, and incarceration are addressed, communities of color will never be whole ... will never be healthy ... will never be safe.

Medical Violence Against People of Color and the Medicalization of Domestic Violence

Ana Clarissa Rojas Durazo

He said, "Do you want to press charges?" He stood tall in front of me, in uniform and with might, and right, on his side. I lay on the hospital bed, recently emerging from a protective unconscious sleep. I wanted it all to go away. The second my head hit the steel door, I remember having a choice to go down, so I took that path. I was unsure of where it would lead, but I knew that's what I had to do. My eyes rolled back, body crumbled before me and everything turned dark. I couldn't take the light of day where the failure of love cuts deeply into already festering wounds. It's like when you're naked in the daylight, it's different, you know? You can't hide anything. This is where the real monsters stand at your feet ready to devour. Monsters don't hide in the light of day.

So I went with it, took to the floor like I was meant for it. It was quiet. All the yelling stopped; the still darkness was like a soft warm blanket. It was a fleeting moment, it passed by quickly, like the flick of hummingbird wings. But you know when something seems to pass in real slow motion and real quick at the same time? I guess that's when fear takes over, or is it wisdom, being so deeply present. I liked it quiet. But slowly the sounds of life came back kind of like at a *feria* or an arcade, intense, loud. I couldn't hear her but I began to make out her head and then the side of her. She stood over me crying, surprised at what she had done. As I held on tightly to the feeling of calm, of quiet and dark, I knew it was time for me to go.

And then she took me to the hospital, found someone with a car and I remember the silence returning. The longest car ride ever. Nobody spoke. Next thing I remember I'm laying on the hospital bed. It's really cold, hospital cold, you know—when they give you those paper thin *batas* to wear? And she was still standing over me, unsure, watching everything. The bright white ominous lights of hospitals glared at me and the ice-cold hospital air ate at my skin.

That's when the cop approached and said "Do you wanna press charges?"

I didn't even know what he meant at first, I literally didn't understand him. I don't know if that was because I had no idea what he was talking about, or if my preoccupation with holding onto the quiet helped me erase everything around me. Or maybe the quiet doesn't want me to get all caught up in those English words. It just didn't register, but somehow, after a moment of silence, I said "no." And then I understood, and I couldn't believe I was supposed to make that kind of a decision. It was as if my "no" followed the cop until he was out of my sight, and I suddenly understood what he was asking, as well as the consequences of saying "no." And everybody knew. The doctors, the nurses, the patients all around, the tall white cop, and she knew. She knew I hadn't pressed charges.

What kind of position is that to put someone in? Like the world needs another reason to hate lesbians? Like I need another reason not to feel welcomed since I came to this country? How did they even know? Who told them? I didn't say anything. And I'm supposed to just say "yes" or "no?" I didn't even wanna come to the hospital. I was just trying to hold on to the quiet, and I didn't think the choice to press charges would help me do that—what kind of choice is that? I was just trying to hold on to the quiet.

February, 2006

Starting in the late 1970s and increasingly thereafter, state funding encouraged a strong, system-based response to domestic violence. This funding brought together the criminal justice system, hospitals, and social service agencies to intervene in domestic violence. Prior to this, some antiviolence laws were on the books, but there was minimal prosecution and limited law enforcement involvement. As the state moved in, the real need for survivor safety came increasingly to be translated into a "need" for prisons and for social services. This logic supported the strategic expansion of the prison industrial complex (PIC), and domestic violence came to be seen as a crime. It also supported the development of the nonprofit industrial complex, as nonprofit agencies were set up and funded by the state to provide counseling and shelter services, with scant funding for social change work. As the criminalization and non-profitization of domestic violence were underway, the medicalization of domestic violence also ensued.

On Medicalization

When institutionalized, "mainstream" or western medicine reconstitutes social problems as "diseases" or individual pathologies in need of medical intervention, we can call this medicalization.[1] Medical intervention is increasingly deemed indispensable in eliminating the epidemic of domestic violence, and the "medical industrial complex" (MIC) is beginning to shape how we think about domestic violence, as well as how we prevent—or intervene and treat—the "disease."[2] Like criminalization, medicalization represents a deep threat to the movement, because it uproots the conceptualization of domestic violence as a social problem. Instead, it replaces the ideology and structures of social movements with the ideology and structures of (western) medicine, subsuming grassroots to state and capital interests.

This is particularly dangerous to women of color and our communities because we have suffered a long and continuing history of (western) medical violence. In fact, the institution of (western) medicine has served the interests of colonial, slavery, capitalist and racist systems by excluding us from needed care, and has administered death, disease, and injury. The medicalization of domestic violence is also structured to be interdependent with the criminalization and non-profitization of domestic violence. For example, as in the opening story, a stop at the hospital can lead to criminal charges—sometimes *without* survivor consent—which potentially enlists processes of incarceration, detention, and deportation.

The object of medical inquiry (disease/illness) is "not necessarily inherent in any behavior or condition, but [it is] constructed."[3] Just as we call into question what, when, and why something is considered a crime, we can also question what, when, and why something becomes a medical issue. Thus, when we reflect and interrogate medicalization, we can critically consider the ways medicine, as a tool of social control, has been extended to more and more aspects of our lives. This extension bears the interests of the MIC—the relationship between medicine, capital, and the state.[4] The structured goals of the medical industrial complex are to heighten profits, legitimate the state, and maintain the dominance of the western medical model, which, in turn, perpetuates racism, classism, and heterosexism. The institution of medicine is organized and structured to reflect and reproduce society's class, racial, and gendered hierarchies, and as it mirrors and purports injustice, it also produces ideology that legitimates it.

For example, the racist and capitalist class structures in medicine are transparent in the maintenance of an elite corporate/upper class which makes health policies and reaps the financial benefits of the "business," while an exploited class is made responsible for low-wage dirty work, including janitorial, nursing assistance, and administrative work. Not surprisingly, class lines in medicine are also racial lines, and people of color are overrepresented in the exploited groups. When we examine the phenomena of medicalization, we see systemic legitimation, or hegemony maintenance, and the efforts of a particular institution (medicine) to maintaining inequality.[5]

Furthermore, the medical gaze transposes a disease model that sets out to deflect attention away from social injustices, while highlighting individual pathology.[6] Social phenomena come to be understood as problems that western medicine can solve; some call this the MIC's habit of turning "badness into sickness."[7] Not coincidentally, medicalization expands during times of social protest. For example, state expenditures on public health usually rise during periods of social protest (as they did in the late 1960s and 1970s), while cutbacks in public health services were instituted in the early 1980's, following a decline in social protest by low-income communities.[8]

Understanding medicalization can help us map out—or prevent—the cooptation of a social movement. So as women of color working against violence, it is imperative that we recognize that reliance on the medical industrial complex is deeply problematic, as its unjust institutional structure, as well as its racist, classist, and sexist interests, always come along with the package. What, then, does the medicalization of domestic violence mean for our safety as women of color, and what does it imply for the movement's goal of eliminating domestic violence?

The Medicalization of Domestic Violence

In the latter part of the twentieth century, increased federal funding was allocated for a strong, system-based domestic violence response in the US. Initially, this funding was geared toward increasing law enforcement response to domestic violence.[9] Criminal justice agencies, medical institutions and social service agencies were enlisted to respond to domestic violence. In 1978, officials from these agencies, along with activists and academics, were invited to participate in the United States Commission on Civil Rights' "Consultation on Battered Women: Issues of Public Policy." This marked a historic first: a state-coordinated assessment of domestic violence. Although mainstream medicine had given some attention to domestic violence before this, and there were laws on the books which deemed it a crime, this new funding—combined with new policies and criminal legislation—jump-started the criminalization, non-profitization and medicalization of domestic violence. Shortly thereafter, the categories "battered spouse" and "battered woman" were added to the international classification of diseases.[10] In the 1980s, the Center for Disease Control (CDC) began funding research on domestic violence, while the American Association of Obstetrics and Gynecology instituted an initiative to educate physicians on domestic violence screening and referral.

In 1992, during his tenure as president of the American Medical Association (AMA), Robert McAfee started the AMA's initiative against family violence. Later that year, the AMA released its "Guidelines for the Screening of Domestic Violence." That same year, the US Surgeon General ranked abuse as the leading cause of injury for women aged 15-44, and the Family Violence Prevention Fund in San Francisco was funded by the Department of Health and Human Services to create the National Health Resource Center, a national clearinghouse to promote medical intervention in domestic violence. Since then, the Family Violence Prevention Fund/National Health Resource Center has played a central role in efforts to medicalize domestic violence within the antiviolence movement. For instance, a 1993 study by the organization found that most battered patients were not identified as such by hospital emergency room staff, and that these staff lacked training in identification or referral procedures. This research study ushered in two policies, enacted first in California then throughout the US, that drastically extended medicalization. In California, health care providers were required to receive training in the detection of domestic violence, and hospitals had to adopt written policy on how to treat battered people. The second law required medical practitioners to report to the police when a patient sustained an injury that was the "result of assaultive or abusive conduct" and/or "the injury is by means of a firearm." Any attending physician who failed to report would face criminal penalties, and the latter policy buttressed the implementation of the former.[11]

Other key events which furthered the medicalization campaign included the annual "Health Cares about Domestic Violence Day," and the manual *Preventing Domestic Violence: Clinical Guidelines on Routine Screening*, sponsored by the American Medical Association (AMA); the American Nursing Association (ANA); and the American College of Physicians (ACP). The Family Violence Prevention Fund/National Health Resource Center coordinated these efforts. The FUND/NHRC also issued the "State-by-State Report Card on Health Care Laws and Domestic Violence," funded by the US Department of Health and Human Services, which shamed states for poor performance in enacting laws that "help doctors and nurses aid victims," and pressured them into crafting policies that medicalized domestic violence.

By the late 1990's, the medical industrial complex had become a crucial site in responding to the domestic violence "epidemic." We were often reminded, in press releases, reports and other propaganda, that "medical practitioners are often the first, and sometimes the only, professionals to whom an abused woman turns for help ..."[12] Interestingly, just as the criminalization of domestic violence directly supported the growth of the prison industrial complex, the medicalization of domestic violence heightened as the corporatization and privatization of health care gained velocity.

Indeed, a shift in the conceptual framework surrounding domestic violence was occurring, as the problem was being publicly recognized as a medical issue. This shift had some problematic underpinnings: the historic and dominant medical understanding of domestic violence had been psychiatric, which maintained that masochism was an integral aspect of female psychology. Consequently, women interpreted the suffering of violence as a sexually gratifying experience. An article in the *Archives of General Psychiatry*, a journal of the American Medical Association, claimed that women have a masochistic need that is fulfilled by their husband's aggression.[13] This psychiatric approach revictimized survivors by asserting that they "provoked" their husband's abusive behavior through, for example, nagging, disagreement, and withholding of sex. It also suggested that we should understand violence as an individual behavior; it was, therefore, decipherable and solvable in the individual. This incomplete psychiatric model provided a logic which bolstered counseling as an essential vaccine against domestic violence, and buttressed the non-profitization of domestic violence while deterring social change work.

Medical Violence Against People of Color

Couched in a deceptive framework of benevolence, (western) medicine is a violent institution that has, in fact, been dangerous to the health and well-being of women of color and women in the Third World since its imposition. This is medicine's double discourse of care: expressed interest in the provision of care, while making people of color sick. Historically, medicine has always worked for the colonial state; for example, institutional practices quelled indigenous resistance by drawing indigenous communities into colonial structures and relationships. Medicine arrived in the Americas, and throughout the world, as an integral arm of European colonial invasion: land grants were given to doctors who settle areas and develop medical institutions. And medical institutions served as sites where indigenous communities were actively subordinated, regulated, tracked, and counted. As Fanon argues in *A Dying Colonialism*, medicine makes colonial interests palatable so that slowly, over time, we are "reduced to saying yes to the innovations of the occupier."[14]

This "provision of care" subjugates women of color and our communities by negating indigenous knowledges of the body, health, and healing and by superimposing western values and colonial racist epistemologies and figures (e.g., the all-knowing patriarchal doctor). Thus, the power of healing is displaced from women and indigenous communities.[15] bell hooks reminds us, "conscious of race, sex, and class issues, I wondered how I would be treated in this white doctor's office. Through it all, he talked to me as if I were a child …"[16]

Medical violence is deployed from etiology (diagnosis, naming of disease and establishment of cause), to prevention (or lack thereof), treatment ("care" potentially injurious or unavailable), and research (treating people of color as guinea pigs).[17] And as discussed earlier, the MIC buttresses racist and colonial state needs by surveilling and reporting on communities, regulating human bodies, and by further dominating the colonized by imposing docility.[18]

The irony is that colonial invasion and war often create "needs" for medical intervention, as was the case with one of the most lethal forms of colonial violence throughout the Americas: the intentional spread of infectious diseases such as tuberculosis, measles and smallpox to indigenous communities.[19] Once this need is bolstered, additional forms of medical violence—such as active exclusion and withholding of treatment—emerge, and become tools of social control; the MIC determines who is treated, who lives, who dies. Even if treatment is provided, violence persists as the delivery of medical "care" is still rife with racism, classism, and sexism, as well as state and colonial interests and structures.[20]

For example, historically the "sick role" has been assigned to marginalized communities in the US, as it implies "deviance" in need of medical intervention. Through medicine, colonial racist archetypes of the "diseased and uncivilized" other were legitimated, and the "other" was created.[21] Medicine's professional and eurocentric shroud confirms and grants the authority to define sickness, name the sick, identify the "healthy," and prescribe what is biologically normal and what is not, thereby discerning between what should be called "natural," and what should be called "unnatural."[22]

"Drapetomania" stands among the first medical diagnoses in the United States. Samuel Cartwright, a physician in New Orleans defined it as "the desire for a slave to run away."[23] Among the causes listed were laziness and poor intellectual capabilities.[24] Only slaves were able to contract this "disease," much like only slaves were able to violate the first criminal laws enacted in this country.[25] In the *New Orleans Medical and Surgical Journal*, Dr. Cartwright argued that the tendency of slaves to run away was a treatable medical disorder, believing that with "proper medical advice, strictly followed, the troublesome practice that many Negroes have of running away could almost entirely be prevented." Whipping was prescribed as the most effective treatment of the disorder and amputation of the toes was prescribed for cases that failed to respond to whipping.[26] This is an early example of the violence of western medical thought and practice. First, an ideological marker of disease is inflicted on a resistant slave's plight to recapture his/her liberty and humanity; then, an ideological shift displaces consideration of an unjust social order, replacing it with a medical diagnosis present in an individual and curable under the jurisdiction of medical purview. Finally, as a result, slavery is legitimized and buttressed by medicine.

Given this history, it's not surprising that people of color—especially poor people of color—often have served as the guinea pigs of the Medical Industrial Complex, suffering poor health and death as consequences. Among the most flagrant historic examples of the MIC's use of poor people of color as guinea pigs is the Tuskegee syphilis experiment. In 1932 government doctors began a study on the effects of the illness. Their project deemed "expendable" the bodies of southern Black sharecroppers by withholding treatment and lying about treatment; for example, excruciatingly painful spinal taps were performed under the guise of treatment. While the medical community failed to note any wrongdoing, the research project continued for many years.[27] Well into World War II, the lead scientific investigators even secured government exceptions from military recruitment for the research subjects, because the military provided treatment for syphilis. As a result, nearly one hundred men died and many more lived with chronic and serious health complications.

Indeed "the burden of scientific investigation has rested on those that are socially and therefore medically disenfranchised."[28] In Puerto Rico in the 1960's, birth control pills three to four times the hormone dosages of today's birth control pills were tested on women without their consent. Many were killed and injured while being used as guinea pigs. Eugenecist Margaret Sanger, the mother of the (western interventionist) birth control movement and founder of Planned Parenthood, went to Puerto Rico to support "administering physicians."

Sterilization

Attacks on our sexual and reproductive systems are among the most pervasive types of medical violence against women of color. Medicine furthers colonial attacks through eugenics and population control. The eugenics movement set out to reproduce "the superior stock of the nation." In the early 20th century, Margaret Sanger argued that birth control would be an effective way to reduce the size of "undesirable" populations who would become a hindrance to the development of the idealized white supremacist nation-state.[29] In her essay "Better Dead than Pregnant," Andrea Smith notes, "women of color become particularly dangerous to the world order as they have the ability to reproduce the next generations of communities of color."[30] In the United States, sterilization has been practiced on Japanese women while they were detained in internment camps in WWII, Mexican immigrants and Chicanas, Native and Puerto Rican women. In her book, *Birthing the Nation: Strategies of Palestinian Women in Israel*, Rhoda Ana Khanaaneh argues that "female, nonwhite and poor bodies are seen as population growth vessels that must be stopped."[31] In *Killing the Black Body*, Dorothy Roberts wrote that "regulating Black women's reproductive decisions has been a central aspect of racial oppression in America."

From the 1930s to the 1960s, close to one half of Puerto Rican women of childbearing age were sterilized without their informed consent.[32] The procedure came to be called simply "la operación" ("the operation") because it was so common. Population control rhetoric claimed that the island population was "exploding" while at the same time multinational corporations had relocated the garment industry to Puerto Rico, which heightened their need for female "unattached" (childless) workers. The US Agency for International development later promoted sterilization and birth control in developing nations to prevent revolutions.[33]

> In 1977, R. T. Ravenholt, from the US Agency for International Development (AID), announced the plan to sterilize a quarter of the world's women because, as he put it, population control is necessary to maintain "the normal operation of US Commercial interests around the world."[34]

Exclusion from Care

Exclusion from medical care is yet another form of medical violence. First, the medical model is based on the archetype of the white male body; people of color as recipients of care and healing are an afterthought to the Medical Industrial Complex. We are also structured as an afterthought in access to care as high costs, lack of insurance, withholding of referrals to specialists and specialized procedures often keep care out of our reach. A marker for access to healthcare, though not the only one, is insurance. Latinos have reported uninsured rates of 33% compared to 11% of whites, while 84% of all uninsured women are women of color.[35] The current political direction of actively eroding access to insurance—through cuts to Medicaid to support the unfathomable costs of war, for example—helps us see whose lives are deemed expendable by each of the MICs' (Military and Medical Industrial Complex).

African-Americans, Latinos, and American Indians have the highest rates of death attributable to preventable diseases that include heart disease, cancer, strokes, diabetes and AIDS. Medical care is structured for whites to access it earlier, one of the reasons their life expectancy is highest in the US, whereas people of color often cannot access care until the disease is too advanced for successful treatment. Multiple variables are responsible for the proliferation of these illnesses in our communities, including overexposure to toxic environmental conditions, limited access to healthy foods, and migrant displacement from land and families; each of these factors is a consequence of racism and social inequalities.

While African-American women are approximately 13% of the population, they account for 63% of new AIDS cases. African-Americans and Latinos make-up a third of the US population, yet account for 82% of pediatric AIDS cases, 69% of new HIV and AIDS cases, and 62% of everyone living with AIDS.[36] These astronomical rates of AIDS are primarily a result of education, prevention, and treatment being unequally distributed across racial and socio-economic lines. There are other factors, rooted in racism and social inequality. For example, immigration policies and the conditions of migrant farm work have also historically created conditions where single men are kept away from families and their primary sexual partners, which can lead to practices which increase exposure to HIV.[37]

The recent loss of cherished Chicana/Mexicana warrior Gloria Anzaldúa from diabetes-related complications reminds us that the rate of diabetes among Latinas is twice that among white women. Furthermore, Latinas and African-American women are most likely to have undiagnosed diabetes, which can lead to other preventable but serious complications and death.[38] Another important finding is that a patient's race negatively affects referral to accessing potentially lifesaving treat-ments, which translates to higher heart disease mortality rates for women of color, especially African-American women.[39]

Dangerous to Our Health

The medicalization of domestic violence embeds domestic violence within a con-text (the Medical Industrial Complex) that has proven an enduring and powerful threat against women of color and our communities. Furthermore, to the extent that the Medical Industrial Complex is organized in a manner that reflects, legiti-mates and promotes capitalism, racism, colonialism and sexism and to the extent that domestic violence in our communities emerges out of these violent processes, the Medical Industrial Complex is invested in maintaining domestic violence.[40] So, how can women of color rely on the Medical Industrial Complex for care and respect? In fact, can't women of color instead expect revictimization when coming into contact with the MIC? Can't we expect our autonomy and self-determination to be inhibited, and our safety to be threatened?

Almost all interviewees in a recent study of survivors of sexual abuse said they were re-traumatized by the medical examination procedures.[41] First, because there is an underlying assumption that they are not to be believed, material evidence must be collected from their bodies as they are objectified and invaded, penetrated a second time by medical intervention. And like mandatory arrest policies, the now common medical mandatory reporting policies also deem the survivors inau-dible and irrelevant by insisting that criminal charges be imposed without their consent.[42] Consequently, bias in reporting is sure to arise in domestic violence cases, as has been demonstrated in child abuse reporting where medical providers reported low-income families and people of color at higher rates.[43] In addition, a study of physicians found that emergency care providers were more likely to report than private physicians. Since uninsured poor communities and communities of color are more likely to seek care in emergency care facilities, we are also more likely to be reported.[44]

Mandatory reporting policies are particularly dangerous to immigrant women because the immigrant experience is already replete with an incessant and over-whelming fear of deportation and lack of access to care and services. When ser-vices are available, the fear of deportation is so pronounced, especially in an era where violence against immigrants has become increasingly prevalent, that immi-grants are likely to deter care because of the link to law enforcement.

> Because one is an immigrant, as an illegal in this country one be-lieves that in the moment in which one will ask for help … they will return you to your country and this is something that perhaps we the Latina women are obligated to put up with—this type of (domestic) violence—for fear that we will be deported.[45]

Immigrant women already face the sociocultural stresses present in expe-riences of migration and displacement, in addition to struggling to survive an encounter with a white American hegemonic culture, all factors which exacerbate the lethality of domestic violence.[46] Mandatory reporting policies and the medicalization of domestic violence heightens the grave danger immigrant survivors already face.[47]

Conclusion

Medicalization transforms the survivor into a patient, presenting with an injury/medical need which can be addressed by the presiding (and often paternalistic) physician, law enforcement and the state. The medical response does not address domestic violence as a consequence of structured inequalities and social processes: "The narrowing of the analysis of sexual crimes to evidentiary, medical and legal aspects strips away the context of oppression." [48] Medical interventions in domestic violence are constructed as acts of "sensitivity" provided to survivors, and related to improving service delivery through identification and screening procedures. The focus is not on injustice and inequality. With medicalization, the oppositional thinking of social movements is swallowed up and a prescription is rendered as social change work is quietly sent into oblivion.

Medicalization is a tool used by the MIC to heighten profits, legitimate the state, maintain medical dominance, reproduce social inequalities, and co-opt social movements (by expanding at times of social protest.) The lived experiences of women of color and our communities can dislocate the assumption that medicine will heal.[49] Frantz Fanon relates the example of a "non-compliant"Algerian patient who would not divulge any information about his health.[50] He knew he faced not only a doctor but the colonizer, so he resisted. We all know the "ordeal" it is to go to the doctor's. We come to expect racist and classist treatment. Acts of refusal or resistance to medical treatment are acts against medical violence. Perhaps sister Audre, in her struggle with cancer, was invoking our survival and resistaince of medical violence when she said that as women of color, to take care of ourselves and our health is an act of political warfare.

Lastly, let's challenge the calls for a "system-based" response to domestic violence; it is this very call that gave heed and runway to criminalization and medicalization. Let's call out and stop relying on violent institutions to attempt to solve violence, i.e. the Medical Industrial Complex, Military Industrial Complex, PIC, etc. Isn't domestic violence an outgrowth of these very institutions? Instead, let's build movements for healing that are accountable to us and our communities and that don't reproduce oppressive relations. Let's call out the medicalization of domestic violence and re-invigorate a grassroots movement against domestic violence that doesn't shy away from asking, or isn't paid to forget to ask "what's it really gon'na take to live lives free of violence?"

III
BUILDING MOVEMENT

22

Unite and Rebel!
Challenges and Strategies in Building Alliances

Elizabeth (Betita) Martínez

Women of color have come together against violence—and expanded the very meaning of the term—as never before in US history. In their organizing, scholarship, and advocacy work, initiated at the first Color of Violence Conference in 2000, INCITE! Women of Color Against Violence demonstrates the electrifying capacity of women of color to organize against that common enemy across racial and ethnic lines. As we engage this mission more broadly and deeply, we learn more about both the strengths and challenges that confront us in working together toward unity.

Sharing experiences of violence, in one form or another, provides the foundation for alliance-building between women of color. But, as the late and beloved Gloria Anzaldúa said in her book *Making Face, Making Soul/Haciendo Caras*, "Shared oppression by itself does not override the forces that keep us apart." In fact, white supremacy encourages the forces that divide us. "Divide and Conquer" has been a major strategy for maintaining white supremacy for centuries.

We see intensified efforts at division today, as changing demographics promise that whites will be a minority in this country relatively soon. Divisive tactics feature emphasis on job competition between the native-born and immigrants. We also hear the counterattack, accusing people of color of being "racist" toward each other or against whites. This tactic reminds us that we should understand racism to be an entire structure of power relations best called white supremacy. Communities of color rarely have structural power over each other (much less over white people) except in very limited situations such as on the job or in local political structures. At the same time, we can be prejudiced toward each other and act in racist-like ways. This does not mean we have the power to be racists, but such prejudice, such actions can be a serious barrier to alliance-building.

White supremacy not only encourages subtle and not so subtle expressions of racist-type attitudes between women of different colors. It also encourages internalized racist attitudes toward oneself as an individual, and toward one's own group. This too can undermine alliance-building, by fomenting a narrow nationalism intended to restore necessary self-respect in ways that can backfire against long-range, collective goals.

Anticipating Challenges

Working in a group of women that combines different racial or national origins, we should assume problems will develop and strategize how to address them. It helps to think about those problems as rooted in differences of class, race, color (and other physical characteristics), as well as nationality, culture, sexuality, and age. Disability is also an issue; failure to recognize it can generate a sense of apartness, of isolation and indifference. All of these "differences" are linked to historical experience. All are interconnected and cannot be discussed in isolation from each other.

Before looking at each area of difference and its specifics, let's reaffirm our goals. First, we want to build our united strength so as to help transform this society into one of justice and peace for all. We are all in it together, and transforming this society would be a precious achievement for us all. Is anything else more worthwhile?

Second, we should think in terms of building not only coalitions but also alliances. In a coalition, separate groups come together to address a common, usually immediate, single, problem or set of related problems. Coalitions are often necessary and even vital. They have potentially great immediate impact, and can pave the way for alliance-building.

Alliances should be broader in their focus, more profound, and more long-range, more lasting. The forces of white supremacy and imperialism are too strong for us to battle separately. Alliance can bring us together and give greater power to our resistant efforts over the years. Strong alliances make it possible for us to dream of someday seeing a global women of color movement to create a more just global society.

Finally, dealing with our differences and divisions cannot be left to casual concern or spontaneous resolution. It has to be one of our organizational priorities, a clear-cut part of program. That is the basic message of this article.

Learning Our Herstories

As we begin to examine the forces that obstruct alliance-building, we can see that ignorance and lack of understanding about our different communities greatly affect the influence of those forces. To combat the forces of division, we need to learn much more about the history of each community. Today, as Arab and Islamic people, as well as others of Middle Eastern/South Asian backgrounds have become the most recent, most visible victims of extreme racist oppression, we see yet another example of widespread ignorance. How much about the history and struggles of Arab, Islamic, Middle Eastern/South Asian communities is actually known by US-women of color not from these communities? How much is known about the long Palestinian struggle against US-supported Israeli expansion?

For women of color all over the world, the most common and destructive experiences of violence have come from war. In modern times, at least, war has consistently left more women and children dead than soldiers. Here in the United States, we find that women of color have been subjected to racist violence in both similar and different ways. If we look at their different herstories, we find that war is not uncommon.

For Native Americans, the experience begins with invasion of their homeland, seizure of that land, and genocide. Genocide is mass murder, and much more than that. It aims to eliminate the present and future existence of an entire people. Its goal is so thorough, it barely leaves room for colonization. As intended, millions of indigenous people were wiped off the hemisphere; nations, tribes, and languages simply ceased to exist.

For African Americans, securing their labor was the goal in European eyes. The essence of their historical experience has been uprooting, massive kidnapping, enslavement, and the murder of millions. It could be called a more utilitarian form of genocide: reduce the populations to nonexistence as actors in history while guaranteeing possession of their labor.

Once genocide of the Natives had provided the European invaders with their land base, slavery provided their labor base. It played the crucial role of facilitating the country's nascent economy—a role that Indian and imported European labor were insufficient to play.

If land theft and genocide defined Native experience and slavery defined the Black experience, for people of Mexican decent it was war. First came Spain's military invasion of Mexico, then its colonization, and then the United States, which seized almost half of Mexico by war in 1848. In the newly enlarged US, Mexican labor became crucial to US nation-building west of the Mississippi. Like other communities of color, Mexicans experienced brutal repression including lynching and murder by colonial forces.

The exploitation and oppression of Mexicans and other Latinos has had a unique characteristic: the artificially created US-Mexico border which officially requires the legal right to cross. Although ignored by thousands of poor Latinos, the border has provided bosses with a certain means of control that can sustain exploitation. Utilizing its legal demands, Anglos have not infrequently reduced Mexican and other undocumented Latino labor to modern slavery or peonage. Promised wages at the end of a season, for example, many will work unpaid for months and then the boss calls immigration authorities to deport them—all free of charge. Fear of deportation is used all over the United States to intimidate desperately poor workers into accepting many forms of abuse.

Like Mexicans, those of Pacific Island origin share the racist experience of colonization, with Hawai'i, the Philippines, and Guam as classic examples whose struggles continue today. In the US, Asian immigrant workers all share the commonality of stolen labor, going back to the nineteenth century when they were brought over for railroad building, mining, and agricultural work.

Many examples can be mentioned of similarities with other groups of color. The lynching of Chinese miners in the 1880s in Wyoming, which sometimes amounted to massacres, is a horrible reminder of Black experience. In the area of immigration abuse, the Chinese Exclusion Act remains an unforgettable milestone.

Strategies for Alliance Building

The similarities and differences in historical experiences of racism mean that women of color have different collective memories of violence, and, therefore, they may relate differently to each other without always realizing it or knowing why. Dissimilar sources of pain may keep us focused on what separates rather than unites. For example, an African American may associate state violence with her color while a Mexican/Latina will associate it with her language or accent.

   In addressing these and other challenges, each group of women of color could put together its own lists of do's and dont's based on real-life experiences; we each have different strategies to deal with the challenges, and to expand our strengths. Some will be very general and far-ranging, like the need to understand the different herstories and cultures of each racial group that have been discussed here. Yet, there are more specific rules and procedures centered on establishing mutual respect that can be drawn up.

   For example, when a group of women goes to meet or work in a different setting from their own, be very aware of how the women in that unfamiliar setting do things: what are the spoken and unspoken rules, the protocols, the established values for human interchange. Don't be a know-it-all, but don't fail to share everything that might be helpful. Don't be in a hurry, too impatient to listen.

   We also say, stick to dialogue. Don't give up, even if it becomes difficult. It's normal. There can be enormous resistance to speaking openly about one group's issues with another. And women are often especially afraid of hurting someone's feelings, stepping on toes, or sounding racist by bringing up feelings that might sound like stereotypes.

   The Institute for MultiRacial Justice, whose mission is to help build alliances between peoples of color and combat conflicts, has experience with these barriers and inhibitions. One lesson has been the difficulty of having such dialogue in a large, public gathering. This was what happened at three forums with multicultural panelists in the late 1990s in the Bay Area. At the third session, the panelists included an African American journalist who came close to provoking real discussion when she described the feelings of some African Americans about bilingual education. She was not afraid of being provocative, which is often what we need most. But we often censor ourselves in public spaces. So the Institute tried smaller workshops as a way of facilitating dialogue. At one session, mixed-race participants expressed dissatisfaction with not having their own caucus like the race-specific people. This could be corrected.

   What should we do, given the reluctance to speak openly? We must acknowledge our tendency toward silence around race and difference and work on solutions. Role-playing about some divisive issue can open people's eyes and generate discussion. Humor and a few provocative questions can loosen the grip of self-consciousness. It might help to set up a task force to undertake some specific project, like Black/Brown people working together to win more affordable housing.

   Culture can also help generate communication and build bridges between different communities, as youth have shown with hip-hop, spoken word, and other forms of cultural expression. It can be a way for women to make fun of the differences or celebrate similarities, as the Latina Theater Lab did together with young Asian women actresses a few years ago in San Francisco. Cultural expression can liberate our alliance-building energy and talents.

   Building an alliance comes most easily when it emerges organically from a conflict situation. After the so-called "Rodney King riots" in Los Angeles, as clashes continued between African Americans and Koreans, church leaders from San Francisco's Black community invited their members to meet and talk about the conflict with Koreans and other Asian Americans. Again it was a large public meeting without a collective, in-depth analysis of problems. Still, I felt encouraged that the discussion happened at all.

Let me add one last comment about an elusive problem related to building cross-racial respect and solidarity. There is a kind of spiritual violence that women working together for social justice sometimes inflict on one another. Those with more standing, influence, and power within a group dynamic can unthinkingly do violence to the spirit of someone with less power in the group. To deprecate or humiliate a sister out of competitiveness, or out of habits of domination that sometimes accompany leadership skills and intelligence, is to do a harmful violence to her spirit.

This is an insidious kind of personal violence that must never be ignored, for when others say nothing, this second act of violence compounds the damage that's already been done. Silences can feed the cancer of unaddressed conflict, and this has destroyed more than one project, group, or organization. This is a matter of organizational integrity: we cannot righteously continue our struggle, any struggle, without facing it.

Women of color need to act with integrity, speak with honesty, and reject any fear of our differences and conflicts. To transform the goal of unity into a reason for denying conflict, as we sometimes do, is self-defeating. Today, as reactionary forces work to aggravate rather than diminish racism in this society, the times call for courage more than ever. Let us create a stubborn, imaginative, honest, powerful insurgency. Let us counter the enemy forces of divide and conquer with our strategy of unite and rebel!

23

Sistas Makin' Moves
Collective Leadership for Personal Transformation and Social Justice

Sista II Sista

Sista II Sista Collective Poem
Of Woman Born and lives we live
Afro-Latina groove together as unique sisters
Women raised sometimes to depend on and comfort men
We take command over our bodies and our souls
How hard we struggle with the pain we went through
I have come and I have gone;
What women have come through in the past and present
and what we will go through in the future.

Hermanas somos, pedazos de la tierra
giving of ourselves sometimes unwillingly
Hot air cold feet;
we allow ourselves to be mistreated no more.
We understand the irony of power,
that those who are vulnerable,
in fact are a source of strength,
Because the meek shall inherit the earth

I am Black, I am Latina, I am the hip-hop, merengue,
reggae, salsa, calypso, bachata rich woman who gave you life.
I am the dark chocolate, caramel butter pecan, complexion
filled with *sazon* and spices
of my ancestors that gave me life,
my history, my hope, my dreams of becoming a woman.

But this is only the beginning of my struggle,
This is only a mystery to be unfolded, to expand and soar
like butterflies going from destination to destination,
telling the Queens of our past and present
to bring our journey home to the future
through the words of wisdom that our mothers have taught us.

Editorial note: In keeping with their organizational model and practice, Sista II Sista wrote this piece, as well as their poem, collectively, which means they labored and labored over several drafts and all of Sista II Sista's membership reached consensus on the entire piece and jointly created the title.

Us, Mothers, daughters, sisters, aunts, girlfriends,
and grandmothers—the source to which we will return.
We are the alpha and omega, the beginning and the end.

Introduction

We at Sista II Sista wrote this article to share our experiences and learnings with those young women of color who are struggling to find meaning and purpose; for those of you who are doing work with young people; those who are doing work around violence (state or interpersonal); those of you who are trying to develop new ways of organizing, building community, and developing organization; and, lastly, for those of you who think that change is not happening. Since 1996 we have been building a grassroots organization called Sista II Sista. This is who we are.

Who We Are

Sista II Sista (SIIS) is a Brooklyn-wide, community-based organization located in Bushwick. We are a collective of working-class, young and adult, Black and Latina women building together to model a society based on liberation and love. Our organization is dedicated to working with young women to develop personal, spiritual and collective power. We are committed to fighting injustice and creating alternatives to the systems we live in by making social, cultural, and political change.

Our goal is to promote the holistic development of young women of color, ages 13 to 19, and to inspire them to take strong leadership roles in their local communities. We nurture the personal development of young women which incorporates physical, emotional, spiritual, and intellectual growth, linked to community-based, political action. Sista II Sista remains grounded in its principle of self-determination with respect to young women's personal, spiritual, and political empowerment processes. Self-determination promotes the idea that all groups are able to identify and work toward solving their own problems and creating their own liberation.

How We Came to Be

In 1996, a group of working-class young women in our early twenties began looking at how we had been marginalized growing up. We felt that existing institutions did not speak to our life experiences. The schools and youth centers we had been a part of did not address our experiences as young women of color. As a group facing a braid of oppression (racism, classism, sexism, ageism, etc.), we deal with multiple challenges. In a low-income community organization, the experiences of youth from the community are not central; in a youth-focused organization, the experiences of young women are not central; in a women's organization, the experiences of poor and working-class women of color are not central. We found that there was no place to nurture the voices of young women of color to participate fully and to build collective power to transform the society we are a part of. From this space, the vision for Sista II Sista was developed.

We started meeting to plan a summer Freedom School for young Black and

Latina teen women. In a matter of months, we developed a vision for a holistic personal and political space where we could support young women's leadership through workshops and activities that focused on building physical, intellectual, creative, spiritual, and emotional power. Even though our advisors felt we should first raise money, we decided to jump right into launching a summer program with no money and no infrastructure. The first Freedom School was eight weeks long and had twenty-five young women participants and fifteen young adult women volunteers to coordinate and facilitate. We obtained free space at a Beacon Center in a public school in Bedford-Stuyvesant and got donated food and supplies. A Beacon Center in New York City is a public school that is open during summer and after school for community groups to use the classrooms for free. We were excited to share our skills in workshops on sexism in hip-hop, holistic community organizing, the feelings and politics of hair, revolutionary women of color in history, martial arts, b-girlin, and the creation of photo autobiographies.

At the first graduation of our Freedom School for Young Women of Color there were drummers, dancers, photoautobiographical displays, and lots of love. In her closing comments, one volunteer stated, "Young women do not suffer from low self-esteem. It's about the struggle to defend (ourselves from) it, to live and move in it every day." Finally, the collective poem that young women wrote declared in its last line, "Not ONE more strangled, stabbed, shot sista anywhere. Together, forever, sistahoood." That was the very successful summer of 1996.

From there, the growing pains began. We were constantly outreaching to young women of color that shared our vision, vibe, and politics to join our crew. We kept meeting and talking about how to develop Sista II Sista as a year-long program, not just a summer Freedom School. We decided that we wanted to be a young women of color organization, not just a program. We began putting these ideas into practice and ran into one of our biggest challenges: creating an organizational structure that was in line with our vision of the society we wanted to create.

How We Became a Collective

We started to build with each other personally—the volunteers and the young women participants. We started to build strong ties of love and friendship and we started to really feel connected to each other. We saw ourselves grow politically and personally in each other's lives, experiences, and ideas, and the power of Sista II Sista began to emerge. (We could keep telling the story, year by year, but y'all would probably get bored.) To make a long story short, we researched the infrastructures of other organizations. Then we spent lots of time developing our own structure based on the information we gathered, and our own imaginations. So we never had an executive director or a secretary. From the beginning, we decided that these titles had no place in an organization like ours because we wanted everyone to feel valuable. We wanted to recognize everyone's labor, as equals.

After long dinners, meetings, visioning sessions, and hangouts at people's houses, we decided that Sista II Sista would be a collective. Visually, we saw this as a flower, and the petals were the different areas of work: organizational development, Freedom School program, outreach and organizing, financials, and fundraising. (Recently, we added a membership petal.) And, back then, the center of the flower was the collective—a leadership body of ten to fifteen people made up of members who made the time commitment. Now, our center includes the Sista Squad (young women leadership body); the collective (young and adult women who meet monthly); the advisory board and our general membership. These bodies decide on the direction and vision of the organization together twice a year at retreats. The Sista Squad and the collective make the day-to-day decisions that need to be made outside of those retreats.

Ten years later, our collective structure reflects the ideals of a society that approaches all its members as equals—instead of following a model of one or two directors, our organization's leadership and decision-making model is nonhierarchical and one of inclusion. In spite of the challenges, we are working to create sustainable leadership centered on a diverse group of women sharing power and creating a vision together. Prior to 2000, the organization functioned through volunteer efforts. All the work of the collective has remained volunteer-based and all members are asked to volunteer with SIIS for at least three to six months before joining the collective. Though some collective members are now staff members, they also participate in the collective as volunteers.

Major decisions are made by a consensus-based decision making process. This is based on the principle that the voices of minority or dissenting opinions are as important as the majority, and the most powerful ideas come from putting many perspectives and experiences together. Not every member of SIIS is not involved in every single decision; different teams are empowered to make decisions. Though this model is time consuming and difficult, this process has proven to be richer and more rewarding than any other work experience we've been a part of.

Our collective style has yielded better ways to structure our work because when something isn't working and the issue gets raised, we all pay attention. For example, until 2002, we had a Freedom and an Action Squad: the Freedom Squad developed, coordinated, and facilitated the holistic leadership development work of the Freedom School, and the Action Squad members coordinated the community organizing work of SIIS. But at the 2002 fall retreat, members expressed concern that the division of work between Freedom and Action Squad members had, at times, created a false division between "personal" (Freedom Squad) and "political" (Action Squad) work. This division was clearly contrary to our mission, and we recognized that it created a dynamic which privileged the work of the Action Squad over the Freedom Squad. So, shortly after the retreat, we created mixed "work teams" which incorporate Freedom and Action Squad members. Squad members, collective members, and general membership have divided themselves into interdisciplinary work teams focused on different issues and areas of work, including programming, organizing, video, and grassroots fundraising.

Our model ensures growth and continued relevance of the organization by incorporating graduates of the Freedom School into all levels of the organization (Sista Squad, collective, board). The Sista Squad is a concrete vehicle for young women's leadership and ownership of the organization. All of SIIS's organizing issues are chosen by young women members based on their real-life experiences, and they are also responsible for developing and implementing organizing strategies.

Furthermore, Sista II Sista's Freedom School programs are developed and facilitated with the leadership of the Sista Squad, who build relationships with new incoming members and create evaluation systems for programs. The role of the Sista Squad in SIIS is critical because it is a tangible mechanism for young women to have on-going decision-making power over the direction of the organization. It also serves as a place for young women to develop as strong leaders who are invested in SIIS, which will ensure the sustainability of the organization and will continue to bring forth change in their day-to-day lives and surrounding communities.

What We Believe in and What Guides Us

Sista II Sista promotes the principles of self-determination, interconnected personal and social transformation, and collective action against injustice. We believe that the perspectives of young women of color are critical to the survival and flourishing of our communities, so our approach focuses on young women's innate power as organizers for social change.

Unfortunately, many programs geared toward youth utilize a service approach that frames young people in terms of their deficiencies, and very few organizations address the experiences of young women of color in particular. Taking the principle of self-determination as a starting point, Sista II Sista has created an organization where young women of color take the leadership in transforming themselves and their communities. Though it is true that more services are needed for young women, if we are truly committed to the creation of a society based on social justice, we must encourage young women to actively struggle for the creation of this vision. It is important to have spaces where young women can be more than recipients, or "victims in need of services," and can fulfill their potential as leaders and creators of a more just community and society.

While we clearly believe that there is tremendous potential in sisterhood, we also believe that it is not an automatic thing—it must be built, and is part of a process of struggle. Our membership is African American, Afro Caribbean, and Latina young women at various stages in their lives, which provides a rich forum for personal and political development. Rooting ourselves within our membership's diverse experiences, cultures, and realities, we express our visions for a more just society through cultural mediums such as dance, media, music, and poetry. We recognize these areas as places where culture is created and promoted, and use these mediums to foster critical thinking and challenge dominant culture, which often degrades our very existence.

Lastly, as mentioned above, although we do not promote individual leaders, we recognize the uniqueness of every individual involved. We practice this in all aspects of the organization, not just the collective and squad. We have no "founders," our staff is nonhierarchical, division of labor is not traditional, and the pay scale is flat —everyone is paid the same wage, regardless of age, formal education, or how long they've been a member. Our experiences continue to show us that real and long-lasting change comes through collective leadership and struggle.

What We Do

In the past seven years SIIS has established a strong membership base through our holistic leadership development program, the Freedom School for Young Women of Color. For the first three years we didn't take on organizing projects and campaigns, instead we focused on building our base, developing collective leadership and consciousness, and supporting the organizing work of our allies. Once we had established a strong base of members through the Freedom School, we began to develop our organizing work.

The Freedom School operates as a year-round program with three cycles: fall, spring, and summer. Through their participation in the Freedom School, young women are engaged in a variety of activities designed to spark their development as critical thinkers, physically strong women, creative performers, and as community organizers. The five main components of our Freedom School are: political education, physical health and power, nourishing our bodies, video, and community action projects. Political education links the personal experiences of young women to larger issues of oppression and resistance. Using principles and techniques of popular education, workshop topics include women in hip-hop, confronting sexual harassment, the braid of oppression, sex and relationships, and many more. Physical health and power allows young women to explore their physical power through classes such as break-dancing, self-defense, boxing, and Afro-Brazilian and Afro-Dominican dance. Nourishing our bodies provides an opportunity for participants to share healthy recipes and meals.

The video component trains young women of color as media makers, puts the word out on the street about an issue, and supports our community organizing in a creative way. Video production has shown us how different forms of media can help us get our message across to larger audiences; SIIS's message is reaching more people in the neighborhood, citywide and nationally through regular screenings and discussions. Since adding the video component in 2001, we have purchased equipment, expanded our video work, and developed an organizing plan using video as a political education and organizing tool. Finally, our Community Action Projects are chosen by SIIS members and led by Squad members in conjunction with the Outreach and Organizing petal. Through discussions with the Freedom School participants, Squad members facilitate the identification of issues that the young women feel should be addressed. Once an issue is identified, Squad members outline an organizing strategy and take leadership in involving other Sista II Sista members in the campaign.

Organizing against Violence Targeting Young Women of Color

Sparked by the murder of two teen women of color in Bushwick by a police officer and an auxiliary policeman, in the summer of 2000, young women identified violence against young women of color in Bushwick as our main area of organizing work. We realized that the majority of our membership had faced some level of violence in their lives, but, by launching a community survey of four hundred young women in Bushwick, we were able to confirm what a serious issue this was.

We started our work in 2001 with Street Theater, skits about sexual harassment. SIIS members performed skits on the streets of Bushwick with the objective of raising consciousness about the issue. We also held a community forum in October 2001 with INCITE! to strategize about community solutions to the issue of violence in our communities. These solutions would be later incorporated into Sista's Liberated Ground.

In 2002, we launched Action Summer to do ongoing organizing around these issues. As part of Action Summer, we did a video documenting police harassment of young women in Bushwick called "You Have the Right To Break the Silence." The video project was really successful in putting into action the research (surveys and statistics) and documenting the on-the-street perspectives of young women, community activists, and local police officers on this issue. We also held an end-of-summer Action Day in front of the 83rd Precinct in Bushwick to strongly address the issue of accountability. Over 250 community members attended the event and close to two hundred petitions were signed demanding an end to police violence and harassment of young women in Bushwick. The action included testimonies, breakdancers, poetry, and a screening of our video.

This cultural event/action sent a loud message that harassment of young women by the police would not be tolerated by a unified community. The action served as an opportunity to put into practice our model of organizing, and it succeeded in publicly embarrassing the local precinct in front of many local residents and the press, putting the police on notice that they were being watched. But it also sparked serious harassment and surveillance of SIIS. The day after, there was a mini-precinct mobile unit of the New York Police Department (NYPD) parked outside of the SIIS space. They were messing with the phone wires on the pole outside and the mini-precinct stayed parked there for two weeks, 24/7, with a cop inside at all times. It definitely planted some fear in us. But in the era of the "war on terror," we were aware that this was not only a random retaliation from this particular precinct. Through our coalition work we knew that our allies were going through similarly heightened surveillance and harassment.

We initially met with fellow organizers to document our experience and to strategize a response. In terms of our work, we realized that our conversations and actions were being watched more closely. We did additional "Know Your Rights" trainings for all members, and everyone carried our pro-bono activist lawyer's card with them at all times. Though most of our members stayed focused and committed, parents of families who were undocumented became less active and encouraged their daughters to stop participating. We had a lot of deep conversations with mothers, and understood that everything was now more complicated. We couldn't really do much about the harassment but document it and proceed with greater caution to ensure all our safety. Irrespective of these methods of intimidation, our work continued on.

At SIIS we feel that true social transformation is holistic, that change comes from inspiration, emotional and cultural expression, and a strong political message. The video, Action Day, trainings, self-defense workshops, and day-to-day organizing work, such as door-knocking and flyering, strengthened community support for our organizing work. SIIS went from getting bottles thrown at our doors by young men who didn't understand the need for a women's space to gathering hundreds of neighborhood supporters—who were multigenerational, and not just female—at street actions against the police and military. This took many years of street outreach and conversations. As our work around violence has grown, we've divided it into three areas: challenging the police around issues of sexual harassment and violence against young women of color in Bushwick; building an alternative to the police for women to turn to in cases of interpersonal violence; and creating solidarity with women facing violence in the Third World.

We have learned from our experiences that, along with taking a strong public stance against police abuse of young women, we must also find practical ways of implementing creative solutions to this issue. In 2002, our efforts coincided with citywide press coverage of the NYPD backlog of domestic violence cases against women: more than one hundred thousand reported cases had not been followed up on—this gross inaction further endangered women's lives. This information supported our critique of the police as an inherently oppressive institution, and as an impractical and ineffective agency to end violence against women. But to truly build collective power, we need to do more than strongly critique an institution or system—we must also begin to envision and create what we want to replace it with! We needed a concrete option for sistas to count on when dealing with the constant gendered violence on the streets, at school, at work, and at home. Sista II Sista's overall vision for our organizing campaign is to work on institutional change, as well as social and cultural change, while creating alternatives at the same time. Sista's Liberated Ground (SLG) is our local alternative to the police.

SLG has been the most challenging social change work that SIIS has ever engaged in. We began strategizing within SIIS, held local meetings and built on strategies from our October 2001 community forum. In February 2003, we hosted a two-day gathering sponsored by INCITE!. The meeting brought together thirty-five young and adult women of color from around the country who are working on models of community accountability for violence against women. At this gathering, SIIS members presented SLG and drew from other concrete models, and many presented interesting reflections and observations. With the knowledge gained from that meeting, squad members improved the project model and presented it to the whole SIIS membership for a consensus approval in May of 2004.

Since then, we've declared our territorial zone: Sista's Liberated Ground, a space where violence against sistas is not tolerated, and where women turn to each other instead of the police to address the violence in their lives. SLG includes extensive outreach with flyers, posters, T-shirts, stickers, and murals to mark the territory. There is also an action line, a phone number that women can call to get involved in SLG. The squad members are also developing a series of workshops for young women from the community on sexism, conflict resolution, collective self-defense, and other topics to raise consciousness and build relationships with other women in the neighborhood. Our new video, *No More Violence Against Our Sistas!*, will be used for political education within the community. SLG is also organizing Sista Circles, collectives of support and intervention for cases of gender violence with groups of sistas that are friends, neighbors, and coworkers. We will first practice these Sista Circles in the Freedom School with our members to see what creating collective support and real accountability looks like.

The inauguration of SLG took place on June 28, 2004, at our block party. Amid performers and music, community members signed on to and shouted the Sista's Liberated Ground Pledge:'

> I believe that in the struggle for justice, women's personal safety is an important community issue.
>
> Violence against women hurts families, children and the whole community.
>
> As a member of this community, I commit myself to ending violence against women!
>
> I stand in support of Sista's Liberated Ground, a territory where violence against women is not tolerated.
>
> I commit myself to working with the community to collectively confront cases of violence against women without the police and to work together so that violence against women stops happening.
>
> I will dedicate myself to creating relationships based on respect, love and mutual support and to struggling for justice and liberation on a personal and community level.

This innovative organizing project created by the young women of SIIS is beyond anything any of our staff or volunteer collective has concrete experience with, and we've been surprised by the challenges and rewards. Through meeting other national groups, we've also learned that there aren't established on-the-ground models to help us figure out how to put these ideas into practice. We've also looked at and learned from many current models in revolutionary movements and community struggles in the Third World. We looked at the occupation safety systems and the gender teams of the Landless Workers' Movement (MST) in Brazil, the autonomous territories of the Zapatistas, and many less-known community accountability action groups of poor women that live in places where the police wouldn't come even if called. These creative intervention models were built upon strong community connections and relationships.

And in the United States, in a lot of places like Bushwick, community has been undermined—that's what keeps us all alienated. So doing this type of work inside the empire is extra hard. We know this work will take years and a lot of sista power to fully implement, but we are excited and challenged by this project.

Another area of social change work that SIIS members have taken on is solidarity with other women in the Third World. We began with a solidarity campaign with young women in Júarez, Mexico. Squad members saw the parallels between how violence affects poor young women in Bushwick and in Júarez. The work included an action at the Mexican Embassy with hundreds of petitions presented to the head consul on the same day that actions were happening all over Mexico, in late November 2002.

From there, attention turned to the impending war and the solidarity team began organizing with citywide coalitions against the war. In Third World Within (a citywide people of color social justice network), SIIS squad members were the only youth (under 21) at organizing and work meetings. But our participation brought energy, ideas, and creativity to the larger group. We successfully helped organize actions on February 15, 2003, the day after the bombing began, and on May 19, Malcolm X's birthday.

Along with the citywide work, the solidarity team also did local neighborhood antiwar organizing by doing outreach and education on the issue, holding a candle-light vigil the night the bombing began, and by doing ongoing antimilitary recruit-ment outreach which culminated in an action called Recruitment for Justice. On June 17, outside the local ROTC recruitment center in Bushwick, antiwar stickers, posters, and CDs were given for free to those who would register with SIIS (by join-ing our mailing list) instead of the armed services.

How We Fund Our Work

SIIS functioned during its first three years without any foundation funding. We had an all-volunteer collective that helped coordinate and facilitate our Freedom School, and we maintained our programming through in-kind donations from volunteers and local community businesses, t-shirt sales, and cultural fundraising events. In the past three years, our foundation funding has increased significantly. We expanded our grassroots fundraising with individual donor drives, speaking engagements, and workshops, events, and collectively-made products.

In the fall of 2002, spurred by the realization that we were increasingly work-ing harder and harder to become ever-dependent on foundation grants, we priori-tized non-foundation, grassroots fundraising strategies by creating two working groups dedicated to raising money. One group promotes and markets SIIS prod-ucts, which include T-shirts, sweatshirts, massage oils, bath salts, and other SIIS-created and creative products. This group also began promoting the Sista Solidarity Products, crafts, such as earrings, blouses, and hand bags, made by women's coop-eratives in the Third World; these sales provide funding to the cooperatives as well as SIIS.

The other fundraising work team is the Big Mouth Project, made up of a small group of collective and squad members who have developed a national SIIS speaker's bureau. The team created a base of thirteen workshops and talks based on SIIS's curriculum and model of organizing, and began outreaching to public schools, community groups, colleges and universities, and foundations to set up paid speaking engagements for SIIS. The Big Mouth Project team schedules and coordinates the engagements, but all SIIS members are expected to facilitate the workshops and give talks. The prices are on a sliding scale depending on the type of organization. This project has turned out to be one of our most successful grass-roots fundraising initiatives, because it raises money, supports the development of SIIS members' leadership abilities, and spreads our mission and vision nationally.

A Few Words on Our Vision from Our Members

What would Brooklyn look like if it was against the community law
to tear and claw
at a woman's bra

or to break her jaw?

Would Brooklyn be a better place for the human race
if there were no more bruises
on a woman's face?
—*Rafia, 13 years old*

Today I walked down the street and I felt relaxed but strange. I had on a halter top with shorts and some sneakers. And let me tell you, I was looking REAL good. Had my hair flowing with a huge Kool-aid smile plastered on my face. But I still felt strange. I strutted my stuff. Hips swaying to the rhythm of my own music while my breasts bounced to a different tune. I felt so good and relaxed I didn't even notice that for the past half an hour, while I walked through the crowded street filled with men, no one called out at me. For once I didn't hear, "Yo shorty with the big ass," or "Yo ma, can I holla at you?" or even "damn, shorty!" For the first time, I walked down the street and noticed how beautiful the sky looks on a sunny day, how green the grass truly is, and I even noticed the many colors of a tree's leaves. It's bad that it took me so long to notice these things because for years I walked around with a screwed-up face just daring someone to look or say something so I could curse them out. But today I smiled. Free to be me and not having to apologize for being a woman. So you know what I'm going to do as I walk? I'm gonna thank everyone in my community for making this possible. Although it took years, my sistas can finally smile. We are free.
—*Keisha, 18 years old*

As I walk I find
As I walk I see
As I walk yo recojo los pedazos
Que me han tratado de quitar
Caminando me comunico con mis
Angeles, con mis antepasados
Regreso al lugar onde vivi
Una existencia completa
Caminando recupero la fe, vuelvo
A creer en la posibilidad
De un mundo más humano
Un mundo que valorize la vida
Y no la destrucción
Caminando I find mi camino de
Paz, justicia y verdad.
—*Loira, 24 years old*

At the End of the Day
Since we wrote this, we have made some tough decisions at Sista II Sista. One of our major decisions was not doing foundation fundraising anymore. What happened? 9/11 happened. Foundations started moving in more conservative direc-

tions, reflecting the larger climate in the US. Sista II Sista had also ridden a wave of being the "flavor of the month" among the foundations and that time was coming to an end. The progressive funders didn't understand our new organizing work, SLG. If we weren't "targeting institutions" like the police anymore, then they thought we weren't doing "real organizing." Simultaneously we started feeling more and more constrained by the amount of grant writing, administration, site visits, and reports. We were drained by the rejections, the waiting, and the constant explanations of our work to people who just didn't get it. It got tiring fitting our work into quantitative outcomes. Morale was low and SIIS went from being a labor of love to a job.

So we made the leap of faith. We are transitioning back to being an all-volunteer collective. Things move slower now. We've lost a few people in the transition. Our lives are crazy. On the other hand, young women have stepped up and their leadership is more prominent than ever in SIIS. It's empowering to know that people are open to finding alternative ways to building and working in this movement.

Conclusion

We have written many things about ourselves and our work in this piece, but without a doubt there are many more things to be said about Sista II Sista. Over the years, we have learned many lessons and faced many challenges. Some of the lessons stand out more than others.

Among the brightest is our collective understanding that justice is not a product that you arrive at. It's not an "end." Justice is something we have to continually imagine, envision, construct, and practice. It is something that you have to incorporate into your daily life and interactions with those around you in your home, work, organization, spiritual/religious space, and in all the other aspects of a human being's existence. Because of this, Sista II Sista will be constantly reshaping and reorganizing itself to respond to our responsibility to model an organization based on the principles of liberation, self-determination, and love.

The other lesson in the shine-so-bright category is that it is not enough to criticize systems that we find to be oppressive. It is a lot easier to say what's wrong with something than it is to sit with a group of people and imagine what would be better for everyone. It's easier, but it doesn't get us any closer to achieving justice for our communities. We can't tell those who are in power that what they are doing is wrong and then let them decide what would be better for us. We have to create that collectively for ourselves. That is the challenge that lies ahead of us.

24

Disloyal to Feminism
Abuse of Survivors within the Domestic Violence Shelter System

Emi Koyama

A telephone rings at a feminist domestic violence shelter and a worker picks up. First, the caller requests an Arabic-English translator to help her communicate, so the worker calls in a telephone translation service. The caller identifies herself as an immigrant who had come to the United States two years ago, who had never left her house by herself in these two years—until just now. Today she is calling from a local clinic, where she had sought emergency medical care for injuries arising from the battering by her husband the night before. She is afraid for her safety, but there is more than just the immediate safety that she is worried about: Where will she go? How will she take care of herself financially? Can she stay in this country, or can she even go back?

The worker proceeds to screen her for services, but before the worker tells the woman that she is welcome to come over and stay at the shelter, her supervisor leaves a note on her desk saying, "DON'T TAKE HER." Puzzled, the worker puts the woman on hold and speaks to the supervisor. "We're seeing all those women of color come in, fail our program, and get kicked out," says the supervisor, "We can't even get Spanish-speaking women to succeed in our program. I think it's a mistake to accept someone who only speaks Arabic." Protest ensues, but in the end the worker tells the woman, who has been waiting on hold for several minutes, that she may not come to the shelter. No reasons are given; she is just not "appropriate" for the shelter.

Feminist movements have struggled to confront abuses of power and control within our very movements, even as we critique and resist the abuse of women within our sexist society. On a theoretical level, at least, we now know that not all women's experiences are the same nor necessarily similar, that claiming universality of women's experiences inherently functions to privilege white, middle-class, heterosexual, and otherwise already privileged women by making their participation in these systems of oppression invisible. We now know, for example, that fighting racism requires not only the obliteration of personal prejudices against people of different races, but also active disloyalty to white supremacy and all of the structures that perpetuate systems of oppression and privilege.[1]

In practice, however, these are difficult concepts to implement. The need to address the issue of abusive power and control within our movements is often minimized, or deprioritized as less urgent than addressing men's abuse of power and control. This has been especially true within the movement against violence against women, which, in addition to naming such widespread, but previously unspoken practices as wife battering, sexual harassment, and date rape, viewed violence against women as part of the "conscious process of intimidation by which all men keep all women in a state of fear."[2] By adopting the view that domestic violence is not an act of one abuser against his or her victim, but all men against all women, we have made it easier to frame the violence and abuse by women against other women within the anti-domestic violence movement as individual rather than systemic, and thus, less worthy of our collective attention.

This article is about the abuse of power and control within the feminist movement against domestic violence. It primarily focuses on the imbalance of power between the workers who provide services and the survivors who receive them, but is also informed by the work of women of color, working-class women, and other feminist women who have confronted power imbalances within feminist movements. It also acknowledges that frontline direct service workers are not directly to be blamed, as they are frequently dehumanized by the contradiction of having to respond to and face extraordinary responsibilities while having too little actual institutional power to affect the larger system.

I am a survivor of domestic violence. I am someone who stayed in a shelter, back in 1994. My experience there was horrendous; I constantly felt the policing gaze of shelter workers across the half-open door, and feared "warnings" and punishments that seemed to be issued arbitrarily. No, to describe the practice as "arbitrary" would be inaccurate; it was clearly selective in terms of who got them most frequently—the poor Black and Latina women with children, especially if they were in "recovery" from alcohol or drug "abuse."

Snitching on other residents was actively encouraged. Residents were rewarded for reporting rule violations of other residents and their children, even when the allegations were not exactly accurate. I did not know whom to trust, especially after some staff or volunteer slipped the fact that I was a prostitute running away from an abusive live-in relationship. They denied ever breaking confidentiality, but how else would other residents know?

Eventually, the feeling of constant siege by shelter staff and all the "crazy-making" interactions pushed me over the edge, and I cut myself with a knife. They put me in a mental hospital, effectively ending my stay at the shelter before I could find a permanent, safer space to live. And I was not helped by the fact that the shelter staff told the State hospital about my background. After I learned to answer "correctly" to all of the insensitive and dehumanizing questions, including those about my work, they released me back on to the streets.

When I began volunteering for a rape crisis center and then for a domestic violence shelter, I believed that if I worked on the other side of the half-open door—if I could run these shelters—things could be drastically different. I believed that shelter rules could be modified for the better, that shelter workers and volunteers could be trained differently. Like every abused woman, I believed that I could make the shelter system change, that I could help make it stop being abusive and become loving and caring. I was trapped in what Jennifer Baumgardner calls "Battered Women's Movement Syndrome."[3]

After working at several domestic violence shelters in various capacities, I realize that my thinking has changed. While I still believe that there can be better rules, better trainings, and better volunteer screening procedures for domestic violence shelters than those currently employed, I now feel that these reforms do not fundamentally change the dynamic of power and control within the shelter system. In the absence of more radical changes, I fear that these reforms will only make us more benevolent and manipulative abusers, the kind that buys a woman flowers, kisses her, and says "I love you."

The shelter worker described at the beginning of this article is me. I am the worker who told the woman, who had no other place to turn to, who would probably be beaten again if she went back, that she may not come to the shelter. This episode marked my last day working at the domestic violence shelter, more than two years ago, but I continue to ache from this experience. Of course, this was not the first time that I questioned how shelters were being run. I questioned everything: the "clean and sober" policy regarding substance use; the policy against allowing women to monitor their own medications; the use of threats and intimidations to control survivors; the labeling of ordinary disagreements or legitimate complaints as "disrespectful communication"; the patronizing "life skills" and "parenting" classes; the seemingly random enforcement of rules that somehow always push women of color out of the shelter first. I hated just about everything that went on in a shelter, and I refused to participate in the enforcement of most of these regulations. I never issued formal "warnings" against any of the residents, preferring instead to have dialogues about any problems as casually as possible. I pretended that I did not smell the alcohol on the women's breath, so long as their behavior did not cause any problems for other residents. I never ever walked a woman to the bathroom and watched her as she peed into a little cup for drug tests, as shelter policy expected me to do. I did everything I could to sabotage the system I viewed as abusive—I was disloyal.

But in many other situations, I failed. To this day, I ask myself why I did not simply ignore my supervisor's order on that day, let the woman come to the shelter and deal with the consequences later. I ask myself how many times I must have misused what little power I had without even realizing it, or failed to use it positively when I could have. In the end, my greatest failure was not the failure to always be the sane voice in an insane environment, but the fact that I relied on my own feminist conscience to keep me from taking part in the abuse of women within the shelter system, not realizing that institutional structures would force me to play out that role as long as I was part of the shelter system, whether or not I liked it.

Like white antiracists who must recognize the impossibility of purifying themselves of their racist white privilege, I came to realize the limitation of feminist consciousness. I came to understand that we need structural changes, rather than better rules, staffs, trainings, or consciousness-raising conversations, in order to make social interventions that can make domestic violence activists and shelter workers more accountable to the actual needs and demands of survivors. The focus of my activism began to shift from domestic violence to the domestic violence industry.

Lulu's Story

"After I left my second husband, I went back on cocaine," recalls Lulu, a white forty year-old former street prostitute who has survived various forms of violence and abuse throughout her life.[4] "In order to support my cocaine habit, I went out with a big-time drug dealer who was also a gang member. I was his girl: I stayed at home, dressed nice, took care of his daughter and house. I gave him sex, and he gave me dope." But at some point he became very violent, with events culminating the last time she left him, when he stabbed Lulu with a knife and fork, and punched her in the face for nearly eight hours straight. "The next day, I went to stay at the battered women's shelter."

Yet even at the shelter, Lulu felt under siege. "I couldn't tell the shelter staff what was really going on. I didn't tell them about the gang, or about drugs, nothing about that. Nothing about prostitution certainly. I lied about most things." She lied because of the fear that she would be judged and mistreated if the shelter staff actually knew what she was going through.

One day, she and another resident drove together to a nearby convenience store. She was sitting on the passenger side when her abusive ex-boyfriend abruptly showed up at her window, angry. Instead of driving, the woman on the driver seat ran out of the car and into the store, and the ex-boyfriend began punching and kicking Lulu in an attempt to drag her into his van. "No one at the store intervened; no one even called the police, including the woman I was with, or the store employees." Eventually the ex-boyfriend's cousin told him to stop because he was afraid that someone had seen the license plate, and they both ran, leaving Lulu bloody and bruised.

"Police didn't show up, so I called up the police myself to make a report. And when I went back to the shelter, covered in blood, bruises, cuts, and bleeding out of my mouth, they accused me of lying. They believed that I willingly went to see him, and told me to stay away from him. They never believed me. I left the shelter when I got money from welfare. I went back to prostituting on the street," she said.

Akasha's Story

Akasha is a younger woman from California, who has also been homeless many times in her life. "I am a young, trans, queer, sex worker woman survivor of domestic violence and sexual assault," she says. Since Akasha came out as a trans woman and "transitioned" in her early twenties, she has been not only targeted by abusive partners, but also ostracized by and isolated from her family. "I was homeless on and off for about three years, and during this time I stayed with numerous abusive friends and sugar daddies. I was repeatedly blamed for the poverty and homelessness I felt trapped in. My health deteriorated to the point where I was sick eight months out of the year, had frequent panic attacks, got raped by a 'trick' and found myself sleeping outdoors in the middle of winter rains."[5] Akasha ended up in a domestic violence shelter after one of her sugar mommas became so violent that she found herself on the run for her life.

"How was your experience of being in a shelter, as a homeless person, as a trans woman, and as a sex worker?" I asked. "Well, for starters, I pretty much knew from the start that I couldn't afford to be out as a sex worker. Being the first trans woman at the shelter was trouble enough," she said. "The staff demonstrated the complete lack of training" on trans issues, Akasha says. "Apparently [the shelter] only bothered to offer any accommodations because of the local trans civil rights ordinance. They violated my confidentiality and outed me as transgendered to other residents."

But transphobia was not the only problem she experienced at the shelter. "Amazingly, the shelter staff showed overwhelming disdain for all the women there, treating us as if we were all 'abuse addicts' looking for our next fix, as if we craved the abuse we received. Like many women at the shelter I was frequently written up for missing my curfew, not doing my chores 'right,' and 'disrespectful communication' for standing up for myself and refusing to comply with their unreasonable demands. This is how I ended up having panic attacks almost every day towards the end of my stay. These panic attacks in turn were used by staff to justify further write-ups and threats of eviction."

Akasha continues: "During my stay at the DV shelter I was unable to do sex work at all because of the curfew and other restrictions, and fear of staff finding out. And my 'straight' job was also threatened by the demands placed on my time due to my weekly chores, which usually added up to about ten hours a week of cleaning and cooking during my regular work hours. This forced me to disclose to my boss that I was living in a shelter, and obviously, this compromised my job security."

"Another complaint I have is about what they called 'support' groups that we were required to attend at the shelter," she said. "These groups encouraged residents to disclose personal information that would often be later used against me by staff and opened us up to judgment from other residents. For instance, the pronoun that I used to describe my batterer distinguished me as the only out queer and made me vulnerable to ridicule by other residents. Also staff played on [the fact that I was] given a separate room to incite the envy of other residents who were forced to share rooms—sometimes up to four women to a room. Nevertheless, I felt more supported by other residents than by the staff."

"I saw widespread abuse of single mothers, especially those who were poor and in recovery from substance abuse. One single mom was harassed and then kicked out onto the street with her one-month-old daughter and three-year-old son while she and her daughter were detoxing off heroin, all because the three-year-old was rambunctious and demanded more time from the mom. So she got in trouble not just for her son's behavior but for missing her chores."

I know these stories are true, because I saw the same pattern when I stayed at the shelter back in 1994. I know they are true, because as a shelter worker I unintentionally participated in maintaining this pattern. Yet even if I did not have firsthand experiences of them, it's not hard to see why these problems occur; they are bound to when there are few, if any, institutional mechanisms to hold service providers accountable to the actual needs and perspectives of people receiving services. At most shelters, the only internal grievance procedures lack real teeth.

As a result, I am no longer able to delude myself with the self-indulgent fantasies that I can be a different kind of shelter worker, or that things would be different if I could be a shelter director. In fact, it is this self-indulgent feminist fantasy that we have about ourselves as feminists that often individualizes obvious problems, invisibilizes more subtle ones, and minimizes the urgent need for institutional, rather than individual, remedies. We need to not only criticize individual acts of mistreatment of survivors by the shelter system, but also instigate an active disloyalty to feminist utopianism which perpetuates the institutional abuse of survivors and forestalls structural changes.

Professionalization = Depoliticization

The process of "institutionalization" and "professionalization" of the "battered women's movement" and its ills have been widely discussed among long-time activists who created early domestic violence shelters.[6] Patricia Gaddis tells a typical radical feminist version of how it took place:

> Only a short time after the Feminists had fallen asleep, mainstream professionalism infiltrated battered women's programs, bringing forth a new and unpleasant hierarchy within the movement, a hierarchy that undermined the Feminists' effort to eradicate the root causes of domestic violence. Shared power among employees was quickly discarded and ethical practices that included the voices of battered women, basic training on the dynamics of domestic violence, and the power of shared experience among women was frowned upon...[u]nqualified executive directors were brought in from the mainstream to tell shelter staff and court advocates that they were not as important to the program as the licensed professionals...[b]attered women seeking refuge were held captive by the never-ending shelter rules that were put into place by the mainstream professionals who thumbed their noses at the original founders. Many safe houses now seemed more like prisons, or "social" bed and breakfasts, that prevented the disabled and women of all races, ages, classes, and religions and ethnic groups from entering. Victims were referred to as "crazy" and whips were cracked upon the backs of advocates or victims who dared question the professional task master's authority...[s]helter programs were no longer a safe place for all battered women.[7]

Radical feminists view the institutionalization and professionalization of the movement as a continuous process of "depoliticization," fueled by the patriarchal backlash and cooptation. Nancy J. Meyer of the Washington, D.C., Coalition Against Domestic Violence defines "depoliticization" as "a reframing process that directs attention away from (and recreates knowledge about) sexism, male dominance, patriarchy, and female subjugation." She argues that there "is nothing inherently wrong with trying to improve the conditions in which battered women live, but when putative efforts to just 'make it better' become the end goal, the political vision and motivation to address the real exegesis of male violence becomes sublimated."[8]

Aided by stronger laws against domestic violence, this "growing paternalism of the state" has resulted in many unintended negative consequences for survivors of domestic violence. For example, a report by the Family Violence Project of the Urban Justice Center on the impact of the mandatory arrest law in New York City discovered a dangerously high frequency of "victim arrest"—that is, when victims of domestic violence are arrested because of false or exaggerated allegations by their abusers, or because the victim fought back to defend herself or her children. The report states, "The negative effects of victim arrest were wide-ranging and lasting ... many women reported that their physical and mental health and well-being, financial status, educational goals, personal relationships and their family's physical and mental health and well-being were adversely affected by the arrest."[9]

According to Juley Fulcher, the public policy director of the National Coalition Against Domestic Violence, women are being evicted from their public housing when they report being abused, because the Anti-Drug Abuse Act of 1988 calls for an eviction when any resident or visitor is arrested for drug-related or violent crimes.[10] A recent ruling by a federal judge in Brooklyn found that child protection services routinely removed children from mothers who were abused by their partners under the premise that the mother failed to protect her children.[11] In Kentucky, a municipal judge was praised in the pages of the *Wall Street Journal* for fining two battered women for going back to their abusive partners after they had been granted restraining orders.[12]

Paternalism and bureaucratic procedures flourish also within the shelter systems. "Lately I've begun to wonder exactly who it is that domestic violence programs do shelter," writes Patty Neal Dorian. "It seems the list of 'we don't shelter those women' just keeps growing: women with substance abuse issues, homeless women, women with mental illnesses, women who are HIV-positive, women who won't attend parenting classes, women with physical disabilities, women who don't want protective orders, women who won't submit to drug tests and searches... [a]nd just to be completely sure this woman can't 'use' the system, these names get shared with every program within a 50-mile radius."[13]

In 1999, a jury in South Carolina found Cumbee Center, the local domestic violence shelter, negligent in the murder of a resident by her abusive husband, rewarding a claim of more than one hundred thousand dollars to the victim's mother. A local newspaper simply reported that the shelter drove Sebrenia Russaw Neal to see her husband "just nine days after she and her three children had left him and moved into the shelter," but Rita Smith and Gretchen Eckroate of the National Coalition Against Domestic Violence point out that the realities were much more complex.[14] According to Smith and Eckroate, it was the mother of the woman who relayed her husband's request to meet at an attorney's office, supposedly for some legal purpose. "When Sebrenia arrived at the office, she found out that her husband had lied about having an appointment with the lawyer, but he begged her to talk to him anyway. The advocate that escorted Sebrenia to the office advised her not to do so and told her she did not have to stay." However she "decided to talk to him anyway" and was shot and killed.

The most disturbing aspect of the Cumbee Center case, aside from the murder of the victim, was the fact that it was the domestic violence "experts" and their rhetoric that aided the verdict against the shelter. Smith and Eckroate write: "The plaintiff's expert witness ... testified that all women who came into the shelter suffered from battered women's syndrome and post-traumatic stress disorder and that they should not be allowed to make decisions for themselves for at least six months."[15] This episode illustrates how the rhetoric of "battered women's syndrome"—originally invented to explain why some women end up murdering or injuring their abusers rather than simply escaping and to help free or reduce sentences for women charged with such crimes—is now being used by domestic violence "experts" to negate survivors' agency and thus justify paternalistic rules and actions by the legal and shelter systems.

Not surprisingly, poor women, women of color, and their communities are among the groups impacted most harshly by the domestic violence movement's overreliance on the state. As Angela Davis pointed out during her keynote address at the historic Color of Violence Conference in 2000, "... the primary strategies for addressing violence against women rely on the state and on constructing gendered assaults on women as 'crimes,' the criminalization process further bolsters the racism of the courts and prisons. Those institutions, in turn, further contribute to violence against women. I suggest that we focus our thinking on this contradiction: Can a state that is thoroughly infused with racism, male dominance, class-bias, and homophobi, and that constructs itself in and through violence, act to minimize violence in the lives of women?"[16]

Andrea Smith voices some of the same sentiments expressed by Gaddis, Meyer, and Levey: "As the antiviolence movement has gained greater public prominence, domestic violence and rape crisis centers have become increasingly professionalized to receive accreditation and funding from state and federal agencies." Smith continues, "Rather than develop peer-based services in which large groups of women can participate, they [domestic violence and rape crisis centers] employ individuals with the proper academic degrees or credentials. This practice excludes most women from full participation, particularly women of color and poor women."[17]

However, unlike those of Gaddis and Meyer, the visions of women who gathered at the Color of Violence Conference extended beyond refocusing on men's dominance over women as the fundamental root of violence against women. Illustrating mainstream domestic violence activists' refusal to "address sexual and domestic violence within the larger context of institutional inequality and violence," Smith criticized such narrow approaches as problematic because "violence within communities of color cannot be addressed seriously without dealing with the larger structures of violence, such as militarism, attacks on immigrants and Indian treaty rights, police brutality, the proliferation of prisons, economic neocolonialism, and institutional racism.... [I]t makes no sense to say that it is not okay for a man to hit his wife, but it is okay for him to bomb civilians in Iraq."[18] Thus Smith's and Davis' calls for political mobilization within the antiviolence movement are substantially different from those of white radical feminists.

White radical feminists such as Gaddis and Levey romanticize the "battered women's movement" that once was, where things were run collectively rather than hierarchically and all women were welcome and equal. Indeed, their cries of "depoliticization" naturally lead to calls for "repoliticization," to put the critical analysis of men's overwhelming dominance over women and other oppressions as subsystems of the patriarchy first—rather than seeing them as separate, interlocking mechanisms.

Mazie Hough and Ann Schonberger of the University of Maine have documented a radical feminist "success" story of Spruce Run, a collectively run domestic violence agency. Founded in 1972 by a group of feminists that included "a handful of women going through marital crises," Spruce Run initially supported itself through creative fundraisers. But in the late 1970s, it became "clear to Spruce Run that more secure funding sources were needed to help the organization thrive," and thus it began appealing for funding from the state and from the United Way. Shortly thereafter, the Steering Committee of Spruce Run decided to appoint one of the women as the executive director of the staff of four, and "others began to question a structure which gave one staff member more power than the others." After much discussion, the organization abolished the hierarchal structure, and has since implemented further policies to "eliminate status differences between administrators and service providers" and to reduce the pay gap based on longevity in order to remain true to the ideal of nonhierarchical organization.[19] Women involved in Spruce Run apparently believed that in order to make an institution equitable they needed to eliminate differences, be it authority, salary, or roles (administrative versus service provider).

But by this token, would it not become necessary to eliminate race in order to end racism? Hough and Schonberger do not explore how Spruce Run deals with any of the actual differences and imbalances that simply cannot be eliminated at the Steering Committee's whim, such as the power imbalances between women of color and white women, US-born women and immigrants, paid staff and volunteers, and service providers and recipients. Are the radical feminist recollections about the "battered women's movement" reality, or selective memories that require active overlooking of power imbalances?

I argue that, far from being an innocent victim of the patriarchal backlash, the flawed assumptions and analyses of the white radical feminism that shaped the early "battered women's movement" are partially responsible for the movement's uncritical collusion with racist, imperialist state interests, as well as the abuse of women within the shelter system. By focusing excessively on "the power of shared experiences among women," these radical feminists created a movement that discourages and suppress the discussions about the specificities of each woman's experiences within a complex matrix of social inequalities and examinations of ways in which some well-intentioned feminist women can and do abuse power over other women.

If we were to truly "repoliticize" the antiviolence movement, it would be more helpful to acknowledge that there are many power imbalances among women that are very difficult to eliminate than to hastily move to make them disappear. That way, we could hope to create structures that would actively counter the power relationships that already exist, that would hold ourselves accountable to each other.

We need to resist the anachronistic urge to accept eulogies as history, and instead build a multi-issue movement whose scope includes, but does not necessarily center, men's dominance over women, among many other structures of inequalities and injustices.

Implementing Strategies for Accountability

In 1992, the Coalition on Homelessness of San Francisco successfully lobbied the Social Services Commission of the City and County of San Francisco to adopt the "universal grievance procedure," which all homeless shelter agencies that receive city funding are required to comply with when clients appeal an agency's decision to deny or terminate services. In addition, the Department of Human Services was mandated to hire two client advocates to represent homeless people in internal and external hearings. These actions were in response to what was viewed by the Coalition as a prevalent problem within homeless shelters: unequal and arbitrary enforcement of agency rules that resulted in unfair evictions from housing and denial of services.[20]

Even though some people initially questioned whether or not such a policy was even needed, the increase of grievances filed against service providers following the implementation proved the successfulness of the new policy: at last, clients had a realistic chance of appealing and overturning unfair evictions and denial of services. According to the Coalition on Homelessness:

> In the first year of implementation there were 360 requests for shelter hearings regarding denials of services. At the shelter level, 49% of the denials were overturned or modified, and 51% were upheld or the client failed to appear at the internal hearing. Of the denials upheld at the shelter level, 31 clients requested a hearing with an arbitrator. The arbitrator overturned or modified the shelter's decision in 31% of the cases and upheld the shelter decision in 69% of the cases. Over the next three years the numbers of clients requesting appeals have steadily increased. During the time period from February 1996 through January of 1997, 690 clients requested to appeal a denial of services. Of those, 309 (45%) were overturned, 82 (12%) had the penalty modified, 135 (19%) were upheld, and 164 (24%) clients failed to appear at the shelter hearing. There were 43 arbitrations during the same time period with 10 shelter decisions upheld, 15 overturned, 5 with a modified penalty, and 13 clients who failed to appear.[21]

Riding on this success, the Coalition on Homelessness has been working to create similar grievance procedures for "transitional" housing facilities, which include substance abuse, youth, mental health, and domestic violence facilities. But the adoption of client-centered grievance procedures has been minimal outside of homeless shelters. In addition, while good grievance procedures can make the arbitrary application of policies less frequent, they cannot change unfair or paternalistic policies themselves. "We tried to get it to include policy changes too, but most providers here are adamantly opposed to homeless people having rights," says an activist with the Coalition on Homelessness, also noting that the Coalition's effort is "seen as us trying to change their programs."[22]

Part of the reluctance on the part of the domestic violence shelters to embrace client-centered grievance procedures and agency policies such as those advocated by the Coalition (and the motivation on the part of the City of San Francisco to exempt domestic violence shelters from the structures it deemed necessary for homeless shelters) comes from our pervasive tendency to uncritically accept domestic violence shelters as organizations that are wholeheartedly committed to the empowerment of women, and therefore, cannot possibly mistreat their clients the same way homeless shelters might. These stereotypical presumptions about women as naturally compassionate, caring, loving, sympathetic, fair-minded, and peaceful allow us to underestimate women's capacity to use power and control over other women. We also underestimate the fact that despite the talks of "sisterhood," women as a group do not necessarily share the same interests, and that allowing feminist service providers to set agency policies with little or no input from service recipients silences survivors, resulting in an intensified hostility and paternalism toward women accessing services.

The work of the Coalition on Homelessness, and its insistence on putting service recipients at the center of program design and implementation, fit in the broader context of the harm reduction movement. Harm reduction is a philosophy initially developed and adopted by people organizing around the HIV/AIDS crisis and other health issues among injection drug users, but its impact and implication for the rest of the progressive social change movement is far-reaching.

The Harm Reduction Coalition defines harm reduction as "a set of practical strategies that reduce negative consequences of drug use" that "meet[s] drug users where they are at." It demands that "interventions and policies designed to serve drug users reflect specific individual and community needs." According to the Coalition, "Harm reduction stands in stark contrast to the law enforcement efforts to criminalize and prosecute drug use as well as to the medical community's efforts to pathologize it."[23]

Harm reduction demands that the goals of any social intervention be determined by communities and individuals receiving the intervention, and that any such intervention needs to be evaluated by these goals, rather than that of the government or the service provider. For example, if the goal of the drug user community was to reduce the risk of HIV and Hepatitis C transmission, any intervention would have to be evaluated on the basis of how successfully it achieves this goal, rather than how successfully it reduced drug use, as government, religious, medical, and other institutions frequently demand.

In 1997, the American Medical Association (AMA) released a position paper on the use of harm reduction strategy. While maintaining abstinence as the ultimate, most desirable goal, the AMA acknowledges that harm reduction mechanisms such as needle exchange programs are "effective" in "reducing the spread of HIV and other pathogens ... as demonstrated by extensive programs in Europe and more limited experience recently in this country."[24] With the AMA's somewhat reluctant admission that employing harm reduction strategies saves lives, funding for needle exchange and other harm reduction–based programs from local health departments and mainstream foundations is increasing.

Harm reduction is the opposite of paternalism, which unfortunately is rampant within antiviolence agencies that are based on the social service model. Redefined in terms of survivor advocacy, harm reduction could provide a set of practical strategies to reduce negative consequences to survivors' lives, while honoring each survivor's own goals and coping strategies. This includes behaviors that have been traditionally labeled as "maladaptive" or "unhealthy," such as alcohol and drug use, self-harm, sex work, irregular eating and sleeping, and staying in contact with the perpetrator—behaviors that could get a woman evicted from domestic violence shelters today.

In practice, of course, this shift would require us to acknowledge complex social issues that contribute to individual survivors' unique visions and methods of survival, which in turn would force us to be politicized around a multitude of violence and oppression issues, rather than just sexism or even just domestic and sexual violence. It would also require the institutionalization of methods which guarantee that survivors are regarded as agents of their own survival, and could be given real power in shaping interventions designed to assist them, including opportunities to lead antiviolence efforts within our communities.

The successful organizing efforts of the Coalition on Homelessness and the harm reduction movement speak volumes about the importance of creating mechanisms to ensure that communities that receive services are given realistic power to design, critique, and challenge any services. Social workers, medical professionals, and others who are genuinely committed to "helping" others—homeless people, drug users, or domestic violence survivors—need to be made to stop disempowering the communities they serve through their paternalism. Harm reduction needs to be explicitly adopted as one of the core principles for any organization providing social services, including those working with survivors of domestic violence. Within the movement against domestic violence, however, the pervasive notion of "women's shared experiences" and other feminist euphemisms hinder our ability to recognize our paternalism and to create structures that are truly survivor-driven.

Worse, even when survivors' voices are centered, we frequently end up creating a similarly faulty notion of "survivors' shared experiences," which works to invisibilize specificities of each survivor's experiences within the complex matrix of social identities, roles, and oppressions, usually to the detriment of women of color, poor women, immigrant women, and others marginalized and underrepresented within the domestic violence movement. Knowing this, we need to create explicit structures to counter this effect, rather than relying on our feminist consciousness to eventually "address" it.

What if we had an organization that did not provide any services itself, but organized survivors and advocates to fight for survivors' collective as well as individual interests, similar to what the Coalition on Homelessness does for homeless people? What if every woman coming into a domestic violence shelter received a telephone number for this organization, and she could bring in an advocate from this organization to help her appeal the decisions and policies of the shelter? What if shelters were made to defend their decisions and policies in front of an independent arbitrator? Only then could survivors begin to have a realistic say in the design and delivery of services at domestic violence shelters.

To move this strategy one step further: what if exploited and overworked employees of the shelter also organized to defend their collective and individual interests through a union? What if employees were given a realistic chance to protest the fact that they are made to take on unreasonable amounts of responsibility with too little actual power and too little pay? If we are truly committed to ending violence against women, we need to begin by refusing to buy into the Battered Women's Movement Syndrome, where we remain silent about abuses we receive in order to protect the agency, hoping that the abusive system will change if we just stay long enough.

The strategy I am talking about is hyper-institutionalization. Whereas some radical feminists wish to reverse the institutionalization of the antiviolence movement in order to return to the utopian "battered women's movement," I view this approach as anachronistic, historically revisionist, and hopelessly unrealistic. Instead, I am arguing for further institutionalization which would compensate for the negative impacts of one-sided institutionalization. This one-sided institutionalization has increased the powers of the state and of service providers, while leaving survivors and frontline workers without institutional backing. By creating structures to advocate for the interests of survivors and workers, we can hope to make various interests and values that enter into our discussions about how to operate social service agencies explicit, and these dynamic interactions would ultimately result in the redistribution of powers, and in a system of checks and balances for all parties.

Radical feminists who created and fostered early domestic violence shelters may view this approach as the ultimate disloyalty to their founding principles: (presumed) women's shared experiences, (presumed) equality of all women, (presumed) consensus decision-making, and communal power structure. I agree. Those shelters that opposed the initiatives of the Coalition on Homelessness are right: We are changing their programs.

The Limits of the Shelter System
The concept of an organization that advocates for survivors so that they can receive better services from domestic violence shelters is not necessarily new. In fact, many organizations set up by and for women of color and immigrant women have historically played this role across the country.

For example, Korean American Women In Need (KAN-WIN) was founded in Chicago in 1990 by seven Korean American women activists because traditional domestic violence shelters did not provide culturally sensitive materials and services, nor did they adequately address the impact of social injustices other than sexism, such as racism and classism, on Korean women's lives. KAN-WIN now provides some direct services, such as a crisis hotline. They also serve "as a liaison between battered Korean women and services," participate in "immigrant rights demonstrations and labor rights rallies," and mobilizes around issues such as the Korean "comfort women" during the Second World War.[25]

But even with outside advocates to push for better services and reforms, to change the design and delivery of services, shelter systems remain an expensive Band-Aid solution to domestic violence, something that is necessary only because we cannot rely on our friends, neighbors, and communities to adequately hold perpetrators accountable and support survivors. Many of us are struggling to develop grassroots community organizing that focuses on community accountability, community support, and prevention.

Women's Legal Alternative Collective (WLAC) of Olympia, Washington, is one of the groups that has a good grasp of the problems with the existing legal and medical remedies to domestic violence, but seems to be having difficulty articulating a clear, realistic alternative. Mainly made up of young white women active in the local "radical" and "anarchist" communities, reflecting the "alternative" culture of this town, WLAC believes in building an overwhelming community response against rape and abuse within "radical" communities to hold perpetrators accountable without utilizing the legal system. But if they were to bypass the legal system, how would they establish what actually took place when the allegation of rape or abuse was contested? After internal debates, women of WLAC decided that implementing quasi "community court" would be in contradiction to its original mission to do away with the legal system, and instead chose to not question women's stories. However, this approach is likely to result in the phenomenon of "retaliatory arrest," the term used by the Urban Justice Center to refer to the specific form of "victim arrest" where the perpetrator reports false or exaggerated allegations of abuse in order to silence and punish the real victim.[26]

Community accountability is a laudable philosophy, but in many cases its application lacks structures to ensure motivation for those being held accountable to respond in good will or to comply. While I have heard about some organizing efforts that have implemented community accountability within specific small communities (a South Asian immigrant community, a particular Native nation, etc.) with varying degrees of success, it is unrealistic as an alternative to the racist criminal justice system if the scheme requires the revival of the romanticized communities, the "village that raises a child." Considering the fact that we live in a society where the vast majority of people we meet every day are complete strangers, romantic communitarianism offers no more realistic vision for social justice than radical feminist utopianism does.

Northwest Network, a Seattle-based organization working within bisexual, transgender, lesbian, and gay communities, offers both radical analyses of social injustices and concrete strategies to prevent abuse through community organizing without euphemistic idealization of what "community" is supposed to be. For example, whereas mainstream antiviolence organizations view violence as an anomaly, a result of the conscious choice by the perpetrator, Northwest Network director Connie Burke believes that abuse of power is so prevalent in this society that each of us needs to make conscious choices not to misuse our individual as well as institutional power and privilege, lest we would be participating in abuse of some kind by default. Unlike the radical feminist presumption that all women have shared experiences in relation to the patriarchy, this analysis allows for the exploration of specificities of each woman's experiences, and for constructing systems of internal and external accountability within our movements.[27]

"Friends Are Reaching Out" (F.A.R. Out) is a particularly inspiring program model from Northwest Network. Initially designed for communities of queer people of color, this "radical organizing project to strengthen friendships and build accountability in our relationships with each other" facilitates intentional dialogues about relationship abuse among close friends. This approach is based on participants' shared commitment to staying connected to each other, while building the capacity of friendship networks to resist isolation, and hold each other accountable.[28]

The basic assumption of the F.A.R. Out program is that even though we may love and care for our friends, we are unreliable to each other in the face of abuse unless we work in advance on building the capacity to respond. In addition to clarifying our expectations for what roles friends should play when one is in a troubling relationship so as to "take the guesswork out of how to support your friend when they're in need," the strategy of staying connected may prevent relationship abuse because "isolation from friends and family is the most common tactic used by abusers in establishing control patterns."[29]

The particular challenge to those of us who work within the feminist antiviolence movement is to confront and dispel the myths we have created about ourselves as women and as feminists. We need to challenge the notion of women's shared experiences and accept specificities of women's experiences in relation to the complex matrix of social institutions, not just the patriarchy. We need to challenge the notion that women do not have real power in this society, and address how all of us are capable of using our various powers and privileges lovingly or abusively. We need to acknowledge the limitation of our feminist consciousness and ethics, and pursue structural remedies to hold ourselves accountable to each other as women and as fellow human beings.

Once we cease to fear being tagged as disloyal to these feminist myths, once we cease to allow the use of feminism to preserve the status quo, we can begin the true transformation of our feminist movements against all forms of violence and oppression, a revolution. When the rebels take down the walls of feminist pretenses and the castle of self-serving feminist make-believe, feminism will survive, more powerful than ever.

25

Gender Violence and the Prison-Industrial Complex

Statement by Critical Resistance and INCITE! Women of Color Against Violence

We call social justice movements to develop strategies and analyses that address both state *and* interpersonal violence, particularly violence against women. Currently, activists/movements that address state violence (such as anti–prison, anti–police brutality groups) often work in isolation from activists/movements that address domestic and sexual violence. The result is that women of color, who suffer disproportionately from both state and interpersonal violence, have become marginalized within these movements. It is critical that we develop responses to gender violence that do not depend on a sexist, racist, classist, and homophobic criminal justice system. It is also important that we develop strategies that challenge the criminal justice system and that also provide safety for survivors of sexual and domestic violence. To live violence- free lives, we must develop holistic strategies for addressing violence that speak to the intersection of all forms of oppression.

The antiviolence movement has been critically important in breaking the silence around violence against women and providing much-needed services to survivors. However, the mainstream antiviolence movement has increasingly relied on the criminal justice system as the frontline approach toward ending violence against women of color. It is important to assess the impact of this strategy.

1) Law enforcement approaches to violence against women may deter some acts of violence in the short term. However, as an overall strategy for ending violence, criminalization has not worked. In fact, the overall impact of mandatory arrest laws for domestic violence have led to decreases in the number of battered women who kill their partners in self-defense, but they have not led to a decrease in the number of batterers who kill their partners.[1] Thus, the law protects batterers more than it protects survivors.

2) The criminalization approach has also brought many women into conflict with the law, particularly women of color, poor women, lesbians, sex workers, immigrant women, women with disabilities, and other marginalized women. For instance, under mandatory arrest laws, there have been numerous incidents where police officers called to domestic incidents have arrested the woman who is being battered.[2] Many undocumented women have reported cases of sexual and domestic violence, only to find themselves deported.[3] A tough law-and-order agenda also leads to long punitive sentences for women convicted of

killing their batterers.[4] Finally, when public funding is channeled into policing and prisons, budget cuts for social programs, including women's shelters, welfare, and public housing, are the inevitable side effect.[5] These cutbacks leave women less able to escape violent relationships.

3) Prisons don't work. Despite an exponential increase in the number of men in prisons, women are not any safer, and the rates of sexual assault and domestic violence have not decreased.[6] In calling for greater police responses to and harsher sentences for perpetrators of gender violence, the antiviolence movement has fueled the proliferation of prisons which now lock up more people per capita in the United States than any other country.[7] During the past fifteen years, the number of women, especially women of color, in prison has skyrocketed.[8] Prisons also inflict violence on the growing numbers of women behind bars. Slashing, suicide, the proliferation of HIV, strip searches, medical neglect, and rape of prisoners have largely been ignored by antiviolence activists.[9] The criminal justice system, an institution of violence, domination, and control, has increased the level of violence in society.

4) The reliance on state funding to support antiviolence programs has increased the professionalization of the antiviolence movement and alienated it from its community organizing, social justice roots.[10] Such reliance has isolated the antiviolence movement from other social justice movements that seek to eradicate state violence, such that it acts in conflict rather than in collaboration with these movements.

5) The reliance on the criminal justice system has taken power away from women's ability to organize collectively to stop violence and has invested this power within the state. The result is that women who seek redress in the criminal justice system feel disempowered and alienated.[11] It has also promoted an individualistic approach toward ending violence such that the only way people think they can intervene in stopping violence is to call the police. This reliance has shifted our focus from developing ways communities can collectively respond to violence.

In recent years, the mainstream anti-prison movement has called important attention to the negative impact of criminalization and the buildup of the prison-industrial complex. Because activists who seek to reverse the tide of mass incarceration and criminalization of poor communities and communities of color have not always centered gender and sexuality in their analysis or organizing, we have not always responded adequately to the needs of survivors of domestic and sexual violence.

1) Prison and police accountability activists have generally organized around and conceptualized men of color as the primary victims of state violence.[12] Women prisoners and victims of police brutality have been made invisible by a focus on the war on our brothers and sons. It has failed to consider how women are affected as severely by state violence as men.[13] The plight of women who are raped by INS officers or prison guards, for instance, has not received sufficient attention. In

addition, women carry the burden of caring for extended family when family and community members are criminalized and warehoused.[14] Several organizations have been established to advocate for women prisoners; however, these groups have been frequently marginalized within the mainstream anti-prison movement.[15]

2) The anti-prison movement has not addressed strategies for addressing the rampant forms of violence women face in their everyday lives, including street harassment, sexual harassment at work, rape, and intimate partner abuse. Until these strategies are developed, many women will feel shortchanged by the movement. In addition, by not seeking alliances with the antiviolence movement, the anti-prison movement has sent the message that it is possible to liberate communities without seeking the well-being and safety of women.

3) The anti-prison movement has failed to sufficiently organize around the forms of state violence faced by Lesbian, Gay, Bisexual, Transgendered, Two-spirited, and Intersex (LGBTTI) communities. LGBTTI street youth and trans people in general are particularly vulnerable to police brutality and criminalization.[16] LGBTTI prisoners are denied basic human rights such as family visits from same-sex partners, and same-sex consensual relationships in prison are policed and punished.[17]

4) While prison abolitionists have correctly pointed out that rapists and serial murderers comprise a small number of the prison population, we have not answered the question of how these cases should be addressed.[18] The inability to answer the question is interpreted by many antiviolence activists as a lack of concern for the safety of women.

5) The various alternatives to incarcaration that have been developed by anti-prison activists have generally failed to provide sufficient mechanisms for safety and accountability for survivors of sexual and domestic violence. These alternatives often rely on a romanticized notion of communities, which have yet to demonstrate their commitment and ability to keep women and children safe or seriously address the sexism and homophobia that is deeply embedded within them.[19]

We call on social justice movements concerned with ending violence in all its forms to:

1) Develop community-based responses to violence that do not rely on the criminal justice system and which have mechanisms that ensure safety and accountability for survivors of sexual and domestic violence. Transformative practices emerging from local communities should be documented and disseminated to promote collective responses to violence.

2) Critically assess the impact of state funding on social justice organizations and develop alternative fundraising strategies to support these organizations. Develop collective fundraising and organizing strategies for anti-prison and antiviolence organizations. Develop strategies

and analyses that specifically target state forms of sexual violence.

3) Make connections between interpersonal violence, the violence inflicted by domestic state institutions (such as prisons, detention centers, mental hospitals, and child protective services), and international violence (such as war, military base prostitution, and nuclear testing).

4) Develop an analysis and strategies to end violence that do not isolate individual acts of violence (either committed by the state or individuals) from their larger contexts. These strategies must address how entire communities of all genders are affected in multiple ways by both state violence and interpersonal gender violence. Battered women prisoners represent an intersection of state and interpersonal violence and as such provide an opportunity for both movements to build coalitions and joint struggles.

5) Put poor and working-class women of color in the center of their analysis, organizing practices, and leadership development. Recognize the role of economic oppression, welfare "reform," and attacks on women workers' rights in increasing women's vulnerability to all forms of violence, and locate antiviolence and anti-prison activism alongside efforts to transform the capitalist economic system.

6) Center stories of state violence committed against women of color in our organizing efforts.

7) Oppose legislative change that promotes prison expansion and criminalization of poor communities and communities of color—and thus state violence against women of color—even if these changes also incorporate measures to support victims of interpersonal gender violence.

8) Promote holistic political education at the everyday level within our communities—specifically, how sexual violence helps reproduce the colonial, racist, capitalist, heterosexist, and patriarchal society we live in, as well as how state violence produces interpersonal violence within communities.

9) Develop strategies for mobilizing against sexism and homophobia within our communities in order to keep women safe.

10) Challenge men of color and all men in social justice movements to take particular responsibility to address and organize around gender violence in their communities as a primary strategy for addressing violence and colonialism. We challenge men to address how their own histories of victimization have hindered their ability to establish gender justice in their communities.

11) Link struggles for personal transformation and healing with struggles for social justice.

We seek to build movements that not only end violence, but that create a society based on radical freedom, mutual accountability, and passionate reciprocity. In this society, safety and security will not be premised on violence or the threat of violence; it will be based on a collective commitment to guaranteeing the survival and care of all peoples.

26

Trans Action for Social and Economic Justice

Statements by TransJustice, a Project of the Audre Lorde Project

The following statements were issued in 2005 by TransJustice, a political group created by and for trans and gender nonconforming people of color. It is a project of the Audre Lorde Project, a community organizing center for Lesbian, Gay, Bisexual, Two-Spirit, and Transgender People of Color in the New York City area. TransJustice works to mobilize its communities and allies to act on the pressing political issues they face, including gaining access to jobs, housing, and education; obtaining trans-sensitive job training, healthcare, and HIV-related services; and resisting police, government, and anti-immigrant violence.

On April 24, 2002, the New York City Council amended the city's Human Rights Law to prohibit discrimination against transgender people, making it the third jurisdiction in New York State to enact such legislation. Two states, Minnesota and Rhode Island, and thirty-nine other municipalities have enacted similar laws. On December 22, 2004, two and a half years after the city's Human Rights Law was amended to preclude discrimination based on gender identity and expression, the New York City Human Rights Commission finally released its "Compliance Guidelines Regarding Gender Identity Discrimination."

The June 2005 Day of Action was endorsed by over one hundred organizations and individuals, including INCITE! Women of Color Against Violence. The trans and gender nonconforming community and its allies marched— more than two thousand strong—to link struggles and rally for the rights of all New Yorkers. Drawing from the success and momentum of the Day of Action, TransJustice organized a job fair in December 2005 to highlight the barriers to employment and education for trans and gender nonconforming people of color, and the challenges all people confront in trying to secure a living wage, health benefits, and access to educational opportunities.

CALL FOR A TRANS DAY OF ACTION

We invite our trans and gender nonconforming people of color communities (TGNC), and our allies, to march with us in the **First Annual Trans Day of Action for Social and Economic Justice** in New York City on June 24, 2005.

Visibility of Trans and Gender Nonconforming People
Communities of color have histories that are rich with multiple gender identities, experiences, and expressions, but today the two-gender system is enforced against us everywhere: in health care, immigration, bathrooms, clothing, shelters, pris-

ons, schools, government forms, job applications, and identity documents.

- Gender policing has always been part of the United States' bloody history. State-sanctioned gender policing targets Trans and Gender Non-Conforming people first by dehumanizing our identities. It denies our basic right to gender self-determination, and considers our bodies to be property of the state.
- Gender policing isolates TGNC people from our communities, many of which have been socialized with these oppressive definitions of gender. As a result, we all too often fall victim to verbal and physical violence. This transphobic violence is justified using medical theories and religious beliefs, and is perpetuated in order to preserve US heterosexist values. Gender policing and violence denies our existence and is used to maintain control over us and keep our communities divided.

Our Struggles and the Broader Community

The specific issues that TGNC people of color face mirror those faced by broader communities of color in New York City: police brutality and harassment; racist and xenophobic immigration policies; lack of access to living wage employment, adequate affordable housing, quality education, and basic health care; and the impact of US imperialism and the so-called US "war on terrorism" being waged against people at home and abroad. These issues are compounded for TGNC people of color by the fact that homophobia and transphobia are so pervasive in society. As a result, our community is disproportionately represented in homeless shelters, in foster care agencies, and in jails and prisons.

- In April 2002, the city of New York passed a nondiscrimination law that included gender identity as a protected category under the city's human rights law, yet it took the Bloomberg administration two years to create and release a set of guidelines to define what this meant. Meanwhile, TGNC people continue to experience high levels of violence and harassment everywhere we go.
- Across the country, people of color communities face high levels of unemployment. For example, it is widely known that the unemployment rate for Black men in New York City is now at 50%. We can only deduce that the rate of unemployment for TGNC people of color is likely to be much higher, since there is hardly any New York State employment data for our community. Due to the lack of employment opportunities, many of us are forced to accept work that is criminalized by the government, stigmatized by society, and offers very little safety.
- The anti-immigrant REAL ID act not only blatantly violates the rights of immigrants, but also has a direct impact on the lives of all TGNC people. This is especially relevant for people

of color, who since 9/11 have experienced rising levels of policing and scrutiny from state agencies such as the Department
of Motor Vehicles and Social Security. TGNC people are portrayed as frauds and potential so-called "terrorists," and then
targeted or denied rights.

- The police, as agents of the government, have brutalized and
  murdered multitudes of people in our communities over the
  past few years. Many of them are people of trans experience
  who have had no recourse because the violence perpetuated
  against them was, and still is, state-sanctioned.

As trans and gender nonconforming people of color, we see that our struggle today
is directly linked to many struggles here and around the world. *We view the June
24 Trans Day of Action for Social and Economic Justice as a day to stand in solidarity
with all peoples and movements fighting against oppression and inequality.* We also
view this action as following the legacy of our trans people of color warriors, such
as Sylvia Rivera, and others who with extreme determination fought not only for
the rights of all trans and gender nonconforming people, but also were on the
frontlines for the liberation of all oppressed peoples. In this spirit, we as trans and
gender nonconforming peoples of color call on all social justice activists, lesbian,
gay, bi, and trans movements, immigrant rights organizations, youth and student groups, trade union and workers' organizations, religious communities, and
HIV/AIDS and social service agencies to endorse this call to action and to build
contingents to march in solidarity together on June 24. With this march we com-
memorate the lives of those who came before us, and honor the courage of all our
communities that continue to struggle and fight for liberation and self-determination every day.

CALL FOR THE FIRST NEW YORK CITY
TRANS AND GENDER NONCONFORMING
PEOPLE OF COLOR JOB AND EDUCATION FAIR

We invite our trans and gender nonconforming people of color communities and
our allies within employment and educational institutions, as well as GED and
job readiness programs, to participate with us in the historic celebration of the
first-ever New York City Trans and Gender Non-Conforming People of Color Job
and Education Fair on Saturday, December 3, 2005, from 10 am to 6 pm at the
Pennsylvania Hotel.

Although trans and gender nonconforming peoples, especially of color, comprise a diverse skill-based population, our talents are often underutilized because
of societal stigma and discrimination within employment and educational institutions. In December 2004, the New York City Commission on Human Rights
(CHR) added new antidiscrimination guidelines to the Human Rights Law that
prohibits discrimination against trans and gender nonconforming people on the basis

of gender identity or expression in regards to employment, housing, and public accom- modations, including city agencies. Nationally, over 236 employers, including 53 Fortune 500 and 104 private sector companies, have adopted gender identity guidelines within their hiring policies.

We, as trans and gender nonconforming people of color living in New York, are taking the initiative to ensure that our communities reap the full benefits of the CHR guidelines by organizing the *New York City Trans and Gender Noncon- forming People of Color Job and Education Fair.* We see this endeavor as part of the dismantling of the oppressive standards of the two-gender system that have disenfranchised our communities, reducing us to second-class status. We strive to change the political climate in this country that has historically forced many Trans and Gender Nonconforming people to have few economic opportunities and/or be dependent on substandard governmental programs for our survival. We demand:

- The right to secure the basic human entitlements of jobs and educational opportunities
- An end to the daily harassment, discrimination, and violence we encounter in the workplace or at schools
- The right to the proper recognition of our identities, pronouns, or the freedom to not use pronouns
- The right to use the restrooms, locker rooms, or living accom- modations of our choosing, free from gender profiling and the fear of possible arrest.

Moreover, we are organizing *the New York City Trans and Gender Nonconforming People of Color Job and Education Fair* to spotlight the historical class, racial, sex- ual, and gender oppression of poor and communities of color for centuries in this country. The recent blatant governmental negligence in the Gulf region during Hurricane Katrina—particularly in New Orleans, Louisiana, a cultural center for African American trans and gender nonconforming people—is a glaring example of how economic disenfranchisement plagues poor people and communities of color in the United States.

As all people living in the United States face record unemployment and under- employment, while the Bush administration continues to spend billions of dollars on the war in Iraq, we as trans and gender nonconforming peoples of color stand in solidarity with all working and poor people who are struggling for the right to a living-wage job, health benefits, and access to affordable education.

27

"The Personal is the Private is the Cultural"
South Asian Women Organizing Against Domestic Violence

Puneet Kaur Chawla Sahota

Women of color have participated in and changed the movement against domestic violence in the United States. South Asian women are an important part of this story. Here, the term "South Asia" refers to countries found within the "Indian subcontinent," including India, Pakistan, Bangladesh, Nepal, Bhutan, Sri Lanka, and the Maldives. First-generation immigrant women who came to the United States in the 1960s, 1970s, and early 1980s founded the first South Asian women's organizations (SAWOs), all of which work to end domestic violence in South Asian immigrant communities. Since then, second-generation South Asian women—those who were born in the United States or immigrated before the age of five years—have also founded SAWOs. Today, there are SAWOs in most of the urban areas in the United States where there are significant South Asian immigrant populations, and new organizations continue to emerge. These organizations constitute a new movement, with increasing numbers of South Asian women joining grassroots efforts to improve their communities. As a South Asian woman, I am deeply grateful to the activists who work in SAWOs. We can honor these activists by including their stories as part of the history of women's movements in the United States.

In this chapter, I first discuss the personal and political factors that influenced first- and second-generation South Asian activists to form anti-domestic violence organizations. Then, I examine some of the strategies these activists have used to work most effectively with their communities on issues around domestic violence. All of the information presented in this chapter is from interviews I conducted with first- and second-generation founders of SAWOs from 2002–2003. I interviewed first-generation activists who founded three SAWOs: Manavi of New Jersey, Sakhi of New York City, and Apna Ghar of Chicago. I also interviewed second generation founders of Raksha of Atlanta and Chaya of Seattle. In addition, I interviewed second-generation activists who have become involved in the SAWOs that were founded by first-generation women.

The activists who participated in interviews have my deepest gratitude. Only a portion of the interviews could be included in this chapter, but I appreciate all who shared their stories with me. Their work is vital to the health of the South Asian community and I thank them for their tireless dedication. This research was funded by the Katherine L. Krieghbaum Scholarship at Northwestern University. Many thanks to my thesis advisor, Professor Ji-Yeon Yuh, for her encouragement, wisdom, and thoughtful guidance throughout this work. I am also grateful to students and faculty in the American Studies program at Northwestern University, especially Professor Nicola Beisel, for their insightful comments.

Roots of Activism

In 1965, the Immigration Reform Act opened US borders to immigrants in "preferred" categories of employment, which included science, engineering, and medicine. A large wave of Asian immigrants who had these "preferred" occupations followed. Immigrants from India who came to the United States early in this wave were the first generation to come of age after Indian independence. As a result, the independence movement had a profound influence on them. Several of the women who founded SAWOs in the United States had family members who protested and participated actively in the struggle for India's independence. Even those without family members in this movement experienced post-Independence optimism and the faith in political activism that accompanied it. In describing "her generation," Anannya Bhattacharjee, one of the founders of Sakhi in New York, said:

> Our parents experienced the independence movement. They may not have been part of it directly, but there is this very visceral sense of colonialism and the importance of Third World power, and India was a very important decolonized country ... You could not grow up without admiring the independence movement in India, without knowing all the icons and where they lived and what they ate. I basically arrived here with the importance of independence of colonialism ingrained in my head.

She also noted that the state she grew up in, Bengal, was especially active in political struggles. Student movements and peasant movements that were underway while she was still a child may not have been comprehensible to her; however, they formed "part of the background noise" that shaped her ideology and motivated her to pursue a life of community organizing and activism.

Shamita Das Dasgupta, one of the founders of Manavi in New Jersey, also came from a family where political engagement was very important. In describing the development of her social consciousness, Shamita said:

> In my family we talked about imperialism and colonization since I can remember. We heard stories, read stories of the independence movement. There were women involved, and men involved in the revolutionary parts of it. It wasn't as if it [her social consciousness] was something that suddenly happened, it was something I was very conscious of. And it wasn't something that was invisible in my mind, it was very clear. And my school—this was after independence, so everything was possible. The idea was that you were supposed to change the world. Our school encouraged us to go into the *bastis* ... you know, the tenements, the huts, and work with kids there. So you know, we really were very conscious that we had a responsibility to our society and to our environment. This wasn't something that happened to me because I came here [to the United States]. I came here and got involved [in the women's movement] *because* those things were already there.

Thus, the development of an activist sensibility did not depend on South Asian immigrants' exposure to the women's movement in the United States. The ways in which their activism manifested itself were certainly influenced by their immigration, but they "came with" the initial motivation to effect social change. Shamita explicitly stated that her identification of herself as "a feminist" did not simply begin when she came to the United States. She said:

> It's not just the USA. I was very much influenced by a history of resistance in India, women's resistance as well as resistance to imperialist forces, peasant movements. So there's a long history of activism in India. It's always been a part of my reality. It's not something new … I'm in a long line of people that were influenced by what happened.

While India's hard-won independence gave future immigrants confidence in political action, other movements in India also provided a source of inspiration. Even if they had remained in India, women that shared Anannya and Shamita's political and family influences might still have worked for social change.

Prem Sharma, one of the founders of Apna Ghar in Chicago, said that her parents' activism had a significant influence on her own desire to engage in community service activities. Her father was a physician who donated his services for free, and she described her mother as a "reformer." When I asked Prem where she got her activist energy, she said:

> I think it came from my mother. My mother was this activist … she brought a lot of reforms in the families back home. She was not a degree holder or anything. Actually she only went to school up to second grade. She was a very, very amazing woman, very dynamic. She would just offer her services to anybody, even strangers, and helped them out. She … brought people home from nowhere, helped them out, cooked dinners for them, found their families. I mean, you name it, she would do it, anything. And I think I saw when I was growing up, that without any expectations of any return or anything, she would just offer … [a]nd although she herself didn't go to school she made sure her children and her daughters were all highly educated. She was a reformer … [s]he had some sort of a power that people would listen to her.

Prem's mother passed down her passion for activism and community service to her daughter. Prem has founded several community organizations, beginning with the Chicago-area Club of Indian Women in 1977. This group was initially a social one, but the women soon looked for a need that they could fill in the South Asian community. In 1983, Prem founded a crisis hotline for Chicago-area Indians. People who called the number were then connected with Indian professionals who donated their services, such as physicians, lawyers, and counselors. Women in abusive relationships were referred to mainstream battered women's shelters, but these shelters were not able to cater to the specific needs of South Asian women. As Prem said, she soon "realized there was a problem because our women had different food habits … religious, languages, clothing, the whole attitude and culture was different." Five years after the crisis hotline was founded, volunteers analyzed the type of calls and found that domestic violence was second only to requests for divorces. Based on this knowledge, Prem set out to found a shelter for South Asian women. In her networking efforts, she met Kanta Khipple, who was working as a counselor for Asian Human Services at the time. Together, the two women founded Apna Ghar, which means "our home," along with four other women from around Chicago. Apna Ghar was incorporated in 1989 and is now open to immigrant women of all backgrounds in the Chicagoland area, although the majority of women who come to the shelter are South Asian.

Kanta Khipple came to the United States with an activist mindset, and, like Shamita Das Dasgupta, she soon found ways to engage in activism through participating in United States. social movements. Kanta was involved in social justice work in India and continued this type of work after immigrating to the United States. One of her many projects was cofounding Apna Ghar. At the time of India's independence in 1947, she had a successful career in public health. She worked with the World Health Organization and was one of the first professionals to perform family planning education in developing countries. She was also a member of an intellectual cadre of politically liberal scholars. She and her husband, a journalist, would gather for frequent political talks with such noted independence era intellectuals as Khushwant Singh. Soon after immigrating, she jumped into community struggles in Chicago. As a social worker and counselor, she worked with women and people of color, including Hispanic migrant workers, residents of Chicago's public housing in Robert Taylor Homes, and Asian immigrants in Chicago's Uptown area through her affiliation with Asian Human Services. She observed that conditions for women in the Cook County Hospital were atrocious in 1967, and set up demonstrations to protest the hospital's maltreatment of pregnant women. Kanta became a national leader, both in the South Asian community and in the mainstream women's movement because of her tireless activism. In addition, she worked for Planned Parenthood in its infancy and was in charge of the organization's professional training program for international students where she taught other women how to spread awareness of family planning in their communities.

The Civil Rights movement was an important influence on many first-generation activists and also served as an arena for their work. Kanta Khipple named Martin Luther King Jr. as one of the people who had influenced her ideas; conversely, she influenced civil rights leaders' ideas about reproductive rights. She told me the story of her discussions with Jesse Jackson:

> Jesse Jackson was a young man when he came to visit me at Planned Parenthood Association … [h]e came to ask me … [t]hey thought if we are focusing on the Black population to prevent further babies, their population will go down. They wanted to have an increasing population. We had a long discussion. I told Jesse Jackson I believed

... family planning means plan your family. Plan reproduction, not just one or two. If your means allow you to have three children, you can have three children. If you don't have a child, I would even help sterile couples to have children, to adopt children. So it has to be a balance. Where a movement fails it is because you don't create a balance. I told Jesse Jackson I want whatever colors, white, or Asian children, they should be healthy. Parents should be able to send them to school. Parents should be able to educate them properly and to feed them. And also, to reduce the infant mortality, because if there is one after the other, they will die, some of the children will die. And he was very much impressed ... [h]e would come to talk to me when he used to work in Woodlawn. It's the [civil rights movement] leadership with whom I have worked very closely.

The engagement of South Asian activists in the Civil Rights movement and the mainstream women's movement was similar: the activists influenced these movements, and in turn, were influenced by them. Many first-generation activists attended lectures on their college campuses on feminist struggles, and some participated actively in feminist groups. International attention was focused on the political struggles in the United States during this volatile time. As Shamita Das Dasgupta said,

> I came here in 1968. It was the time of the Vietnam War, the feminist movement, and the Civil Rights movement. I knew about some of that while I was in India. I became very interested and especially thought that the way I could engage in the social change that was going on around me was to get involved in the feminist movement.

Shamita returned to school in 1974, where she got involved with campus feminism groups. She participated in consciousness-raising groups. She said, "Because I happened to be at that time one of the very small handful of people of color, women of color who was engaged, I ended up rising through the ranks very quickly." Although Shamita held leadership positions at a national level in the mainstream women's movement, she had an ambivalent relationship with this movement. Shamita said, "I questioned at that time the way the movement was structured and who was involved in it and what issues were being addressed ... I started thinking about women of color and immigrant women and what was our space in there, what was our role." Thus, while the "[mainstream] feminist movement was a big part of our conscious influences," as Shamita said, first-generation South Asian women felt that this movement did not fully address issues faced by South Asian women, or immigrant women more generally.

Radha Hegde, who cofounded Manavi (an antiviolence organization for South Asian women in New Jersey) with Shamita in 1985, eloquently described the disconnect between the immigrant experience and the language used by the mainstream women's movement:

> This whole idea in the 1970s, many of us were so moved by the women's movement here, the personal is political and so on. We led this divided existence where you're out listening to the personal is the political, you're listening to Gloria Steinem and reading Germaine Greer and so on. And then you come to the immigrant front where it's the personal is the private is the cultural, it's not the political. So then you're faced ... everything is cultural. Wife-beating is cultural, docility is cultural, everything is cultural. It's the reign of cultural, and nothing is political. The idea to reinstate our immigrant lives and to see the "cultural" through a more organized lens ... to see the political complexity within our lives ... was, I think, very exhilarating.

Radha's story demonstrated the complex interaction between political, personal, and professional factors that motivated many South Asian women to found SAWOs. She immigrated to the United States in her early twenties as a graduate student in journalism. As a South Asian immigrant, she faced prejudice in graduate school, including racial slurs and anxious inquiries as to when she would return to India. Her exposure to women's issues during graduate school, both in and out of the classroom, strongly influenced her decision to concentrate her research on reproductive rights in India. As she said, "This country provided me with a new context" with which to view India. Her scholarly work on women's issues in India and her personal experiences as an immigrant woman in the United States both eventually led to her to cofound Manavi.

Second generation women also felt a dissonance between the discourse of the mainstream women's movement and their experiences as South Asian women. Soniya Munshi, who was the program director at Manavi when I interviewed her, began organizing against domestic violence in the mainstream women's movement in Minnesota as an undergraduate student. She later moved to Manavi because she felt "a lack in the women's movement of immigrant rights' issues." Tanmeet Sethi, a founding member of Chaya, felt similarly about the lack of attention to immigrant issues in the mainstream women's movement:

> In just becoming more aware of the women's movement and "feminism" in America in college ... I definitely identified with it because I grew up here, but I also felt very much apart from it because I felt like it really focused on the Western white woman. So for me, I felt it was a necessary and great, empowering movement, but in many ways I felt it was really not about me. It affected me in ways, but in other ways I almost rebelled against it.

South Asian women are not alone in their dissatisfaction with the mainstream women's movement—they are part of a larger movement of women of color creating their own spaces for dialogue.

Although the mainstream women's movement was a key motivating influence for many first- and second-generation activists, there have also been other political factors that have inspired second-generation women to become involved with SAWOs. South Asians, along with other Asians, have been stereotyped in America as a "model minority"—highly educated, professionally successful, quiet, obedient, politically apathetic, and quickly assimilated into the American mainstream. Personal experience with the model minority myth moved some second-generation women toward activism. As is evident in the stories of these activists, South Asians have been far from politically indifferent! However, South Asian communities in the United States have attempted to adhere to the seemingly positive aspects of the model minority stereotype, particularly by encouraging children to be highly educated and choose "safe" professions. These pressures from within her community motivated Shaila Bheda, a second-generation woman in Atlanta, to become involved with youth outreach activities. At the time I interviewed her, Shaila was the program coordinator for youth activities at Raksha. She said that although her own parents did not pressure her to choose a specific career, many of her peers did feel that their families were pushing them into medicine or engineering. Shaila said that if she is able to help other young South Asians discover their own aptitudes and dreams, as her parents did for her, she will have a fulfilling career:

> I talk to a lot of people my age when I'm doing this youth program now, and they say, "Oh my gosh, if I had this when I was a kid!" And that's exactly one of the reasons why I wanted to do something for South Asian youth in particular in the same way I wanted to do this for South Asian women when we first started is because there are specific challenges that South Asian youth face because they are South Asian. Adolescence is difficult for everybody, you know, it's just a hard, ugly time for most kids ... But for South Asian youth, you have the added challenges of a different skin color, language barriers, you have religious differences, potentially, you have a different name, you have, once again, that whole myth of the model minority concept to be living up to, a lot of community pressure. Just a lot of things that a lot of people face, but there's a cultural variable there. I felt it would be important to have programs that specifically dealt with those issues ... that were run by other South Asian people. South Asian people still think there's three professions you can have: physician, engineer, lawyer ... those are great professions, but there are many other options out there as well.

In sum, several important social movements influenced first-generation South Asian immigrants to become activists in their communities, including the Indian independence movement, the Civil Rights movement, and the mainstream women's movement in the United States. For second generation activists, both the mainstream women's movement and frustration with the model minority myth were motivating factors. The stories of these activists help to explain how they became politicized and why they decided to form groups focused on the needs of South Asian women.

Organizing Against Domestic Violence

While these women had diverse backgrounds and reasons for becoming involved in activism, they all chose to focus on the same cause: domestic violence. They noticed that there was a strong need in their communities for resources to address the specific needs of South Asian women facing violence. Mainstream battered women's shelters were unable to adequately serve the needs of South Asian women. These facilities did not have translation services for women who did not speak English, lacked dietary accommodations for vegetarians, and were not always tolerant of South Asian cultures. Some South Asian women even left mainstream shelters to return to their abusers because of the isolation and discrimination they experienced. SAWOs attempt to provide services tailored to the needs of South Asian immigrant women.

Manka Dhingra said that she trains volunteers to treat South Asian women with extra sensitivity because of their increased need for social support. Manka is a second-generation activist who set up the advocacy program at Chaya in Seattle. Before designing Chaya's programs, Manka had volunteered with a mainstream domestic violence organization and with Narika, a crisis hotline for South Asian women in California. She drew on the philosophies of both when she designed Chaya's programs. She said:

> I liked the professionalism that existed in the mainstream domestic violence (DV) shelters. There were very clear lines on what was whose role. I liked the fact in Narika that you did develop more of a personal relationship [with clients], but there were a lot of complications that occurred because of that. A lot of the volunteers got very personally involved, more so than they should have. There was a lot of relaxation around rules of safety for the volunteers. So when I was setting up the program for Chaya, I wanted to make sure that the volunteers would be very clear as to what their role would be or should be. That they're not the client's best friend, but that they are an advocate. On the other hand, they needed to understand that they were probably this person's only social support. There had to be some balance where you can provide the client with what they want, which was someone who they could talk to, who they could open up to, and in the South Asian culture that meant you had to share a little bit of your own life with them. But it was important to me that all the volunteers understood there had to be that line where it's OK to say, "Let's not talk about my background, let's go back to talking about you."

Thus, Manka attempts to combine South Asian and mainstream American approaches into a better whole. She values the warmth of extended familial relationships in South Asian cultures as well as the professionalism of American clinical relationships.

Despite a clear need for culturally sensitive services for South Asian women, many SAWOs were not welcome in their communities at first. Founding members of Manavi commented that they were accused of being "home wreckers" when they began doing domestic violence work. Sakhi was excluded from cultural celebrations by larger pan-India organizations in New York City. Many of the activists I interviewed found that it was challenging to work in a community where there was complete silence around issues of domestic violence. This silence was often attributed to the model minority myth. As Sujan Dasgupta, who is Shamita's husband and an active volunteer with Manavi, said:

> In 1985, Manavi was founded. Before that, when we started hearing things [about domestic violence] no one would believe we had a problem. The model minority makes South Asians feel they are different from Blacks and Latino/as. It puts them into a good book of white society, law-abiding society. They think they can work here, earn a living and then die. It is very difficult to accept that there is domestic violence ... They don't want to talk about it and don't want to discuss it with outsiders.

Although Sujan and other activists did describe a silence around domestic violence, they also expressed optimism. Several activists told me that the silence has decreased somewhat because the South Asian community now has a higher level of awareness about domestic violence than when they first founded their organizations.

Activists also face different challenges based on the region of the United States in which their organization is located. South Asian communities in the South are smaller than those in the Northeast and were established later, as Aparna Bhattacharyya commented. Aparna is a second-generation activist and the executive director of Raksha in Atlanta. She said:

> We are a newer immigrant base. We haven't been in the South as long as we have been in New York and California and Chicago ... When I see South Asians from New York and Chicago, the comfort with their sexuality, the comfort with a lot of things is really different than from the South. I think we're still trying to be the middle ground ... [W]e have to take a different approach because of the community we are dealing with ... [T]he Northeast, Midwest and West are more progressive anyway than the South, the South is still kind of coming along ... We meet the community where it's at. It's a ... subtle kind of activism. We can't be shoving things down their throats when they're not ready to deal with it because it's going to alienate [them from] us more and when people need us ... the last thing we want to do is alienate our community from seeking help from us.

Activists in each SAWO have made careful choices in how they have represented their organizations and in their programmatic structures based on the community in which they work. They have had incredible insight into the most effective ways to work with different South Asian communities in different regions of the country. In Raksha's case, the activists developed savvy strategies for effectively working in the conservative southeastern United States. First, they broadened the scope of their programs: they have a peer support program for domestic violence survivors, but they also have a youth outreach program, community education resources, and an HIV program, among many other activities. Through addressing a wide variety of issues, not just domestic violence, they have been able to serve a larger number of people.

Second, Raksha joined forces with other immigrant groups in the Atlanta area. Aparna forged strong ties with other immigrant advocacy organizations such as Refugee Family Violence Prevention and Caminar Latino. She and a few other Atlanta-area immigrant leaders founded International Women's House, a domestic violence shelter for refugee and immigrant women. Eventually, several immigrant advocacy organizations united to form Tapestri, an umbrella organization that promotes the interests of immigrants and refugees in Atlanta. Individual immigrant advocacy organizations found strength by working together. As Aparna said:

> We [the immigrant organizations] were all really small. Raksha had no staff at that time. Refugee Family Violence Prevention had maybe four staff. Caminar Latino had like three to four staff. [There was one woman who] was doing the only domestic violence work in the Korean community … .Since we were all really small organizations, we provided some support for each other, and we were also working a lot on our philosophy … We used to meet like every two weeks at the time … We all started working together [on domestic violence issues], and what we realized was that a lot of these issues were similar, and it makes a much bigger difference if we all work together as a team … [If we stayed in our own communities] there's no way we could do it. Plus we loved working together! We had so much fun hanging out. We learned from each other continually.

The founders of Apna Ghar of Chicago also formed coalitions with other immigrant groups and broadened the population they serve. As the organization's Web site states:

> Apna Ghar … was originally founded to meet the expressed need for appropriate cultural social services for women and children victims of domestic violence who came from the Asian Subcontinent countries of India, Pakistan, Nepal, Bangladesh, Bhutan and Sri Lanka. Today, all services are free and open to families irrespective of ethnic origins, socio-economic status, and racial identity.

Thus, both Apna Ghar and Raksha, which are located in regions with smaller South Asian populations, adapted to their communities through building partnerships with other immigrant groups.

Second-Generation Activists and the Future of SAWOs

Second-generation women have enriched the South Asian women's movement, bringing their experiences and perspectives from growing up in America to their activism with SAWOs. These women have added new programming to SAWOs that were founded by first-generation activists, and some second-generation women have also founded new SAWOs, including Raksha and Chaya. One of the most important new dimensions to SAWOs that second-generation women have added is a focus on youth programming. They have expanded the services provided by SAWOs to include issues faced by young second generation South Asians such as formation of cultural identity and questions about how to bridge the gap between South Asian and American cultures. Second-generation activists have also brought attention to the needs of young South Asians struggling with problems around dating, sexual behavior, and drug use.

The broad spectrum of services offered by Raksha illustrates the vision of its second-generation founders. While domestic violence work is an important part of Raksha's mission, the organization also provides services to South Asians who are HIV positive and has a strong youth outreach program. Activists working in the youth outreach program have worked hard to raise awareness about the destructive effects of the model minority myth in their community. Raksha holds a bimonthly "Chai House" (a South Asian play on having a "coffee house" event), where they invite young South Asians to come together to discuss a wide variety of issues, including gender roles and their experiences growing up stereotyped as a "model minority." In February 2002, Raksha held a Chai House where young South Asians that did not fit the model minority stereotype each told their stories. According to the *Atlanta Journal-Constitution* coverage of this event, of the four young South Asians, "One had married an African American man. Another chose the wrong career. One is openly gay. The fourth, well, she just isn't submissive enough." An explicit focus on the model minority myth is one important contribution second-generation activists have made to the larger South Asian women's movement. While first-generation activists crecognized the model minority myth as a problem, second-generation activists have gone one step further by criticizing the myth and creating a forum for young South Asians to openly discuss it.

Second-generation women have also become a part of SAWOs that were founded by first-generation women. In doing so, second generation activists have expanded the focus of these groups. Monika Sharma's work at Apna Ghar is one example. She founded the Junior Board of Apna Ghar to create a space within the organization to address a wide variety of second generation concerns, including date rape and alcohol abuse. The Junior Board is made up of young South Asian men and women who organize community outreach events and an annual fundraiser aimed at young professionals and college students. Monika commented that the work of the Junior Board might help to raise awareness and prevent abusive relationships among young South Asians, which is part of Apna Ghar's broader mission of organizing against domestic violence. The Junior Board has become a successful part of Apna Ghar, and has raised thousands of dollars at its fundraisers. Today, Apna Ghar has a three-tiered board structure that fosters intergenerational communication. First-generation founders, including Kanta Khipple and

Prem Sharma, are members of the Alumni Board which serves in an advisory capacity to the organization. There is a board of directors that is responsible for direct oversight of Apna Ghar, and, finally, the Junior Board focuses on programming for second generation South Asian youth.

Conclusion

The activists that work to end violence in their communities have touched many lives. These organizations have provided a muchneeded space for South Asians of diverse backgrounds to discuss important social issues, including gender roles, the model minority myth, and the needs of second-generation youth, to name just a few. South Asian communities have been strengthened by the presence of these organizations. SAWOs have also been impressively flexible over the last two decades since the first ones were founded. Activists have carefully adapted their programming in order to tailor it to the needs of their communities. The future of these organizations is strong—South Asian women across generations are working together to address needs that might otherwise not be met. SAWOs provide a successful example of how women of color have organized against domestic violence in their communities. The story of South Asian activists is part of a larger emerging movement—that of women of color united against violence in all its forms.

28

An Antiracist Christian Ethical Approach to Violence Resistance

Traci C. West

As Black women initiate resistance on their own behalf and, in so doing, advance the broader interests of a civil society, it is incumbent upon their communities to continue that momentum. Of course, sustaining a deliberate commitment to end violence in women's lives represents a formidable challenge. We need agreement on certain elements that might comprise the kind of ethical analysis and practice we desire.

In this essay, I suggest that we must embrace and envision not only inclusive, truth telling, moral communities which resist violence against women; we must also help build social movements that could bring such communities into existence. These priorities have specific implications for crafting a community-based Christian social ethic that are considered here, along with concrete strategies for community action that emphasize how local churches might become involved in this effort.

Rationale for Christian Involvement

A primary task of Christian communities is to provide leadership in the midst of a desperate and urgent crisis; this would certainly include the crisis created by social and intimate assaults on women.[1] Engagement in practices that uphold women's genuine moral worth can be called "truth-work." Truth-work exemplifies an important aspect of Christian faith.[2] It involves reaching outside oneself and growing toward an embodiment of justice, and reaching within oneself to tap inner resources of courage and passion. To recognize what is truly just, Christians rely upon their ability to access power from God, their communities of accountability, and resources within themselves. They can live out this realization of truth by creating conditions in the world that reflect it; this requires engagement with distorting human realities such as violence, white supremacy, and male dominance.

Churches can play a critical role in organizing, sponsoring, and engaging in truth-work, because it is possible for them to possess an independence from corporate and state control. If they choose to excercise this autonomy, they can play a unique advocacy role in community life. Churches can function as effective and vital organs of the Christian faith by offering victim-survivors needed confirmation of the death-dealing realities that threaten their lives, and by opposing those realities. They have the chance to act compassionately by offering support to those caught in the anguishing circumstances and consequences of intimate violence.

When Aisha, one of the women I interviewed, founded a church comprised primarily of urban Black women, she included a ministry to respond to the marginalized concerns of women victimized by intimate violence as a fundamental component of the church's mission. She was convinced that the women in her ministry needed reinforcement of the fact that God does not require them to suffer abuse. "That's why it was important to me to have a different type of ministry than what I see being performed in traditional churches, because of my own pain and the pain of so many women around me that was going unaddressed," she said.

Church Resistance Strategies: Self-Critique

Churches must be engaged in a continual self-critique focused on eliminating acts of violence among members, and ferreting out messages within traditions and practices that reinforce the acceptability of antiwoman violence. Churches must be accountable for the ways that scriptures, liturgies, icons, policies, and teachings uphold the subjugation of women. One way to do this is by conducting a regular and periodic audit of practices within existing committee and organizational structures. For example, the worship committee could audit liturgy, and the trustees could audit icons in stained glass windows and paintings on display. Christian traditions that even imply that God is not concerned about women who are victim/survivors of violence must be openly challenged and reinterpreted.

Furthermore, churches must identify and reject all theological tenets and organizational strictures that deny women authority and autonomy. This includes explicit affirmations of the integrity and worth of women's bodies and sexuality, with direct references to the inclusion of lesbian, bisexual, and transgender identities, alongside of heterosexual ones.

Moreover, violence and abuse that occurs at the center of church life, perpetrated by clergy and/or laity against their own family members or other members of the faith community, has to be confronted. When the church ignores abuse against these women and children that people within the faith community, a blatant lie is maintained, and the messages which advocate loving, trusting, right relationships are deeply betrayed.[3]

If they fail to activate direct methods of resistance, churches will continue to be thoroughly complicit in male violence, functioning as simply another cultural conveyer of indifference to women's torment.

Resistance Rituals

Churches can integrate antiviolence rituals into their internal practices, as well as their community outreach efforts. For instance, in a discussion about thwarting existing forms of social bias and exploitation, theologian Delores Williams suggests that Black faith communities create rituals based on African American people's experiences and cultural sources. She explains that the doctrine they use would be decoded of androcentric, gender, homophobic, class, and color bias."[4] These rituals should be enacted "as regularly in the African American denominational churches as the eucharist," so that they are firmly implanted in the community's minds and memory.[5] Though not specifically mentioned by Williams, this proposal could also incorporate opposition to male violence. By naming it and ritually denouncing it on a frequent basis, recognition of the cultural sanctioning of male violence could be cultivated among church members. Ceremonial affirmations that offer alternatives to debasing and trivializing Black women's sexuality and emotional needs might also be woven into these rituals.[6]

Moreover, churches should gather across racial and neighborhood boundaries for public rituals that witness their insistence on women's freedom from male violence, emphasizing the unique spiritual orientation that faith communities contribute to communal work on this problem.[7] The rituals might include prayer vigils outside police stations, courthouses, town halls, or municipal buildings. The group would need to offer specific prayers for judges, prosecutors, legislators, and bureaucratic officials who make daily decisions that affect women's safety.

Relinquishing Male Dominance

It is also essential for churches to challenge men to interrogate how dominance over others is linked to cultural definitions of manhood. Of course, this interrogation would be inadequate without attending to intersecting issues of social power, like race and sexuality, and this training process must involve repeated or continuing opportunities for men to become conscious about what constitutes controlling and abusive behavior toward women. Models for the kind of consciousness needed can be found in Latin American Christian-based communities.[8] It is especially appropriate for churches to sponsor investigations of maleness in Sunday school classes, confirmation classes, and youth group programs. Adult education forums and men's group meetings should additionally be utilized as venues for male reeducation about violence resistance, and men could be trained as peer counselor-educators. Special emphasis has to be given to the topic of sexually appropriate behavior toward children. In addition to fostering respectful attitudes and behavior, male peer educators and other church leaders must directly confront sexually harassing and abusive acts that occur. Again, ongoing opportunities for men to engage in discussions about how to prevent and stop this behavior are critical.

These discussions could utilize exercises which promote a deeper understanding of a male abuser's self-justifications and popular legitimations of white supremacy. Paul Kivel, an activist and writer on antiracism and men against domestic violence, offers categories like denial and blame that are ideal for grasping this concept.[10] For instance, just as abusers refuse to accept responsibility for their actions by blaming the women for "having asked for it" or instigated it by their "henpecking" behavior, whites try to avoid responsibility for racism by blaming Blacks with accusations like "if they weren't so lazy" or "if they didn't spend so much time complaining about racism." In creative exercises based on these types of blaming statements, Black participants would gain a systemic understanding of male violence, internalized racism, and the way power interests are defended and sustained.

Reliance on Communal and Peer Resources

In every way possible, church education and advocacy efforts need to involve a peer approach. An over-reliance on "expert" professionals must be actively discouraged. When church resistance efforts are developed, it is essential to invite women to represent themselves, including them as strategists and colleagues. Obviously, victim-survivors must not be pitied or "helped" in a paternalistic fashion; the insights they bring concerning their experience of intimate and social assaults must be highly valued.

An acute consciousness of which organizational models churches emulate is imperative as they reach out to women in crisis situations. In what ways is the treatment of a victim-survivor at the church-sponsored program like the process and assumptions she finds at the "welfare" office or the hospital emergency room? How should it be different? Church crisis intervention efforts must consciously attempt to reflect their solidarity with victim-survivors. This commitment requires churches to maintain their independence from state and corporate control. When these interest fund and regulate church programs it is especially difficult (if not impossible) to create a countercultural structure and climate.

Documentation

Churches need to assist in the documentation of women's stories of abuse and resistance. Distortions contained in "official transcripts" of violence against women should be countered with subversive record keeping. Documentation not only validates women's experiences, but also serves as an inhibitor and sanction against perpetrators.

Churches could devise a means for logging women's depictions of the violence they encounter in their daily lives. It should take every site of community contact into consideration, including interactions within their congregations. For instance, a women's group might sponsor a session for writing prayers of petition about various assaults the women have endured, with an accompanying opportunity to write prayers of thanksgiving that name their concomitant modes of defiance. Another approach might enjoin an administrative body within the congregation to design a process for receiving written testimony about abusive behavior that may have taken place in the home, church, or community. The design would incorporate guidelines for the content and, when appropriate, a mechanism for response to women's testimony. This process would have to be structured so that it is easily accessed by the women of the congregation. These written statements would be a constant source of accountability for the faith community.

Monitoring

Congregations should engage in monitoring the public and private neighborhood and community agencies that immediately respond to the crisis of violence against women. There are numerous areas to be evaluated, such as: How promptly do the police respond to women's calls? In their general region, does the police-response time differ according to the racial and ethnic makeup of the community or neighborhood? How are women's spiritual and emotional needs attended to by the nearest battered women's shelter? Have hospital emergency room personnel been provided with antiracism training? Since church staff must often make referrals in situations of violence to local social service agencies, the quality of those services must be routinely assessed.

Personal inquiries to community agencies that are the most crucial in providing services to women must be made; hospital administrators, doctors, police officers, prosecutors, social workers, and judges should be invited into the churches and questioned about their practices with regard to violence against women. The results of this monitoring should be publicized through every available means, ranging from the church newsletter or Web site to the local news media. Battered women's shelters, rape crisis intervention programs, and even private therapists should also be contacted and their work evaluated in terms of their treatment of Black women victim-survivors. Community service providers have to be held accountable for adequately serving African American women.

Advocacy

Solidarity with victim-survivors must literally be embodied by advocates who serve in these women's interests. Certain women and men of the congregation could be trained as advocate-friends working against violence and abuse toward women. These individuals would ensure that issues related to this abuse are consistently aired in the congregation and integrated into its mission and structures. Also, in the event that a complaint about sexual harassment or domestic violence surfaces against the pastor, this group would provide an advocate to support the woman (or spouse) who brings the complaint.

This group could help generate ideas for political action in the community such as prayer vigils at the local police precinct or posters that voice community concern about violence against women. Advocacy could also include support for progressive national and local legislative initiatives relevant to ending the violence. In its internal monitoring duties, the congregation's violence-resistance advocates would ensure that these legislative concerns were included on the agenda of the appropriate church social concerns committee.

Churches should also advocate for connections between violence against women, white supremacy, and patriarchy to be spelled out and incorporated into the law school education and law enforcement training of prosecutors, judges, and police personnel. At the initiative of churches, methods could be devised for monitoring and evaluating the extent to which officials in their communities have received this kind of education. Congregations might also join together to create ecumenical and interfaith coalitions that work with local activists to write local ordinances that contribute to this struggle.

In these advocacy efforts, churches must insistently make the traumatizing consequences of violence a public priority. Churches should track administrative policies and laws that are directly responsive to the anguish visited upon women victim-survivors. They should explore the question of what legislative changes could be made to send a clear signal of community intolerance for this behavior. For instance, what if, in the prosecution of perpetrators of male violence, the traumatizing of a woman was considered one of the crimes that was committed? Testimony about the emotional and spiritual agony involved in incidents of violence could be solicited from neighbors, friends, and relatives and considered pertinent evidence of such a crime.

We need more communities with crisis support teams to be available to women when they request emergency assistance from the police. These persons can hold the victim-survivor's hand, cry with her, be silent with her, or be supportive in whatever way she wishes. Furthermore, church advocates could press for a wide range of support services for women victim-survivors of male violence to be established as part of all health care insurance policies, including government-funded health services for poor women.

Organizing Strategic Conversations

Churches should initiate consultations to strategize about specific racial and gender issues that reinforce violence against Black women. They could do so by bringing together small groups of victim-survivors, service providers, activists, scholars, and community leaders who are already actively working on this issue. These consultations might explore some of the ethical problems that arise in devising community responses that are both feminist and antiracist.

One subject for such a consultation should be a candid discussion about how to address the dual realities of white supremacist assaults against Black men and Black male violence against Black women. The session should seek appropriate responses to the competing agendas that these realities create. They could discuss questions like: When launching a public campaign to mobilize community concern, how do you oppose the silencing of violence against Black women without contributing to the degradation of Black men? How should the issue of Black men's violence against Black women be raised with Black audiences? With predominantly white audiences? With audiences comprised of diverse racial/ethnic groups? Should whites be spokespersons on this issue? How should persons of color who are not African American speak about Black male violence against Black women? How can they do so in an antiracist manner? Should Black women's photographs be featured in advertising campaigns to raise public consciousness about domestic violence? If so, what are the possible sociopolitical implications of doing this? It is important that such strategic conversations not follow an academic model of one "expert" person delivering a monologue to an audience. Instead, churches should use a consultation model that facilitates dialogue and encourages the joint development of concrete suggestions.

As we face these challenges we can find hope in the reality that society evolves continuously, and that shared moral commitment and communal effort can help shape the direction of these changes. We can move toward becoming a less violent environment for African American women if we seize and hold fast to a radical vision for freedom from the violations that besiege women. This liberation can take place if we commit ourselves to participate in an ethic of resistance that will not give up the struggle. As Denise, a woman I interviewed, describes it, this involves a conscious decision,

> And the times that I decided to live and what I wanted to do—you know, like trying to resist, being in the spaces of resistance, were the most empowering.... I made a commitment to live and to resist this world's oppression. That is the only place [in which] I could live. I mean, that's the only space of actually living. It is in resistance, or else I give up and that's—it's too terrifying there.

29

Taking Risks
Implementing Grassroots Community Accountability Strategies

Written by a collective of women of color from Communities Against
Rape and Abuse (CARA): Alisa Bierria, Onion Carrillo, Eboni Colbert,
Xandra Ibarra, Theryn Kigvamasud'Vashti, and Shale Maulana

Sexual violence is often treated as a hyperdelicate issue that can only be addressed by trained professionals such as law enforcement or medical staff. Survivors are considered "damaged," pathologized beyond repair. Aggressors are perceived as "animals," unable to be redeemed or transformed.[1] These extreme attitudes alienate everyday community members—friends and family of survivors and aggressors—from participating in the critical process of supporting survivors and holding aggressors accountable for abusive behavior. Ironically, survivors overwhelmingly turn to friends and family for support, safety, and options for accountability strategies.[2]

Communities Against Rape and Abuse (CARA), a grassroots anti-rape organizing project in Seattle, has worked with diverse groups who have experienced sexual violence within their communities to better understand the nature of sexual violence and rape culture, nurture community values that are inconsistent with rape and abuse, and develop community-based strategies for safety, support, and accountability. Using some general guidelines as the bones for each community-based process, we work with survivors and their communities to identify their own unique goals, values, and actions that add flesh to their distinct safety/accountability models. In this paper, we discuss these community accountability guidelines and provide three illustrative examples of community-based models developed by activists in Seattle.

Because social networks can vary widely on the basis of values, politics, cultures, and attitudes, we have found that having a one-size-fits-all community accountability model is not a realistic or respectful way to approach an accountability process. However, we have also learned that there are some important organizing principles that help to maximize the safety and integrity of everyone involved—including the survivor, the aggressor, and other community members. An accountability model must be creative and flexible enough to be a good fit for the uniqueness of each community's needs, while also being disciplined enough to incorporate some critical guidelines as the framework for its strategy.[3] Below is a list of ten guidelines—our accountability principles—that we have found important and useful to consider. (We've chosen to alternate personal pronouns throughout, as this reflects the realities of our work.)

Recognize the humanity of everyone involved.

It is imperative that the folks who organize the accountability process are clear about recognizing the humanity of all people involved, including the survivor(s), the aggressor(s), and the community. This can be easier said than done. It is natural, and even healthy, to feel rage at the aggressor for assaulting another person, especially a person that we care about. However, it is critical that we are grounded in a value of recognizing the complexity of each person, including ourselves. Given the needs and values of a particular community, an accountability process for the aggressor can be confrontational, even angry, but it should not be dehumanizing.

Dehumanization of aggressors contributes to a larger context of oppression for everyone. For example, alienation and dehumanization of the offending person increases a community's vulnerability to being targeted for disproportional criminal justice oppression through heightening the "monster-ness" of another community member. This is especially true for marginalized communities (such as people of color, people with disabilities, poor people, and queer people) who are already targeted by the criminal justice system because of their "otherness." When one person in our community is identified as a "monster," that identity is often generalized to everyone in the community. This generalization can even be made by other members of the marginalized community because of internalized oppression.[4]

Also, dehumanizing the aggressor undermines the process of accountability for the whole community. If we separate ourselves from the offenders by stigmatizing them then we fail to see how we contributed to conditions that allow violence to happen.

Prioritize the self-determination of the survivor.

Self-determination is the ability to make decisions according to one's own free will and self-guidance without outside pressure or coercion. When a person is sexually assaulted, self-determination is profoundly undermined. Therefore, the survivor's values and needs should be prioritized, recognized, and respected.

The survivor should not be objectified or minimized as a symbol of an idea instead of an actual person. It is critical to take into account the survivor's vision for when, why, where, and how the abuser will be held accountable. It is also important to recognize that the survivor must have the right to choose to lead and convey the plan, participate in less of a leadership role, or not be part of the organizing at all. The survivor should also have the opportunity to identify who will be involved in this process. Some survivors may find it helpful for friends or someone from outside the community to help assess and facilitate the process with their community. To promote explicit shared responsibility, the survivor and his community can also negotiate and communicate boundaries and limits around what roles they are willing to play and ensure that others perform their roles in accordance with clear expectations and goals.

Identify a simultaneous plan for safety and support for the survivor as well as others in the community.

Safety is complex and goes far beyond keeping your doors locked, walking in well-lit areas, and carrying a weapon or a cell phone. Remember that a "safety plan" requires us to continue thinking critically about how our accountability process will impact our physical and emotional well-being.[5] Consider questions such as: How will the abuser react when he is confronted about his abusive behavior? How can we work together to demechanize the aggressor's strategies? Remember, one does not have control over the aggressor's violence, but one can have control how to prepare and respond to it.

Violence can escalate when an aggressor is confronted about his behavior. Threats of revenge, suicide, stalking, or threats to disclose personal information, or threats to create barriers for you to work, eat, sleep, or simply keep your life private may occur. The aggressor may also use intimidation to frighten the survivor and others. He or she may use privilege such as class, race, age, or sociopolitical status to hinder your group from organizing. While planning your offense, organizers must also prepare to implement a defense in case of aggressor retaliation. If your situation allows you to do so, organizers can also alert other members of the community about your plan and prepare them for how the abuser may react.

Organizers must also plan for supporting the survivor and themselves. It is easy to become so distracted with the accountability process that we forget that someone was assaulted and needs our emotional support. It is likely that there is more than one survivor of sexual assault and/or domestic violence in any one community of people. Other survivors within the organizing group may be triggered during the community accountability process. Organizing for accountability should not be just about the business of developing a strategy to address the aggressor's behavior, but also about creating a loving space for community-building and real care for others. Organizers should also try to be self-aware about their own triggers and create a plan for support for themselves as well. Sometimes it's helpful to have a separate group of friends that can function as a support system for the survivor as well as for the organizers.

Carefully consider the potential consequences of your strategy.

Before acting on any plan, always make sure that your group has tried to anticipate all of the potential outcomes of your strategy. Holding someone accountable for abuse is difficult and the potential responses from the abuser are numerous. For example, if you choose to use the media to publicize the aggressor's behavior, you might think of the consequences on the safety and privacy of the survivor and the organizers involved. But you will also have to consider the chances of the media spinning the story in a way that is not supportive to your values, or the possibility that the story outrages another person outside of your community so much that she decides to respond by physically threatening the aggressor, or the chance that the media will give the aggressor a forum to justify the abusive behavior. This need to "what if" an accountability strategy is not meant to discourage the process, but to make sure that organizers are careful to plan for possible outcomes. Your first plan may need to be shifted, modified, and tweaked as you go. You may find that you are working to hold this person accountable for a longer period of time than you expected. There may be a split in your community because of the silence surrounding abuse, especially sexual and domestic violence. You may feel that you are further isolating the survivor and yourselves from the community. Think of the realistic outcomes of your process to hold someone accountable in your community. Your process may not be fully successful or it may yield constructive results. Whatever your outcome, you may find that you are more prepared and skilled to facilitate a process of holding others in your community or circle of friends accountable in the future.

Organize collectively.

It is not impossible to organize an accountability process by one's self, but it is so much more difficult. A group of people is more likely to do a better job of thinking critically about strategies because there are more perspectives and experiences at work. Organizers are less likely to burn out quickly if more than one or two people can share the work as well as emotionally support one another. It is much harder to be targeted by backlash when there is a group of people acting in solidarity with one another. A group of people can hold each other accountable to staying true to the group's shared values. Also, collective organizing facilitates strong community-building, which undermines isolation and helps to prevent future sexual violence.

Make sure everyone in the accountability-seeking group is on the same page with their political analysis of sexual violence.

Sometimes members of a community organizing for accountability are not working with the same definition of "rape," the same understanding of concepts like "consent" or "credibility," or the same assumption that rape is a manifestation of oppression. In order for the group's process to be sustainable and successful, organizers must have a collective understanding of what rape is and how rape functions in our culture. For example, what if the aggressor and his supporters respond to the organizers' call for accountability by demanding that the survivor prove that she was indeed assaulted or else they will consider her a liar, guilty of slander? Because of our legal structure that is based on the idea of "innocent until proven guilty," and rape culture that doubts the credibility of women in general, it is a common tactic to lay the burden of proof on the survivor.[6] If the group had a feminist, politicized understanding of rape, they might be able to anticipate this move as part of a larger cultural phenomenon of discrediting women when they assert that violence has been done to them.

This process pushes people to identify rape as a political issue and articulate a political analysis of sexual violence. A shared political analysis of sexual violence opens the door for people to make connections between moments of rape and the larger culture in which rape occurs. A consciousness of rape culture prepares us for the need to organize beyond the accountability of an individual aggressor. We also realize we must organize for accountability and transformation of institutions that perpetuate rape culture such as the military, prisons, and the media.

Lastly, when the aggressor is a progressive activist, a rigorous analysis of rape culture can be connected to that individual's own political interests. A political analysis of rape culture can become the vehicle that connects the aggressor's act of violence to the machinations of oppression in general, and even to his own political agenda. Sharing this analysis may also help gain support from the aggressor's activist community when they understand their own political work as connected to the abolition of rape culture and, of course, rape.

Be clear and specific about what your group wants from the aggressor in terms of accountability.

When your group calls for accountability, it's important to make sure that "accountability" is not simply an elusive concept that folks in the group are ultimately unclear about. Does accountability mean counseling for the aggressor? An admission of guilt? A public or private apology? Or is it specific behavior changes? Here are some examples: You can organize in our community, but you cannot be alone with young people. You can come to our parties, but you will not be allowed to drink. You can attend our church, but you must check in with a specific group of people every week so that they can determine your progress in your reform.

Determining the specific thing that the group is demanding from the aggressor pushes the group to be accountable to its own process. It is very easy to slip into a perpetual rage that wants the aggressor to suffer in general, rather than be grounded in a planning process that identifies specific steps for the aggressor to take. And why not? We are talking about rape, after all, and rage is a perfectly natural and good response. However, though we should make an intentional space to honor rage, it's important for the purposes of an accountability process to have a vision for specific steps the aggressor needs to take in order to give her a chance for redemption. Remember, the community we are working to build is not one where a person is forever stigmatized as a "monster" no matter what she does to transform, but a community where a person has the opportunity to provide restoration for the damage she has done.

Let the aggressor know your analysis and your demands.

This guideline may seem obvious, but we have found that this step is often forgotten! For a number of reasons—including being distracted by the other parts of the accountability process, the aggressor building distance between himself and the organizers, or the desire for the organizers to be anonymous for fear of backlash—we sometimes do not make a plan to relay the specific steps for accountability to the aggressor. Publicly asserting that the person raped another, insisting that he must be accountable for the act, and convincing others in the community to be allies to your process may all be important aspects of the accountability plan—but they are only the beginning of any plan. Public shaming may be a tool that makes sense for your group, but it is not an end for an accountability process. An aggressor can be shamed, but remain unaccountable for his behavior. Organizers must be grounded in the potential of their own collective power, confident about their specific demands as well as the fact that they are entitled to make demands, and then use their influence to compel the aggressor to follow through with their demands.

Consider help from the aggressor's community

Family and friends can be indispensable when figuring out an accountability plan. Organizers may hesitate to engage the aggressor's close people, assuming that friends and family may be more likely to defend the aggressor against reports that he has done such a horrible thing. This is a reasonable assumption—it's hard to believe that a person we care about is capable of violently exploiting another—but it is worth the time to see if you have allies in the aggressor's close community. They have more credibility with the aggressor; it is harder for her to refuse accountability if she is receiving the demand for accountability from people she cares about; it strengthens your group's united front; and, maybe most interestingly, it may compel the aggressor's community to critically reflect on their own values and cultural norms that may be supporting people to violate others. For example, this may be a community of people that does not tolerate rape, but enjoys misogynist humor or music or doesn't support women in leadership. Engaging friends and family in the accountability process may encourage them to consider their own roles in sustaining rape culture.

Also, the participation of the aggressor's close people ensures long-term follow through with the accountability plan. Friends can check in with him to make sure he is attending counseling, for example. Also, the aggressor may need his own support system. What if the intervention causes the aggressor to fall into a deep suicidal depression? The organizers may not have the desire or the patience to support the aggressor, nor should they need to. However, the aggressor's family and friends can play an important role of supporting the aggressor to take the necessary steps of accountability in a way that is sustainable for everyone.

Prepare to be engaged in the process for the long haul.

Accountability is a process, not a destination, and it will probably take some time. The reasons why people rape are complicated and it takes time to shift the behavior. Furthermore, community members who want to protect the aggressor may slow down or frustrate organizing efforts. Even after the aggressor takes the necessary steps that your group has identified for him to be accountable, it is important to arrange for long-term follow-through to decrease the chances of future relapse. In the meantime, it's important for the organizers to integrate strategies into their work that make the process more sustainable for them. For example, when was the last time the group hung out together and didn't talk about the aggressor, rape, or rape culture, but just had fun? Weave celebration and fun into your community; it is also a reflection of the world we want to build.

Also, the change that the organizing group is making is not just the transformation of the particular aggressor, but also the transformation of our culture. If the aggressor's friends and family disparage the group, it doesn't mean that the group is doing anything wrong: it's just a manifestation of the larger problem of rape culture. Every group of people that is working to build a community accountability process must understand that they are not working in isolation, but in the company of an *ongoing* vast and rich global movement for liberation.

These principles are merely bones to be used as a framework for a complex, three-dimensional accountability process. Each community is responsible for adding its own distinctive features to make the body of the accountability process its own. What follows is a description of three very different scenarios of community groups struggling with sexual violence and mapping out an accountability plan. These accountability scenarios occurred before the folks at CARA crafted the principles listed above, but they were important experiences that gave us the tools we needed to identify important components of accountability work.

Scenario One

Dan is a Black man in an urban area who is active in the movement to end racial profiling and police brutality.[7] He is also works with young people to organize against institutional racism at an organization called Youth Empowered. He is well-known by progressives and people of color in the area and popular in the community. Over the course of three years, four young Black women (ages twenty-one and younger) who were being mentored by Dan approached CARA staff with concerns about ongoing sexual harassment within their activist community. Sexual harassment tactics reported by the young women included Dan bringing young people that he mentored to strip clubs, approaching intoxicated young women who he mentored to have sex with them, and having conversations in the organizing space about the size of women's genitals as it relates to their ethnicity. The young women also asserted that institutional sexism within the space was a serious problem at Youth Empowered. Young women had fewer leadership opportunities and their ideas were dismissed.

Organizers at CARA met with Dan in an effort to share with him our concerns and begin an accountability process, but he was resistant. Women of color who were Dan's friends, who did not want to believe that Dan was capable of this behavior, chose to protect Dan from being confronted. Instead, several young women were surprised by an unscheduled meeting within Youth Empowered, facilitated by an older woman of color, where they were bullied into "squashing" their concerns about Dan. They were accused of spreading lies and told that they should be grateful for the organizing opportunities afforded to them by Dan. In one of these meetings, a young woman was shown a letter from the police department that criticized Dan about organizing a rally in an attempt to make her critique of Dan's behavior seem divisive to the movement against police brutality. After these meetings, each young woman felt completely demoralized and severed all ties with Youth Empowered.

Black activists have struggled with the tension of patriarchy within our social justice movements since the movement to abolish slavery. Women who identify the problem and try to organize against sexism and sexual violence within our movements are often labeled as divisive, and even as FBI informants. Their work is discredited and they are often traumatized by the experience. As a result, they often do not want to engage in an accountability process, especially when they are not getting support from people they thought were their comrades, including other women of color.

Over the first two years, CARA made several attempts to hold Dan accountable and each effort was a struggle. An attempt to connect with women of color who organized with him only strained the relationship between our organizations.

We also realized that our staff members were not on the same page with each other about how to support young women who were aggravated with one organization discussing the problem at our organization. How did that impact our ability to build strategic coalitions with Youth Empowered? How were we going to support the young women to tell their truth without the story descending into a feeling of hopelessness? Was this a problem about Dan or was this a problem with the organizational culture within Youth Empowered?

We realized that it was not enough to recognize Dan's behavior as problematic and try to appeal to the consciences of the people around him. We needed a thoughtful plan supported by everyone in our organization and we needed to identify folks within CARA who would take the necessary leadership to map out the plan for all of us. We decided that the women of color would meet separately from the general CARA membership to develop an analysis and strategy and the rest of CARA would follow their lead. The women of color decided that our struggle with Dan and his behavior had also become an organizational issue for CARA—it was not solely a community issue—and we identified it as such. We named Dan as a person who had ongoing chronic issues with sexual harassment. Surprisingly, this intentional defining of the problem had not yet happened among our staff. We had talked about his behavior as problematic, unaccountable, and manipulative, but we had not collectively and specifically named it as a form of sexualized violence.

Importantly, we decided that our analysis of his behavior was not secret information. If people in the community asked us our opinion about Dan or disclosed that they were being sexually harassed at Youth Empowered, we decided that our analysis would not be confidential, but would be shared in the spirit of sharing information about destructive behavior. In the past, we struggled with whether or not sharing this information would be useless or counterproductive gossip. We knew the risk of telling others that a well-known Black man who organized against police violence was responsible for sexualized violence. But we decided that it was safer for our community for us to not allow ourselves to be silenced. It was also safer for Dan if we supported our community to move along in its process of struggling with his behavior and eventually demanding accountability. If our community didn't hold him accountable and compel him to reform his behavior, we worried that he would step over the line with a woman who would not hesitate to report him to the police, which would give the police the ammunition they needed to completely discredit Dan, as well as our movement against police violence. Therefore, we made a decision to tell people the information if they came to us with concerns.

We decided that instead of meeting with all the women of color in Dan's ranks, we would choose one Black woman from CARA to invite one Black woman from Youth Empowered to have a solid, low-drama conversation. We also asked another Black woman familiar and friendly with both groups and strong in her analysis of sexual violence within Black communities to facilitate the conversation. The woman from Youth Empowered had positive experiences organizing with CARA in the past and, though our earlier conversations about Dan were fraught with tension and defensiveness on all our parts, she was willing to connect with us. The participation of the third woman as a friendly facilitator also helped our representative to be more relaxed in our conversation.

The first meetings with these women went very well. The CARA representative was clear that the organization's analysis was that Dan had a serious problem with sexual harassment, and we were specifically concerned about the fact that he was working with young people. We were specifically concerned about Dan's engagement with young people because of the power Dan had in choosing which young person would get internships, go to out-of-town conferences, or receive leadership opportunities. Dan's friend received the information with very little defensiveness and was eager to have more conversations about Dan's behavior. This one-on-one strategy seemed to relax the tension between the two progressive organizations; instead we became three sistas intentionally unpacking the problem of misogyny in our community.

The outcome of these meetings was the healing of the strategic relationship between our organizations, which was important for movement-building, but we still had not moved to a place where we could hold Dan accountable. We struggled with the specific thing we wanted to see happen. The women whom he'd sexually harassed were not asking for anything in particular; they understandably just wanted to be left alone. We decided that we did not want him ejected from the activist community, but that it was not safe for him to mentor young people.

It was at this time that a seventeen-year-old Black woman, Keisha, connected with us through Rashad, a seventeen-year-old Black man who was organizing both with CARA and with Youth Empowered. (Rashad was referred to CARA through Dan's organization because the rift between the two groups had significantly healed. If we had not accomplished this, Keisha may not have found CARA.) Keisha was an intern at Youth Empowered and had written a four-page letter of resignation that detailed Dan's sexist behavior. The women at CARA listened to Keisha's story, read her letter, and decided to share with her our collective analysis of Dan's behavior. Because Dan is so deeply supported at Youth Empowered, CARA's response helped her feel affirmed and validated. CARA's organizers helped Keisha strategize about sharing the letter at Youth Empowered by asking her what she wanted to achieve, how she wanted to be supported, and what she wanted her next steps to be after the meeting.

Keisha read her letter aloud to Youth Empowered members that night, with Rashad acting as her ally. She received some support from some women in the community, but she was also told that her letter was very "high school" and immature, by a Black woman within the organization who was also a mentor. Dan pulled Rashad aside after Keisha read her letter and told him that he was making a mistake by organizing with CARA because "those women hate Black men." It was a very painful event, and yet both Keisha and Rashad felt positive about the fact that they followed through with their plan and publicly revealed the same problems that other young Black women before Keisha had named but privately struggled with.

The Black woman from Youth Empowered who had been engaging with CARA was stunned by Keisha's letter, and quickly organized a meeting with Dan, Keisha, Rashad, her CARA contact, and other Youth Empowered orga-

nizers, along with the same Black woman facilitator. Keisha and CARA organizers prepared for tactics that Dan and his supporters would use to discredit
Keisha. Though each organizer admitted that there was a problem with institutional sexism within Youth Empowered, they belittled the conflict, as if it were a
misunderstanding between Keisha and Dan. They said she was "acting white" for
putting her thoughts on paper and for wanting to resign her internship. Keisha,
being the youngest person at the meeting, was mostly intimidated and silenced
by these hurtful tactics. The CARA organizer who was there, however, carefully
challenged each attempt to discredit Keisha. We continued to support Keisha during and after this meeting.

Keisha's letter, however, had a strong ripple effect that continued to impact
Youth Empowered. The Youth Empowered organizer who had been talking with
CARA was moved by Keisha's letter, and committed to figuring out an accountability plan for Dan that made sense for her organization. She began to organize
discussions to clarify the issues that included organizers from CARA, Dan, and
organizers from Youth Empowered. These conversations were very different than
when we had started. We no longer had to convince folks that institutional sexism
existed in the organization, or that Dan's behavior was a form of sexualized violence. Dan eventually resigned from his mentorship position at the organization,
but it's not known if this was because of the pressure created by Keisha's letter and
CARA's stronger connections with women of color at Youth Empowered. With
his absence, the new leadership at Youth Empowered began to more confidently
address the institutional sexism issues within the organization.

Although we think that this work has created a safer environment at Youth
Empowered, Dan still has not been accountable for his behavior. That is to say, he
has not admitted that what he did was wrong or taken steps to reconcile with the
people who he targeted at Youth Empowered. However, at the time of writing, we
expect that he'll continue to go to these meetings where these conversations about
sexual violence (including his own) will be discussed in the context of building a
liberation movement for all Black people.

Working the Principles

In the above scenario, CARA organizers utilized many of the community
accountability principles discussed above. We were sure to respect the autonomy
of the young women. They needed distance from the situation, so we did not pressure them to participate in the often-grueling process. However, we did regularly
update them on our progress, keeping the door open if they changed their minds
about what they wanted their role to be. In the meantime, we set up support systems for them, making sure we made space for Black women to just relax and talk
about our lives instead of spending all of our time processing Dan.

Because the issue was complicated, we planned together as a group, running strategies by one another so that many perspectives and ideas could help
improve our work. We also learned from our mistakes and learned to consider
more carefully the consequences of strategies such as calling a big meeting rather
than working with individuals. Also, working with the Black woman from Youth
Empowered, a friend and comrade of Dan's, was really critical in bringing Dan

closer to the possibility of accountability. Her participation brought important credibility to the questions we were asking.

However, the most important principle that we exercised in this process was taking a step back and making sure we were all on the same page with our analysis of what we were dealing with. Our frustration with Dan was a little sloppy at first—we weren't sure what the problem was. For example, there was a question about whether or not he raped someone, but we had not spoken to this person directly and, therefore, had no real reason to think this was true other than the fact that he was exhibiting other problematic behavior. We had to decide that the behavior that we were sure about was enough for which to demand accountability. The power of naming the problem cannot be underestimated in this particular scenario. Because the behavior was not intensely violent, such as sexual assault, we were searching for the right to name it as sexualized violence. Sexual harassment often presents this problem. There is no assault, but there are elusive and destructive forms of violence at play including power manipulation, verbal misogynist remarks, and the humiliation of young people. Once we reached consensus in our analysis, we were prepared to receive the opportunity that Keisha's letter and work offered and use it to push the accountability process further along.

Scenario Two

Kevin is a member of the alternative punk music community in an urban area. His community is predominantly young, white, multigendered, and includes a significant number of queer folks. Kevin and his close-knit community, which includes his band and their friends, were told by two women that they had been sexually assaulted at recent parties. The aggressor, Lou, was active and well-known in the music community, and he was employed at a popular club. Lou encouraged the women to get drunk and then forced them to have sex against their will.

One of the survivors and her friends did a brief intervention with Lou, confronting him in person with the information. She reports that at first he was humbled and apologetic, but, after leaving them, reversed his behavior and began to justify his actions.

Frustrated with Lou's lack of accountability and with sexual violence in the music community in general, Kevin's group began to meet and discuss the situation. They not only reflected on the survivors' experiences, but also how the local culture supported bad behavior. For example, they discussed how a local weekly newspaper, popular in the alternative music community, glamorized the massive amount of drinking that was always prevalent at Lou's parties. Kevin's group decided that there was a real lack of consciousness about the issue of sexual violence and the community needed to be woken up. To that end, they designed flyers that announced Lou's behavior and his identity, asserted the need for Lou's accountability as directed by the survivors, included a critique of the newspaper, and suggested boycotting Lou's club. With the survivors' consent, the group then passed the flyers out at places where members of their community usually congregated.

A couple of weeks later, the newspaper published an article defending Lou by implying that, since the women that he allegedly assaulted had not pressed criminal charges, the allegations could not be that credible. Kevin's group realized that they needed to do a lot of reeducation about sexual violence within the music community. At the same time, they were being pressured by Lou with threats to sue for libel. The group had not planned for this possible outcome, but instead of backing off, they re-grouped and used anonymous e-mails and the Internet to protect their identities.[8]

They proceeded to write a powerful document that shared the survivors' experiences (written by the survivors), defined sexual violence, and addressed issues of consent and victim-blaming. Using a mixture of statistics and analysis, they challenged the criminal legal system as an effective source for justice, thereby undermining the newspaper's absurd assertion that sexual violence can only be taken seriously if the survivor reports it to the police. Most importantly, the group clearly articulated what they meant by community accountability. With permission, we have reprinted their definition of accountability below:

> We expect that the sexual perpetrator be held accountable for their actions and prevented from shifting blame onto the survivor. We expect that the perpetrator own their assaultive behavior and understand the full ramifications their actions have and will continue to have on the survivor and the community. The perpetrator must illustrate their compliance by making a public apology and, with the help of their peers, seek counseling from a sexual assault specialist. It is equally important that they inform future partners and friends that they have a problem and ask for their support in the healing process. If the perpetrator moves to a new community, they must continue to comply with the community guidelines set forth above. We believe that by working with the perpetrator in the healing process, we can truly succeed in making our community safer.[9]

They released their full statement to the press and also posted it to a Web site. The statement had an important impact. A reporter from the popular weekly newspaper contacted them and admitted that the statement compelled her to rethink some of her ideas about sexual violence. It also kindled a conversation in the larger music community about sexual violence and accountability.

Other than making threats of a lawsuit to the group, Lou mostly ignored the group until the boycott of the club where he worked started to gain steam. Soon, bands from out of town also began to avoid playing at the club. This pressure compelled Lou to engage in a series of e-mail discussions with Kevin with the goal of negotiating a face-to-face meeting. Engaging through e-mail was a difficult and frustrating process. Lou was consistently defensive and wanted "mediation." Kevin was clear about his group's analysis and goals and wanted accountability. Eventually, they gave up on setting a meeting because they couldn't agree on terms.

Throughout this process, Kevin's group experienced a great deal of exhaustion and frustration. During the periodic meetings that CARA staff had with Kevin for support and advice, he often expressed feeling really tired of the project of engaging with Lou at all. Slowly, Kevin and his group switched tactics and focused more on community-building, education, and prevention. It's a critical shift to decide to use your resources to build the community you want rather than expend all of your resources by fighting the problem you want to eliminate. They began a process of learning more about sexual violence, safety, and accountability. They hosted benefits for CARA and other antiviolence organizations. They prepared themselves to facilitate their own safety and accountability workshops. They did all of this with the faith that they could transform their music community to reach a set of values that were consistent with being fun, sexy, and liberatory and explicitly anti-rape and anti-oppression.

Working the Principles

Similar to the first scenario, this community engaged in some trial and error and learned a lot about different strategies. They were careful to check in with survivors about each of their strategies. It's important to note that one survivor changed her role as the process continued. At first, she was the main person who drove the initial confrontation with Lou. As the group pressured Lou more indirectly, she chose to stay on the sideline. The group did a good job of being flexible with her shifting role.

The fact that the group worked collectively was also very critical. We had the impression that sometimes their work was more collectively driven and sometimes only one or two people were the main organizers. When only one or two people were doing the work, it was clear that the process lost some sustainability. However, we must also reflect a lot of compassion on the reality that some folks who initially began to organize realized down the line that they needed stronger boundaries between themselves and the process. In terms of planning, it may be helpful to do ongoing self-checks to note how the work may be triggering one's own experience of surviving violence or to determine if one just generally has a low capacity for doing this kind of accountability work. Perhaps the type of strategy is not a good match for the culture of the group. As this group moved into a different direction that focused more on raising consciousness and building stronger community connections, we noticed a significant revival in the energy of the organizers.

Finally, we think that the most important principle that made a difference in this community's work was when they presented a critical analysis of sexual violence and rape culture to the larger community of rock musicians and alternative artists. It seemed important to sap the arrogance of the newspaper's uncritical defense of Lou, given how much influence the newspaper has within the larger community. We also think that creating and sharing the statement was important in light of the group's flyering strategy. There's very little one can say on a flyer and sexual violence can be very complicated. Their statement did a great job of demonstrating the full dimension of sexual violence by weaving in the survivors' voices in their own words, using statistical information to show why people do not believe survivors, and presenting a liberatory vision of accountability and justice.

Some members of the community may regret that they were ultimately unable to compel Lou to follow their demands. However, CARA feels that it's not unreasonable to think that their work did have a significant impact on Lou. After experiencing the full force of collective organizing which asserted that his behavior was unacceptable, we venture to guess that Lou might be less likely to act in manipulative and abusive ways. In any case, we think their work may have also compelled other members of the community to think critically about the way in which consent operates in their sexual encounters, which is important work in preventing future sexual violence. Also, it's important to remember that this community did, in fact, stay with their accountability process for the long haul—they now simply have their sights set higher than Lou.

Scenario Three

Marisol is a young, radical Chicana activist who organizes with CARA as well as the local chapter of a national Chicano activist group, Unido. While attending an overnight, out-of-town conference with Unido, a young man, Juan, sexually assaulted her. When she returned home, she shared her experience with organizers at CARA. She told us how hurt and confused she felt as a result of the assault, especially since it happened in the context of organizing at Unido. The organizers validated her feelings and supported her to engage in a healing process. We then began to talk with her more about Unido to get a better grasp on the culture of the organization as a whole and if they had the tools to address sexual violence as a problem in their community.

Marisol realized that she needed to discuss the problem with other young women at Unido. Through conversations with them, she learned that Juan had an ongoing pattern of sexually assaulting other young women organizing with Unido. She found three other women who had had similar experiences with the same activist. This information led Marisol to organize an emergency meeting with the women of Unido to discuss the problem. At this meeting, she learned that this behavior had been happening for years and women before her had tried to address it and had demanded that Juan be ejected from the position of power he possessed within the organization. However, though Unido's leadership had talked to Juan about his behavior, there was no real follow-up and there were no consequences.

The young Chicanas of Unido decided to devise a plan to confront the organization's largely male leadership about the problem of sexual violence in general, and Juan's behavior specifically. Identifying the criminal justice system as a real problem in their community, they did not want to pursue law enforcement–based responses. Also, Marisol did not want the episode to end with Unido simply isolating the aggressor without resolving Juan's abusive behavior. The young women decided on a plan that included demanding that Juan step down from leadership positions in Unido, that he pursue counseling and that his friends support him to go to appropriate counseling, and that Unido pursue intensive educational work on sexual violence.

The women's collective strength and demands were so powerful that Unido's leadership agreed to remove Juan from the organization's ranks and to sponsor trainings on sexual violence—not just within Unido's local Seattle chapter, but to prioritize the issue throughout Unido's national agenda. The workshop curriculum focused on the connection between liberation for Mexicans and Chicanos and the work of ending sexual violence.

Also, because of the help of his friends and community, Juan was supported to go to culturally specific counseling addressing power and control issues, particularly for aggressors of sexual violence. Marisol also worked to build a strong community of support for herself and other survivors within Unido. Eventually she decided it was better for her health to create a boundary between herself and this particular chapter of Unido, but, after a year's break, she is organizing with another chapter of Unido. There, she is incorporating a consciousness of sexual violence and misogyny into the local chapter's political agenda.

Working the Principles

Compared to the other two scenarios, this scenario had a pretty short timeline. While the first scenario has taken over two years (so far), the second scenario has been happening for a little over a year, and the third lasted for a mere two months. One reason is the ease with which a strong accountability process can be facilitated when the community is a specific group of people rather than an unstructured and informal group. If there is a system of accountability within the community that is already set up, organizers can maximize that tool to facilitate an accountability process for sexual violence.

Interestingly, organizers at Unido previously attempted to hold the aggressor accountable using the same means, but their demands were not taken seriously. We think the attempt led by Marisol was more successful for two reasons. First, survivors were backed up by a collective of people instead of just a few folks. This lent credibility and power to the group of organizers as they approached Unido's leadership. Second, the organizers were clearer about what they wanted to see happen with Juan, as well as with Unido. Instead of a vague call for accountability, the women asserted specific steps that they wanted Juan and Unido to take. This clarity helped pressure Unido to meet the challenge by complying with the specific demands that the women called for.

Also, the fact that Juan's friends agreed to support him to attend counseling was a great success. Support from friends and family is perhaps one of the most effective ways to ensure that aggressors attend counseling, if that is the goal. They can be more compassionate because they love the person, they are more integrated in the person's life, and they have more credibility with the person. Support from the aggressor's friends and family can be a precious resource in securing an aggressor's follow through with an accountability process.

A Note on Credibility

We hope that the above scenarios reveal the "jazziness" often needed for a community to negotiate itself through a complex process that has multiple components. (We've borrowed the concept of jazziness from Cornel West, who describes it as a reliance on "simultaenous improvisation and structure," as well as community accountability.) While organizers should be committed to some fundamental political principles (womanism/feminism, antiracism, and pro-queer), and can build on the organizing principles we have listed above, the context of any situation will likely be complex; therefore organizers must also be flexible enough to modify and improve tactics as the process unfolds.

To underscore the need for jazziness, we want to briefly explore a problem that comes up frequently in community accountability work: How do the community and the organizers think about the *credibility* of survivors and of aggressors? Because of oppression, people of color, women, young people, queer people, and people with disabilities are often not believed when telling their stories of being violated and exploited. In our first scenario, for example, one of the Black women who experienced sexual harassment wasn't believed because of the racialized and gendered stereotypes of Black women as promiscuous. For this reason, the wider feminist antiviolence community has a principle of always believing women if they report being sexually violated.

CARA also leans in this direction, but we do not do so uncritically. We try to develop a process of engagement with a person's story of being violated, rather than thinking of the process as a fact-finding mission with an end goal of determining the Objective Truth of What Really Happened. It is almost impossible to prove a sexual assault happened—and when it is possible, it is incredibly time- and resource-consuming. The reality is that a perfectly accurate account of an incident of sexual violence is difficult to attain. Though everyone has an obligation to recount their experience as accurately as they can, sometimes survivors do not get every detail right or their story may be inconsistent. That's understandable—the experience of sexual violence can be extremely traumatic, and trauma can impact a person's memory and perception. Furthermore, the person's age or disability may impact their capacity to convey their story with perfect accuracy. This does not necessarily undermine their credibility. Sometimes aggressors can have what seems to be a very polished account of what happened. That does not necessarily mean that they ought to be believed.[10]

As a strategy to step around this problem of credibility, we implement a method that demands an intentional engagement of organizers with the people and the context of the situation. Organizers are not objective, coolly detached receivers of a report; rather, they are helping to build and create the way to think about what happened and what should happen next.

Critically engaging an account of sexual assault means actively considering it in multiple contexts. For example, we come to this work with an understanding that we live in a culture in which sexual violence is, sadly, a regular occurrence. We consider how institutional oppression informs people's choices within the situations in question. We look at people's patterns of behavior. We think about other information that we know about the community in which the violence happened that may be helpful. Because we understand that we are also not objective, we reflect on how our own biases might be informing the way in which we perceive information, and whether this is helpful or not. We help each other think critically around hard corners of the story so that our analysis doesn't become narrow or develop in isolation. In short, we critically engage the story to come up with our best assessment of its most important elements, and then develop a plan to address the situation based on solid political values and organizing principles.

Conclusion

Given the intensity of addressing sexual violence in a community, naming an aggressor will almost necessarily cause some community upheaval and hurt. We urge people organizing for community accountability to be prepared for the risks involved in leading a community accountability process. This work will be hard and messy, but it is also work that is vital, deeply liberatory, meaningful, and geared toward movement building. Engaging with communities to do this work helps to reconnect people to one another, potentially strengthening our relationships and making our communities more resilient and prepared for other political work. Instead of depending on institutions to support us—institutions that will often respond oppressively if they respond at all—community accountability work helps us to develop a practice of liberation in our personal lives, our community lives, and our political lives. Revolutionary movement-building will only happen if we can build the systems and practices that affirm our liberation-based values of connection, agency, respect, self-determination, and justice. Community accountability work provides us with a critical opportunity to transform our relationships and communities to reflect these liberatory values.

30

poem on trying to love without fear

maiana minahal
*dedicated to Shu Hung and Sheila Quinlan, makers of the documentary
on queer women of color, "Does Your Mother Know?"*

well
i'm not stupid
i'm not blind
just scared
scared to say
i love you
scared you won't
love me
cuz at thirteen
when i told my manong*
i like girls
he turned away
from my face
scared
so then i asked a boy to prom
my mom n pop said
good girls don't
but bad girls do
so which are you
scared so i
shut the door
shut love out
of my house
n never let
never let
anyone in
to love me

n maybe they're scared too
cuz love hurts too much
hurts like children
like sisters who leave home
like me
hurts like funerals
old age

* manong—older brother

hurts like funerals
old age
disease
suicide

n i'm not crazy
i'm not bitter/but
this is not just a poem
it's me
naked on the page
these are not just words

n there are times
when i want to love without fear
i just want to love without fear
don't you?

and i hear people say
what if we really are alone
in this world
what if
none of it/matters
well
let's suppose
they're right
let's suppose
my mom n pop
want the one thing
i can't give
let's suppose
i need to hear
what my brothers
won't say
let's suppose
they're right

let's suppose
that right and wrong
is as black and white
as heaven and hell
or good and evil
n even if it all ends
in nothing
does that change
anything

like your flesh
my blood
our need
for love

n i'm not stupid
i'm not blind
just scared
scared to say
i love you
scared you won't
love me
but
i want to love
without fear
i said
i want to love
without fear
don't
you?

ENDNOTES AND WORKS CITED

Chapter 1 Lessons from the Black Women's Movement in Britain

1 The author is very grateful to members of Southall Black Sisters who generously gave their time to be interviewed and provided materials. This article would not have been possible without the important work that SBS women have carried out as trailblazers within the Black women's movement in Britain.

2 In Britain, the term "Black" was adopted by the antiracist movement in the 1960s as a political designation for people of African, Asian, and Caribbean descent. The term pointed to shared experiences of racism and common histories of anticolonial struggle. In this paper, I follow the British usage of "Black" when referring to the British situation, that is, the Black Women's Movement.

3 Susan Edwards, "Beyond Belief—the Case of Zoora Shah," *New Law Journal* (1999): 667.

4 Southall Black Sisters, *Free Zoora Shah!* (London: Southall Black Sisters, 1998), leaflet.

5 Interview with Hannana Saddiqui, Southall Black Sisters, June1999.

6 Southall Black Sisters, "Campaigns: Zoora Shah," Web site article, 2006, http://www.southallblacksisters.org.uk/campaign_zoora.html (accessed March 7, 2006).

7 Justice for Women, "Current Campaigns: Zoora Shah," http://www.jfw.org.uk/current.htm (accessed March 7, 2006).

8 Kiranjit Ahluwalia and Rahila Gupta, *A Circle of Light: The Autobiography of Kiranjit Ahluwalia* (London: Harper Collins, 1997).

9 Interview with Hannana Saddiqui, Southall Black Sisters, June1999.

10 Uma Narayan, *Dis/locating Cultures: Identities, Tradition and Third World Feminism* (New York: Routledge, 1997).

11 British Home Office, *Statistics on Race and the Criminal Justice System—2004* (London: Home Office, 2004).

12 Ahluwalia and Gupta, *A Circle of Light*, 361. A commentator in *The Times* of London argued: "To permit women to claim that they were provoked into killing their husbands even though the act was committed with forethought would be to permit premeditated murder. It is no good saying: 'But she couldn't have done it any other way.' The object is not to give everyone an equal crack at murder to level the playing field." (*The Times*, "When Marriage Turns Bloody," September 29, 1992).

13 Pat Carlen, *Sledgehammer: Women's Imprisonment at the Millennium* (Basingstoke, UK: Macmillan, 1998), 51.

14 *The Sunday Times*, "All for Love? Violence by Women," July 7, 1992.

15 *The Times*, "Girls Gunning for Revenge," July 9, 1993.

16 See Ann Jones, *Women Who Kill* (Boston: Beacon Press, 1996); Coramae Richey Mann, *When Women Kill* (Albany, NY: State University of New York Press, 1996); Patricia Pearson, *When She Was Bad: Violent Women and the Myth of Innocence* (New York: Viking, 1997); Alice Myers and Sarah Wight, *No Angels: Women Who Commit Violence* (London: Harper Collins, 1996).

17 Stuart Hall et al., *Policing the Crisis: Mugging, The State and Law and Order* (London: Macmillan, 1978).

18 Readers familiar with Freda Adler's controversial book *Sisters in Crime* may have a sense of déjà vu. Adler's claim that women's crime was the "darker side" of the women's liberation movement spurred a similar panic in the United States and Britain in the 1970s (New York: McGraw Hill, 1975), 13. Her hypothesis was later discredited at a scholarly level, but not erased from common-sense explanations of crime. See Meda Chesney-Lind, *The Female Offender: Girls, Women and Crime* (Thousand Oaks, CA: Sage Publications, 1997), 37.

19 Anne Worrall, *Offending Women: Female Lawbreakers and the Criminal Justice System*

(London: Routledge, 1990), 33.

20 Karlene Faith, *Unruly Women: The Politics of Confinement and Resistance* (Vancouver: Press Gang Publishers, 1993), 265.

21 Interview with Hannana Saddiqui, Southall Black Sisters, June1999.

22 Ibid.

23 Tariq Modood, "The Changing Context of 'Race' in Britain," *Patterns of Prejudice* 30, no. 1 (1996): 3–13.

24 Hannana Siddiqui, "Black Women's Activism: Coming of Age?" *Feminist Review* 64 (2000): 83–96.

25 Angela Y. Davis, "Race and Criminalization: Black Americans and the Punishment Industry," in *The Angela Y. Davis Reader*, ed. Joy James (Malden, MA: Blackwell Publishers, 1998), 61–73.

26 Julia Sudbury, *Global Lockdown: Race, Gender and the Prison-Industrial Complex* (New York: Routledge, 2005).

27 Joel Dyer, *The Perpetual Prisoner Machine: How America Profits from Crime* (Boulder, CO: Westview Press, 2000); Marc Mauer, *Race to Incarcerate* (New York: The New Press, 1999).

28 Sudbury, *Other Kinds of Dreams: Black Women's Organizations and the Politics of Transformation* (London: Routledge, 1998).

29 Amina Mama, *The Hidden Struggle* (London: Race and Housing Research Unit, 1989).

30 British Home Office, *Statistics on Women and the Criminal Justice System   2004* (London: Home Office, 2004).

31 British Home Office, *Statistics on Race*, 44.

32 Assata Shakur, *Yesterday Is Not Too Soon* (San Francisco: Legal Services for Prisoners With Children, 1996), video recording.

33 Kemba Smith, "Modern Day Slavery: Inside the Prison-Industrial Complex," in Sudbury, *Global Lockdown*.

34 Recognizing the connection between her freedom and that of all women, Kemba has dedicated her life post-incarceration to revealing the devastating impact of the war on drugs on communities of color and transforming drug law. She is founder of the Kemba Smith Foundation, http://kembasmithfoundation.org/.

35 HM Prison Service Women's Policy Group, *Women and Girls in Prison*, Quarterly Bulletin 5, February 1999.

36 Kim Pate, "CSC and the 2 Per Cent Solution: The P4W Inquiry," *Canadian Woman Studies* 19, nos. 1 and 2 (1999): 145–153. Systemic racism in the Canadian criminal justice system particularly impacts aboriginal women, who represent 3% of Canadian women, but 29% of all women serving more than two years of imprisonment and 46% of women in maximum security. Canadian Human Rights Commission, *Protecting Their Rights: A Systemic Review of Human Rights in Correctional Services for Federally Sentenced Women* (Ottawa: CHRC, 2003).

37 African Americans are eight times more likely to be imprisoned than whites, and Latinos are three and a half times more likely. See Vincent Shiraldi, Jason Ziedenberg, and John Irwin, *America's One Million Nonviolent Prisoners* (Washington, DC: Justice Policy Institute, 1999). The Native American rate of incarceration is nearly two and a half times that of whites and their confinement in local jails is four times the national average. See National Criminal Justice Association, "Native Americans and the Criminal Justice System," July 22, 2003, http://www.ncja.org/native_americans_and_the_crimi.html (accessed March 7, 2006).

Chapter 2   Disability in the New World Order

Abbasi, K. 1999. "Under Fire: The World Bank and World Health." http://bmj.com/cgi/content/full/318/7189/1003 (accessed 2006).

Beneria, L. & Feldman, S. eds. *Unequal Burden: Economic Crises, Persistent Poverty, and*

Women's Work. New York: Westview Press, 1992.

Chang, G. 1997. Structural Adjustment Undermines Social Welfare Around the World. http://irr.org/news/archivednetnews/strucadu.htm (accessed 2006).

Charlton, J. I. *Nothing about Us without Us: Disability, Oppression, and Empowerment*. Berkeley, CA: University of California Press, 1998.

Elson, D. "From survival strategies to transformation strategies: Women's needs and structural adjustment," in *Unequal Burden: Economic Crises, Persistent Poverty, and Women's Work*. Edited by L. Beneria & S. Feldman. New York: Westview Press, 1992.

Elwan, A. "Poverty and Disability: A Survey of the Literature," in the Social Protection Discussion Paper Series. Washington, DC: The World Bank, 1992.

Erevelles, N. "(Im)Material Citizens: Critical Race Theory, Disability Studies, and the Politics of Education." *Disability, Culture, and Education* 1, no.1 (2002): 5–26.

Feldman, S. "Crisis, Poverty, and Gender Inequality: Current Themes and Issues," in *Unequal Burden: Economic Crises, Persistent Poverty, and Women's Work*, edited by Beneria & S. Feldman. New York: Westview Press, 1992.

Ferguson, P. "The Social Construction of Mental Retardation." *Social Policy*, Summer (1987): 51–56.

Kabeer, N. *Reverse Realities: Gender Hierarchies in Development Thought*. Verso: New York, 1994.

Kalyanpur, M. "The Influence of Western Special Education on Community-Based Services in India." *Disability and Society* 11, no. 2 (1996): 249–270.

Kittay, E. F. "At Home with my Daughter," In L. P Francis & A. Silvers *Americans with Disabilities: Exploring Implications of the Law for Individuals and Institutions*, pp. 64–79. New York: Routledge, 2000.

McClintock, A. *Imperial Leather: Race, Gender, and Sexuality in the Colonial Context*. New York: Routledge, 1995.

Mies, M. *Patriarchy and Accumulation on a World Scale: Women in the International Division of Labor*. New Jersey: Zed Books, 1986.

Mohanty, C. T. "Cartographies of Struggle: Third World Women and the Politics of Feminism," in *Third World Women and the Politics of Feminism*, edited by C. T. Mohanty, A. Russo, and L. Torres. Bloomington: Indian University Press, 1991.

Pandey, R. S. & Advani, L. *Perspectives on Disability and Rehabilitation*. Delhi: Vikas Publishing House, 1996.

Patnaik, P. "International Capital and National Economic Policy: A Critique of India's Economic Reforms." *Economic and Political Weekly*, March (1994): 683–689.

Russell, M. *Beyond Ramps: Disability at the End of the Social Contract*. Maine: Common Courage Press, 1998.

Thomas, M. "Community-Based Rehabilitation: What does it Mean? Changes." *The Action Aid Magazine* 1, no. 2 (1992): 8–10.

Thomson, R. G. *Extraordinary Bodies: Figuring Physical Disability in American Culture and Literature*. New York: Columbia University Press, 1997.

Werner, D. "Turning Health into an Investment: Assaults on Third World Health Care." *Economic and Political Weekly*, January (1995): 147–151.

World Bank. *World Development Report 1993: Investing in Health*. New York: Oxford University Press, 1993.

Chapter 3   Federal Indian Law and Violent Crime

Allen, Paula Gunn. *The Sacred Hoop: Recovering the Feminine in American Indian Tradition*.

Boston: Beacon Press, 1986.

Beloof, Douglas E. *Victims in Criminal Procedure.* Durham: Carolina Academic Press, 1999.

Bigfoot, Dolores Subia. 1999. History of Victimization in Native Communities. Center on Child Abuse and Neglect: Native American Topic-Specific Monograph Series. http://ccan.ouhsc.edu/History_of_Victimization_Issues.pdf (accessed February 22, 2006).

Bradford, W. "With a Very Great Blame on Our Hearts: Reparations, Reconciliation, and an American Indian Plea for Peace with Justice." *American Indian Law Review* 27, no. 1 (2003): 1–175.

Brave Heart, M.Y.B. and L.M. DeBruyn. "The American Indian Holocaust: Healing Historical Unresolved Grief." *American Indian and Alaska Native Mental Health Research* 8, no. 2 (1998): 60–82.

Butcher, John V. "Federal Courts and the Native American Sex Offender." *Federal Sentencing Reporter* 13, no. 2 (1998): 85.

Clinton, Robert N., Carole E. Goldberg, and Rebecca Tsosie. *American Indian Law: Native Nations and the Federal System.* Newark: LexisNexis, 2003.

Coughenour, J.C., et al. "The Effects of Gender in the Federal Courts: The Final Report of the Ninth Circuit Gender Bias Task Force." *Southern California Law Review* 67 (1994): 745–993.

Cross, T.L. 2003. This Nation has Failed Indian Children. http://www.oregonlive.com/special/warmsprings/index.ssf?/special/oregonian/warmsprings/commentary_121303.html (accessed February 22, 2006).

Daugherty v. Thompson, 322 F.3d 1249 (10th Cir. 2003).

Department of Interior, office of the Inspector General. 2004. Improvements Needed in the Bureau of Indian Affairs Process for Conducting Background Investigations of Indian Education Employees. http://www.oig.doi.gov/upload/2004-I-00362.pdf (accessed February 22, 2006).

EchoHawk, Larry. "Child Sexual Abuse in Indian Country: Is the Guardian Keeping in Mind the Seventh Generation?" *NYU Journal of Legislation and Public Policy* 5 (2001): 83–127.

Ex Parte Crow Dog, 109 US 556, 3 S. Ct. 396, 27 L.ed 1030 (1883).

Executive Committee for Indian Country Law Enforcement Improvements, US Department of Justice. 1997. Final Report to the Attorney General and the Secretary of Interior. http://www.usdoj.gov/otj/icredact.htm (accessed February 22, 2006).

Fletcher, M.L.M. "Sawnawgezewog: 'The Indian Problem' and the Lost Art of Survival." *American Indian Law Review* 28 (2004): 35–105.

Frickey, P.P. "Domesticating Federal Indian Law." *Minnesota Law Review* 81 (1996): 31–95.

Goldberg, Carole and Duane Champagne. 1996. A Second Century of Dishonor: Federal Inequities and California Tribes. http://www.aisc.ucla.edu/ca/Tribes.htm (accessed February 22, 2006).

Gover, Kevin. 2000. Remarks at the Ceremony Acknowledging the 175th Anniversary of the Establishment of the Bureau of Indian Affairs.

Harring, Sidney L. *Crow Dog's Case: American Indian Sovereignty, Tribal Law, and United States Law in the Nineteenth Century.* New York: Cambridge University, 1994.

Hinkle, J. A Law's Hidden Failure. *American Indian Report* 14, no. 1 (2001): 12–14.

Lawrence-Turner, J. 2004. Chemawa Teen's Death Won't Result in Criminal Charges. http://news.statesmanjournal.com/article.cfm?i=82714 (accessed February 22, 2006).

Lee, Gloria. 1996. Defining Traditional Healing. http://www.usask.ca/nativelaw/publications/jah/lee.html (accessed February 22, 2006).

Massey, J.W. "A Proposal to Narrow the Assault and Battery Exception to the Federal Tort Claims Act." *Texas Law Review* 82, no. 6 (2004): 16–21.

McBride, B.A. "Aspects of Community Healing: Experiences of the Sault Sainte Marie Tribe of Chippewa Indians." *American Indian and Alaska Native Mental Health Research* 11, no. 1 (2002):67–83.

McColl, K. 2004. "If Two White Girls had Been Butchered, there Would've Been Arrests that Night." *JANE Magazine,* March 2004: 136–139.

Melton, A.P. and J. Gardner. 2000. Public Law 280: Issues and Concerns for Victims of Crime in Indian Country. Center on Child Abuse and Neglect: Native American Topic–Specific Monograph Series. http://www.tribal-institute.org/articles/gardner1.htm (accessed February 22, 2006).

Million, D. "Policing the Rez: Keeping No Peace in Indian Country." *Social Justice* 2, no. 3 (1999): 101–119.

Norrell, B. "Native Women are Prey; Communities and Courts Fail Native Women." *News From Indian Country* 9 (2003).

O'Brien, Sharon. "The Concept of Sovereignty: The Key to Indian Social Justice," in *American Indians: Social Justice and Public Policy.* Madison: The University of Wisconsin Press, 1991.

Pevar, Stephen L. *The Rights of Indians and Tribes.* Carbondale: Southern Illinois University Press, 1999.

Porter, R.B. "The Meaning of Indigenous Nation Sovereignty." *Arizona State Law Journal* 83 (2002):75–112.

Porter, R.B. "Strengthening Tribal Sovereignty through Peacemaking: How the Anglo-American Legal Tradition Destroys Indigenous Societies." *Columbia Human Rights Law Review* 28 (1996): 235–304.

Poupart, L.M. The Familiar Face of Genocide: Internalized Oppression Among American Indians. *Hypatia* 18, no. 2 (1999): 86.

——, Crime and Justice in American Indian Communities. *Social Justice* 29, no. ½ (2002): 144–159.

Reno, Janet. 1996. Testimony Before the Senate Indian Affairs Committee. http://www.usdoj.gov/archive/otj/Congressional_Testimony/attgensiac.htm (accessed February 22, 2006).

Shibles, Jill. 1998. National American Indian Court Judges Association: Prepared Statement of President Jill E. Shibles." http://www.naicja.org/legislation/shibles_testimony.asp (accessed February 22, 2006).

Smith, Andrea. "Sexual Violence and American Indian Genocide," in *Remembering Conquest: Feminist/Womanist Perspectives on Religion, Colonization and Sexual Violence.* Binghamton: Haworth Press, 1999: 31–52.

Song, S.C. and V.J. Jiménez. "Concurrent Tribal and State Jurisdiction Under Public Law 280." *American University Law Review* 47 (1996): 1627–1707.

US Commission on Civil Rights. 2002. A Quiet Crisis: Federal Funding and Unmet Needs in Indian Country. http://www.usccr.gov/pubs/na0703/na0731.pdf (accessed February 22, 2006).

US Department of Justice. Bureau of Justice Statistics. *American Indians and Crime,* by L.A. Greenfield and S.K. Smith. Washington DC, 1999.

US Department of Justice. Bureau of Justice Statistics. *Full Report of the Prevalence, Incidence, and Consequences of Violence Against Women: Findings from the National Violence Against Women Survey,* by Patricia Tjaden and Nancy Thoennes. Washington, DC, 1999.

US Department of Justice. Bureau of Justice Statistics. *Special Report on Violence Victimization and Race,* by Callie Rennison. Washington, DC, 2001.

Valencia-Weber, G. and C.P. Zuni. "Domestic Violence and Tribal Protection of Indigenous Women in the United States." *Saint John's Law Review* 69 (1995): 69–135.

Vicenti, Carey N. "The Social Structures of Legal Neocolonialism in Native America." *Kansas Journal of Law and Public Policy* 10, no. 3 (1999).

Waller, M.A., et al. "Harnessing the Positive Power of Language: American Indian Women, A Case Example." *Journal of Poverty* 2, no. 4 (1998): 63–81.

Weston, R. "Facing the Past, Facing the Future: Applying the Truth Commission to the Historic Treatment of Native Americans in the United States." *Arizona Journal of International and Comparative Law* 18 (2001): 1017–1059.

Yost, Pete. "FBI Whistle-blower in Sept. 11 Matter Seeks New Probe." *Associated Press,* November 6, 1999.

Chapter 4   Feminism, Race, and Adoption Policy

1   Administration for Children and Families, US Department of Health and Human Services, The AFCARS Report: Current estimates as of October 2000.

2   Natalie Pardo, "Losing Their Children," *Chicago Reporter* 28 (January 1999): 1, 7.

3   Martin Guggenheim, "Somebody's Children: Sustaining the Family's Place in Child Welfare Policy," *Harvard Law Review* 113 (2000): 1716, 1718n11.

4   US Department of Health and Human Services, Children's Bureau, *National Study of Protective, Preventive, and Reunification Services Delivered to Children and Their Families* (Washington, DC: US Government Printing Office, 1997).

5   US Department of Health and Human Services, *National Study,* Executive Summary Finding 4, 3 (emphasis added).

6   Mark E. Courtney and Vin Ling Irene Wong, "Comparing the Timing of Exits from Substitute Care," *Child & Youth Services Review* 18 (1996): 307; Loring P. Jones, "Social Class, Ethnicity, and Child Welfare, *Journal Multicultural Social Work* 6 (1997): 123.

7   Mark E. Courtney, "The Costs of Child Protection in the Context of Welfare Reform," *Future of Children* (Spring 1998): 88, 100.

8   Administration for Children and Families, US Department of Health and Human Services, *Child Maltreatment 1998: Reports from the States to the National Child Abuse and Neglect Data System* (Washington, DC: US Government Printing Office, 2000).

9   LeRoy H. Pelton, *For Reasons of Poverty: A Critical Analysis of the Public Child Welfare System in the United States* 146 (New York: Praeger, 1989).

10   Mitchell H. Katz et al., "Returning Children Home: Clinical Decision Making in Cases of Child Abuse and Neglect," *American Journal of Orthopsychiatry* 56 (1986): 253, 257.

11   Carole Jenny et al., "Analysis of Missed Cases of Abusive Head Trauma," *Journal of the American Medical Association* 281 (1999): 621.

12   Wendy G. Lane et al., "Racial Differences in the Evaluation of Pediatric Fractures for Physical Abuse," *Journal of the American Medical Association* 288 (2002): 1603.

13   Mark Testa, presentation at conference on the impact of the Adoption and Safe Families Act on minority communities, Child Welfare League of America, Chicago, IL, November 13, 2000.

14   Michael C. Dawson, *Behind the Mule: Race and Class in African-American Politics* (Princeton, NJ: Princeton University Press, 1994), 15–34.

15   Don Terry, "US Child Poverty Rate Fell as Economy Grew, But Is Above 1979 Level," *New York Times,* August 11, 2000.

16   Dorothy Roberts, *Killing the Black Body: Race, Reproduction, and the Meaning of Liberty* (New York: Pantheon, 1997), 3–21.

17 Donna M. Bishop and Charles E. Frazier, "Race Effects in Juvenile Justice Decision-Making: Findings of a Statewide Analysis," *Journal of Criminal Law & Criminology* 86 (1996): 392, 407–8.

18 US Department of Health and Human Services, *National Study.*

19 Martha Albertson Fineman, *The Neutered Mother, the Sexual Family, and Other Twentieth Century Tragedies* (New York: Routledge, 1995); Eva Feder Kittay, *Love's Labor: Essays on Women, Equality, and Dependency* (New York: Routledge, 1999).

20 Gwendolyn Mink, *Welfare's End* (Ithaca, NY: Cornell University Press, 1998); Linda Gordon, *Pitied But Not Entitled: Single Mothers and the History of Welfare,* 1890–1935 (Cambridge, MA: Harvard University Press, 1994).

21 Dorothy E. Roberts, "Kinship Care and the Price of State Support for Children," *Chicago-Kent Law Review* 76 (2001): 1619.

22 Jane Mansbridge, "Using Power/Fighting Power: The Polity," in *Democracy and Difference: Contesting the Boundaries of the Political,* ed. Seyla Benhabib (Princeton, NJ: Princeton University Press, 1996), 46, 58.

23 Center for an Urban Future, "Race, Bias, and Power in Child Welfare," *Child Welfare Watch* (Spring/Summer 1998), at 1, 6.

24 Somini Sengupta, "Parents in Poor Neighborhoods Wary of Child Welfare Agency," *New York Times,* May 31, 2000.

25 Marc Mauer, *Intended and Unintended Consequences: State Racial Disparities in Imprisonment,* The Sentencing Project (1997); Jamie Fellner, *Losing the Vote: The Impact of Felony Disenfranchisement Laws in the United States,* The Sentencing Project and Human Rights Watch (1998).

26 Katha Pollitt, "Subject to Debate: Republican Party and Unwed Mothers," *The Nation,* December 12, 1994.

27 Amanda Spake, "Adoption Gridlock," *US News and World Report,* June 22, 1998.

28 Dorothy Roberts, *Shattered Bonds: The Color of Child Welfare* (New York: Basic Books, 2002), 3.

29 Ibid, 13.

30 Donna Coker, "Crime Control and Feminist Law Reform in Domestic Violence Law: A Critical Review," *Buffalo Criminal Law Review* 4, no. 2 (2001), 801, 808, citing Angela Davis in her keynote address to the Color of Violence Conference.

31 Beth E. Richie, "A Black Feminist Reflection on the Antiviolence Movement," *Signs* 25 (Summer 2000): 1133.

32 Lawrence Sherman et al., "Symposium on Domestic Violence: Studies: The Variable Effect of Arrests on Criminal Careers: The Milwaukee Domestic Violence Experiment," *Journal of Criminal Law and Criminology* 83 (Spring 1992), 137, 139.

33 Kimberle Crenshaw, "Mapping the Margins: Intersectionality, Identity Politics, and Violence Against Women of Color," *Stanford Law Review* 43 (1991): 1241.

34 Linda Mills, "Killing Her Softly: Intimate Abuse and the Violence of State Intervention," *Harvard Law Review* 113 (December 1999), 550–1.

35 Stephanie Simon, "Judges Push for Abused to Follow the Law," *Los Angeles Times,* January 22, 2002.

36 Mills, "Killing Her Softly," 613.

37 See *Nicholson v. Scoppetta,* 202 F.R.D. 377 (E.D.N.Y. 2001).

38 Rickie Solinger, *Beggars and Choosers: How the Politics of Choice Shapes Adoption, Abortion, and Welfare in the United States* (New York: Hill and Wang, 2001).

39 I borrow this story from Roberts, *Killing the Black Body,* 275–6.

40 Elizabeth Bartholet, *Nobody's Children* (Boston: Beacon Press, 1999), 6.

Chapter 5   The Color of Choice

1   I write this essay from the perspective of an African American woman, sterilized by the Dalkon Shield intrauterine device in the 1970s, when I was 23 years old. I have since been active in the movement for reproductive justice, trying to ensure that what I experienced will never happen to another woman, even though I am a grandmother now. Rather than perceiving my lived experience as a deficit as a writer (or myself as a victim), I prefer to see it as an asset in understanding how the politics of race intertwine with the politics of class and gender in the United States. My body has served as a site of many of the battles over reproductive politics in this country. My passion now is borne of the conviction that population control is not a hysterical conspiracy offered by people of color but a real determinant of many conditions in our lives.

2   Asian Communities for Reproductive Justice, "Reproductive Justice: A New Vision for Advancing our Movement for Reproductive Health, Reproductive Rights and Reproductive Justice," http://www.reproductivejustice.org/download/ACRJ_A_New_Vision.pdf (accessed October 15, 2005).

3   Ibid.

4   Founded in 1997, the SisterSong Women of Color Reproductive Health Collective is the only national coalition of women of color organizations and individuals in the United States that unites our collective voices to ensure "Reproductive Justice" through securing human rights for communities of color. Reproductive Justice is a fresh and exciting human rights–based analysis offered by women of color that is increasingly being used by many organizations to link reproductive health and population concerns to environmental, economic, racial, and other social justice issues. With our national office in Atlanta, Georgia, the SisterSong Collective is now comprised of seventy-six local, regional, and national grassroots organizations representing six populations in the United States: Native American/indigenous, Black/African American/Caribbean, Latina, Middle Eastern/North African, and Asian/Pacific Islander, as well as individual women of color affiliated with mainstream organizations, and white and male allies. The Collective is governed by the Management Circle, a board of directors composed of twenty-one organizational and individual members. Membership in the Collective is open: everyone can be a member of SisterSong. The mission of SisterSong is to amplify and strengthen the collective voices of indigenous women and women of color to ensure reproductive justice through securing human rights. Our core strategic goals are to: 1) Create opportunities for women of color to build a national movement for reproductive justice in the United States; 2) strengthen women of color organizations by providing training, information, and analyses on reproductive health and organizational development issues; and 3) build alliances among women of color and between women of color and the mainstream movement through shared advocacy work. SisterSong publishes a national newspaper by and for women of color on reproductive justice issues called *Collective Voices* and can be reached at www.sistersong.net.

5   Quoted in Andrea Smith, *Conquest: Sexual Violence and American Indian Genocide* (Cambridge, MA: South End Press, 2005), 80.

6   Abby L. Ferber, *White Man Falling: Race, Gender and White Supremacy*, (New York: Rowman & Littlefield, 1998), 9.

7   Human Rights Watch, "All Too Familiar: Sexual Abuse of Women in US State Prisons," Summary and Recommendations, December 1996, http://hrw.org/reports/1996/us1.htm (accessed March 18, 2006).

8   Rosalind Pollack Petchesky, *Abortion and Woman's Choice: The State, Sexuality and Reproductive Freedom* (Boston: Northeastern University Press, 1990), 70.

9   John T. Noonan, *Contraception: A History of Its Treatment by the Catholic Theologians and Canonists* (Cambridge, MA: Harvard University Press, 1966), 21–2.

10   Rickie Solinger, *Pregnancy and Power: A Short History of Reproductive Politics in America*

(New York: New York University Press, 2005), 3.

11 World Watch Institute, "State of the World 2005 Trends and Facts—Population and Security," http://www.worldwatch.org/features/security/tf/2 (accessed July 30, 2005).

12 Leila Hessini, "Globalizing Radical Agendas," *Collective Voices* 1, Issue 1, www.sistersong.net (accessed August 8, 2005).

13 World Health Organization, "World Health Report 2005," http://www.who.int/whr/2005/whr2005_en.pdf (accessed September 9, 2005).

14 Heritage Foundation, "Where We Stand: Our Principles on Building on Welfare Reform," http://www.heritage.org/research/features/mandate/2005/topic.cfm?topic=17   (accessed November 15, 2005).

15 Zillah Eisenstein, "Katrina and Her Gendering of Race and Class," Women's Human Rights Net, www.whrnet.org/docs/issue-katrina.html (accessed September 30, 2005).

16 Ruth Dixon-Mueller and Paul K. B. Dagg, *Abortion and Common Sense* (Philadelphia: XLibris Corporation, 2002), 225–6.

17 Ibid, 226.

18 James Ridgeway, *Blood in the Face: The Ku Klux Klan, Aryan Nations, Nazi Skinheads, and the Rise of New White Culture* (New York: Thunder's Mouth Press, 1990), 174.

19 Betsy Hartmann, "The Greening of Hate at Home and Abroad," *ZNet*, December 10, 2003.

20 Izaak Walton, League of America, http://www.overpopulation.org (accessed August 8, 2005).

21 Smith, *Conquest*, 78.

22 Rhonda Copelon and Rosalind Petchesky, "Reproductive and Sexual Rights as Human Rights," in *From Basic Needs to Basic Rights,* ed. Margaret Shuler (Washington, DC: Women, Law and Development International, 1995), 355.

23 John J. Donohue III and Steven D. Levitt, "The Impact of Legalized Abortion on Crime," *The Quarterly Journal of Economics* 116, Issue 2 (May 2001), 379.

24 Alexander Sanger, *Beyond Choice: Reproductive Freedom in the 21st Century* (New York: Public Affairs Books, 2004), 67.

25 William Saletan, *Bearing Right: How the Conservatives Won the Abortion War* (Berkeley, CA: University of California Press, 2003), 2.

26 Martha C. Ward, *Poor Women, Powerful Men: America's Great Experiment in Family Planning* (Boulder: Westview Press, 1986), 31.

27 Thomas B. Littlewood, *The Politics of Population Control* (Notre Dame, IN: University of Notre Dame Press, 1977), 51, 139.

28 Ward, *Poor Women,* 59.

29 Littlewood, *Politics of Population Control,* 54.

30 Ibid, 56.

31 Jean Hardisty, "Hurricane Katrina and Structural Racism: A Letter to White People," October 2005, http://www.jeanhardisty.com/blog_katrina.html (accessed October 1, 2005).

32 Dorothy Roberts, *Shattered Bonds: The Color of Child Welfare* (New York: Basic Books, 2002), 237.

33 Solinger, *Pregnancy and Power*, 38.

34 Quoted in Rickie Solinger, "Poisonous Choice," in *"Bad" Mothers: The Politics of Blame in Twentieth-Century America*, eds. Molly Ladd-Taylor and Lauri Umansky (New York: New York University Press, 1998), 385.

35 Smith, *Conquest*, 96.

36 National Council of Negro Women, editorial, *Black Woman's Voice* 2, no. 2 (January/February 1973).

37 Dan T. Carter, "George Wallace and the Rightward Turn in Today's Politics," the *Public Eye* magazine, Winter 2005, http://www.publiceye.org/magazine/v19n3/carter_wallace.html

(accessed July 20, 2006).

38 Solinger, *Pregnancy and Power*, 137.

39 Jael Silliman et al., *Undivided Rights: Women of Color Organize for Reproductive Justice* (Cambridge, MA: South End Press, 2004), 42–3.

40 Asian Communities for Reproductive Justice, "Reproductive Justice."

Chapter 6   Heteropatriarchy and the Three Pillars of White Supremacy

1 Angela P. Harris, "Embracing the Tar-Baby: LatCrit Theory and the Sticky Mess of Race," in *Critical Race Theory*, eds. Richard Delgado and Jean Stefancic, 2nd ed., (Philadelphia: Temple University Press, 2000), 440–7. I also thank Sora Han and Jared Sexton for their illuminating analysis of Blackness.

2 Ella Shoat and Robert Stam, *Unthinking Eurocentricism*, (London: Routledge, 1994), 118–119.

3 Rayna Green, "The Tribe Called Wannabee," *Folklore* 99, no. 1 (1988): 30–55.

4 Sora Han, *Bonds of Representation: Vision, Race and Law in Post-Civil Rights America* (Santa Cruz: University of California-Santa Cruz, 2006).

5 Juan Perea, "The Black/White Binary Paradigm of Race," in *Critical Race Theory*, Delgado and Stefancic, 2nd ed.

6 Angela P. Harris, "Embracing the Tar-Baby."

7 William McLoughlin, *Cherokees and Missionaries, 1789–1839* (Norman, OK: University of Oklahoma Press, 1995).

8 Charles Colson, "Societal Suicide," *Christianity Today* 48, no. 6 (June 2004): 72.

9 Charles Colson and Anne Morse, "The Moral Home Front," *Christianity Today* 48, no. 10 (October 2004): 152.

10 Ralph Reed, *After the Revolution* (Dallas: Word, 1990).

11 Ibid.

12 Ann Burlein, *Lift High the Cross* (Raleigh, NC: Duke University Press, 2002).

13 Andrea Smith, *Conquest, Sexual Violence and American Indian Genocide* (Cambridge, MA: South End Press, 2005).

14 Cathy Cohen, *The Boundaries of Blackness* (Chicago: University of Chicago Press, 1999).

Chapter 8   The Color of Violence

1 David E. Stannard, *American Holocaust: Columbus and the Conquest of the New World* (New York: Oxford University Press, 1992), 21–22.

2 Ibid, 137.

3 Ibid, 144.

4 Ibid, 146.

5 United Nations, *Convention on the Prevention and Punishment of the Crime of Genocide*, 78 UNTS 277, adopted December 9, 1948, entered into force on January 12, 1951; also reprinted in Richard B. Lillich and Hurst Hannum, *International Human Rights: Documentary Supplement* (Aspen, CO: Aspen Law and Business, 1995), 17–22.

6 James H. Blount, *Report of the Commissioner of the Hawaiian Islands*, 53rd Cong., 2d sess. (Washington, DC: Government Printing Office, 1893).

7 Frantz Fanon, *The Wretched of the Earth*, trans. Constance Farrington (New York: Grove Press, 1968), 81.

8 David F. Stannard, "The Hawaiians: Health, Justice, and Sovereignty," *Cultural Survival Quarterly* 34 (Spring 2000): 15–20.

9 Andrew Hacker, *Two Nations: Black and White, Separate, Hostile, Unequal* (New York: Ballantine, 1992).

10 Haunani-Kay Trask, *From a Native Daughter: Colonialism and Sovereignty in Hawai'i*, rev. ed. (Honolulu: University of Hawai'i Press, 1999), 10. (Original publication: Monroe, ME,

Common Courage Press, 1993.)

11 Zohl de Ishtar, ed., *Pacific Women Speak Out for Independence and Denuclearisation* (Christchurch, NZ: The Raven Press, 1998).

12 Kyle Kajihiro, "Nation Under the Gun: Militarism and Resistance in Hawai'i," *Cultural Survival Quarterly* 24 (Spring 2000): 28–33.

13 Darlene Keju-Johnson, "For the Good of Mankind," in Ishtar, *Pacific Women Speak Out*, 16.

14 Ibid, 17.

15 Ibid, 18.

16 Fanon, *The Wretched of the Earth*.

17 Lijon Eknilang, "Learning From Rongelap's Pain," in Ishtar, *Pacific Women Speak Out*, 21–6; Jacqui Katona, "No Uranium Mining on Mirrar Land," in Ishtar, *Pacific Women Speak Out*, 27–42; and Josephine Kauona Sirivi, "Surviving a Nine Year War," in Ishtar, *Pacific Women Speak Out*, 52–8.

Chapter 11 The Forgotten "–ism"

1 The first version of this paper was published under the Arab Women's Solidarity Association, San Francisco Chapter, and gained nationwide recognition as "The AWSA Paper" among US activists in the aftermath of September 11th, when the solidarity movement with Palestinian liberation gained increasing recognition alongside intensified Israeli aggression. It is important to note that since we wrote the first version of this paper in 2001, the San Francisco chapter of the organization AWSA, or AWSA SF is no longer active and has been transformed into Sunbula: Arab Feminists for Change (www.sunbulawomen.org). This third version was revised collectively, in consultation with the original team of researchers and advisors from the former organization, AWSA SF. Also, we define Zionism as a settler-colonial political movement that seeks to ethnically cleanse historical Palestine of the indigenous population and repopulate as a Jewish-only state. See Part A. Zionism and Colonialism for a comprehensive definition of Zionism.

2 Quoted in Joanna Kadi, "Introduction," *Food for Our Grandmothers: Writings by Arab-American and Arab-Canadian Feminists*, ed. Joanna Kadi (Boston: South End Press, 1994).

3 We are indebted to the Women of Color Resource Center for including an earlier version of this study in their publication, *Time to Rise*, prepared for the United Nations Third World Conference Against Racism, Racial Discrimination, Xenophobia and Related Intolerance. We are also indebted to INCITE! Women of Color against Violence for supporting the publication and distribution of this essay. Both organizations have been critical to efforts aims at coalition building between Arab women activists and US women of color movements and to countering attempts to exclude critiques of Zionism from progressive politics.

4 Non-Jews can be "citizens" of Israel, but only Jews are "nationals."

5 For more information on Zionism and racism, see the International Organization for the Elimination of all forms of Racial Discrimination (1977). For more information on the global dimensions of Zionism see Noam Chomsky, *The Fateful Triangle: The United States, Israel & the Palestinians* (Boston: South End Press, 1986); and Benjamin Beit-Hallahmi, *The Israeli Connection: Who Israel Arms and Why* (New York: Pantheon Books, 1987).

6 For information on the relationship between Zionism and racism, see International Organization for the Elimination of All Forms of Racial Discrimination, *Zionism and Racism* (Great Britain: Billings and Sons, 1977). For information on the global dimensions on Zionism see Chomsky, *Fateful Triangle* and Beit-Hallahmi, *Israeli Connection*.

7 See Joel Beinin and Lisa Hajjar, *Palestine, Israel and the Arab-Israeli Conflict: A MERIP Primer. Middle East Research and Information Project*. Retrieved from http://www.merip.org/palestine-israel_primer/toc-pal-isr-primer.html.

8 See Walter Laquer and Barry Rubin, eds., *The Israel-Arab Reader: A Documentary of the*

Middle East Conflict (New York: Penguin Books, 1984).

9   "The state to be created must be Jewish. But not in the same way as the Congo was Belgian or Algeria was French. The Jewish state must be composed primarily, and, ideally, exclusively, of Jews (since they had no metropolis). Thus it was not a question of 'exploiting' the manpower, resources, and markets of another human community, as the colonial powers had done, but rather of finding a 'legitimate' way to exclude the Palestinian community from its own territory" (Guy Bajoit, "Zionism and Imperialism," in *Zionism and Racism,* International Organization for the Elimination of All Forms of Racial Discrimination, 136).

10   Quoted in Rafael Patai, ed., *The Complete Diaries of Theodore Herzl, Vol I.* (Herzel Press, 1960).

11   Quoted in Arthur Hertzberg, *The Zionist Idea: A Historical Analysis and Reader* (Philadelphia: Jewish Publication Society, 1997).

12   Quoted in, Rafael Patai, ed., *The Complete Diaries of Theodore Herzl, Vol I.* (Herzel Press, 1960).

13   See Salman Abu-Sitta, *The Palestinian Nakba, 1948: The Register of Depopulated Localities in Palestine* (London: Palestinian Return Center, 1998); and Benny Morris, *The Birth of the Palestinian Refugee Problem, 1947–1949* (New York: Cambridge University Press, 1987).

14   See Tom Segev, *The Seventh Million: The Israelis and the Holocaust* (New York: Hill and Wang, 1993).

15   See Lee O' Brien, *American Jewish Organizations & Israel* (Washington, DC: Institute for Palestine Studies. 1986).

16   Other countries where Israel cooperated and aided oppressive regimes: East Timor, Colombia, Honduras, Sierra Leone, Ghana, Algeria, and Tunisia (The Muslim Student Association of UCLA 2000; Shahak 1997).

17   See Paul Findley, *Deliberate Deceptions: Facing the Facts about the US–Israeli Relationship* (Brooklyn: Lawrence Hill Books, 1993; Lee O' Brien, *American Jewish Organizations & Israel* (Washington, DC: Institute for Palestine Studies, 1986). During the 1940s, a sign of the ADL's early interest in information gathering and suppression of opinion was its active participation in the witch hunt of that time by providing information to the US Civil Service Commission on thousands of Americans whom the ADL considered unpatriotic. Such information was later used by the infamous House Un-American Activities Committee and the FBI. The Middle East Labor Bulletin, in its Spring 1993 issue, states that, of the 487,033 cards on individuals found in the Commission's New York office alone, six to seven thousand were compiled in cooperation with the ADL.

18   Quoted in Rachelle Marshall, "Spy Case Update: The Anti-Defamation League Fights Back," *The Washington Report on Middle East Affairs* (July/August 1993).

19   For further analysis of the ADL spy case, see Elias A. Rashmawi, "A Journey Through the Palestinian Experience in the United States. In the Company of the ADL: A Case Study in Subverting the US Constitution and Intimidating Dissent," 1992. During the 1940s, a sign of the ADL's early interest in information gathering and suppression of opinion was its active participation in the witch hunt of that time by providing information to the US Civil Service Commission on thousands of Americans whom the ADL considered unpatriotic. Such information was later used by the infamous House Un-American Activities Committee and the FBI. The Middle East Labor Bulletin, in its Spring 1993 issue, states that, of the 487,033 cards on individuals found in the Commission's New York office alone, 6000 to 7000 were compiled in cooperation with the ADL.

20   Quoted in Marshall, "Spy Case Update."

21   See Rashmawi, "A Journey Through the Palestinian Experience in the US."

22   For example, in the February 8, 2002 speech, "New Excuses, Old Hatred: Worldwide Anti-Semitism in the Wake of 9/11," ADL's national director argued that, "anti-Zionism is anti-Semitism, period. There is no debate about it.... It is pure, simply, unadulterated

anti-Semitism" (Foxman 2002). Also see Noam Chomsky's *Necessary Illusions* for an analysis of the ADL's contention that criticism of Israeli is Anti-Semitism: "The ADL has virtually abandoned its earlier role as a civil rights organization, becoming 'one of the main pillars' of Israeli propaganda in the US…. These efforts, buttressed by insinuations of anti-Semitism or direct accusations, are intended to deflect or undermine opposition to Israeli policies, including Israel's refusal, with US support, to move towards a general political settlement."

23 See Marshall, "Spy Case Update," 20; and Rashmawi, "A Journey Through the Palestinian Experience in the US."

24 For information on Zionism and labor, see the *Middle East Labor Bulletin*; on Zionism and religious institutions in the United States, see Basheer K. Nijim, ed., *American Church Politics and the Middle East* (Belmont, MA: The Association of Arab-American University Graduates, 1982); on Zionism and politics, see Cynthia McKinney, "A Celebration of Culture and Resistance." Speech given at the American-Arab Anti-Discrimination Banquet, San Francisco, CA, May 26, 2001; on Zionism and the media see Edward Said, *Covering Islam: How the Media and the Experts Determine How We See the Rest of the World* (New York: Pantheon Books, 1981).

25 Hatem Husseini writes that "By 1970, the Arab-Americans and Arabs in the United States were faced with a comprehensive campaign of investigation and surveillance carried out by a number of government agencies, including the Federal Bureau of Investigation, the Justice Department, and the Immigration Department. This campaign of 'spying, wiretapping, and burglaries' was instituted on orders from the White House in an attempt to uncover the activities of so-called saboteurs. Leonard Garment, White House adviser for Jewish affairs, was ordered to contact Jewish intelligence to assist in this campaign of surveillance…. Since 1968, Zionist and pro-Israeli Jewish organizations in the United States have been pressing Congress and the White House for action against Arabs and Arab-Americans critical of Israel" ("The Impact of the Arab-Israeli Conflict on Arab Communities in the United States" in *Settler Regimes in Africa and the Arab World: The Illusion of Endurance*, ed. Ibrahim Abu-Lughod and Baha Abu-Laban, [Wilmette, IL: The Medina University Press International, 1974] 216).

26 Here, we borrow from Michael Omi and Howard Winant's analysis of the processes by which racist notions become "common sense" (*Racial Formation in the United States:From the 1960s to the 1990s* [New York: Routledge, 1994]).

27 It was after the 1967 Arab-Israeli war when the United States solidified its alliance with Israel. It was also after the 1967 Arab-Israeli war when systematic, racist images of Arabs emerged within the US media. Edward Said writes, "During and after the June War few things could have been more depressing than the way in which the Arabs were portrayed…. The symbolism repeated the simple pattern of a Cooper novel— was not the June War the conflict between the white European bravely facing the amoral wilderness in the person of savage natives bent on destruction? As an intelligible unit in the mind, the Arab has been reduced to pure antagonism to Israel" (Edward Said, "The Arab Portrayed" in Arab-Israeli Confrontation of June 1967, ed. Ibrahim Abu-Lughod [Evanston, IL: Northwestern University Press, 1970] 6.)

28 African-American politics are a central site where Zionists interfere to sabotage the possibilities for Arab-Americans to build solidarity with potential allies. In a speech written by Congresswoman Cynthia McKinney, [D-GA] and addressed to an American Arab Anti-Discrimination Committee banquet on May 26, 2001, McKinney, referring to a memorandum from the Counter Intelligence Program stated, "the purpose of the memorandum was to fashion a strategy at the highest levels of the US government that would preserve white superiority and white privilege in the United States and in Africa." McKinney then quoted from the memorandum which read, "In the above context we must envisage the possibility, however remote, that Black Americans interested in African Affairs may refocus their

attention on the Arab-Israeli conflict. Taking into account the African descent of American Blacks, it is reasonable to anticipate that their sympathies would lie with the Arabs who are closer to them in spirit and, in some cases, related to them by blood. Black involvement in lobbying to support the Arabs may lead to serious dissension between American Blacks and Jews."

29 We use Omi and Winant's definition that "racial formation" is "the sociohistorical process by which racial categories are created, inhabited, transformed, and destroyed" (Omi and Winant, *Racial Formation*).

30 See Mohja Kahf, *Western Representations of the Muslim Woman: From Termagant to Odalisque* (Austin: University of Texas Press, 1999).

31 Quoted in Leila Ahmed, *Women and Gender in Islam: Historical Roots of a Modern Debate* (New Haven, NJ: Yale University Press, 1992).

32 This image emerged in the context of the Intifada that began in October 2000 as part of the Zionist project's strategy for justifying and explaining the Israeli state's brutal aggression against Palestinian civilians.

33 All the names of interviewees in this chapter have been changed for purposes of confidentiality.

34 For a study of the "Holocaust Industry," see Norman G. Finkelstein, *Image and Reality of the Israel-Palestine Conflict* (London: Verso Books, 2001).

35 According to Webster's Encyclopedic, unabridged dictionary, the term Semitic is a biblical term including any of the descendents of Shem, the oldest son of Noah. This includes Akkadians, Canaanites, Phoenecians, Hebrews, and Arabs.

36 Per the request of an editor of the original anthology, we wish to clarify that this interviewee is not referring to the 20-year anniversary edition of *This Bridge Called My Back: Writings By Radical Women of Color* (1981/2001).

Chapter 12 Reflections in a Time of War

1 CorpWatch Website, "Company Profiles," http://corpwatch.org/article.php?list-type&type=8 (accessed July 15, 2005).

2 West Asia/North Africa: This term is used to include all peoples from the region who are not necessarily Arab or identify as Arab, as well as Kurds, Assyrians, Celdanis, Berbers, Iranians, and more.

3 Please refer to the chapter on "The Forgotten '-ism': An Arab American Women's Perspective on Zionism, Racism and Sexism."

4 "Overall, over 30 percent of enlisted personnel but only 12 percent of officers are people of color, who are then disciplined and discharged under other than honorable conditions at a much higher rate than whites. When recent studies showed a slight dip in young African-Americans' (disproportionately high) interest in the military, the Pentagon reacted with a new ad campaign. They're targeting Latino youth with special Spanish-language ads. The recruiters' lethal result: tracking high achieving young people in communities of color into a dead-end, deadly occupation." http://www.objector.org/before-you-enlist/hazardous.html (accessed February 2006).

Chapter 13 Don't Liberate Me

1 Red and white or black and white Arab headdress.

Chapter 14 "National Security" and the Violation of Women

1 This article is concerned with human rights violations committed by US officials and does not discuss the role of Mexican officials in committing acts of rape.

2 For this article, I selected a few cases that were representative of other cases of abuse. Due to space limitations and underreporting, I can provide only a glimpse of human rights vio-

lations regarding violence against women. The small number of cases discussed here does suggest important directions for future research. My intent is to exemplify the violation of women's human rights via cases of militarized border rape.

3   For the purposes of this article, I refer to INS officials as INS officials because that was their identity at the time of the incidents even though in reality, the INS does not exist anymore. That said, the militarization efforts continue to grow in a post-9/11 world so that the US public can feel the state is providing them with security, which is why the creation of the Department of Homeland Security is the new home for immigration issues.

4   Amnesty International, United States of America: Human Rights Concerns in the Border Region with Mexico, 1998, http://web.amnesty.org/library/Index/engAMR510031998 (accessed March 13, 2006).

5   Timothy Dunn, *The Militarization of the U.S-Mexico Border 1978–1992: Low-Intensity Conflict Doctrine Comes Home,* (Austin, TX: University of Texas, Center for Mexican American Studies, 1996), 13.

6   Dunn, *The Militarization of the U.S-Mexico Border,* 21.

7   Susan Brownmiller, "Making Female Bodies the Battlefield." *Newsweek,* January 4, 1993.

8   Beverly Allen, *Rape Warfare: The Hidden Genocide in Bosnia-Herzegovina and Croatia* (Minneapolis: University of Minnesota Press, 1996),159.

9   The Chicana/o saying "We didn't cross the border; the border crossed us" is a powerful reminder to all of us about this colonial legacy.

10 Nicole Gaouette, "Immigration Proposals Include Arizona Fence," *Los Angeles Times,* March 10, 2006, Part A, 1.

11 It is not my intention (nor Enloe's) to suggest that militarized prostitution is not also violent and a form of rape. Militarized prostitution has a history of being forced an inflicted on women from all sides of a military conflict.

12 Cynthia Enloe, *Maneuvers: The International Politics of Militarizing Women's Lives* (Berkeley, CA: University of California Press, 2000),111.

13 Enloe, *Maneuvers: The International Politics of Militarizing Women's Lives,* 124.

14 Susanne Jonas, "Rethinking Immigration Policy & Citizenship in the Americas: A Regional Framework." *Social Justice* 23 (1996): 72.

15 *Time Magazine,* "Day of Infamy," September 12, 2001, at http://www.time.com/time/nation/article/0,8599,174502,00.html (accessed March 13, 2006).

16 Dan Glaister, "Schwarzenegger backs Minutemen," May 2, 2005, http://www.guardian.co.uk/international/story/0,3604,1474559,00.html (accessed March 13, 2006).

17 Enloe, *Maneuvers: The International Politics of Militarizing Women's Lives,* 134.

18 Elizabeth Martínez, *De Colores Means All of Us: Latina Views for a Multi-Colored Century* (Cambridge, MA: South End Press, 1998), 58.

19 Rape convictions in the United States are extremely low [see Catherine Mackinnon, "Reflections on Sex Equality Under the Law," *Yale Law Journal* 100 (1991):1281].

20 Human Rights Watch (1995) acquired the information in this account through interviews with the victim, her lawyer, the Office of the Inspector General, and press reports.

21 Human Rights Watch, *Crossing the Line: Human Rights Abuses Along the US Border with Mexico Persist Amid Climate of Impunity* (New York, NY: Human Rights Watch, 1995), 12–13.

22 "Ex-Border Guard Indicted on Federal Charges," *Phoenix Gazette,* April 6, 1995.

23 "Women Raped by Border Patrol Agent Awarded $753,000" *Associated Press, State and Local Wire,* October 14, 1999.

24 Ibid; Human Rights Watch, *Frontier Injustice: Human Rights Abuses Along the US Border with Mexico Persist Amid Climate of Impunity,* (New York, NY: Human Rights Watch, 1993), 13.

25 "INS Officer Pleads Not Guilty in Rape, Kidnapping," *Los Angeles Times,* May 16, 1990.

26 Michael Connelly and Patricia Klein Lerner, "INS Agent Faces More Sex Charges," *Los*

Angeles Times, June 15, 1990.

27 Ibid.

28 Refer to http://www.ins.usdoj.gov/graphics/glossary.htm#E (accessed March 13, 2006).

29 Michael Connelly, "Jury Acquits INS Officer in Rapes," *Los Angeles Times,* February 28, 1992.

30 Human Rights Watch, "Frontier Injustice," 8. See also *People v. Luis S. Esteves,* Case number 14855, Imperial County, CA, 1992.

31 Human Rights Watch "Frontier Injustice," 8 and Patrick J. McDonnell, and Sebastian Rotella. "Crossing the Line: Turmoil in the US Border Patrol," *Los Angeles Times,* April 23, 1993.

32 Amnesty International "Human Rights Concerns in the Border Region."

33 Ibid.

34 Ibid.

35 United Nations Economic and Social Council. "Question of the Violation of Human Rights and Fundamental Freedoms in Any Part of the World, with Particular Reference to Colonial and Other Dependent Countries and Territories. Rape and Abuse of Women in the Territory of the Former Yugoslavia. Report of the Secretary-General." Document E/CN.4/1994/5, June 30, 1993, 5.

36 Dunn, *The Militarization of the U.S-Mexico Border,* 31.

37 State Advisory Committees to the United States Commission on Civil Rights (Arizona, California, New Mexico and Texas), *Federal Immigration Law Enforcement in the Southwest: Civil Rights Impacts on Border Communities* (Washington, DC: US Government Printing Office, 1997), 24), [CR 1.2: IM6]. See also McDonnell and Rotella, "Turmoil in the US Border Patrol."

38 In San Diego, the Border Patrol launched an aggressive recruitment campaign geared toward military officers. In March 1999, the INS organized the "Southern California All-Military Recruiting Events," where teams of Border Patrol recruiting agents visited 5 to 10 military bases to talk about the Border Patrol as a possible career. Following this intensive recruitment effort, the INS stated, "with the advent of new initiatives such as the 'all-military' campaign in the San Diego sector, we hope to see an even greater number of applicants from this key group in the coming year" (US Immigration and Naturalization Service, "INS Recruiting Update: Spotlight on San Diego Sector Recruitment Efforts," communiqué, February, 1999: 11).

39 State Advisory Committees 10. See also US Congress, House Committee on Government Operations, *The Immigration and Naturalization Service: Overwhelmed and Unprepared for the Future.* 193rd Congress, First session, H.R. Rep 216 (Washington, DC: US Government Printing Office, 1993), 2), [Y1.1/8:103–216].

40 Human Rights Watch "Crossing the Line," 21.

41 Ibid.; Amnesty International "Human Rights Concerns in the Border Region"; State Advisory Committees "Federal Immigration Law Enforcement in the Southwest"; and US Immigration and Naturalization Service, *Citizens' Advisory Panel Report to the Attorney General* (Washington, DC: US Government Printing Office, 1997) [J 21.2:C 49/10].

42 US Immigration and Naturalization Service, "Citizens" Advisory Panel Report," 6.

43 On September 29, 1993, the House Subcommittee on International Law, Immigration, and Refugees held a hearing on the House of Representatives (H.R.) 2119 bill. This bill wanted to establish an independent review commission to investigate complaints of civil rights abuses in the border region (US Congress. House. Committee on the Judiciary, Subcommittee on International Law, Immigration, and Refugees, *Border Violence* (Washington, DC: US Government Printing Press, 1993), [Y4.J 89/1:103/14]. As of October 7, 1994, the bill was stalled in committee (Lexis-Nexis, *Bill Tracking Report,* HR 2119, 1995). Establishing an independent review commission to investigate border violence continues to be an important goal for immigrant rights groups.

44 Amnesty International "Human Rights Concerns in the Border Region."

45 US Immigration and Naturalization Service, "Citizens' Advisory Panel Report."

46 The overwhelming theme of migration literature is people migrate for labor. However, women may be fleeing from domestic violence and therefore, once in the United States, are in search for employment. Therefore, it is important to not reduce their narratives to be one of searching for work when the motivation may actually be escaping domestic violence.

47 Leo Chavez, *Shadowed Lives: Undocumented Immigration in American Society* (Orlando, FL: Harcourt Brace College Publishers, 1998), ix. See also Vicki Ruiz and Susan Tiano, eds., *Women on the US-Mexico Border: Responses to Change* (Boulder, CO: Westview Press, 1991).

48 Mallika Dutt, *With Liberty and Justice for All: Women's Human Rights in the United States* (New Brunswick, NJ: Center for Women's Global Leadership, 1994), 6–7.

49 R. W. Connell, "Sociology and Human Rights," *The Australian and New Zealand Journal of Sociology* 31 (1995): 26.

50 The US efforts to exempt its military units from prosecution in the International Criminal Court (ICC), a court that investigates war crimes as of July 1, 2002 of which gender-based violence such as military rape is prosecutable, is deeply troubling and problematic. Even though President Clinton signed ICC Treaty to begin the process of institutionalizing the court, Bush "unsigned" the United States's name to the treaty (Neil A. Lewis, "US Is Set to Renounce Its Role in Pact for World Tribunal," *The New York Times*, May 5, 2002), a blatant act of defiance to the international community and a clear message that the United States is accountable to no one. However, the international community responded back to the United States and moved forward with the ICC by obtaining sufficient signatories for official approval. Although the United States initially hoped to halt the creation of the ICC altogether, the international community continued to move forward to conduct the world's affairs without the United States. Hoping for permanent exclusion from all ICC prosecutions, the United States received an annual approval from the UN Security Council for exclusion from the ICC, which is renewable (William M. Reilly, "Analysis: US, UN Dent Int'l Court," *United Press International (UPI)*, June 12, 2003) meaning that the UN Security Council will not require the ICC investigate and prosecute the actions of the US military. To clarify, the International Criminal Court and the United Nations operate separately. First, for the court to have jurisdiction, the state where the crimes occurred must have agreed to the treaty or the (accused) individual's country (of nationality) must have agreed to the treaty. Second, prosecutors can initiate an investigation on their own as long as the state (or states) involved has already agreed to the treaty. A 3-judge panel reviews the case to ensure it meets with the requirements of the court. Third, the United Nations Security Council can refer a case to the court, even if a country has not ratified the treaty; the court's jurisdiction is broadest with the UN Security Council. So the United States is ensuring that it is protected from all angles, which is why they pushed for the immunity from the UN Security Council and are for the bi-lateral agreements with other states. The United States is also in the process of passing legislation, which would prevent federal and state agencies from cooperating with the ICC unless the Court is trying Osama Bin Laden, Sadaam Hussein, and/or Slobodan Milosevic. For more information, please refer to Women's Initiatives for Gender Justice (formerly the Women's Caucus for Gender Justice) based in The Hague, The Netherlands at www.iccwomen.org. Furthermore, as another layer of protection for the US military, the government obtained official bi-lateral agreements from other governments confirming that they will not attempt to prosecute the US military through the ICC either. Obtaining these exemptions to the ICC is a result of US government manipulation and not from a conviction that the US military should be above international law. The United States threatened to remove peacekeeping troops in Bosnia and withhold foreign aid to countries who refused to the agreement. See Serge Schmemann, "US May Veto Bosnia Force In a Dispute Over New Court," *The New York Times*, June 29, 2002 and Thom Shanker and James Dao, "US Might

Refuse New Peace Duties Without Immunity," *The New York Times*, July 3, 2002.

51 UN Economic and Social Council "Situation of Human Rights in the Territory of the Former Yugoslavia, Report on the Situation of Human Rights in the Territory of the Former Yugoslavia Submitted by Mr. Tadeusz Mazowiecki, Special Rapporteur of the Commission on Human Rights," Document E/CN.4/1993/50, 10 February 1993, 67.

52 The Statute of the International Criminal Tribunal for the Former Yugoslavia of May 1993 identified rape as a crime against humanity. This statute took an important step toward recognizing armed conflict affects women differently from men, but did not take the issue far enough. That is, the statute characterized rape in a limiting manner by considering it within the context of ethnic cleansing, rather than serving "purposes which are central to the enterprise of war-making" (Liz Philipose, "The Laws of War and Women's Human Rights," *Hypatia* 11(1996):46–62.

53 Allen, *Rape Warfare: The Hidden Genocide in Bosnia-Herzegovina and Croatia*, 39.

Chapter 15 The Complexities of "Feminicide" on the Border

1 Jane Caputi and Diana E.H. Russell first coined the term "femicide" as a homology to "homicide." In Latin America and Europe the preferred term is "feminicide," which emphasizes the structural and institutional forces, as well as the culture of impunity productive of "gender-based hate crimes."

2 Ciudad Juárez is the fourth-largest city in Mexico. During the 1990s, the city was host to five hundred export processing factories (*maquiladoras*) employing three hundred thousand workers. The maquila industry dates back to Mexico's Border Industrialization Program of 1965, when the country created an export processing zone along the Mexico-United States border, the industry was given a boost in 1993 with NAFTA (North American Free Trade Agreement).

3 Factual information contained in this section has been culled from various sources, including the research of Mexican journalists working independently from the state, who have based their findings on the examination of the files of 137 victims murdered between January 1993 and December 1998. The results have been published in Benítez et al. (1999). See also Monárrez (1999).

4 The majority of the victims were dark and thin, with long black hair. Of 137 victims, 5% were light-skinned, 41% dark. Information is not available for the other 54%. Many of the murdered women had been gagged, raped, strangled, and mutilated, with nipples and breasts cut off and buttocks lacerated like cattle, or they had been penetrated with objects. The number of murders tabulated as sexual killings is disputed because city authorities don't count it as rape if an object was used in penetration. For example, a woman found with a blanket in her anus was not recorded in police investigations as having been raped. See Benítez et al. (1999).

5 I am building upon my previous characterization of the state's interpretive framework as the "discourse of morality," which I have since modified to draw attention to the state's shifting framework of interpretation (Fregoso 2000: 137-56).

6 I am indebted to George Lipsitz for bringing to my attention the literature on nonheteronormative sexuality, especially Ferguson (2000: 419-44) and Shah (2001). See also Benítez et al. (1999: 110).

7 My translation: *"Visitaba un centro en el que se dan cita homosexuales y lesbianas"; "Gustaba salir con diferentes hombres y era asidua asistente a salones de baile."*

8 My translation: *"¿Qué, no tienen otra cosa que inventar? De todos los casos han dicho lo mismo: Que la manera de vestir, su supuesta doble vida."*

9 And while the incorporation of women into wage employment has been growing in export-processing zones throughout the Third World, to some extent the situation on Mexico's border cities differs. The traditionally female workforce of the maquiladora industry peaked

in the 1960s. Due in large measure to Mexico's economic crisis of 1982, border cities like Ciudad Juárez experienced a drop in female participation in the *maquiladora* labor force, from 68 to 53% in the years between 1981 and 1989, with the hire of men rising in matching proportions. Transnational corporations on the border export zone took advantage of the cheap male labor force produced by high unemployment and inflation during the Mexican recession of the 1980s, creating the phenomenon researchers are calling "the remasculinization of *maquila* labor" in Ciudad Juárez. Another factor, according to Maria de la O Martínez (1995: 261), is that *maquila* technology and organizational structures have become increasingly complex, leading to the perceived need for more highly trained technicians—typically, men. De la O Martínez argues that today "women are marginalized by the hierarchical structures now in place in the *maquiladora* industry."

10 See for example Laundau (2002).

11 A poem read at the Burials on the Border gathering.

12 Until Guillermina González announced the "disintegration" of Voces sin Eco in July 2001, its members had gathered every weekend to paint more crosses as a symbol of their struggle for social justice. For an excellent analysis of the political resistance of mothers of the disappeared young women in Juárez, see Bejarano (2002).

13 Interview of Mrs. González in the documentary *Maquila: A Tale of Two Mexicos* (2000).

14 President Vicente Fox continues government inaction even as he pays lip service to women's groups by speaking on behalf of gender equality and against gender violence. During International Women's Day, at the official ceremony for the appointment of Patricia Espinoza Torres (a feminist, ex-PAN deputy) as head of the Instituto Nacional de la Mujer, Fox broached the issue of gender and human rights: *"En las ciudades, las mujeres sufren aún discriminación; en el campo, su situación es muchas veces violatoria de los derechos humanos y clama por una pronta y clara justicia."* (In the cities, women still suffer discrimination; in the rural areas, the violation of their human rights is greater and it demands a clear and swift justice.) See Cruz and Garduño (2001: 41).

Chapter 17 Law Enforcement Violence Against Women of Color

1 Glennda Chui, "More Than 100 People March in Protest of San Jose Shooting," *San Jose Mercury News*, July 16, 2003.

2 Hector Castro, "Pregnant Woman 'Tasered' by Police is Convicted," *Seattle Post-Intelligencer*, May 10, 2005.

3 "City Misses Opportunity," Editorial, *Greensboro News & Record*, March 10, 2005; Margaret Moffett Banks and Eric Collins, "Witnesses Say Police Conduct Fine," *Greensboro News & Record*, November 9, 2004; Margaret Moffett Banks, "Muslims Ask Apology in Arrest," *Greensboro News & Record*, November 8, 2004; "Condemn Attack on Mrs. Afaf Saudi," Letter to the Editor, *Greensboro News & Record*, November 8, 2004.

4 "Video Captures Police Handcuffing 5-year-old Girl," Associated Press, April 22, 2005; "A Current Affair to Show 5-year-old's Arrest Today," April 24, 2005, http://www.acurrentaffair.com/daily/todayshow/index.html.

5 Patrick Gallahue, "Family: Cops Attacked Us," *The Brooklyn Paper*, August 18, 2003.

6 Press release issued by survivor's attorney in preparation for officer's sentencing, March 16, 2005 (on file with author).

7 The Stolen Lives Project, *Stolen Lives: Killed by Law Enforcement,* 2nd ed. (New York: October 22nd Coalition, 1999), 171.

8 *Brandon v. County of Richardson*, Brief of the Gender Public Advocacy Coalition, et al., *amici curiae*, at 8 (Neb. Sup. Ct. 2000), citing *Lamot v. City of New York*, (S.D.N.Y. Nov. 23, 1999).

9 Jane Doe, personal communication,

10 Dayo Foyalan Gore, Tamara Jones, and Joo-Hyun Kang, "Organizing at the Intersections:

A Roundtable Discussion of Police Brutality through the Lens of Race, Class, and Sexual Identities," in *Zero Tolerance: Quality of Life and the New Police Brutality in New York City*, ed. Andrea McArdle and Tanya Erzen (New York: New York University Press, 2001).

11 "Call to Action," Black Radical Congress, April 2002, on file with author.

12 ACLU, The Brennan Center for Justice at NYU, and Breaking the Chains, "Caught in the Net: The Impact of Drug Polices on Women and Families" report, March 15, 2005, 16–18; Marc Mauer, Cathy Potler, and Richard Wolf, "Gender and Justice: Women, Drugs, and Sentencing Policy," report for the Sentencing Project, November 1999, available at http://www.sentencingproject.org/pdfs/9042.pdf.

13 Mary Haviland et al., "The Family Protection and Domestic Violence Intervention Act of 1995: Examining the Effects of Mandatory Arrest in New York City," report by the Family Violence Project of the Urban Justice Center, May 2001.

14 Ibid.

15 Amnesty International, *Stonewalled: Police Abuse and Misconduct Against Lesbian, Gay, Bisexual and Transgender People in the US* (London: Amnesty International Publications, 2006).

16 Ibid.

17 Angela Y. Davis, "Violence against Women and the Ongoing Challenge to Racism," in *The Angela Y. Davis Reader*, ed. Joy James (Malden, MA: Blackwell Publishers, 1998).

18 Evelyn A. Williams, "Statement of Facts in the New Jersey Trial of Assata Shakur," June 25, 2005, available at http://www.assatashakur.org/appeal_case_facts 2005.htm (accessed August 29, 2005).

19 Angela Y. Davis, "Violence against Women and the Ongoing Challenge to Racism."

20 Joy James, *Resisting State Violence* (Minneapolis: University of Minnesota Press, 1996).

21 Terry Morris, *No Justice, No Peace: From Emmett Till to Rodney King* (Brooklyn: Afrocentric Productions, 1993), 41; Selwyn Raab, "Officer Indicted in Bumpurs Case," *New York Times*, February 1, 1985; Selwyn Raab, "Ward Defends Police Actions in Bronx Death," *New York Times*, November 3, 1984; "Then, After the Killing," Editorial, *New York Times*, November 2, 1984.

22 Darryl Fears and Greg Krikorian, "Family Asks Why Police Shot Woman," *Los Angeles Times*, December 31, 1998; "Riverside, CA, Officers Who Shot Tyisha Miller Fired From Force," *Jet* magazine, July 5, 1999.

23 Amnesty International, *A Briefing for the UN Committee against Torture* (London: Amnesty International Publications, 2000); Earl Ofari Hutchinson, "New Menace To Society? Police Shootings of Black Women Are the Deadly Consequence of Stereotypes," *Christian Science Monitor*, June 8, 1999.

24 Rebecca Young, presentation at the National Development and Research Institutes, summarizing the results of an extensive study of the treatment of lesbians within the criminal justice system, drug treatment facilities, and homeless shelters, February 23, 2004.

25 Ibid.

26 Kara Fox, "Maryland Lesbian Alleges Metro Police Abuse in Arrest," *Washington Blade*, April 26, 2002.

27 A significant number of Native Americans do not identify as "gay," "lesbian," "bisexual," or "transgender," associating these identities with predominantly white communities. Many Native Americans, particularly those living in urban areas, have adopted the term "Two Spirit" to include individuals living alternative gender identities and expressions as well as those living same-gender-loving existences. See Sue Ellen Jacobs, Wesley Thomas, and Sabine Lang, ed., *Two Spirit People: Native American Gender Identity, Sexuality, and Spirituality* (Urbana: University of Illinois Press, 1997); Lester B. Brown, ed., *Two Spirit People: American Indian Lesbian Women and Gay Men* (New York: Haworth Press, 1997).

28 See Audre Lorde Project, "Police Brutality against Lesbian, Gay, Bisexual, Two Spirit and

Transgender People of Color in New York City," draft report, July 14, 2000 (on file with author).

29 "In the era of Stonewall, laws against cross dressing were common. Indeed, the most recent case of such archaic laws being struck down was in San Diego, just a handful of years ago. It would not surprise me if there are locales in the United States where such laws are still on the books. Many of them required that a person, if so dressed, had to be wearing three items of their birth gender's clothing. Some were more stringent, with some biological females having to get special licenses in order to wear pants in public." Gwen Smith, "Transsexual Terrorism," *Washington Blade*, October 3, 2003; see also Leslie Fineberg, *Trans Liberation: Beyond Pink or Blue* (Boston: Beacon Press, 1998); Phyllis Frye, http://www.transhistory. org/history/TH_Phyllis_Frye.html (citing Houston Code struck down in 1981). These laws, known as "sumptuary laws," required that individuals wear a minimum number of articles of "gender appropriate" clothing. Such regulations persist to this day inside correctional facilities in the United States.

30 Sylvia Rivera Law Project, *Toilet Training*, video (New York: Sylvia Rivera Law Project, 2003); People in Search of Safe Restrooms Web site, http://www.pissr.org.

31 Young, presentation at the National Development and Research Institutes.

32 Kate De Cou, "US Social Policy on Prostitution: Whose Welfare is Served?" *New England Journal on Criminal and Civil Confinement* 24 (1998): 427, 435–437.

33 See Amnesty International, *Stonewalled.*

34 C. Nicole Mason, Executive Director, National Women's Alliance, personal communication with author, October 10, 2003.

35 Young, presentation at the National Development and Research Institutes.

36 Ibid.

37 Mason, personal communication with author, October 10, 2003.

38 Young, presentation at the National Development and Research Institutes; Mason, personal communication with author, October 10, 2003; see also Amnesty International, *Stonewalled.*

39 Kendall Thomas, presentation at Lavender Law Conference, New York, NY, October 18, 2003; Joey Mogul, presentation at Lavender Law Conference, New York, NY, October 18, 2003.

40 Joey Mogul, People's Law Office, personal communication with author, November 2003.

41 Jennifer Rakowski, Communities United Against Violence, personal communication with author, October 2003.

42 Ujima Moore, personal communication with author, November 2003.

43 "Behind Closed Doors: An Analysis of Indoor Sex Work in New York City," report by the Sex Workers Project of the Urban Justice Center, 2005; "Revolving Door: An Analysis of Street-Based Prostitution in New York City," report by the Sex Workers Project of the Urban Justice Center, 2003. Both are available at http://www.sexworkersproject.org (accessed August 29, 2005).

44 Sex Workers Project, "Revolving Door."

45 Sex Workers Project, "Behind Closed Doors."

46 Simmi Ghandi, personal communication with author, November 2003; Amnesty International, *Stonewalled.*

47 Amnesty International, *Stonewalled.*

48 Young, presentation at the National Development and Research Institutes; Amnesty International, *Stonewalled.*

49 Young, ibid.

50 Amnesty International, *Stonewalled.*

51 Ibid.

52 Kathryn Russell, *The Color of Crime: Racial Hoaxes, White Fear, Black Protectionism, Police*

Harassment, and Other Macroaggressions (New York: New York University Press, 1999).

53 This account is based on a feature aired on the NBC news program *Dateline,* entitled "Road Warrior," in which the video tape of the incident is shown, and Ms. Antor and Officer Beckwith are interviewed. See also "Black Woman Abused by White South Carolina State Trooper Sues State," *Jet* magazine, April 29, 1996; "White South Carolina State Trooper Fired After His Video Camera Shows Him Abusing Black Woman," *Jet* magazine, April 8, 1996; "Woman Dragged From Car by Police Sues State," *CNN* News Briefs, April 4, 1996, http://www.cnn.com/US/9604/04/newsbriefs/index1.html; Fred Bruning, "Rogue Cops and Civilian Beatings," *Newsday,* April 1996.

54 "Justice on the Line: The Unequal Impacts of Border Enforcement in Arizona Border Communities," Border Action Network report, 2000, 11. Available at http://www.borderaction.org/PDFs/BAN-Justice.pdf (accessed July 26, 2006).

55 "Rights for All," Amnesty International report, 1998, available at http://www.rightsforall.amnesty.org/info/report/index.htm (accessed July 26, 2006).

56 Geneva Horse Chief, "Amnesty International Hears Testimony on Racial Profiling," *Indian Country Today,* October 16, 2003.

57 Shelly Feuer Domash, "A Few Bad Cops, or a Problem with the System?" *New York Times,* February 11, 2001.

58 Andy Newman, "Suffolk County Officer Is Charged in Abuse of Female Drivers," *New York Times,* March 29, 2002.

59 Domash, "A Few Bad Cops, or a Problem with the System?"

60 Al Baker, Janon Fisher, and Matthew Sweeney, "Two Officers Are Charged in Sex Attack," *New York Times,* November 22, 2005; "Woman Says Officers Sexually Abused Her," *New York Times,* November 21, 2005.

61 See, for example, Dorothy E. Roberts, "Punishing Drug Addicts Who Have Babies: Women of Color, Equality, and the Right of Privacy," *Harvard Law Review* 104 (1991): 1419–87; Lynn M. Paltrow, "Background Concerning Ferguson et al. v. City of Charleston et al.," National Advocates for Pregnant Women report, available at http://www.advocatesforpregnantwomen.org/issues/ferguson_history.htm (accessed July 26, 2006); Lynn M. Paltrow, "McKnight Background," National Advocates for Pregnant Women report, available at http://www.advocatesforpregnantwomen.org/issues/mcknightbckrd.htm (accessed July 26, 2006).

62 Dorothy E. Roberts, *Shattered Bonds: The Color of Child Welfare* (New York: Basic Books, 2003).

63 "Police Killing in San Jose Raises Questions," Asian Pacific Islander Legal Outreach report, August 1, 2003, available at http://www.geocities.com/apilegaloutreach/Uploads/CauTran.htm (accessed August 29, 2005).

64 Stolen Lives Project, *Stolen Lives: Killed by Law Enforcement,* 200.

65 Ibid.

66 Ibid.

67 Ibid.

68 Ibid.

69 Ibid.

70 *Applewhite v. City of Baton Rouge,* 380 So. 2d 119 (La. App. 1979).

71 "Ga. Deputy Acquitted of Raping Lesbian, Found Guilty of Violating Oath of Office," *Washington Blade,* March 26, 2004; "Lesbian Rape Trial Begins in Georgia," the *Advocate,* March 17, 2004; Joe Johnson, "Alleged Rape Victim Testifies in Court," *Online Athens,* March 16, 2004, available at http://www.amren.com/news/news04/03/17/onelessdyke.html (accessed August 29, 2005); "No Hate Crime Charge in 'One Less Dyke' Rape Case," *Online Athens,* August 26, 2003, available at http://www.queerday.com/2003/aug/26/no_hate_crime_charge_in_one_less_dyke_rape_case.html (accessed August 29, 2005).

72 "Former INS Officer Gets 4-year Prison Term," *Los Angeles Times*, November 23, 2004.

73 See chapter 14 in this anthology, Sylvanna Falcón, "Securing the Nation through the Violation of Women's Bodies: Militarized Border Rape at the US-Mexico Border"; see also Coalición de Derechos Humanos/Alianza Indigena Sin Fronteras, *Violence on the Border*, press release, February 25, 2004.

74 "Ex-officer Accused Again of Telling a Woman to Disrobe," *Chicago Sun-Times*, July 23, 2005.

75 "Eugene, Oregon, Settles Two Suits with Women Abused by Cops," Associated Press, August 12, 2005; C. Stephens, "Magana Verdict," KVAL 13 News, June 30, 2004; "Trial Begins For Perverted Eugene Cop Roger Magana: Media is Shut Out," Portland Independent Media Center, June 4, 2004, available at http://www.publish.portland.indymedia.org/en/2004/06/290053.shtml (accessed August 25, 2005); "Victim Speaks Out About Perverted Eugene Cop," KVAL 13 News, March 13, 2004; "Magana Records Revealed," KVAL 13 News, March 4, 2004; "Four More Women Accuse Eugene Officer of Abuse," KATU 2 News, December 11, 2003.

76 See Sista II Sista, "Sistas Makin' Moves: Collective Leadership for Personal Transformation and Social Justice," in this anthology.

77 Greg Smith and Tara George, "Officers Accused of Beating Woman," *New York Times*, March 2, 2000; Juan Forero, "Two Officers Are Accused of Beating Woman Who Asked for Their Names and Badge Numbers," *New York Times*, March 2, 2000; J. Zamgba Browne, "Two Officers Sentenced in Assault of Black Woman," *Amsterdam News*, November 15, 2001.

78 Forero, "Two Officers Are Accused of Beating Woman.".

79 Smith and George, "Officers Accused of Beating Woman"; Forero, "Two Officers Are Accused of Beating Woman"; "National Briefs," *Pittsburg Post Gazette*, March 2, 2000.

80 Smith and George, "Officers Accused of Beating Woman."

81 Kwame Dixon and Patricia E. Allard, *Police Brutality and International Human Rights in the United States: The Report on Hearings Held in Los Angeles, California, Chicago, Illinois, and Pittsburgh, Pennsylvania, Fall 1999* 10 (London: Amnesty International Publications, 2000).

82 Stolen Lives Project, *Stolen Lives: Killed by Law Enforcement*.

83 Ibid.

84 Ibid; Amnesty International, "Rights for All" report.

85 Horse Chief, "Amnesty International Hears Testimony on Racial Profiling."

86 Stolen Lives Project, *Stolen Lives: Killed by Law Enforcement*.

87 Ibid, 226.

88 Ibid.

89 *Gazette Extra*, July 19, 2005.

90 "Appellate Court Says Officers Can be Held Liable in L.A. Raid," Associated Press, September 22, 2004.

91 See ACLU et al., "Caught in the Net," *supra* note.

92 F., personal communication with author, February 2004.

93 *New York Times*.

94 Leadership Conference on Civil Rights Education Fund, "Wrong Then, Wrong Now: Racial Profiling Before & After September 11, 2001," report, 2003, 22–3.

95 Ibid.

96 See National Law Center on Homelessness and Poverty, "No Homeless People Allowed," report, 1994); Robert C. Ellickson, "Controlling Chronic Misconduct in City Spaces: Of Panhandlers, Skid Rows, and Public-Space Zoning," *Yale Law Journal* 105 (1996): 1165; Dirk Johnson, "Chicago Council Tries Anew with Anti-Gang Ordinance," *New York Times*, February 22, 2000; Steve Miletich, "Sidewalk Law is Posted," *Seattle Post-Intelligencer*, May 19, 1994; Michael Ybarra, "Don't Ask, Don't Beg, Don't Sit," *New York Times*, May 19,

1996.

97 Personal interview with Sylvia Beltran and Alex Sanchez of Homies Unidos, January 29, 2004.

98 Amnesty International, *Stonewalled*; see also Leadership Conference on Civil Rights Education Fund, "Wrong Then, Wrong Now."

99 Desis Rising Up and Moving (DRUM), forthcoming research report; National Economic and Social Rights Initiative (NESRI), forthcoming research report.

Chapter 18 Crime, Punishment, and Economic Violence

1   Paige M. Harrison and Allen J. Beck, *Prisoners in 2004* (Washington, DC: US Department of Justice, 2005), 4.

2   Bureau of Justice Statistics, "Survey of Inmates in State and Federal Correctional Facilities," computer file, 1997.

3   *Personal Responsibility and Work Opportunity Reconciliation Act of 1996*, Public Law 193, 104th Cong., 2nd Sess. (August 22, 1996).

4   This represents a very conservative estimate, because some reporting states provided limited data. For instance, some states only provided incarceration data and not probation data for felony drug convictions, leaving a potentially significant number of women unaccounted for in this estimate. Patricia Allard, "Life Sentences: Denying Welfare Benefits to Women Convicted of Drug Offenses," report for The Sentencing Project, February, 2002, 2–3.

5   The Sentencing Project, "Executive Summary: Life Sentences: Denying Welfare Benefits to Women Convicted of Drug Offenses," report, 2005.

6   *1998 Amendment to the Higher Education Act of 1965*, Public Law 244, 105th Cong., 1st Sess. (October 7, 1998). Most recent amendment found in *Deficit Reduction Act of 2005*, Public Law 362, 109th Cong., 2nd Sess. (February 1, 2006).

7   Until 2006, the education ban applied to people convicted of drug-related offenses whether they were attending a post-secondary institution or not at the time of the conviction. On February 1, 2006, the 1998 Amendment was further amended by Congress under the Deficit Reduction Act of 2005 to limit its application to people convicted while attending an institution of higher learning.

8   Should the young woman be convicted of sale or a distribution offense, she would face a two-year suspension for the first offense and a lifetime ban for a second offense.

9   *Housing Opportunity Program Extension Act of 1996*, Public Law 120, 104th Cong., 2nd Sess. (28 March 1996).

10 Corinne Carey, "No Second Chance," Human Rights Watch report, 2004.

11 *Department of Housing and Urban Development v. Rucker et al.*, 535 US 125 (2002). See Cornell Law School Legal Information Institute, http://www.law.cornell.edu/supct/html/00-1770.ZS.html.

12 Ibid.

13 Beth Richie, *Compelled to Crime: The Gender Entrapment of Black Battered Women* (New York: Routledge,1996).

14 Unfortunately, the following data analysis is limited to African American women and Latinas because the Bureau of Justice Statistics report relied upon does not provide data for any other racial or ethnic group of incarcerated women. The Bureau needs to offer greater racial, ethnic, and gender breakdowns in all its reports, especially its annual prisoner reports and its prisoner survey, which is conducted every five years. With more and more people requesting these types of data from the Bureau, perhaps it will be compelled to provide more to the public. Similar requests should be made of state data agencies.

15 Bureau of Justice Statistics, *Survey of Inmates in State and Federal Correctional Facilities*," (Washington, DC: US Department of Justice, 1997). For all figures, there was a fraction of people who did not respond to the question. In order to keep the results uniform, all per-

centages are of the total state prison population, not simply those who responded. Therefore, we can assume that these estimates are conservative, and may range between 1 and 4 percentage points higher.

16 Coalition for Human Needs, *Analysis of the Bush Administration's FY 2006 Budget* (Washington, DC: Coalition for Human Needs, 2005), 3.

17 Ibid, 10.

18 Ibid, 11.

19 Ibid.

20 "Response to: USDOJ Serious, Violent Offender Reentry Initiative/Application #2002-YO222-FL-RE," Florida Department of Corrections, 2002, 21.

21 Funding for marriage promotion initiatives began in 1996, when Congress earmarked money for marriage education programs as a part of welfare reform. These programs were identified as a way to curb poverty and reduce public assistance rolls. It was not until 2002, however, that the marriage initiative began gaining significant public attention.

22 Rick Lyman, "Marriage Programs Try to Instill Bliss and Stability Behind Bars," *New York Times*, April 16, 2005.

23 Ibid.

Chapter 19 Pomo Woman, Ex-Prisoner, Speaks Out

Costo, Rupert. *Natives of the Golden State: The California Indians*. San Francisco: The Indian Historian Press, 1995.

Greenfield, Lawrence and Smith, Steven. *American Indians and Crime*. Washington, DC: Bureau of Justice Statistics, 1999.

Harring, Sidney. *Crow Dog's Case: American Indian Sovereignty, Tribal Law, and United States Law in The Nineteenth Century*. Cambridge: University Press. 1994.

Kurshan, Nancy. *Women in Prison*. Oakland, CA: Prison Activist Resource Center, 1994.

Reed, Little Rock. *The American Indian in the White Man's Prisons: A Story of Genocide*. Taos: Uncompromising Books, 1993.

Ross, Luana. *Inventing the Savage: The Social Construction of Native American Criminality*. Austin: University of Texas Press, 1998.

Chapter 20 The War Against Black Women, and the Making of NO!

1 In this essay, I use the words "Black" and "African American" interchangeably to describe the descendants of enslaved Africans who were brought over, against their will and in chains, to the mass of land now known as the United States of America.

2 Toni Cade Bambara edited the groundbreaking anthologies *The Black Woman* (1970) and *Tales and Stories for Black Folks* (1971). She authored two short story collections, *Gorilla, My Love* (1972) and *The Seabirds Are Still Alive* (1977); and one novel, *The Salt Eaters* (1980). A noted documentary filmmaker and screenwriter, Bambara's film work includes the documentaries *The Bombing of Osage Avenue* (1986) and *W. E. B. DuBois: A Biography in Four Voices* (1995), both of which were produced and directed by Louis Massiah. After Bambara's untimely death on December 9, 1995, Toni Morrison published two pieces of Bambara's work: *Deep Sightings and Rescue Missions* (1995), a collection of fiction, essays, and conversations, and *Those Bones Are Not My Child* (1999), a novel.

3 Scribe Video Center, a Philadelphia-based nonprofit organization, was founded in 1982 by award-winning documentary filmmaker Louis Massiah as a place where people could work together and gain skills in media-making. Scribe Video Center seeks to explore, develop, and advance the use of video as an artistic medium and as a tool for progressive social change. Central to its mission are efforts to reach communities that traditionally have not had access to video training or production facilities. Scribe Video Center engages people of color, wom-

en, young people, senior citizens, and those with limited economic resources in a dialogue about the potential of the video medium. For more information, visit www.scribe.org.

4 Gloria T. Hull, Patricia Bell Scott, Barbara Smith, eds., *All the Women are White, All the Blacks are Men, but Some of Us Are Brave: Black Women's Studies* (New York: The Feminist Press, 1982).

5 The following interviews and performances are featured in *NO!*: Samiya A. Bashir, poet; Elaine Brown, former chairperson of the Black Panther Party; Johnnetta B. Cole, president, Bennett College for Women; Adrienne Davis, legal scholar at University of North Carolina; John T. Dickerson, Bluegrass Rape Crisis Center; Ulester Douglas and Sulaiman Nuriddin, Men Stopping Violence, Inc.; Farah Jasmine Griffin, scholar and author, Columbia University; Beverly Guy-Sheftall, historian and author, Spelman College; (the late) Essex Hemphill, poet, *To Some Supposed Brothers;* Audree Irons, administrative associate, Spelman College; Honorée Fannone Jeffers, poet, *that's proof that she wanted it*; Reverend Reanae McNeal, Imani Revelations; Charlotte Pierce-Baker, author, *Surviving the Silence: Black Women's Stories Of Rape*; Queen, poet; Loretta Ross, former director, Washington, DC Rape Crisis Center; Gwendolyn Zoharah Simmons, Islamic scholar and former SNCC organizer; Michael Simmons, international human rights activist; Barbara Smith, scholar, author, and activist; Salamishah Tillet, cofounder, A Long Walk Home, Inc.; Scheherazade Tillet, cofounder, A Long Walk Home, Inc.; Reverend Traci West, author, *Wounds of the Spirit: Black Women, Violence and Resistance Ethics*; Aaronette M. White, social psychologist, activist; Janelle White, sociologist, activist; Rosetta Williams, visual artist, poet; Aminata Baruti, choreographer/dancer, *The Migration Dance*; Faith Sangoma Pennant and Moon Wisdom, co-choreographers/dancers, *Black Feminist Dance Statement*; Moon Wisdom, choreographer/dancer, *For Women of Rage And Reason* and *A State of Rage,* a narrative choreopoem; archival footage of Minister Louis Farrakhan, Nation of Islam, and Reverend T. J. Jemison, National Baptist Convention; and vignettes exposing inter- and intra-racial rape and sexual assault during enslavement and Reconstruction.

6 During this time, Gwendolyn Zoharah Simmons was known as Gwendolyn "Gwen" Robinson.

7 The Council of Federated Organizations was made up of four organizations working to achieve racial equality in the United States. The organizations were Student Non-Violent Coordinating Committee (SNCC), Southern Christian Leadership Conference (SCLC), Congress on Racial Equality (CORE), and National Association for the Advancement of Colored People (NAACP).

8 Since its very beginning in 1994, the creative production and advisory team has been inclusive of lesbians, as well as young and older women, most of whom are of African descent. The women and men behind *NO!* are: Tamara L. Xavier, coproducer and director of choreography; Gail M. Lloyd, coproducer and contributing editor; Joan Brannon, associate producer, cowriter, and director of photography; Sharon Mullally, editor; Wadia L. Gardiner, associate producer and production manager; Salamishah Tillet, associate producer and director of archival research; Amadee L. Braxton, associate producer and archival researcher; Giscard (JEE EYE ZEE) Xavier, producer, composer, and performer of original score; Nikki Harmon, assistant director; Kia Steave Dickerson, set decorator; Scheherazade Tillet, production stills photographer; Traci McKindra, NO! logo design and Web site maintenance; Michael Simmons, creative advisor; Tina Morton, post-production consultant. Scholar-activist advisors: Elsa Barkley Brown, PhD; Kimberly D. Coleman, PhD; Charlotte Pierce-Baker, PhD; Aaronette M. White, PhD; and Janelle White, PhD. Legal services: Tonya M. Evans-Walls, Esquire. Fiscal sponsor: Women Make Movies, Inc.

9 Members of Black Men in Support of the Film *NO!*: Deputy Mayor Ras Baraka, Newark, New Jersey; St. Clair Bourne, filmmaker; Tyree Cinque/DJ Drama, DJ, turntablist, producer; Ulester Douglas, co-executive director, Men Stopping Violence; Michael Eric Dyson, Avalon

Foundation Professor in the Humanities, University of Pennsylvania; Alfred A. Edmonds Jr., sr. v.p., editor-in-chief, Black Enterprise Magazine; Dr. Ibrahim Abdurrahman Farajaje', professor of cultural studies/Islamic studies, Starr King School/Graduate Theological Union; Thomas Glave, professor, English, SUNY-Binghamton; Byron Hurt, anti-sexist activist, producer, director, *Beyond Beats and Rhymes*; Christopher C. Logan, visual artist, DJ; Erik McDuffie, scholar, activist, writer; Mark Anthony Neal, professor, English, SUNY-Albany; Sulaiman Nuriddin, manager, men's intervention programs; Jeffrey O. G. Ogbar, professor, history, University of Connecticut; Eternal Polk, writer/director, producer, NFL Films; Kevin Powell, poet, journalist, activist; founder, Hiphop Speaks; Marcus Reeves, writer, publisher, Romarc Media; Michael Simmons, regional director for Europe, American Friends Service Committee; Tyrone Smith, co-chair, Mayor's Commission on Sexual Minorities, Philadelphia, PA; Alvin Starks, associate director, Open Society Institute; Brook Stephenson, thought organizer, city manager, *Rolling Out Urbanstyle Weekly*; Kalamu ya Salaam, editor, writer, filmmaker, teacher, moderator of e-drum Listserv for Black writers; Yemi Toure, director, The Black Man Film Festival, Atlanta; Cheo Tyehimba, writer, educator, activist.

10 Hiphop Speaks was created by Kevin Powell and April Silver in 2001, and is a series of quarterly forums (March, June, September, and December of each year). The forums are geared toward the healthy exchange of social and political ideas related to the hip-hop generation/era and beyond (as the rap group Dead Prez has stated, it is bigger than hip-hop, after all), and are led by voices from the hip-hop community.

11 For a complete listing of all of the major supporters of *NO!*, please visit www.NOtheRapeDocumentary.org/supporters.html.

Chapter 21 The Medicalization of Domestic Violence

1 Peter Conrad, "Medicalization, Genetics, and Human Problems," in *Handbook of Medical Sociology, 5th Edition*, ed. Chloe E. Bird, Peter Conrad, and Allen Fremont (Upper Saddle River, NJ: Prentice Hall, 2000).

2 C. L. Estes, C. Harrington, and D. N. Pellow, "Medical Industrial Complex," in *Health Policy*, ed. C. Harrington and C. L. Estes (Boston: Jones & Bartlett Publishers, 2001).

3 C. Estes and R. Beard, "Medicalization of Aging," in *Encyclopedia of Aging*, ed. David J. Ekerdt et al. (New York: MacMillian Reference, 2002).

4 Estes et al., "Medical Industrial Complex."

5 Antonio Gramsci, *Selections From The Prison Notebooks of Antonio Gramsci*, ed. Quintin Hoare and Geoffrey Nowell Smith (New York: International Publishers, 1999).

6 Howard Waitzkin, "Social Structures of Medical Oppression: A Marxist View" in *Perspectives in Medical Sociology*, ed. P. Brown (Belmont, CA: Wadsworth, 1989).

7 Conrad, "Medicalization, Genetics, and Human Problems."

8 Waitzkin, "Social Structures of Medical Oppression."

9 Susan Schecter, *Women and Male Violence: The Visions and Struggle of the Battered Women's Movement* (Boston, MA: South End Press, 1982).

10 Emerson R. Dobash, *Violence Against Wives: A Case Against the Patriarchy* (New York: The Free Press, 1979).

11 Ariella Hyman, *Mandatory Reporting of Domestic Violence by Health Care Providers: A Policy Paper* (San Francisco, CA: Family Violence Prevention Fund, 1997).

12 Family Violence Prevention Fund, *San Francisco Domestic Violence Health Care Proposal* (San Francisco, CA: Family Violence Prevention Fund, 1997).

13 J. E. Snell, R. J. Rosenwald and A. Robev,. "The Wife-beater's Wife: A Study of Family Interaction," *Archives of General Psychiatry* 11 (1964): 107–113

14 Frantz Fanon, *A Dying Colonialism* (New York: Grove Press Inc., 1967).

15 Aihwa Ong, "Making the Biopolitical Subject: Cambodian Immigrants, Refugee Medicine and Cultural Citizenship in California," *Social Science and Medicine* 40, no. 9 (1995): 1243–

57.

16 bell hooks, "Violence in Intimate Relationships: A Feminist Perspective," in *Gender Violence: Interdisciplinary Perspectives,* ed. Laura O'Toole and Jessica Schiffman (New York: New York University Press).

17 Gary King, "Institutional Racism and the Medical/Health Complex: A Complex Analysis," *Ethnicity and Disease* 6 (1996): 30–46

18 Michel Foucault, *The Birth of the Clinic: An Archaelogy of Medical Perception* (New York: Vintage Books, 1975).

19 Fanon, *A Dying Colonialism.*

20 Fanon, ibid.

21 Aihwa Ong, "Making the Biopolitical Subject."

22 Eliot Freidson, *Profession in Medicine: A Study in the Sociology of Applied Knowledge* (Chicago: University of Chicago Press, 1970).

23 "An irrestrainable propensity to run away." The term is derived from Greek *drapeto* (to flee) and *mania* (obsession or madness).

24 P. Brown, "The Name Game," *Journal of Mind and Behavior* 11 (1990): 385–406.

25 Randall Kennedy, *Race, Crime and the Law* (New York: Vintage Books, 1997).

26 Samuel A. Cartwright, "Report on the Diseases and Physical Peculiarities of the Negro Race," *The New Orleans Medical and Surgical Journal* (1851): 691–715.

27 James H. Jones, *Bad Blood: The Tuskegee Syphilis Experiment* (New York: The Free Press, 1981).

28 *The Deadly Deception.* PBS/NOVA: Science Programming on Air and Online, 1993.

29 Dorothy Roberts, *Killing the Black Body: Race, Reproduction, and the Meaning of Liberty* (New York: Pantheon., 1997).

30 Andrea Smith, "Better Dead than Pregnant: The Colonization of Native Women's Reproductive Health," in *Policing the National Body: Race, Gender, and Criminalization,* ed. Jael Sillman and Anannya Bhattacharjee. (Cambridge: South End Press, 2002).

31 (Berkeley, CA: University of California Press, 2002).

32 Iris Lopez, "Agency and Constraint: Sterilization and Reproductive Freedom Among Puerto Rican Women in New York City," in *Situated Lives: Gender and Culture in Everyday Life,* ed. Louise Lamphere, Helena Ragone and Patricia Zavella (New York: Routledge, 1997).

33 Ana Maria Garcia, *La Operacion.* (New York: Latin American Film Project, 1982).

34 Statements by INCITE! 2003, see http://www.incite-national.org/.

35 Apryl Clark, Claire Fong, and Martha Romans, *Health Disparities Among US Women of Color: An Overview* (Washington, DC: Jacobs Institute of Women's Health and The Commonwealth Fund, 2002).

36 Statements by Center for Disease Control, see http://www.cdc.gov/.

37 Xóchitl Castañeda and Patricia Zavella, "Changing Constructions of Sexuality and Risk: Migrant Mexican Women Farmworkers in California," in *Journal of Latin American Anthropology* 8, no. 2 (2003):126–150.

38 Clark et al., *Health Disparities Among US Women of Color.*

39 K. A. Schulman, K.A., J. A. Berlin, W. Harless et al., "The Effect of Race and Sex on Physicians' Recommendations for Cardiac Catheterization," *New England Journal of Medicine* 340 (1999): 618–626; J. G. Canto, J. J. Allison, C. I. Kiefe et al., "Relation of Race and Sex to the Use of Reperfusion Therapy in Medicare Beneficiaries with Acute Myocardial Infarction" in *New England Journal of Medicine* 342 (2000): 1094–1100; and Clark et al., *Health Disparities Among US Women of Color.*

40 Waitzkin, "Social Structures of Medical Oppression."

41 Nadera Shalhoub Kevorkian, "Imposition of Virginity: A Life-saver or a License to Kill?" in *Social Science and Medicine* 60 (2005): 1187–1196.

42 Penal Code 11160–11163.

43 Hyman, "Mandatory Reporting of Domestic Violence by Health Care Providers: A Policy Paper."

44 Ibid.

45 Michael Rodriguez, "Mandatory Reporting of Domestic Violence: What Do Patients and Physicians Think?" in *Wellness Lecture Series* (San Francisco: California Wellness Foundation, 1997).

46 R. Rodriguez, "Family Violence and Migrant Women: Implications for Practice. Migrant Clinicians Network Clinical Supplement," in *Migrant Health Newsline* 10, no. 3 (1993): 1–3.

47 C. Hoagland and K. Rosen., *Dreams Lost, Dreams Found: Undocumented Women in the Land of Opportunity* (San Francisco: Coalition for Immigrant and Refugee Rights and Services, Immigrant Women's Task Force, 1990); Yvette Flores-Ortiz, "La Mujer y La Violencia: A Culturally Based Model for the Understanding and Treatment of Domestic Violence in Chicana/Latina Communities," in *Chicana Critical Issues*, ed. Norma Alarcon, Rafaela Castro, Emma Perez, Beatriz Pesquera, Adaljiza Sosa Riddell, and Patricia Zavella (Berkeley, CA: Third Woman Press, 1993).

48 Kevorkian, "Imposition of Virginity: A Life-saver or a License to Kill?" 1195.

49 Irving Zola, "Medicine as an Institution of Social Control" in *The Sociology of Health and Illness*, ed. P. Conrad (New York: St Martin's Press, 1997).

50 Fanon, *A Dying Colonialism.*

Chapter 24 Disloyal to Feminism

1 The use of the word "disloyal" in this context is a reference to Adrienne Rich's "Disloyal to Civilization," from her 1979 book, *On Lies, Secrets and Silences.*

2 Susan Brownmiller, *Against Our Will: Men, Women And Rape* (New York: Simon and Schuster, 1975), 15.

3 Gloria Stymied, "Ms.ery," *BUST* no. 2 (Spring 1999), 15; Jennifer Baumgardner and Amy Richards, *Manifesta: Young Women, Feminism, and the Future* (New York: Farrar, Straus and Giroux, 2001), xviii. Jennifer Baumgardner used the pseudonym "Gloria Stymied" when she wrote the article "Ms.ery," an expose about *Ms.* magazine. Because Baumgardner wrote about the same story under her real name in the book she cowrote with Amy Richards, and because she has since acknowledged that she was Gloria Stymied, who coined the term "battered women's movement syndrome," I chose to name her as the person who coined the phrase.

4 The names of survivors interviewed for this article have been changed to protect their privacy. Lulu and Akasha both picked their own pseudonyms. I plan to expand on these and other interviews I conducted when I write a book-length manuscript on this topic.

5 Akasha and I agreed that the word "trick" should be put in quotation marks because a rapist is not a "trick" any more than a bank robber is a "customer."

6 Nancy J. Meyer and others point out the term "domestic violence" itself is a euphemism designed to dilute feminist critiques of male dominance. I understand and am sympathetic to this concern. However, I am using the term "domestic violence" throughout this article, including in my discussion of radical feminist critiques of "de-politicization," for the sake of consistency and also because I seek to politicize the concept of "domestic violence" differently than they do.

7 Patricia Gaddis, "A Creation Story of Battered Women's Shelter," *off our backs* 31, no.9 (2001): 16.

8 Nancy Meyer, "Now you see it, now you don't: the state of the battered women's movement," *off our backs* 31, no. 10 (2001): 23.

9 Mary Haviland, Victoria Frye, et al., *The Family Protection and Domestic Violence Intervention Act of 1995: Examining the Effects of Mandatory Arrest in New York City* (New York: Urban

Justice Center, 2001), 6. Available from the Urban Justice Center, (646) 602-5612.

10 Torn Schram, "Ruling on Housing Law a Blow to Battered Women," *Women's eNews,* March 31, 2002.

11 Jennifer Friedlin, "Judge Exposes Agency Harm to Battered Mothers, Kids," *Women's eNews,* April 29, 2002.

12 Collin Levey, "Feminists Howl at a Kentucky Judge's Approach to Domestic Violence," *The Wall Street Journal,* February 1, 2002.

13 Patty Neal Dorian, "So Who's Left?" *off our backs* 31, no. 9 (2001), 24.

14 Rita Smith and Gretchen Eckroate, "Have You Been Sued Yet?" *VOICE: The Journal of the Battered Women's Movement,* (2001), no.1; and *The Augusta Chronicle,* "Area briefs," April 8, 1999.

15 Smith and Eckroate, "Have You Been Sued Yet?"

16 Angela Y. Davis, "The Color of Violence Against Women." *ColorLines* 3, no.3 (2000).

17 Andrea Smith, "Colors of Violence." *ColorLines* 3, no. 4 (2000).

18 Ibid.

19 Mazie Hough, Ann Schonberger, and The Feminist Oral History Project, "Spruce Run and the Politics of Empowerment," *VOICE: The Journal of the Battered Women's Movement,* no. 3, (1998).

20 I would like to thank Allison Lum of the Coalition Against Homelessness and others involved in its Shelter Outreach program for providing me with inspiration and detailed information about how the universal grievance procedure worked.

21 Coalition on Homelessness, Web site http://www.sf-homeless-coalition.org (accessed July 25, 2002).

22 Ibid.

23 Harm Reduction Coalition, "Principles of Harm Reduction," Available at http://www.harmreduction.org (accessed July 25, 2002).

24 American Medical Association, "Reduction of the Medical and Public Health Consequences of Drug Abuse," *Report of the Council on Scientific Affairs* (Chicago, IL: American Medical Association, 1997).

25 Bernice Yeung, "Fighting the many faces of violence." *ColorLines* 3, no. 4 (2000). "Comfort women" is a euphemism (hence the quotation marks) used by the Japanese imperial army during the Second World War (when Korea was under Japan's colonial rule) to refer to women who were made to provide sexual services to Japanese soldiers in "comfort facilities" set up inside Japanese bases. Many Korean women were routinely lured into the situation by the false promise of "good employment," but instead they were kept captive and forced to perform sexual acts. In addition, there were some documented instances of forcible abductions of women from Korea and other parts of Asia that Japan controlled at the time. While these "comfort facilities" were technically private brothel businesses that contracted with the government, the Japanese government did little or nothing to discourage or punish this criminal behavior. While diplomatic treaties between Japan and South Korea in the 1960s officially dissolved any claims for compensation between the two nations, many Korean people as well as Japanese activists are demanding that the Japanese government directly compensate the surviving "comfort women" for their suffering and loss.

26 Haviland, Frye, et al., *The Family Protection and Domestic Violence Intervention Act.* This discussion of the Women's Legal Alternative Collective is based on the WLAC's workshop session at the Gender and Sexuality Conference at Evergreen State College in May 2002.

27 I would like to thank Connie Burke, Ellie Kimaro, and Jed Lin of Northwest Network for their work and their willingness to make the time to meet with me during the busy Pride weekend.

28 Northwest Network, "F.A.R. Out! What's It About?" Available from Northwest Network, (206) 568-7777.

29 Northwest Network, "F.A.R. Out!"

Chapter 25 Gender Violence and the Prison-Industrial Complex

1   In a 20-year study of 48 cities, Dugan et al. found that greater access to criminal legal remedies for women led to fewer men being killed by their wives, as women who might otherwise
have killed to escape violence were offered alternatives. However women receiving legal support were no less likely to be killed by their intimate partners, and were exposed to additional retaliatory violence (Laura Dugan, Daniel S. Nagin, and Richard Rosenfeld, "Exposure
Reduction or Retaliation? The Effects of Domestic Violence Resources on Intimate-Partner
Homicide," *Law & Society Review* 37, no. 1 (2003).

2   See Martha McMahon, "Making Social Change," *Violence Against Women* 9, no. 1 (January
2003): 47–74; Sue Osthoff, "But Gertrude, I Beg to Differ, a Hit is Not a Hit is Not a Hit,"
Violence Against Women 8, no. 12 (December 2002): 1521–1544; Susan Miller, "The Paradox
of Women Arrested for Domestic Violence," *Violence Against Women* 7, no. 12 (December
2001). Noting that in some cities, over 20% of those arrested for domestic violence are
women, Miller concludes: "An arrest policy intended to protect battered women as victims is
being misapplied and used against them. Battered women have become female offenders."

3   Women's dependent or undocumented status is often manipulated by batterers, who use the
threat of deportation as part of a matrix of domination and control. Although the Violence
Against Women Act (VAWA 1994 and 2000) introduced visas for battered immigrant wom-
en, many women do not know about the act's provisions or are unable to meet eviden-
ciary requirements. Since the Illegal Immigration Reform and Immigrant Responsibility Act
made domestic violence grounds for deportation, women may also be reluctant to subject
a legal permanent resident spouse to potential deportation proceedings by reporting him
to the police. In addition, women arrested under mandatory arrest laws could themselves
face deportation. See Anita Raj and Jay Silverman, "Violence Against Immigrant Women:
The Role of Culture, Context and Legal Immigrant Status on Intimate Partner Violence,"
Violence Against Women 8, no. 3 (March 2002): 367–398; Deena Jang, Len Marin, and Gail
Pendleton, *Domestic Violence in Immigrant and Refugee Communities: Assessing the Rights of
Battered Women*, 2nd Ed. (San Francisco: Family Violence Prevention Fund, 1997).

4   For example, California Governor Grey Davis, whose tough law-and-order platform included a promise that no-one convicted of murder would go free, has rejected numerous parole
board recommendations on behalf of battered women incarcerated for killing in self defense.
Rebecca Vesely, "Davis' Right to Deny Parole to Abused Women Upheld," *Women's eNews*,
December 19, 2002. For further information and testimonies of incarcerated survivors of
domestic violence, see www.freebatteredwomen.org.

5   Christian Parenti documents the shift in government spending from welfare, education and
social provision to prisons and policing in *Lockdown America: Policing and Prisons in the Age
of Crisis*. (London: Verso Books, 1999).

6   The US prison and jail population grew from 270,000 in 1975 to 2 million in 2001 as legislators pushed "tough on crime" policies such as mandatory minimums, three-strikes-and-
you're out and truth in sentencing (Michael Tonry, ed., *Penal Reform in Overcrowded Times*
[New York: Oxford University Press, 2001], 17). Over 90% of these prisoners are men, and
approximately 50% are Black men. Despite claims that locking more people away would lead
to a dramatic decrease in crime, reported violent crimes against women have remained relatively constant since annual victimization surveys were initiated in 1973 (Bureau of Justice
Statistics, *National Crime Victimization Survey Report: Violence Against Women* [Washington,
DC: US Department of Justice, 1994]

7   In 2001, the United States, with 686 prisoners per 100,000 residents, surpassed the incarceration rate of gulag-ridden Russia. The United States dwarfs the incarceration rate of
Western European nations like Finland and Denmark, which incarcerate only 59 people in
every 100,000. British Home Office Development and Statistics Directorate, *World Prison
Population List* (London: Home Office, 2004). Available at www.homeoffice.gov.uk/rds/

pdfs2/r188.pdf.

8   The rate of increase of women's imprisonment in the United States has exceeded that of men. In 1970, there were 5,600 women in federal and state prisons, by 1996 there were 75,000 (Elliott Currie, *Crime and Punishment in America* [New York: Henry Holt, 1998])

9   Amnesty International's investigation of women's prisons in the United States revealed countless cases of sexual, physical and psychological abuse. In one case the Federal Bureau of Prisons paid $500,000 to settle a lawsuit by three black women who were sexually assaulted when guards took money from male prisoners in exchange for taking them to the women's cells; prisoners in Arizona were subjected to rape, sexual fondling, and genital touching during searches as well as constant prurient viewing when using the shower and toilet; women at Valley State Prison, California were treated as a "private harem to sexually abuse and harass"; in numerous cases women were kept in restraints while seriously ill, dying, or in labor and women under maximum security conditions were kept in isolation and sensory deprivation for long periods (*Not Part of My Sentence: Violations of the Human Rights of Women in Custody* [New York: Amnesty International, 1999]).

10   Andrea Smith "Colors of Violence," *ColorLines* 3, no. 4 (2000).

11   May Koss argues that the adversarial justice system traumatizes survivors of domestic violence. "Blame, Shame and Community: Justice Responses to Violence Against Women," *American Psychologist* 55, no. 11 (November 2000): 1332. For a first person account of a rape survivor's fight to hold the police accountable see Jane Doe, *The Story of Jane Doe: A Book About Rape*, (New York: Random House, 2003). Jane Doe was raped by the Toronto "balcony rapist" after police used women in her neighborhood as "bait."

12   Beth Richie, "The Social Impact of Mass Incarceration on Women," in *Invisible Punishment: The Collateral Consequences of Mass Imprisonment*, ed. Marc Mauer and Meda Chesney-Lind (New York: The New Press, 2003), 136–149.

13   For a comprehensive account of state violence against women in the United States see Annanya Bhattacharjee, *Women of Color and the Violence of Law Enforcement* (Philadelphia: American Friends Service Committee and Committee on Women, Population and the Environment, 2001).

14   Additional burdens on women when a loved one is incarcerated include dealing with the arrest and trials of family members, expensive visits and phone calls from correctional facilities and meeting disruptive parole requirements (Richie, "The Social Impact of Mass Incarceration").

15   In the United States see Justice Now; Legal Services for Prisoners with Children (http://prisonerswith children.org); Free Battered Women (www.freebatteredwomen.org); California Coalition for Women Prisoners (http://womenprisoners.org); and Chicago Legal Advocacy for Incarcerated Mothers (www.c-l-a-i-m-.org). In the UK see Women in Prison (www.womeninprison.org); and Justice for Women (www.jfw.org.uk). In Canada, see the Canadian Association of Elizabeth Fry Associations (www.elizabethfry.ca/caefs_e.htm).

16   According to transgender activists in the Bay Area, the police are responsible for approximately 50% of all trans abuse cases. The Transaction hotline regularly receives reports from TG/TS survivors of police violence who have been forced to strip in order to "verify gender," or subjected to demands for sex from undercover police officers. "Transgender Sues Police," *San Francisco Examiner*, August 9, 2002; "Another Transgender Murder," *Bay Area Reporter* 29, no. 14 (April 8. 1999).

17   Karlene Faith, *Unruly Women: The Politics of Confinement and Resistance*, (Vancouver: Press Gang Publishers,), 211–223.

18   Abolitionists Thomas and Boehlfeld's response to the question: "What Do We Do About Henry?" where Henry is a violent rapist, is an example of this problem. The authors conclude that this is the wrong question since it focuses attention on a small and anomalous subsection of the prison population and detracts from a broader abolitionist vision (Jim Thomas

and Sharon Boehlefeld, "Rethinking Abolitionism: 'What Do We Do With Henry?'" in *We Who Would Take No Prisoners: Selections From the Fifth International Conference on Penal Abolition* [Vancouver: Collective Press, 1993]).

19 Alternatives to the traditional justice system such as Sentencing Circles are particularly developed in Canada and Australia, where they have been developed in partnership with indigenous communities. However, native women have been critical of these approaches, arguing that they fail to address the deep-rooted sexism and misogyny engendered by experiences of colonization and that they may re-victimize women (Patricia Monture-Angus, "The Roles and Responsibilities of Aboriginal Women: Reclaiming Justice," in *Criminal Injustice: Racism in the Criminal Justice System,* ed. Robynne Neugebauer [Toronto: Canadian Scholars' Press Inc., 2000]). See also Barbara Hudson, "Restorative Justice and Gendered Violence" *British Journal of Criminology* 42, no. 3 (Summer 2002).

Chapter 28 An Antiracist Christian Ethical Approach to Violence Resistance

1 This chapter is an excerpt from *Wounds of the Spirit: Black Women, Violence, and Resistance Ethics* (New York: New York University Press, 1999).

2 For a discussion of the critical role of Christian faith communities in developing moral responses to contemporary social crises, see Larry Rasmussen, *Moral Fragments and Moral Community: A Proposal for Church in Society* (Minneapolis: Fortress Press, 1993), especially 150–151.

3 Cornel West, *Prophesy Deliverance! An Afro-American Revolutionary Christianity* (Philadelphia: Westminster Press, 1982), 98.

4 Christine Gudorf, *Victimization: Examining Christian Complicity* (Philadelphia: Trinity Press International, 1992), 92.

5 Delores Williams. *Sisters in the Wilderness: The Challenge of Womanist God-Talk* (Maryknoll, NY: Orbis Books, 1993), 177.

6 Ibid.

7 For a resource that provides rites for women's healing from violence, see Rosemary Radford Ruether, *Women-Church: Theology and Practice* (New York: Harper and Row, 1985), especially 151–161.

8 For some examples of social justice rituals, see George D. McClain, *Claiming All Things for God: Prayer, Discernment, and Ritual for Social Change* (Nashville, TN: Abingdon Press, 1998).

9 In the 1980s, I had the privilege of meeting men from a Christian-based community in Nicaragua who described their process of coming to a greater awareness of the destructive impact that the dynamics of "machismo" can have upon women. The women of that community also testified to the behavioral changes taking place in their community that had resulted in increasing men's participation in child care and women's involvement in formal political leadership.

10 Paul Kivel, *Uprooting Racism: How White People Can Work for Racial Justice* (Philadelphia: New Society Publishers, 1996), 40–46. For his work on domestic violence, see *Men's Work: How to Stop the Violence That Tears Our Lives Apart* (New York: Hazelden/Ballantine, 1992).

Chapter 29 Taking Risks

1 For the purposes of this article, we use the word "aggressor" to refer to a person who has committed an act of sexual violence (rape, sexual harassment, coercion, etc.) against another person. Our use of the word "aggressor" is not an attempt to weaken the severity of rape. In our work of defining accountability outside of the criminal system, we try not to use criminal-based vocabulary such as "perpetrator," "rapist," or "sex predator." We also use pronouns

interchangeably throughout the article.

2   Jacqueline M. Golding et al., "Social Support Sources Following Assault," *Journal of Community Psychology* 17 (January 1989): 92–107. This paper is just one example of research showing that survivors are much more likely to access friends and family for support than they are to access police or rape crisis centers. Golding's research reveals that 59% of survivors surveyed reported that they disclosed their assault to friends and relatives, while 10.5% reported to police, and 1.9% reported to rape crisis centers. Interestingly, Golding's research also asserts that survivors rated rape crisis centers as most helpful and law enforcement as least helpful. She suggests that, since friends or relatives are the most frequent contact for rape victim disclosure, efforts should focus on enhancing and supporting this informal intervention.

3   Borrowing from philosopher Cornel West, we can call this approach of simultaneous improvisation and structure a "jazzy approach." Much like jazz music, a community accountability process can incorporate many different and diverse components that allow for the complexity of addressing sexual violence while also respecting the need for some stability and careful planning. Also, like jazz music, an accountability process is not an end point or a finite thing, but a living thing that continues to be created. Our understanding of community accountability ultimately transcends the idea of simply holding an abusive community member responsible for his or her actions, but also includes the vision of the community itself being accountable for its support of a culture that allows for sexual violence. This latter accountability process truly necessitates active and constant recreating and reaffirming a community that values liberation for everyone.

4   We define "internalized oppression" as the process of a person who belongs to a marginalized and oppressed group accepting, promoting, and justifying beliefs of inferiority and lack of value about her group and, perhaps, herself.

5   Thank you to the Northwest Network of Bisexual, Trans, Lesbian, and Gay Survivors of Abuse for asserting the verb in "safety plan."

6   We do not mean to simply imply that the principle of "innocent until proven guilty" should be completely discarded. However, we also recognize that this particular goal is actually often disregarded in a criminal system that is entrenched with institutional racism and oppression. Our goal is to create values that are independent of a criminal justice–based approach to accountability, including thinking critically about ideas such as "innocent until proven guilty" from the perspective of how these ideas actually impact oppressed people.

7   All names of people and organizations have been changed for the purposes of this article, not because we are concerned about the legal ramifications of slander or because we have a blanket rule about confidentiality, but because we try to be intentional about when and for what reason we publicly identify aggressors.

8   Those of us working on community accountability should have a talk about aggressors' threats of suing for slander and libel. These threats happen often, especially if the aggressor is well-known and has a reputation to defend. However, when suing for slander or libel, one has the burden of proof and must be able to demonstrate that the allegations are false. It's very hard to prove that something is false, especially when it is, in fact, true. Still, the threat of a lawsuit can understandably be frightening and it would be helpful to have more conversations about what the actual danger is and perhaps develop some best practices when considering using public disclosure as a tool to reach accountability.

9   Press release, January 25, 2003.

10 More thinking may need to be done to address situations in which people are intentionally lying about an account of rape or abuse. What happens if someone uses an accusation of abuse as a tool to isolate, punish, or control the person being accused? This could happen in an abusive relationship, but it could also happen as a function of oppression (for example, a straight woman accuses a queer woman of harassment simply by virtue of her being queer,

or a white woman accuses a Black man of sexual assault because of her own racism). Another problem is when a person experiences an event as violent, but this experience doesn't fit the community's general definition of "violence." The community may need to figure out if it should expand its notion of "violence" or if a different analysis and response is needed. Lastly, while struggling through these questions, we'd like to caution our left/progressive community against creating a culture of endless process that stands in for organized action. Issues of credibility, as well as other controversial issues, are complicated and can sap a group's time and energy. You may not even need to come to consensus about how to finally think about what happened. But this doesn't necessarily mean you can't come to consensus on a plan of action to respond.

INDEX

About the Contributors

Dena Al-Adeeb is a diasporic Iraqi artist, photographer, activist/organizer and journalist currently residing between Cairo, Egypt and San Francisco, California. Her photography has been exhibited in the US and internationally. Her organizing experiences include the Women of Color Resource Center, Racial Justice 911, Arab Women's Solidarity Association San Francisco Chapter, San Francisco Women Against Rape, American Arab Anti-Discrimination Committee San Francisco Chapter, among others. She is presently working towards earning a MA in sociology-anthropology at the American University of Cairo.

Patricia Allard is a lawyer by training and a Black feminist activist and policy analyst in practice. Formerly Associate Counsel at the Brennan Center for Justice at NYU School of Law, Pat has authored many articles, including "Claiming Our Rights: Challenging Post-Conviction Penalties Through an International Human Rights Framework." Pat is a graduate of Queen's University Law School and received her MA in criminology from the University of Toronto.

Lina Baroudi immigrated from Syria with her family in 1983. She holds a BA in sociology, which focused on the intersection of queer theory and postcolonial studies. Since graduating, Lina has been employed with the Law Office of Robert B. Jobe, an immigration and nationality firm, where she mainly works on federal litigation focused on deportation defense. She is also an evening law student.

Communities Against Rape and Abuse (CARA) is a vibrant, women of color–led, grassroots antiviolence project in Seattle that advances a broad agenda for liberation and social justice while prioritizing anti-rape work as the center of our organizing. CARA activists create community-based systems of accountability, safety, and support in order to build healthy relationships and communities free of both community violence and state-sponsored violence. We use community organizing, critical dialogue, and collective action as tools to build safe, peaceful, and sustainable communities.

Critical Resistance (CR) is a national grassroots group that fights to end the prison industrial complex (PIC) by challenging the belief that policing, surveillance, imprisonment, and similar forms of control make our communities safer. We believe, by contrast, that basic necessities like food, shelter and freedom create the conditions for more genuine forms of security. For that reason, our work involves both relieving the burden of the PIC on the lives of people across the country and empowering those communities that are most directly affected by its intrusions.

Sarah Deer (Muscogee) works at the Tribal Law and Policy Institute in St. Paul, Minnesota and is the author of several books and articles on violence against Native women.

Eman Desouky was born in Chicago and grew up in Saudia Arabia, New York, Georgia, and Egypt. Currently, she has one foot in Oakland, California and the other foot in Alexandria, Egypt. Her work has ranged from counseling survivors of sexual assault, organizing community responses to INS detentions and deportations, to producing cultural events for Palestine. She practices centralizing radical cultural work as a revolutionary strategy in her community work.

A Palestinian born in Kuwait, **Dana Erekat** lived in the Levant and Gulf regions before coming to the US. Having traveled to Gaza as a photographer, she was awarded a grant to return to the region. She holds a degree in architecture from UC–Berkeley. Dana teaches Palestinian and standard Arabic at Pacific Arabic Resources.

Nirmala Erevelles is an associate professor in the Department of Educational Leadership, Policy, and Technology Studies at the University of Alabama. Her research and teaching interests are in the areas of education for social justice, transnational feminism, and disability studies.

Sylvanna M. Falcón is a teacher-scholar who completed her PhD from the Department of Sociology with a doctoral emphasis in women's studies at UC–Santa Barbara. Her dissertation is entitled, "Where are the Women? Transnational Feminist Interventions at the United Nations World Conference Against Racism," examines how feminists have irretrievably changed the discourse of racism at the global level. She and her family live in Los Angeles.

Emi Koyama is a third-wavin', multi-issue, social justice activist synthesizing, feminist, Asian, survivor, dyke, queer, sex worker, and gender-queer, as these factors (while not a complete description of who she is) all impacted her life. Emi lives in Portland, Oregon, and is putting the "emi" back in feminism.

Elizabeth "Betita" Martínez is a Chicana writer, activist, and teacher whose many years of social justice work are legendary. In the 1960s and 70s, she worked in the Black civil rights movement and the Chicano movement. Currently active in mobilizing for peace, Martínez also co-founded and chairs the Institute for Multi-Racial Justice, an organization dedicated to building alliances between communities of color. She is the author of six books and numerous articles. Her well-known title *500 Years of Chicano History* became the basis for the video she co-directed. Her most recent book is *De Colores Means All of Us: Latina Views for a Multi-Colored Century* (South End Press, 1998).

maiana minahal is a queer Filipina American poet who was born in Manila, raised in Los Angeles, and currently lives in San Francisco. She began studying and teaching poetry in 1994 with June Jordan's Poetry for the People collective at UC–Berkeley. Her work has been included in *June Jordan's Poetry for the People: A Revolutionary Blueprint* (Routledge, 1995) and anthologies like *inVasian: Asian Sisters Represent* (Study Center Press, 2003).

Nadine Naber is a scholar-activist and an assistant professor in Arab American studies and gender studies at the University of Michigan. Nadine is a co-editor of *Gender, Nation, and Belonging,* a special issue of the *MIT Online Journal of Middle East Studies for Arab American Feminisms.* She is co-founder of such groups as the Arab Women's Solidarity Association (North America) and the Arab Movement of Women Arising for Justice. Naber is a former board member of INCITE! Women of Color against Violence.

Stormy Ogden (Tule River Yokuts, Kashaya Pomo, and Lake County Pomo) is currently involved in the Squaw Name Change Committee and volunteers at the women's federal prison in Dublin, California.

Andrea J. Ritchie is a progressive lesbian feminist of African Caribbean descent who has worked in the women's movement in the United States and Canada over the past 15 years as an advocate and researcher. She graduated from the Howard University School of Law and is currently a member of the National Collective of INCITE! Women of Color Against Violence. Ritchie also served as one of the national coordinators of the Color of Violence III.

Dorothy Roberts is the Kirkland & Ellis Professor at Northwestern University School of Law, with joint appointments in the departments of African American Studies and Sociology. She earned her JD from Harvard Law School and is the author of award-winning books such as *Killing the Black Body: Race, Reproduction, and the Meaning of Liberty* (Pantheon, 1997). From 2002 to 2003, Roberts was a Fulbright scholar at the Centre for Gender and Development Studies at the University of the West Indies, in Trinidad and Tobago.

Ana Clarissa Rojas Durazo was raised in Mexicali, Baja California, Mexico, and Calexico, California. She has organized in raza and communities of color for over 15 years, working to resist violence and injustices committed against and within these communities. She served on the founding national planning committee of INCITE! and chaired the INCITE! anthology committee. Rojas is completing her doctorate degree at UC San Francisco and has taught in raza studies and ethnic studies at San Francisco State University since 1999. Her poetry has appeared in literary journals in the United States and México.

Loretta J. Ross is the national coordinator of the SisterSong Women of Color Reproductive Health Collective, a network founded in 1997 of 76 women of color and allied organizations that work on reproductive justice issues. In 2004, Ross was national co-director of the April 25th March for Women's Lives in Washington, DC, the largest protest march in US history. From 1996 to 2004, she was the founder/executive director of the National Center for Human Rights Education in Atlanta, Georgia. She is a coauthor of *Undivided Rights: Women of Color Organize for Reproductive Justice* (South End Press, 2004).

Puneet Kaur Chawla Sahota is a Punjabi Sikh American woman interested in gender, culture, and ethnic identity. Puneet received her BA from Northwestern University, where she graduated summa cum laude. There, she wrote her senior honors thesis on the history of South Asian women organizing against domestic violence in the United States. She is currently an MD/PhD student at Washington University in St. Louis where she is studying cultural anthropology.

Renee Saucedo is an organizer, an activist, and a lawyer who has played a prominent role in this country's immigrant rights movement at all levels. She founded INS WATCH, a grassroots organization that resists INS enforcement. Saucedo has been honored with numerous community service awards from organizations including the Mexican American Legal Defense & Education Fund.

Aishah Shahidah Simmons is the producer, writer and director of *NO!*. She is an award-winning independent documentary filmmaker and activist based in Philadelphia. In 2006, Aishah received a major grant from the Ford Foundation to support the educational marketing and distribution of *NO!*. The National Sexual Violence Resource Center chose Simmons as the 2006 recipient of their Award for Outstanding Response to and Prevention of Sexual Violence for her work with *NO!*.

Sista II Sista is a Brooklyn-based collective of working-class young and adult Black and Latina women building together to model a society based on liberation and love. The organization is dedicated to working with young women to develop personal, spiritual, and collective power. Sista II Sista is committed to fighting for justice and creating alternatives to the systems we live in by making social, cultural and political change.

Andrea Smith (Cherokee) is a co-founder of INCITE! Women of Color Against Violence and the Boarding School Healing Project. She is the author of *Conquest: Sexual Violence and American Indian Genocide* (South End Press, 2005).

S.R. is an Iraqi-based writer, currently living in the US.

Julia Sudbury is a professor of ethnic studies at Mills College and editor of *Global Lockdown: Race, Gender and the Prison Industrial Complex* (Routledge, 2005). She is a founding member of Critical Resistance and the Prison Justice Action Committee in Toronto. She has been involved in antiviolence, LGBT, anti-racist, global justice, and prison abolitionist activism in the UK, US, and Canada for the past two decades.

Neferti Tadiar is an associate professor in the History of Consciousness Department at UC–Santa Cruz. Her publications include *Fantasy-Production: Sexual Economies and Other Philippine Consequences for the New World Order* (Hong Kong University Press/Ateneo de Manila University Press, 2004), and *Beyond the Frame: Women of Color and Visual Representation*, which she co-edited with Angela Y. Davis (Palgrave Press, 2005).

TransJustice is a political group created by and for trans and gender nonconforming people of color, which works to mobilize its communities and allies to act on the pressing political issues they face. These issues include gaining access to jobs, housing, and education; obtaining trans-sensitive job training, healthcare, and HIV-related services; and resisting police, government, and anti-immigrant violence. TransJustice is a project of the Audre Lorde Project in New York City.

Indigenous nationalist, political organizer, and poet, **Haunani-Kay Trask** is professor of Hawaiian studies at the University of Hawai'i-Manoa. She is the author of three books, including a book of poetry, *Light in the Crevice Never Seen* (Calyx, 1999), and a collection of political essays, *From a Native Daughter: Colonialism and Sovereignty in Hawai'i* (University of Hawai'i Press, 1999).

Traci C. West is an associate professor of ethics and African American studies at Drew University (Madison, NJ). She is the author of *Disruptive Christian Ethics: When Racism and Women's Lives Matter* (Westminster/John Knox, 2006) and *Wounds of the Spirit: Black Women, Violence, and Resistance Ethics* (New York University Press, 1999), as well as articles on justice issues in church and society. She is an ordained minister in the United Methodist Church.

Janelle White is a cofounder of INCITE! Women of Color Against Violence. A longtime antiviolence activist, she is currently executive director of San Francisco Women Against Rape.

ABOUT SOUTH END PRESS

South End Press is a collectively run, nonprofit book publisher with more than 250 titles in print. The majority person of color, majority women collective tries to meet the needs of readers who are exploring or already committed to the politics of radical social change. Since our founding in 1977, our goal has been to publish books that encourage critical thinking and constructive action on the key political, cultural, social, economic, and ecological issues shaping life in the United States and in the world. In this way, we hope to provide a forum for a wide variety of democratic social movements, and provide an alternative to the products of corporate publishing.

From its inception, the Press has organized itself as an egalitarian collective with decision-making arranged to share the rewards and stresses of running the business as equally as possible. Each collective member is responsible for core editorial and administrative tasks, and all collective members earn the same base salary. The Press also has made a practice of inverting the pervasive racial and gender hierarchies in traditional publishing houses; our staff has had a female majority since the mid-1980s, and has included at least 50% people of color since the mid-1990s. Our author list—which includes Arundhati Roy, Noam Chomsky, bell hooks, Winona LaDuke, Manning Marable, Ward Churchill, Cherríe Moraga, and Howard Zinn—reflects the Press's commitment to publish on diverse issues from diverse perspectives.

To expand access to information and critical analysis, South End Press has been instrumental in the starting of two on-going political media projects—Speak Out and *Z Magazine*. We have worked closely with a number of important media and research institutions including Alternative Radio; Political Research Associates; the Committee on Women, Population, and the Environment (CWPE); and INCITE! Women of Color Against Violence. Please consider making a donation to help support South End Press in its mission to continue expanding access and ensure our continued financial viability.

To make a donation or receive a current catalog of our books, please write to us at South End Press, 7 Brookline Street #1, Cambridge, MA 02139 or email us at southend@southendpress.org. To order books, obtain information about author events, or submit a review of a South End Press book, please visit our website: www.southendpress.org.